FAITHFUL IN ADVERSITY

To my children, Rosa, Sophia and David, who each follow in their paternal grandfather's footsteps in different ways. And Dawn, who helps me connect the past to the present.

FAITHFUL IN ADVERSITY

THE ROYAL ARMY MEDICAL CORPS IN THE SECOND WORLD WAR

JOHN BROOM

Pen & Sword
MILITARY
AN IMPRINT OF PEN & SWORD BOOKS LTD.
YORKSHIRE – PHILADELPHIA

First published in Great Britain in 2019 by
PEN AND SWORD MILITARY
An imprint of
Pen & Sword Books Ltd
Yorkshire – Philadelphia

ISBN 978 1 52674 955 0

A CIP catalogue record for this book is available from the British Library.

Typeset in Times New Roman 11.5/14 by
Aura Technology and Software Services, India
Printed and bound in the UK by TJ International

Pen & Sword Books Limited incorporates the imprints of Atlas, Archaeology, Aviation, Discovery, Family History, Fiction, History, Maritime, Military, Military Classics, Politics, Select, Transport, True Crime, Air World, Frontline Publishing, Leo Cooper, Remember When, Seaforth Publishing, The Praetorian Press, Wharncliffe Local History, Wharncliffe Transport, Wharncliffe True Crime and White Owl.

For a complete list of Pen & Sword titles please contact
PEN & SWORD BOOKS LIMITED
47 Church Street, Barnsley, South Yorkshire, S70 2AS, England
E-mail: enquiries@pen-and-sword.co.uk
Website: www.pen-and-sword.co.uk

Or
PEN AND SWORD BOOKS
1950 Lawrence Rd, Havertown, PA 19083, USA
E-mail: Uspen-and-sword@casematepublishers.com
Website: www.penandswordbooks.com

Contents

Acknowledgements

I would like to thank the following relatives of men who served in the RAMC for permission to quote from material held in private family collections: Claire Adler, David Adler, Richard Bradley, Vera Cannell, Michael Cayley, Norah Chown, Sheila Cox, Margaret Ellerington, Michael Haine, Julie Harden-Wells, Sheila Howell, Richard Jevons, Stuart Jebbitt, Laura Kitson, Michael Lacey, Cathy Larwood, Chris Manning, Paul Morrell, Theo Quant, Joseph Ritson, Derek Thorley, Rosie Tobin, Kay Turton, Richard Watts and Joan Willetts.

I was privileged to be able to use material directly provided by the following veterans of the Second World War: Ronald Dickinson, Ruggles Fisher, Bill Frankland and Walter Hart.

I acknowledge the permission of Neil Barber to quote from the memoirs of Captain David Tibbs; and Elizabeth Coward and William Earl to quote from *Blood and Bandages.*

Anne Wickes at the Second World War Experience Centre, Wetherby, has been unfailingly efficient and supportive in the provision of materials from the excellent archive housed there.

Thanks also to Robert McIntosh of the Museum of Military Medicine for permission to reproduce the image from the No. 224 Field Ambulance History.

If I have inadvertently failed to acknowledge any copyright holders in this edition of the book, I shall be glad to rectify this omission in future printings.

To Linne Matthews, Laura Hirst and Jonathan Wright at Pen & Sword, who between them bring encouragement, discipline, creativity and organisation to the writing process.

Glossary

ADMS – Assistant Director of Medical Services
ADS – Advanced Dressing Station
AMD – Army Medical Department
AMPC – Auxiliary Military Pioneer Corps
ARP – Air Raid Precautions
BEF – British Expeditionary Force
BGH – British General Hospital
BMA – British Medical Association
BMU – Brigade Medical Unit
CCP – Casualty Collection Point
CCS – Casualty Clearing Station
CMWC – Central Medical War Committee
DADMS – Deputy Assistant Director of Medical Services
DDMS – Deputy Director Medical Services
DSO – Distinguished Service Order
DUKW – amphibious transport vehicle
FA – Field Ambulance
FDS – Field Dressing Station
FSU – Field Surgical Unit
FTU – Field Transfusion Unit
IWM – Imperial War Museums
KSLI – King's Shropshire Light Infantry
LCT – landing craft tank
LFA – Light Field Ambulance

MAC – Motor Ambulance Convoy
MDS – Main Dressing Station
MO – medical officer
NCO – non-commissioned officer
PoW – prisoner of war
QAIMNS – Queen Alexandra's Imperial Military Nursing Service
RAF – Royal Air Force
RAMC – Royal Army Medical Corps
RAOC – Royal Army Ordnance Corps
RAP – Regimental Aid Post
RASC – Royal Army Service Corps
RMO – Regimental Medical Officer
RN – Royal Navy
RSM – Regimental Sergeant Major
RTU – returned to unit
SWWEC – Second World War Experience Centre
VAD – Voluntary Aid Detachment
TA – Territorial Army
TNA – The National Archives
USAAF – United States Army Air Forces
WWCP – Walking Wounded Collecting Post

List of Illustrations

20. The Red Cross brassard, which probably saved Norman Jevons' life. *(Courtesy of Richard Jevons)*
21. Paul Adler of 13th Nyasa Battalion, Kings African Rifles and No. 6 Field Ambulance, with his wife, Margaret. *(Courtesy of Paul Adler)*
22. Bert Swingler of No. 93 General Hospital. *(Courtesy of Joan Willetts)*
23. & 24. Sketches made by Arthur Atkin of No. 140 Field Ambulance. *(Author's collection)*
25. Fred Cannell of No. 9 General Hospital. *(Courtesy of Vera Cannell)*
26. Christmas celebrations 1945 at No. 9 General Hospital, Ranchi. *(Courtesy of Vera Cannell)*
27. Tom Leak, whose hopes of an early release as a PoW were dashed.
28. Desmond Whyte of No. 11 Field Ambulance. *(Author's collection)*
29. a & b. David Jebbitt of No. 181 Airlanding Field Ambulance, before and after a year as a PoW. *(Courtesy of Stuart Jebbitt)*
30. & 31. Ink drawings created by Gerald Hitchcock of No. 198 Field Ambulance during his time as a prisoner of the Japanese. *(Courtesy of Second World War Experience Centre)*
32. David Paton, Medical Officer with No. 2 Commando Unit. *(Author's collection)*
33. Engraving from *Red Devils*, an account of No. 224 (Parachute) Field Ambulance in Normandy. *(Courtesy of the Museum of Military Medicine)*
34. Casualty evacuation by jeep over Caen Canal, 1944. *(Author's collection)*
35. Jim Whitaker of No. 203 Field Ambulance. *(Courtesy of Second World War Experience Centre)*
36. Members of No. 133 (Parachute) Field Ambulance living rough to evade capture. *(Courtesy of Second World War Experience Centre)*
37. Eric Harden VC. *(Courtesy of Gravesend Borough Council)*
38. The only Second World War RAMC gravestone to bear the Victoria Cross. *(Courtesy of Julia Harden-Wells)*
39. Members of No. 11 Light Field Ambulance, including Clarence Smith (right) inspect the damage caused by a German aerial attack on Belsen concentration camp. (*Courtesy of Colin Culpitt-Smith*)
40., 41. & 42. The degradation of humanity that greeted medical personnel entering Belsen Concentration Camp. *(Courtesy of Second World War Experience Centre)*

Preface

When I was growing up in the 1970s and 1980s, I was vaguely aware that my father had served in the Second World War in the 'Desert Rats', the British Army's 7th Armoured Division. Naively I asked him if he had killed anyone; he answered that he had been in the medical services and it was his role to keep people alive. Unfortunately the conversation never went beyond this and a house burglary in the early 1980s meant that his collection of personal war memorabilia was lost, including a Red Cross armband. My father died in 1991, before I had really taken any interest in the history of the Second World War, and for a decade and a half, any curiosity I had in my father's war service lay dormant. Then, a chance communication from a distant relative revealed that my father's war medals, scrapbook and 170 letters he had sent home to his mother had been preserved, and I was welcome to drive from Barnsley to Colchester to collect them. I did so eagerly and, fifteen years after his death, was rewarded with my father's time in the war being revealed to me through his correspondence. He was a devout Christian, and I have explored the relationships between the world wars and religious faith in other publications. The other main motif of his war experience was the increasing identification he developed with the units in which he served as a private and lance corporal – No. 7 Light Field Ambulance and No. 2 Light Field Ambulance in the Royal Army Medical Corps. Thus this book starts from a desire on the part of the author to place the medical aspects of his war into a wider context. The part played by men of the RAMC features in many publications about the Second World War, and this book brings together much hitherto unused material held in archives and private family collections to shed fresh light on the experiences of medical officers and orderlies across the globe from 1939 to 1945. I hope you derive as much satisfaction from reading it as I have from researching and writing it.

John Broom
Penistone, May 2019

Chapter 1

Recruitment, Organisation and Training

The history of formal medical services in the British Army can be traced back to the reign of King Charles II (r. 1660–85) who established the Standing Regular Army with the provision of medical officers within each regiment, both in peacetime and war. This regimental arrangement continued until 1873, when the Army Medical Department (AMD) was established to work across the entire army. Doctors had to pass a series of practical and written examinations organised by the Army Medical School, which had been established at Fort Pitt in Chatham in 1860 and then moved to Netley, near the river Solent, in 1863. During this period, medical officers did not carry a military rank but did receive pay and other benefits commensurate with officer rank. Meanwhile, the Medical Staff Corps had been established during the Crimean War, composed of 'Men able to read and write, of regular steady habits and good temper and of a kindly disposition'. Their role was to provide support to medical officers, having received specific training for the task.

Recruitment to the Army Medical Department proved a challenge for the army, with no new admissions occurring from July 1887 to July 1889. After pressure from the British Medical Association (BMA) and the Royal College of Physicians, officers and soldiers providing medical services were incorporated into the new Royal Army Medical Corps, established in 1898, with its first colonel-in-chief being HRH the Duke of Connaught.

During the Boer War of 1899–1902, 743 RAMC officers and 6,130 other ranks were lost due to the fighting and outbreaks of epidemic diseases that plagued the British Army during the campaigns. The largely preventable deaths from illnesses such as typhoid, which outstripped the numbers of men lost in battle, led to a reform of military hospitals and the Army Medical School being moved from Netley to Millbank in London. The First World War saw the RAMC and other army medical services become an integral part of the British Army under Sir Alfred Keogh, Director General of Army Medical Services 1905–10 and 1914–18.

A system for the organisation of casualty evacuation was established based on a 'chain of evacuation' in which the sick and wounded were moved backwards by a series of posts: the Regimental Aid Post (RAP), the Casualty Collection Point (CCP), the Advanced and Main Dressing Stations (ADS and MDS), the Casualty Clearing Station (CCS), and finally, the General Hospital, either in France or England, via a hospital ship. Due to the necessity of early treatment, Casualty Clearing Stations were expanded and positioned closer to the front line, accommodating up to 1,000 patients at a time. By 1918, the number of officers in the RAMC had swelled to 13,000, supported by 154,000 other ranks, who served in all theatres of war across Western and Eastern Europe, the Middle East and Africa.

On the eve of the outbreak of the Second World War, the strength of the regular and reserve forces comprising the Army Medical Services, as at 31 August 1939, was 1,453 regular officers, 5,920 other ranks, and 3,401 on the reserve list – a total strength of 9,321.[1] The Territorial Army's medical units comprised:

Field Ambulances	34
Cavalry Field Ambulances	4
Hygiene Companies	4
Motor Ambulance Convoys	2
Casualty Clearing Stations	4
General Hospitals	15[2]

By the end of May 1945, the total number of men serving in the Army Medical Services stood at nearly 18,000, a doubling of forces during the course of the war.[3] In order to address the immediate demand for medical officers at the start of the war, the Central Medical War Committee of the British Medical Association (CMWC) was appointed by the War Office as the instrument for recruitment from the medical profession. The Deputy Director General Army Medical Services was appointed as the representative of the Army Medical Directorate on this body. All medical practitioners in the United Kingdom were contacted and asked for details of their employment and commitments, as well as their willingness to undertake service with the fighting or civil defence forces. It was agreed that in the event of compulsory service, the committee would notify the War Office of their particulars.[4]

During September 1939, the CMWC nominated 110 medical men for commissions as specialists, but only ninety-eight were forthcoming over the subsequent six months. As a consequence, qualification requirements were lowered so younger and less experienced men could take up appointments where they could work under the guidance and supervision of more experienced specialist officers. Known as 'graded' staff, e.g. 'graded surgeon', 'graded physician', these new officers were granted a temporary rank of lieutenant. They immediately replaced those who had been mobilised for field service to reinforce military hospitals, but due to shortages of existing medical staff, some were used to address deficiencies in field medical units due to be despatched overseas. By mid-1941, a total of 869 specialists and 187 graded specialists were serving with the Army Medical Services.[5]

In addition to the efforts made by the BMA to recruit doctors into the military, in September 1939, about 800 medical practitioners volunteered for service in the army.[6] Each one was medically examined, and then interviewed by a Deputy Director of Medical Services (DDMS) at the headquarters of a command. By the end of June 1940, due to the post-Dunkirk realisation that the war would be a long drawn-out affair, this number had risen to nearly 3,000 professionals signing up for the duration of the war.[7]

Despite this increase, it had become apparent that voluntarism would not be sufficient to meet the need for medical officers, so conscription was introduced. The practice of medicine was removed from the list of reserved occupations and medical practitioners became liable for compulsory military service under the National Service (Armed Forces) Act. The CMWC was informed of War Office requirements and established local medical war committees to determine the most suitable recruits from each district. The War Office then notified the individual, offering him a commission in the RAMC. He was informed that if he declined this, he would be liable to be called up for service under the normal arrangements of the National Service Act.

In the midst of this recruitment drive, the Ministry of Health had to be conscious of balancing the medical needs of the armed forces with those of a civilian population under immense strain. The ratio of medical practitioners per 1,000 of population was found, in early 1941, to be:

Civlilian	0.82
Royal Navy	4.1
Army	2.8
Royal Air Force	2.9

The Royal Army Medical College at Millbank, London had been reopened soon after the conclusion of the First World War as a teaching establishment for the postgraduate training of RAMC officers in areas such as military surgery, tropical medicine and hygiene. Other ranks were also trained for technical roles such as radiographers or laboratory assistants. An Army School of Hygiene was established at Aldershot in 1922, with the aim of promoting efficient hygienic practice across the army, as 'nothing less would suffice than that every individual solider should be taught to observe the principles underlying a healthy existence and to live his life according to a regimen based on their application.'[8]

The school featured laboratories and lecture rooms, and outdoor demonstrations including scale models of water supplies, sanitary appliances, disinfectors and mosquito breeding grounds. Officers from outside the medical services also received training here. Subjects included soldier welfare, dietetics, general hygiene, field sanitation and anti-malarial measures. The school was relocated to Mytchett Barracks, near Aldershot on 13 November 1939. Training for those officers wishing to work in specialist branches of surgery such as ophthalmic, thoracic, cranial and maxilla-facial took place in special hospitals and surgical units and was augmented by attendance at lectures and demonstrations. Clinical instruction in wartime medicine and surgery was arranged by postgraduate teaching bodies.

A system for the training of medical orderlies – the men who would work as nurses, stretcher-bearers, theatre assistants, radiographers, laboratory technicians and a host of other technical and support roles within the corps – had to be established. The RAMC had two main training depots in England – one in the north and one in the south of England – in addition to No. 2 Depot at Newbattle Abbey, near Edinburgh. Beckett Park in Leeds had served as a military hospital during the First World War and had been a teacher training college up to 1939. On 1 December 1939, it was established as No. 11 Training Depot RAMC, where recruits would undertake a special intensive course of training in technical subjects extending over two months. Mr R. McFarlane was on the staff at Beckett Park and recalled receiving a new batch of recruits every six weeks.[9] The remit of the staff was to turn civilians into trained troops within that period. Men came from all walks of life and all parts of the country. They were formed into platoons of thirty and were housed in the accommodation blocks, where they were issued with mattress covers that they filled with hay and straw. Every morning they would be woken and given breakfast, and then marched off to the main building where they would receive drill and medical training. As the number of recruits grew, some private houses in the Headingley and Meanwood areas were requisitioned to house them.

Each Sunday, there would be a compulsory church parade, sometimes in the main hall and at other times in St Chad's Church, Headingley. One block at Beckett Park had a swimming pool where the men would be taught how to take casualties over the water. At the end of the training period there was a 20-mile route march, which would take a day to complete. On completion of their training, men would be given a few days' leave before receiving their posting orders, being sent as nursing orderlies to different RAMC units. Sergeants were recruited from other regiments to teach drill to the recruits. Tom Bradley was billeted at 12 Grove Lane, about a mile from Beckett Park.[10] Each morning at 6.30am, his troop would be marched to the depot for breakfast. As it was the middle of winter, men at the front and back of the column would have to carry a lit hurricane lamp.

No. 1 Training Depot RAMC was based at Boyce Barracks at Church Crookham, 5 miles from Aldershot in Hampshire. The barracks had been purpose-built in 1938 to act as the regiment's main depot. The depot could accommodate 2,500 men in peacetime and included a large parade area, gymnasium and cinema. Alexander Adamson recalled a drill square of smooth tarmac, which was a joy to parade on.[11] There were lectures on first aid and the rudiments of nursing, including bandaging, treatments of various types of wounds, burns, snake bites, the use of antiseptics and sterilising instruments for operating. During Adamson's training there was one special parade at Tweseldown Racecourse that was inspected by the king and queen, and the prime minister, Neville Chamberlain.

As the majority of Territorial Army (TA) medical staff had been posted to France in 1939, the Army Medical Services on home soil had to build a comprehensive and versatile organisation to cater for the citizen army then being raised and trained. In addition, RAMC units had to be raised and trained in the technical and professional skills needed to operate in the field in various theatres of war. All new army recruits required a rigorous physical examination to determine their fitness for military service and the category in which they could serve. After this examination, vaccinations and inoculations had to be administered and each individual's documentation completed. As there were not sufficient army medical officers to undertake these tasks, some civilian medical practitioners had to assist in this process.

In order to provide for the rapidly increasing number of sick occasioned by the growth of the army, military hospitals and reception stations had to be expanded. Provision for those suffering from minor ailments or trivial injuries was to be made in small camp hospitals located at RAMC training centres and other camps. Often, Voluntary Aid Detachment (VAD) members were used to supplement the personnel at these hospitals. RAMC officers also worked closely with the Royal Engineers in the design of huge new barracks and camps to house the recruits, ensuring that, as far as possible, sanitation, cooking and lighting supplies were established. However, it was claimed that 'in spite of all efforts to obtain the best that improvisation could achieve, the hygienic and sanitary state of many of these camps was, for a time, far from satisfactory.'[12]

Recruitment

The men who formed the bulk of the RAMC during the war, working as orderlies in a variety of general and specialist technical roles, came from a wide variety of backgrounds, some having already been members of the Territorial Army before the war, others having a general interest in medicine and first aid, and some merely being assigned randomly to the corps. A further group, the conscientious objectors, were posted to the RAMC on the basis that they would have to bear arms against a fellow human.

David Jones, a cost clerk with a gas company, was already a member of a Territorial RAMC unit and so on the Monday following Chamberlain's announcement on the wireless that Britain was at war, he reported to Finsbury Barracks in Central London. After a morning amid confusion as to how the influx of what was now a regular army was to be organised, Jones became one of many men who took a dislike to army drills and the way in which they were conducted:

> When I arrived at the barracks there was chaos and we just sat around in groups waiting for something to happen. At midday they told us to 'fall in' on the parade ground and then they marched us through the streets to the local ABC

> restaurant. We all sat down and had steak and kidney pie with vegetables and some sort of fruit pie with custard.
>
> The next day was a little different and they were more organised. We were taken out onto the parade ground and a little squint-eyed Sergeant called Stanton put us through two hours of marching up and down. He soon got to know me and every so often shouted out 'Jones, take that smile off your face.' Then he would have a go at someone else and it was not long before we all hated him.[13]

Ronald Ritson had left school aged 14 to begin work as a coal miner at Walkmill Colliery in Cumberland. The colliery maintained a branch of the St John's Ambulance, which Ritson joined, competing with other local mines to win a shield for the most efficient unit. Ritson also availed himself of the option to join the unit's Military Hospital Reserve, which afforded him additional opportunities for medical training but also meant that, in the event of war breaking out, he would be liable to an immediate call-up.

On Monday, 4 September, on completion of his shift in the darkness of the pit, Ritson arrived home at 3.00 pm to be greeted with the equally dark news that his call-up papers had arrived and he was to catch a train at Bransty Station, Whitehaven at 7.00 pm. He did not have the opportunity to formally give his notice at work, and had to say a hurried farewell to his parents and siblings.[14]

Paul Watts, a resident assistant golf professional, joined the local Air Raid Precautions (ARP) unit and had become a gas instructor for his home village of Mundesley in Norfolk. He was also the local Scout master and when interviewed for call-up was told that unfortunately, he would not qualify for the infantry as he had flat feet. As someone who earned his living from sport, this amazed him. However, he was not too sorry to miss out on the infantry and pointed out that he had been trained in first aid for his Scout work, suggesting his skills could be used in the RAMC.[15]

Jim Whitaker had worked in a shoe factory in Lancashire before the war. His employer wanted a qualified first-aider on his staff and had offered to pay the course fees of anyone who applied. Whitaker leapt at the opportunity and was able to gain experience in ambulance driving and treating patients in this additional role. However, as he was thus considered a key worker for Civil Defence, he was not permitted to volunteer for the RAMC, as was his wish, and had to wait for his age group to be called up before being assigned to the corps.[16]

Walter Hart, a printer and bookbinder from the Jewish East End of London, was another Territorial, like David Jones, who found his initiation into army food provisions a pleasant experience. Hart was part of the 1st Militia, the first batch of troops to be conscripted, and had been a member of the St John's Ambulance before the war as well as serving as a sergeant in the Jewish Lads' Brigade. Having signed on at a labour exchange in May 1939, he was passed as A1 at a medical and posted to the training depot at Church Crookham:

> On arrival we were told to form a queue, so that we could be checked in. Just then a red tabbed colonel came by and said a few words of welcome. After being booked in we were led by a sergeant to a big mess hall, there meeting our view, were tables placed in pairs end to end. Each table was covered by a white sheet, serving as a tablecloth, and on each was a small vase with flowers. The kindly sergeant told us to sit down and we were served with tea and sandwiches by corporals who were present. The sergeant declared, 'This is only a snack, you will get a proper lunch later.'[17]

However, this kindness was merely for the benefit of the attendant members of the press, out in full force to cover the story of the first batch of conscripts. After they had left, the tablecloths and flowers were removed and a sergeant barked, 'Right, twelve to a table.' The final two men to sit down were appointed mess orderlies for the week, assigned the task of dishing out the food and removing and washing the empty pots afterwards. During the meal an officer came round and asked if there were any complaints. Having been previously warned that if anyone complained, they would be 'in for it, no one raised any objection despite the awfulness of the food.'

Charles Quant had lost the use of an eye in a boyhood accident, and when he went for an initial medical examination to join the army, he was told by the doctor that he was unfit for military service due to only having one working eye:

> I said I was a very good shot with rifle or shotgun, but he said that King's Regulations said that nobody with only one

> eye could shoot. I was cheeky and asked him if he could shoot, he said he did. I asked him which eye he closed and he said the left. I said that my left eye was permanently closed, but he stuck to the point about King's Regulations and sent me home.[18]

Nevertheless, Quant was called for interview a few months later and told there was an opening in the RAMC to train as a radiographer. (Pic 1) He keenly accepted this offer and was sent to the training depot at Church Crookham, and thence to the training college at Millbank, the timing of which coincided with the start of the Blitz.

Norman 'Ginger' Barnett had never planned to become a medic. Before the war he and a friend had calculated that if they waited to be called up there was a chance that they would be directed into coal mining, a fate neither of them surveyed with relish, so they sought to join the TA. Having been rejected by both the Royal Artillery and the Queen's Regiment on account of their Territorial units both being full, they were advised to volunteer for the RAMC, whose local unit was based in a wooden hut in a Croydon back street. Finally they were accepted and Barnett was assigned to No. 133 Field Ambulance.[19]

A similar route into the RAMC was experienced by Frank Turton, a 20-year-old grocery assistant employed by the Brightside and Carbrook Co-operative Society in Sheffield. (Pic 2) Initially, Turton had no intention of joining the Medical Corps and attended an interview to join the RAF. Retrospectively, he felt that the questions were being framed towards assigning him as a rear gunner but he did not provide the required answers, so on 6 June 1940, he was sent to the RAMC training depot at Beckett Park, Leeds. Due to the recent influx of evacuees from Dunkirk into the hospital wards at Beckett Park, there was a shortage of beds, so Turton and his colleagues had to stuff straw palliasses on which to sleep. This provided a taste of things to come, as he was not to sleep in a bed for a further five years of army service.[20] After the period of initial training at Beckett Park, Turton was assigned to No. 132 Field Ambulance, a sister unit to that of 'Ginger' Barnett's No. 133 FA.

A recruit with a different rationale for joining the RAMC was Ernest Grainger. In 1938 he was working as an insurance surveyor in the City of London in a company that encouraged its junior staff to join the Territorial Army. In order not to have his future career prospects blighted, and because he had harboured youthful ambitions to become a doctor, Grainger opted for the RAMC as this was the closest he thought he could come to realising them. Grainger was assigned to No. 10 Casualty Clearing Station and trained as an operating room assistant, a role that included mopping up blood as the surgeon worked, holding clamps in place and generally fulfilling whatever tasks the surgeon found for them.[21]

John Broom was a 23-year-old furniture salesman from Colchester at the time of his call-up and appeared before the medical board on 24 February 1940, being classed as Grade 'A1'. (Pic 3) He was deemed to have enlisted on 15 March 1940, on which date his devoutly Christian parents gave him a pocket bible with the following inscription:

> To my darling John
> With fondest love
> From Mum and Dad
> March 15th 1940
> And when He putteth forth
> His own sheep
> He goeth before them …
> Kept by the Power of God
> Peter 1.5.
> In all thy ways acknowledge Him,
> And He shall direct thy paths
> Proverbs 3.6

This bible was to remain with him throughout the war, and indeed for the rest of his life. His mother Florence, like many women of her generation, had to send her son off to war just twenty-five years after seeing her husband depart for the horrors of the First World War trenches. On his arrival in Leeds, Broom wrote, 'Regarding my departure, you were very brave and the circumstances were the best possible. I realise how very much you must have been dreading it. Truly you all bore yourselves with conspicuous courage. I am glad you didn't break down, though I should have understood it if you had.'[22]

Home comforts he had become used to were not much in evidence once Civvy Street had been left behind. He had to undertake dining hall fatigues, company messenger duties and lighting fires in the company sergeant major's room. Individuality was at a minimum at Beckett Park, with the recruits being allowed just one suitcase in which to keep their personal effects (clothes, kitbag, books and papers), and Broom was forced to parcel up his civilian clothes to send home.

Although many recruits had no previous medical experience, this was not the case with William Earl, a pharmacist's assistant who was called up in late May 1940 and assigned to No. 214 Field Ambulance. Earl reported to Euston Station and found that most of the hundred or so men mustered there that day were pharmacists or assistants, the assumption amongst them being that they had been slotted into a military role based on their civilian jobs.[23]

Geoffrey Haine had been working as a medical officer at Selly Oak Hospital, Birmingham while waiting for his call-up. (Pic 4) Taking matters into his own hands, in July 1940 he wrote to the War Office offering his services to the RAMC. Following a stint as a locum GP, he was instructed to report to the RAMC depot at Church Crookham and gazetted as Lieutenant G.L. Haine, 141998. His attention then turned to practical matters such as getting his service dress made and visiting a local solicitor to have a will drawn up. Haine's arrival at Church Crookham coincided with that of about fifty other doctors, approximately forty of whom were psychiatrists, or 'trick cyclists', as they were referred to in the army. Haine held few fond memories of his initial period of army training:

> I didn't really enjoy being 'turned into a soldier' and thought all the drilling was very pointless, when all I wanted was to do my bit as a doctor to help the wounded and sick. We marched up and down, we had lectures about Army formation and Army discipline and we had 'Tactical exercises without troops', TEWT – and all the while Hitler was massing his troops ready for an invasion.[24]

After six weeks of this unfulfilling work, Haine took part in a passing out parade and was posted as General Duty Officer with the No. 34 British General Hospital (BGH) at Hatfield House, Hertfordshire, and a month later as a medical officer to the Royal Tank Regiment at Bovington in Dorset.

After Haine had served in West Africa with No. 34 BGH, he was transferred to No. 49 Field Surgical Unit (Pic 5) and was struck at how few of the men under his leadership had any pre-war medical experience:

> We went to Warminster for our other ranks to report to us. They consisted of nine nursing orderlies and three drivers. Our corporal had been a salesman in a gents' outfitters in London. The fellow who we trained to look after the theatre was from a timber store in London where he was the chief clerk – the fellow who was to be part-time batman for me came from a shoe factory. None had had any civilian nursing experience.[25]

David Paton had qualified as a doctor at the University of Glasgow in 1938, and having been in the Officers' Training Corps, was called up on 2 September 1939. His pre-war enthusiasm had been based on an understanding of the nature of Hitler's regime: 'I could see Hitler was evil. I had read *Mein Kampf* and I thought "this is evil and somebody ought to fight this" … I was pleased to be called up.'[26]

However, Paton was to find himself mis-posted – 'an awful thing'. He was sent to be the medical officer for the 15th/65th Anti-Tank Regiment, Royal Artillery, stationed at Blandford Forum, Dorset, but on his arrival found that the regiment had left the county some weeks previously. He then went to Tidworth Military Hospital on Salisbury Plain, where a senior officer had no role for him. Paton was then asked, 'Do you know anything about radiology?'

'I said, "No, but I will if you want me to." And he said, "Well, I would like, I am waiting to go to France. I have got my 13CCS here and I want to go to France. We just need a radiologist and we can go so I will tell him I have got my radiologist."'

On being interviewed by the unit's commanding officer, Paton was ordered back to the War Office in London to ascertain where exactly he should be. On arrival he walked straight through the main door without being challenged and found the department that should have been able to clear up the confusion, AMD1.

> I found a couple of Majors in there. One was red haired. He said 'Oh, something has gone wrong,' and he looked and he said 'Oh I tell you what, I have done the wrong thing.

> I have sent all these chaps to the wrong place.' He looked, there were two columns. In one was to go to this unit and the others he had taken the names off and he sent them all to the same place, and they had gone long ago.

The major then sent Paton up to Northern Command, where he was assigned to the 1st Battalion of the York and Lancaster Regiment, who were preparing to go to France. Paton spent a night talking to his new commanding officer over a bonfire and the pair got on well. The following morning, another doctor arrived in camp and he took precedence as he had been sent directly by the War Office rather than via Northern Command. Captain Paton was to experience two further postings before being assigned to a commando unit for the raid on St Nazaire.

Reg Gill was another recruit who brought a pre-war medical expertise to the RAMC. In 1938, Gill was working as a trainee radiographer at Leeds General Infirmary. Having become fully conversant with the X-ray and photographic equipment, Gill and his friend Joe Knapton decided to offer their services to the Territorial Army. A unit was being formed, the core of which would be staff from their hospital. The colonel was to be an ex-consultant, the two lieutenant colonels would be current consultants and the registrars would become majors. Gill and Knapton reckoned that it was best to volunteer and be given the job they wished to do rather than wait to be conscripted and run the risk of being placed in the infantry. Having joined in April 1939, Gill went to camp with the newly formed 1st Northern General Hospital. 'It rained the whole week. It was a deluge, the ground was a swamp, the food terrible. It was bitterly cold and we were permanently wet under canvas. Within my tent, believe it or not, were privates Night, Day, Moon and Love. I was the odd one out as a Gill.'[27]

Not expecting a war to start as early as August 1939, Gill cycled to Rhyl for a holiday, only to hear on the youth hostel wireless that all TA personnel were to report back to their barracks at once. Forgoing the return journey by bike, Gill caught the first train back to Leeds to report to Meanwood dance hall. Having assembled in 'utter confusion', each member of the unit was issued with two blankets and made to sleep on the cold, hard floor. The following day they were marched to Beckett Park and formed into squads. On 3 September, they were told that Chamberlain's ultimatum to Hitler to withdraw his troops from Poland had been ignored, and the country was at war.

Conscientious objectors

The National Service (Armed Forces) Act, which was enacted by Parliament on 3 September 1939, gave provision for those with an ethical, religious or political objection to war to register as a conscientious objector. Some men who had availed themselves of this wished to serve in the Royal Army Medical Corps as they knew they would not be required to bear arms. One such young man was James Driscoll, a recently married Christian from London. Having registered as a conscientious objector, he was ordered to appear before the South-East local tribunal on 19 March 1940, at which he stated, 'I refuse to have any part in the killing and maiming of my fellow beings because it is incompatible with my Christian faith. I am, however, willing to do purely non-combatant duties in the Medical Corps.'[28] Driscoll preferred service in the RAMC to the Pay Corps as he could not bear the thought of sitting behind a desk in a warm office whilst others were fighting and dying. Initially he was directed to undertake agricultural or forestry work, possibly because he had no first aid training. Because of this, he lodged an appeal, for which he made a written submission: 'I did not object to non-combatant duties in the Medical Corps. Indeed, I believe my Christian duty in the present emergency is to help alleviate the sufferings caused by the hostilities.'

The appeal was heard on 6 August 1940 and Driscoll was accepted into the RAMC. In his later years, he reflected on the different experience he would have had as a conscientious objector in Germany, where they frequently faced death by firing squad, hanging or beheading. He had been provided with travelling and subsistence expenses for his appeal but was subsequently dismissed from his employment for his beliefs.

Lacey Tingle, the son of a Methodist minister, would later join the airborne No. 224 Field Ambulance and become a D-Day hero. However, in 1940 his beliefs were dismissed as 'religious claptrap' by a member of the tribunal:

> When Anthony Lacey Tingle, a Wigton Magna (Leicestershire) elementary school teacher told Leicestershire Conscientious Objectors Tribunal yesterday that he believed in the brotherhood of man, Councillor E. Purser, a member of the tribunal, asked 'Where do you get that from?'

> Mr Purser added 'This is the 3,131st case in which applicants have spoke of the brotherhood of man, and I have never discovered any single person who could say where he found it. It is nothing less than religious claptrap.'[29]

Tingle was registered for non-combat service, originally assigned to the Non-Combatant Corps, before volunteering for the RAMC in 1941 and training as a parachutist.

Cases of conscientious objectors were frequently reported in the regional press. The *Lancashire Evening Post* of 22 February 1940 reported the case of one such man whom Judge Burgis, the chairman of the North-West tribunal, used as an example of military service that could be undertaken by objectors:

> 'The applicant has done great service both to the Tribunal and to other conscientious objectors by drawing attention to this matter. It is abundantly clear that there is nothing about the R.A.M.C. that might impinge the consciences of objectors.'
>
> This is how Judge Burgis thanked Wilfred M. Spencer (21), library assistant, of Castle Road, Colne.
>
> Spencer was closely questioned by Judge Burgis on a statement he made that he had heard from a Colne friend now serving with the R.A.M.C. that he (the friend) was trained in the use of the rifle.
>
> Spencer said he did not object to non-combatant duties and was willing to join the R.A.M.C. if he could be assured he would not be compelled to use a rifle. He had intended to volunteer for the R.A.M.C. until he heard, at Christmas, this story from his friend.
>
> The Tribunal ordered that Spencer's name should be removed from the register as liable to be called up for service in non-combatant duties. They recommended, however, that he be posted to the R.A.M.C.
>
> 'This question is causing great misunderstanding in the minds of some conscientious objectors. I make this clear and definite – that every man who joins the R.A.M.C. as a conscientious objector on an order of this Court, will not be trained in the use of firearms.'

Jim Wisewell was 23 years old when he received his call-up papers in 1940, and had been a committed Christian for six years. His father had been killed at Passchendaele in 1917 and Wisewell had left school without completing a secondary education to work as a baker due to straitened family circumstances. Conscription presented him with an ethical dilemma:

> Could I, as a committed Christian, kill my fellow men? I felt I couldn't. I didn't have any blockages politically; I realised that Hitler was an evil genius and his hatred for the Jews wakened a conviction that he needed to be stopped. So I had no problems in supporting the war effort but I felt that I just couldn't personally kill. So I decided I would join the Medical Corps, become a stretcher-bearer and then save men's lives rather than destroy them.[30]

On registering at the local labour exchange, Wisewell elucidated his position to the recruiting sergeant but was told, 'Well you can't do it that way, you'll have to face a tribunal and tell them.' So he went down to Bristol to appear before Judge Weatherhead and the other South-West tribunal members. He explained that he could not kill his fellow men but was more than willing to join the RAMC. Wisewell was granted this request, then called up, graded A1 at his medical and sent to the training depot at Church Crookham in August 1940. While at the Boyce Barracks, Wisewell and his fellow recruits did not receive the number of lectures they should have due to time being spent digging tank ditches around London as the threat of invasion seemed very real. After an initial period at one of the training depots, men were then posted to a specific unit, in Wisewell's case, No. 223 Field Ambulance, which was stationed near Hertford. Further medical and military training was undertaken, along with work in civilian hospitals.

Preparation and training

At whatever level they enrolled, all RAMC recruits had to have various inoculations in order to prevent avoidable diseases spreading through the ranks. John Broom, who had recently arrived at No. 11 Training Depot at Beckett Park, wrote home to his mother:

> We had T.A.B. inoculation abt. 3p.m. which left me with most others with a temporary high fever. We are excused

> for 48 hrs until Thursday afternoon. Some of the chaps fainted. The foolish part about it was that a few minutes after we had been marched back to our quarters, the Fire Drill Bugle sounded so we had to parade again in the freezing cold and with a high wind. After waiting about a quarter of an hour we were told to march inside, and about 200 of us had to herd into a small hall, packed like cattle. There were no windows open. One chap near me fainted & after about twenty minutes wait I felt ready to faint myself. Then the Company Sergeant Major came along & told us that we could go to our rooms. I laid down in bed, and missed tea & supper, whilst I was sweating like a bull.[31]

Further medical checks were made to ensure men were in the best possible health. Broom reported: 'There is the dental business. Did I tell you about that? I had inspection the other day and they, my teeth, have to be attended to. I suppose they will drag out my brute by the excavator method. Other teeth have to be drilled. Sounds inviting doesn't it, dear?'

Leslie Ellis was surprised at the sight of fellow doctors collapsing after their jab: 'We learnt how to salute and also we did a little square bashing. We had to have our hair cut and had to be inoculated, when shamelessly not me but … some of the other doctors having got injected for TAB fainted on the spot.'[32]

For those on the Far East draft at Beckett Park, a vaccination was administered in late September 1940. John Broom described the nauseating vaccine fever that lasted for three days:

> Did I tell you that I had been vaccinated last week? It was actually done on 18th Sept., & I knew all about it these past few days. I spent all Weds. Thurs. & Friday evenings in bed with alternating fits of sweating & shivering, a severe headache, of which I was rid only this morning, backache, which went yesterday & of course arm ache not to mention a royal cold. In this depot it's looked upon with disfavour to fall sick after vaccination, so I didn't do that, but I don't remember feeling worse in all my life! How I got through those 3 days I just don't know & P.T.

> on Fri morning! I couldn't sleep much on any of those nights because of my head, the top of which seemed likely to snap off. One of the masseurs on my draft massaged me last evening – again I went to bed early – & today I'm beginning to take a bit more interest in things. My arm hasn't swollen too much & in a couple of days I shall be right O.K. So don't worry. I've had a touch of vaccine fever, that's all, & I've weathered it. It's really surprising how many chaps here-there are on whom the vaccination doesn't take at all. Lucky fellows, but hardly healthy, I should imagine.[33]

Being amongst the first wave of conscripts, Walter Hart was issued with equipment dating from 1917. This included a gas mask, which, during the retreat from France in the summer of 1940, would have proved useless against new poison gases the Germans had developed, and had to be handed in for modifications.

On arrival at Beckett Park, John Broom was issued with initial basic equipment, allowing men to post their civilian clothes home, garments that most would not wear again for nearly six years:

> Well to start at the beginning, on Saturday morning we received our uniforms consisting of trousers, jacket (battle dress) forage cap, boots & a pair of what they here call shoes but which are really brown canvas topped slippers … Also we had an overcoat (mine hasn't got any brass buttons, praise be) canvas jacket & trousers for fatigues. Mine haven't started yet.[34]

The requirement to have brass buttons maintained with a shiny lustre would cause men many hours of tedious work. Private Paul Watts wrote to his wife shortly after his arrival at the Church Crookham training depot:

> I have now got my uniform and am a full-blown soldier. My kit consists of: hat, blouse, trousers, great coat, heavy pair of boots, pair of plimsoles, 3 pairs of socks, 2 pairs

> of long pants, 3 shirts, pullover, braces, 2 towels, puttees, 2 shoe brushes, toothbrush, clothes brush, shaving brush and razor, button brush. The uniform is quite a good fit but there are 17 buttons to clean and soon there will be badges as well. The boots are greasy and so you can imagine what it is like to polish them. We are expected to get them bright enough to see our faces in them. The discipline here is very strict. No smoking outside the barrack room and if there is a button undone you are really for it. Puttees have to be put on if we leave the Depot or it is raining. I have just been for a walk – blimey these boots!!![35]

Watts found mealtimes to require no table manners, as men raced each other to stick their forks into a jar of jam before it ran out, as hunks of bread were passed down long trestle tables. Arbitrary army discipline could cause anxiety amongst the new recruits. Watts reported: 'A terrible thing happened last night. We got a month's C.B. [confined to barracks] for talking after "lights out". We are hoping to get this either reduced or wiped out as we didn't know that we shouldn't talk.'

Bill Frankland had qualified as a doctor in 1938 and was working as a house physician at St Mary's Hospital, Paddington at the outbreak of war. On 1 September, the same day Germany invaded Poland, he enlisted as a civilian military practitioner and was posted to Tidworth Military Hospital in Wiltshire. Shortly afterwards, Frankland was commissioned as a lieutenant in the RAMC. Going up to London to purchase his equipment, he kept the Sam Browne belt that his father had worn during his service in the First World War in the Royal Army Chaplains' Department. 'It was to me a privilege to wear something that my father had worn in the First World War.'[36]

The syllabus of training for wartime recruits into the ranks initially comprised of 270 hours, nearly 100 hours of which were taken up with physical training and drill, and also included lessons on chemical warfare, anatomy and physiology, first aid and nursing. Drilling for the first wave of militia recruits at the Church Crookham base during the summer of 1939 was initially less rigorous and subject to undertones of militancy.

Barnsley-born Ron Dickinson was called up with the first batch of militia and in July 1939 began what he thought would be a six-month training programme. His immaculate copperplate handwriting recorded the information that he would then strive to commit to memory. (Pic 6) Dickinson had been a member of the St John Ambulance and had consequently been offered the chance to join the RAMC. The six-month training programme became six weeks as he was sent to France shortly after the outbreak of war in September 1939. 'Pack your kit, we're on the move,' Dickinson and his comrades in No. 11 Field Ambulance were told. Seventy-nine years later, Dickinson wryly reflected, 'I went for six months' training. It took me six years to get back!'[37] (Pic 7)

Walter Hart and his comrades were initially subjected to the full weight of army discipline in the first day of training:

> There was a large open space, which formed part of the racecourse, and it was here that we paraded. Having formed up on the square, we were ordered 'Open order march', and the inspection began. The Colonel led the way, followed by the Orderly Officer, RSM and the Orderly Sergeant. Inspection of us, in the militia, was somewhat scanty, in the few days that we had been in the depot. The 'powers that be' had learned that they could not do as they pleased with us. We still had the right to contact newspapers and our MPs, and many did just that.[38]

Hart displayed greater enthusiasm the following Saturday, when stretcher drill was introduced. This required the squad to be able to 'form fours'. The men had to form two lines, the front men numbering from right to left and those in the rear line having to listen to the man in front in order to get his number. When the command 'form fours' was given, all those with even numbers had to take one step back and one step to the right, thus forming four lines. On the command 'form two deep', they had to go back to their original positions. When there was an odd number in the squad there was only one man in the penultimate file. In four's drill he was called blank file and had to always stand in the front line, so that when an 'about turn' was given, he also had to march to what had now become the front line.

The British Army was in the process of changing from four's drill to drilling in three lines; therefore, the corporal in charge of the drill had either not experienced leading this procedure or had forgotten it. As Hart had served as a sergeant in the Jewish Lads' Brigade, where drilling in fours was the usual method, he instructed the instructor in that kind of drill, much to the latter's relief.

All recruits, whatever their rank, had to learn basic army drilling. Like Walter Hart, John Broom was given temporary responsibility of leading a drill:

> Yesterday morning we had to learn to slow march. I was singled out by our Sergeant, Cowell by name (who was in the Cameronians & has been sent here as instructor for drill, so that we learn discipline) to teach the backward chap himself, I had to drill the whole squad of 31. There are 33 in our Section 1 altogether. There are abt. 5 or more sections to our 'A' company. I think that if I were in an infantry regiment I should get promotion fairly quickly, but as I am now you know that I can't very well.[39]

The repetitive drilling took up much of the time of the recruits at Beckett Park: 'A single period of drill sometimes lasts for two hours, and when we get about three periods a day, well there isn't a great time left, taking other duties etc. into consideration.' By the spring of 1940, the Leeds training depot was becoming a hive of activity. Broom continued:

> I see that tomorrow Saturday, I am down for fatigue at Becketts Home, about two and a half miles away. With the others detailed for same fatigue I have to parade at 7.45 am in Khaki, carrying canvas jacket & trousers & march to this place. Hardly anybody has heard of the place which apparently is to be taken over with other building for further intakes of recruits. There was never a time when there were so many chaps here. Some of the new fellows when they arrive will have to sleep in tents.

Ian Campbell had qualified as a doctor in 1939, but his initial offer to join the RAMC had been rejected as it was considered they had sufficient number of qualified medics at that time. When he did eventually receive the call, in late 1940, he was posted to the Leeds training depot. Despite his qualification, he was not exempt from usual army practices. 'We did this two weeks course to learn and salute and to march in Beckett's Park.'[40] John Forfar recalled the yawning gap between the professional skill of the newly commissioned medical officers and the ineptitude of their basic military skills: 'It was quite interesting to watch how the men doctors, of great distinction sometimes because they were all called up at the one time without recognition of rank or status together, and I can remember the oddity with which, for instance, the most distinguished medical men couldn't march in time.'[41]

The enmity that had built up between David Jones and Sergeant Stanton within No. 168 Field Ambulance during initial training in London continued once the unit had landed in Palestine in January 1940, with a less than serious attitude to drilling being used as a reason to discipline Jones and his mate:

> The overall control of the huts was in the hands of the most hated Sergeant Stanton. … On drill parades Stanton frequently shouted at the top of his squeaky voice 'Jones, Masson take that smile off your face.' Sometimes instead of putting Denny and me on a charge he would say 'Report to me after parade.' He would then put us on 'camp duty' white-washing a pile of coal at the beginning of the line of barracks. This huge pile of coal was for use in the barracks if the weather became cold. We were not allowed out if we were on fatigues. Sometimes if the coal was white he would make us wash the coal clean. We hated him and told him that when we went up to the front line not to get in front of us.[42]

On top of drilling, many men found the seemingly pointless demands of military culture irksome. When this was allied with an antipathy towards a hierarchical discipline structure, resentment was occasioned at the loss of precious leisure time.

> You mustn't think that all the Army is as restrictive as this unit. It depends on the Assistant Director of Medical Services for the division & our C.O. who spent some years in Sierra Leone (White Man's Grave) in West Africa where

> he had only to clap his hands & a score of lickspittles would come rushing to him. He treats us like that. By his order we were all on fatigues Sunday afternoon, an unheard-of thing in the Army. After that I had to blanco my equipment & polish all brasses (contrary to War Office Instructions) & thus was prevented from attending chapel in the evening. This, because of the C.O.'s inspection, Monday morning! The order which prevents us going to Tunbridge doesn't apply to other units in the division. The London Rifle Brigade are allowed anywhere within 15 miles radius. We are confined to Groombridge.[43]

Frequently, men of otherwise impeccable morals saw fit to subvert army rules. Paul Watts reported:

> Half a dozen of us have been out and bought some bread and cheese and buns which came out to fourpence halfpenny each. We had a real feed. The only trouble was smuggling the bread back into barracks as we have to pass 3 lots of Regimental Police and we are not supposed to bring food into camp. So we cut the loaf into half (it was one of those long square loaves) and another chap and I took our overcoats off and wrapped the bread up in them and carried over our arms, so we got in alright.[44]

As the flow of men emerging from the training depots had to increase, due to the need to fill posts in the new field and base units being established, a special intensive course of instruction was developed for use at No. 11 RAMC Depot at Beckett Park, which reduced the period of instruction to 164 hours, spread across two months. The three main areas of study were anatomy and physiology, first aid and nursing. All three training depots arranged special courses for different occupations, e.g. dispensers, clerks, cooks and sanitary assistants.

The training of men with a non-medical background to become nursing orderlies was rigorous and left little time for reflection. John Broom had no significant medical experience before being allocated to the RAMC training depot at Beckett Park in 1940. After a few weeks of training, which consisted almost entirely of drilling, the task of turning the Colchester furniture salesman into a nursing orderly began. 'On Friday evening we had a little film show here, dealing with medical stuff like bacteria (three sorts) & blood cells. They put on another film to finish with, starring Deanna Durbin. You may remember her voice singing on the Wireless.'[45]

The speed with which training had to be completed, along with the need to continue to be moulded into members of a military machine, could sometimes leave insufficient time for the learning to become embedded:

> Well, we have had more lectures. The trouble is that they are too intensive & as we have no time of our own to study them up, they tend to become forgotten during drill etc. There are absolutely hundreds of queer names to remember, functions & so on to get the low-down on. If we did nothing else but medical stuff here, I'm sure that we should get on well, but these other duties put the Kybosh on it. I understand however that directly our 2 mths are done, we have no more infantry drill at all. The chief object of it is to smarten us up on it.[46]

Paul Watts found the intensity of the additional learning once he had been posted to No. 6 Light Field Ambulance to be intellectually rewarding:

> I have started on my lectures on Gas and I think they are going to be very interesting. We have to learn all we can and then lecture to others when we have completed the course. I am looking forward to that and then we have to have a course on incendiary and high explosive bombs and of course lecture on that. So I want to learn as much as I possibly can and perhaps if I can prove that I know what I am talking about more than the others I may be able to get the chief lecturers job in the ambulance.[47]

Nevertheless, theories of medical care had been absorbed, although their practical application remained unaddressed. John Broom wrote:

> As for further training, the only kind we haven't had is the actual practical training with real cases, but as far as the theory is concerned, we've been taught all that anyone

> would ever want to know without specialised training in any special branch of the medical work. As I've explained before, the grass hasn't been growing under our feet & the ground covered would astonish you. But I do hope that I shall be moved nearer home.[48]

Physical training remained arduous, with officers frequently setting a good example:

> Last Thursday we went for a route march & travelled 15–16 miles. Not bad, eh? We had the midday meal on the way & a hot dinner when we got back. My feet weren't blistered, though they ached a bit! Just a few chaps fell out by the wayside, but the rest did remarkably well. All the officers who went, about a dozen in all, marched every inch of the way & were a very decent lot.[49]

Men could enjoy a variety of organised sporting activities to supplement the fitness gained from long route marches:

> I've played five [football] games in eight days going to Maresfield & Crowborough besides Grinstead & Groombridge. Last week, too, we had a cross-country run over seven miles on Weds afternoon. I came in first. The next day we had a route march which took us twenty-two miles. The blisters which I collected are still with me, the largest one being pricked yesterday (left heel). All this exercise is besides P.T. & drill. I shouldn't have much fat left, should I?[50]

The religious scruples that many men carried from civilian life into the armed services during the war occasionally brought them into conflict with the expectations of military life. John Broom recounted his refusal to play sport on the Sabbath:

> Just lately we have had compulsory games including football & I have played once or twice. Not being the worst player I was chosen to play for the draft against the 'Cooks Course' but the only time the ground was available was yesterday Sunday

> afternoon, so of course I told them I wouldn't play. A corporal said 'Would you go on parade on a Sunday?' I answered 'Of course.' So he followed up with 'Wouldn't you rather play football?' Whereupon I told him with finality that I drew a strict line between business & pleasure on a Sunday & so on.[51]

Rebellion against military authority was not confined to issues of conscience. Rigid discipline caused discontent in the ranks.

> As our draft is in disgrace we have had all swimming, games & week-end passes cancelled & instead we have had extra drills & P.T. The Riot Act was read to us on two successive days for the fellows are getting very restive about being treated as they are in such a ridiculous manner. One can't wonder at there being a certain amount of mutiny considering that most of the fellows have had long service in the Corps (regulars) & they are being bossed around by a conceited incompetent set of sergeant-dispensers with just a few months service & no experience. And hanging about here for months doesn't help.[52]

Private Arthur Atkin was in the first wave of men to be called up, resulting in him being drafted into an existing unit rather than sent to a training depot. The military side of his training was provided by the personnel of the unit of which he would remain a member for the next six years, the No. 140 Field Ambulance, attached to 168 Brigade in the 56th Division. Atkin learnt the rudiments of medical care in the wards of various civilian hospitals wherever the unit was stationed: London, Folkestone and Newmarket. Eventually he qualified as a Nursing Orderly Class I, before being assigned the role of signwriter in an unofficial tradesmen group of men within the unit headquarters, which also included a barber, tailor, carpenter and boot repairer. The army was keen to utilise any skills that men brought in from civilian life.[53]

Reg Gill found that skills that would have been of invaluable use once he arrived in France in early 1940 with No. 18 General Hospital were not given high priority during his period of training:

> You know we spent all those weeks between September 1939 and the end of the year, marching up and down and

> doing useless drills. Ceremonial drills for stretcher-bearers are complicated. It takes half an hour to sort out 200 men into equal size to carry stretchers but we were never told how to retrieve a casualty who might be lying pinned to barbed wire, or in a bush somewhere, or on uneven ground.[54]

David Jones spent the autumn of 1939 being taken to hospitals around London to be shown how to support surgeons undertaking operations. His unit, No. 168 Field Ambulance, then moved to a country mansion in north-east Lincolnshire where there were daily lectures and lessons on how to use the specialist equipment the unit had been given.

Ronald Ritson had been called up immediately upon Britain's entry into the war, and after some temporary postings through the autumn of 1939, was posted to Ash Vale, Aldershot for field hygiene training, which lasted three months. Upon admission to No. 26 Field Hygiene Section, Ritson was sent to Somerset, where he was appointed to serve as batman to the commanding officer, Major Wright. At the time, Wright, like many veterans of the First World War, was anticipating a similar pattern of warfare as he had experienced two decades previously, and had the men digging trenches to defend Britain in the event of a German invasion.

Forde Cayley had qualified as a doctor in 1938 and was serving as a house physician at Middlesex Hospital. As a member of the Territorial Army, he was called up on the outbreak of war. Having narrowly passed his medical at Millbank – in spite of the medical officer's reluctance because of his poor physique – Cayley was gazetted as a lieutenant and posted to No. 11 General Hospital mobilising at Netley, Hampshire, on 23 September 1939. He recalled the training consisting of 'route marches to the Bugle at Hamble, play[ing] snooker and riotous mess nights'.[55]

Due to fears of imminent German invasion during the summer of 1940, Lieutenant Colonel Marshal, Commanding Officer of the No. 214 Field Ambulance, decided that parade drills should take second place to stretcher exercises, first aid and fieldwork. William Earl recalled training during the day, and camping in the middle of a Kent field at night, watching out for German paratroopers.[56] The training was intense. Lectures were given on anatomy, physiology and first aid, as well as on how to treat broken limbs and shock. In addition to the medical training, camouflage and map-reading had to be mastered, and men needed to be made physically robust, undertaking route marches of up to 20 miles. General hygiene and sanitation was taught, as well as dealing with gas attacks, carrying stretchers and casualty evacuation, both in darkness and daylight. Those assigned to field ambulances had to learn how to rapidly assemble and disassemble dressing stations. Earl was posted to Canterbury Hospital and was taught by nurses how to change dressings, take temperatures, administer enemas, diagnose minor injuries and judge the seriousness of wounds. He watched operations in theatres and witnessed some of his comrades fainting at the sight of blood.[57]

John Broom, posted to No. 7 Light Field Ambulance, experienced plenty of training to ensure that the unit would be nimble during the battles to come in North Africa:

> Yesterday afternoon we had practice in removing. We divided into sections & lugged certain equipment into the lorries, got into the lorries & made a short tour round until we got back to the barracks where we had to unload. I think the chief idea was to find out how many lorries it will take when we move off shortly.[58]

Following the end of initial training, all recruits were required to take an examination. Those with a sufficiently high mark and a 'demonstrable inclination to care for the sick' were awarded the status of Nursing Orderly Class III.[59] Further training could then be undertaken to achieve Classes II and I. Those who did not achieve this initial standard were transferred to other support corps such as the Royal Army Service Corps (RASC), or given supporting roles within the RAMC.

> We were all examined at the end of our training, but only those with sufficiently high results and a demonstrable inclination to care for the sick, were designated the trade of Nursing Orderly Class III. I passed and could therefore undergo further training to become a Class II or Class I. Those that didn't pass joined other units like the Royal Engineers, the RASC or were given supporting roles within the field ambulance.[60]

John Broom described the process he had to go through to pass his nursing orderly examination during the period No. 7 Light Field Ambulance was stationed in the Yorkshire coastal town of Whitby:

> I can't remember telling you, so I'll tell you now. I passed the No. III exam a week or so ago up at our hospital (The Marvic hotel in other days). The officer put me through a regular catechism for thirty minutes & I was glad when it was over. The extra payment of 9d a day will probably take months before it finds its way into my hands, so don't think that I shall be exuding cash.[61]

Walter Hart undertook the examination to be upgraded from Nursing Orderly Class III to Class II while serving with the No.6 British General Hospital in Egypt, being the first man in his unit to do so. This consisted of an eyeball to eyeball examination by the matron, a lady nicknamed 'Dolly' Gray who was held in awe having served in the First World War. The ordeal lasted an hour, with Gray firing questions at Hart, including on how to lay out a tray of instruments for certain operations. At the end, Hart was told he had passed and was congratulated by the matron.

Training for battlefield scenarios was undertaken. It proved difficult to extract a wounded man from a tank without causing him extreme pain and further damage. For this purpose, small ampoules containing 40 minims of chloroform were developed and kept in the first aid kit of a tank. The wounded man would be made to inhale the contents through a strip of gauze and was removed from the tank during the resulting unconsciousness.

The examination to become a Nursing Orderly Class I was naturally more exacting. Private Frank Turton took his test in Syria in March 1943 at No. 3 British General Hospital, answering a series of written questions to prove his worth to a hospital matron. The examination paper read:

> **Military Hygiene and Medicine**
>
> 1. Describe the cause, symptoms, treatment, method of spread, and method of prevention of Malaria.
>
> 2. Describe four types of latrines in detail. What are the special merits and drawbacks of each?

3. A Q.M.S. of the R.E.s has drawn up a plan for a forty bedded hutted hospital ward. He asks you to look it over and criticise. What points would you direct your attention to?

Anatomy, Physiology and Surgery

4. Describe the walls of the cavity of the thorax. Name its contents and state the function of each.

5. Describe the parts of the urinary system.
   How would you test urine:–
   (a) for albumen
   (b) for sugar
   (c) for bile

6. What is shock? Describe in detail how you would treat it.

Answer two questions from Military Hygiene and Medicine and two from Anatomy, Physiology and Surgery. Tabulate your answers as far as possible.

Peter Walker had left school in 1940 aged 17 and had completed his basic training at Church Crookham before undertaking further medical instruction at the Cambridge Hospital, Aldershot and the Royal Herbert Hospital, Woolwich. Following this, in 1942 he was posted to the 43rd Division as a corporal, eventually becoming part of No. 213 Field Ambulance, which provided medical cover for 214 Brigade from late 1943 onwards.

Walker's divisional training was physically gruelling, based as it was around preparing for a probable invasion of the European mainland. Dummy casualties were ferried across difficult ground on stretchers, often in freezing and muddy conditions, providing an excellent foretaste of the conditions that would be encountered during the severe winter of 1944–45 on the Dutch-German border. Walker and his comrades were trained in crawling under barbed wire and climbing up cliffs on scrambling nets, and were taken on 18-mile route marches. The river Medway was used to practise ferrying mock casualties across fast-flowing water at night-time and the anticipated mobile nature of the forthcoming campaign was prepared for by repeatedly pitching and striking tents, testing water for poisons, giving blood transfusions and packing and unpacking medical equipment and stores.

By the end of this training, as well as the physical and technical proficiency Walker and his comrades had gained, the 43rd Division had been formed into a body of men with great mutual respect and confidence. Walker recalled: 'The brigade and divisional training created great confidence in our reliance on each other. Our morale was high, as indeed it needed to be, for a soldier will fight all the better when he knows that if wounded, he will be cared for by competent medical hands.'[62]

As an officer, Ian Campbell and his colleagues were not merely directed to an area of service, but subjected to an admixture of choice and chance: 'We drew cards to see where we would go, would be posted. There were something like twenty postings and we went through this. I volunteered for the Middle East but I drew the two of spades or something and was unsuccessful, but eventually I was posted to Northern Ireland and I got there stationed in Londonderry.'[63]

At this stage of his army career, Campbell was in a field ambulance attached to the 43rd Wessex Division. In order to bring the men to peak fitness, route marches of up to 50 miles were undertaken. Greater challenge was given during a training exercise that took place near the Yorkshire town of Penistone in December 1941. Organised by the King's Royal Rifle Corps, the potential dangers of the battlefield were brought into sharper focus: 'They really got us to understand what fire under live ammunition was like and it was pretty hectic.'[64] Stress levels were further heightened during a training course at Lochailort in Scotland from April to June 1942. For this exercise, the War Office allowed for 10 per cent of the participants to become casualties, although Campbell claimed the figure was much higher. Worse still was the loss of life from fire from one's own guns: 'Quite a lot of people killed on that course on the assault crossings.'

Eric Godwin, a Ruislip GP, volunteered for service in May 1940 and was sent to the RAMC training base at Church Crookham for ten days' training. He recalled doing a lot of drills, and also learning how to purify water using tablets, should the need arise to drink from any available source such as a pond. 'I forget what else. Nothing much.'[65]

Religious provision

Until 1946, it remained compulsory for all those serving in His Majesty's Forces to attend a weekly church parade conducted by an Anglican, Roman Catholic or Free Church chaplain. These chaplains also undertook general pastoral and welfare duties in most units.

The training depot at Beckett Park had a Roman Catholic priest, an Anglican padre and a Methodist minister. They made conscious efforts to reach men who were active Christians. John Broom reported that 'The latter visited my room on Friday & asked us where we came from & if we went to church. He did not say anything, though, of a spiritual nature. I told him I was RM [Railway Mission] like you.'[66]

Claude Jennings, a 21-year-old trainee surveyor from London, received his call-up papers in October 1939 and was posted to a Territorial unit, No. 140 Field Ambulance, based in Regent's Park. The unit already contained some experienced members of the Territorial Army, some of whom had joined to avoid being directed into combat service upon conscription. Sleeping quarters were in a large house near the park, and on the first night, Jennings and another new recruit lay down on the floor of a bedroom containing eight men. 'There was a nervous silence and then they explained that they usually said evening prayers and would we mind? In fact both of us were members of churches, so to great relief there was no problem.'[67]

Dr Kenneth Hulbert, the son of a Methodist minister, had joined the RAMC in June 1940 and had been assigned to Chartham Military Hospital near Canterbury in Kent. This was housed in a newly finished empty wing of the Chartham Mental Asylum, a U-shaped building situated on the top of Chartham Downs. The military ward contained fifty beds, and the nursing sisters and male military staff slept in separate houses in the grounds. Some of the more dependable inmates from the asylum were drafted into working gangs to help the medical orderlies build a sandbag wall around the operating theatre and acute surgical ward.

On 7 July, the day of Hulbert's first ward round, he was perturbed by the sound of aeroplanes overhead as the Battle of Britain raged in the Kent skies. He telephoned his mother and father and felt reassured, then resolved to keep a diary of hymns he had turned to for comfort in the back of the Methodist hymn book, which he had taken with him to the hospital.[68]

The method of ensuring that men attended the correct denominational church parade at Church Crookham was recalled by Walter Hart: 'Next day, being Sunday, there was no drill or lectures. NCOs had been placed around the square with boards on which had been written names of religions, such as C of E, RC, Methodist, Plymouth Brethren, etc. At the end of the parade we were told to go and fall in at the board showing our religion.'[69]

However, there were a handful of men, including the Jewish Hart, whose spiritual affiliation had not been catered for:

> In all there were about 500 conscripts on parade and I found that I was soon left alone with about a dozen others who could not find a board with their religion. A sergeant came and shouted at us, 'What, can't you read or something?' When we said there was no board for us he looked perplexed and asked what we were. Three others, including Monty of course, said they were Jewish. The rest were agnostics or atheists. These he made join the C of E squad, but he had to report to the RSM and orderly officer about us four Jews. We were told to dismiss and make ourselves scarce.[70]

Home Front Service

Whilst many RAMC recruits were being trained for operations in the Mediterranean and the Far East, men were still needed to staff the military hospitals scattered around Britain. In the autumn of 1940, Robert Debenham was promoted to lieutenant colonel as officer-in-charge of the Surgical Division of the No. 7 General Hospital, which was then based in old factory buildings at Leeds. He noted in his diary: 'It has been said and it's true that War consists of long periods of idleness and boredom and short periods of intense activity and excitement.'[71] Intense activity was the experience of medics working in military and civilian hospitals across south-east England as the Battle of Britain was fought in the skies above them during the summer of 1940.

Shorncliffe Military Hospital, standing on a low, sloping hillside facing the English Channel, with the village of Sandgate on the village below, had been built in about 1850. Army surgeon Captain James Ross arrived there in March 1940. Initially the hospital generally catered for run-of-the-mill maladies such as varicose veins, knee sprains and septic lesions. On 14 May 1940, the reality of war came closer, as thirty-one German parachutists, captured in Holland, were brought in. Ross found them less than impressive: 'I never saw such a collection of thugs outside a gangster film – powerfully built, ferocious-looking toughs ... surly, suspicious.'[72] However, particular ire was reserved for a group of officers who followed the parachutists:

> Several tall, fair-haired youths strutting in with haughty airs, demanding boot-brushes, hair-brushes, soap etc., immediately, in perfect English. One's blood boiled at the damned insolence of the Nazi supermen in a British hospital, their hands still reeking from butchering innocent civilians. It maddened us to see how these *Herrenvolk* ['master race'] interpreted our attentions, as if we treated them well because we were frightened of them. 'Swine', 'Bastards', 'Murderers' one could hear one's colleagues murmur, going the rounds.

Ronald Ritson, a private in No. 26 Field Hygiene Section, which was occupying a large house near Ashford, Kent during the summer of 1940, had his first taste of the tragedy of war during a Luftwaffe bombing raid. A bomb was dropped on a nearby row of houses, killing all the inhabitants. Upon investigating the ruins in the hope of recovering any survivors, 'we went round just picking pieces of people up. And what struck me most was when I picked up the little kneecap of a baby. It was very upsetting at the time, very disturbing. However, that was war. It's cruel.'[73]

Having been posted to No. 132 Field Ambulance, a former Croydon Territorial unit that had returned from Dunkirk, Private Frank Turton was briefly stationed in Tickhill, Yorkshire, before undertaking further medical training in military and civilian hospitals in Kent during the summer of 1940, during the time of the Battle of Britain. It soon became clear to him that as well as the saving of life, the practicalities of death would need to be seen to. An army motorcycle despatch rider had been killed in a road traffic accident, and an RAMC veteran from the First World War showed Turton and his comrades how the body should be laid out ready for burial.

Kenneth Hulbert's initial army work took place at Chartham. On 12 July 1940, a German airman was brought into the casualty room. Although he had been shot down, the only injury was to his little toe. Hulbert was struck by the contrast between the ordinariness of the enemy pilot and the hatred that war had unleashed between the peoples of two Christian nations.

> He was a short, fat youth, dressed in blue, who was very polite and did not look a bad sort at all. This was the first Nazi pilot I have seen. I wonder if all of them are so bad as they make out. We all seem to be caught up in some infernal maelstrom in which we do things without thinking.[74]

A month later, Hulbert was brought two German airmen and an American pilot of the Eagle Squadron of the RAF, all with burns to the face and back. They were given an anaesthetic and were cleaned up, and their burnt areas were treated with silver nitrate, tannic acid and gentian violet.

Throughout August and September, Hulbert witnessed the impact of the Battle of Britain on a functioning hospital. On the afternoon of 12 August, while he was on a medical inspection, an air battle took place above the building and bombs were dropped close by, so patients had to be placed on stretchers on the floor. Three days later, while Hulbert was visiting patients in an army unit 2 miles away, the sky became overcast and a large formation of German bombers flew just above the low-lying clouds. The overpowering noise caused him to jump into a slit trench to take shelter until they had passed. On 23 August, the hospital was shaken by prolonged gunfire from 'Hellfire Corner' at Dover. The following day saw continual air raids, and the old hospital siren was in constant use. Hulbert recorded a strange experience with a German airman whom he had given an anaesthetic: 'Some of them have been told that they would not wake up again if they had an anaesthetic in England. One wept when he came round and found himself to be alive and all right.'

Not everyone in England replicated the fair treatment given to a captive by the medics. Hulbert recorded that several Nazi airmen were brought in having been beaten up after being captured. One had had his front teeth knocked out after landing in a field full of Kentish hop pickers, many of whom had been bombed out of their homes in the East End of London.

On one occasion, empty cartridge cases rattled down on the roof of the hospital, the detritus of a dogfight overhead, and one man who had been admitted from Dover as he could not stand the noise of the cross-Channel shooting broke down in a fit of hysterics. By 7 September, it was clear that a systematic bombing campaign was taking place across the flight path to London, so the hospital was temporarily evacuated of patients fit to move. Amongst all the pandemonium, time was found to keep two small black and white rabbits, named Hurricane and Spitfire, who acted as a calming distraction for the RAF fighter pilot patients.

As the Battle of Britain reached its crescendo on 15 September, Hulbert sat in the garden having tea while an enormous formation of German bombers flew over heading for London before returning in twos and threes, dodging in and out of the clouds and being pursued by the RAF. That evening, four very badly injured Nazi airmen were brought in. One died after an operation. 'What a futile waste of life this all is,' noted Hulbert.[75] Four days later, Hulbert and his colleague Captain James Ross witnessed another life slipping through their fingers. A flight lieutenant had been machine-gunned from the air; the bullets had shot through his cervical spine and the damage was irreparable.

An even more agonising case for Hulbert and Ross came about on 28 September. After a dogfight, they saw an RAF pilot bale out and come down in his parachute. Hulbert was dispatched in an ambulance and found the pilot lying in a farmyard, surrounded by clucking hens. The man looked pale, with a smoking wound in his left shoulder caused by a phosphorous shell. Hulbert applied a dressing, freed him from his parachute and got him back to the hospital in the ambulance. After resuscitation he was taken to the operating theatre, where Ross opened up the shoulder wound. The phosphorous burst into flames, so the whole shoulder region had to be opened up and the phosphorous-impregnated tissues excised.

The pilot explained that he had been hit by a Messerschmitt. As his plane hurtled down, he had waited until he was above clear ground before baling out, in order to avoid injury to innocent civilians by landing near houses. Hulbert and Ross worked all day to save the airman, and his wife was sent for before the patient was transferred to a convalescent depot, where he recovered from the wound only to subsequently die of pneumonia. His selfless delay in baling out had possibly cost him his own life.

For those serving as medical officers within other regiments, sometimes a free hand with their work enabled alternative approaches to treatment. In late 1940, Bill Frankland was posted as a medical officer to the Royal Warwickshire Regiment based at Budbrooke Barracks, Warwick. Here he found the hospital to be overstaffed, leaving him largely free of duties from lunchtime onwards. Frankland had a long-standing interest in hypnosis, having seen it demonstrated when he was a medical student, and he was soon able to spot men who might be candidates for that treatment.

In his previous posting to Tidworth Military Hospital, some soldiers had been presented to him who were unable to use their fingers, leaving them unable to pull a rifle trigger. Using hypnosis, he helped them overcome the problem, a feat he described as 'rather showing off' on his part.[76] Nevertheless, these patients were deemed fit for military service and several were sent to serve with the British Expeditionary Force (BEF) in France. At Budbrooke Barracks, Frankland had one patient in his hospital who was suffering from a psychiatric disorder. The disinterested senior medical colonel, who only took one ward round a week (preferring to drink sherry and browse the newspapers), ignored the patient's needs and ordered him to be discharged. This annoyed Frankland as he could see the man was genuinely ill. Therefore, he took it upon himself to hypnotise the man, telling him that when approached by the colonel he should give a Nazi salute. Having trained him to do so, on the morning of the ward round, Frankland duly hypnotised his patient. As the colonel approached the bed and asked why the patient was still in hospital, the man gave a Nazi salute. 'This man is mad,' the colonel said to Bill. 'Yes, Sir, and I have been trying to tell you that for some time.' The ploy worked and the man went on to receive appropriate treatment.

Whilst doctors like Frankland could sometimes enjoy a free hand to engage in unusual medical practices, the same could not be said of young conscripts in the lower ranks. Seventeen-year-old Alexander Keay was sent from his unit, No. 130 Field Ambulance, in late 1939 as they were to be posted abroad. Regulations deemed that he was too young for overseas service so he was dispatched to the Royal Victoria Hospital, Netley to act as a junior nursing orderly in the tuberculosis ward. As this was situated right at the southern end of the hospital, with the kitchens over a quarter of a mile away at the northern end, Keay had to make the round trip to fetch and deliver meals thrice daily, a task he undertook without enthusiasm. It was during this period that a bizarre incident occurred. In order to advance his army career from the status of private, Keay volunteered to train as an operating room assistant, progressing through the various training stages. One afternoon, the main theatre sister, who was a regular army nurse, approached him and said, 'I've got a special mission for you.' Keay followed her into the operating theatre, where she found a long amputation knife, handed it to him and instructed him to go and kill a German officer who had been shot down the previous day and admitted to the hospital. Keay refused and was court-martialled for disobeying an officer's instructions. The legal process was followed to the point where the sister disappeared from the hospital – sent to a mental institution, suspected Keay. This incident shook his faith in the RAMC, and he applied successfully for a commission in the Royal Signals.[77]

In addition to the initial military and medical training, each unit had to have men trained for specialist roles that helped to keep the cogs of efficient organisation whirring. One of these was ensuring that men were promptly and efficiently paid. In March 1942, John Broom made his way by train from Groombridge, on the Kent-Sussex border, to the Pay Duties School in Aldershot. Heavily laden with kit, he reported for a four-day training course on the Monday afternoon. The curriculum was intensive:

> The Course lasted four days – lectures from 9am to 5.30pm after which questions, tea & study. My time was very much occupied. I got writer's cramp too. In four days I took down 180 pages of notes in small handwriting. Takes some doing! The ground covered was terrific. The Course, in other words, was far too crowded. Everybody agreed on that.[78]

Despite this, Broom revelled in having been chosen to undertake this specialised role within his unit, despite being a lowly private:

> There were 4 captains on it, 2 lieutenants & twelve staff-sergeants, six sergeants, three corporals & myself the only

> private. I enjoyed every minute of it. The fellows were a very decent crowd – I shared a room with 2 Tank Corps Sergeants – good beds & all the rest of it. No parades, no duties, just lecture after lecture with a mass of detail & little time to consider & meditate over them.
>
> The exam was on Saturday morning. 15 questions in 3 hours – Good going eh? Especially when one considers that one question took ¾ hour to answer. I did fairly well, I think, though I made some mistakes & my writing, I fear, was as near atrocious as any could be. I'm pretty sure, though, that some of the high-rankers did infinitely worse. A ticklish subject, pay. Very.

Leslie Collier qualified as a doctor in 1942, and after a short period as a house physician at University College Hospital London, was posted to the RAMC depot at Fleet for two weeks' basic training. From there he went to the Army Hygiene establishment at Mytchett, 'where we learned about how to put up loos in the middle of any desert or glacier or wherever we happened to be, and then we had a tropical course which was absolutely splendid. Very good indeed, at The Royal Army Medical College.'[79]

Collier then endured a 'pretty awful' period with a training field ambulance on the Isle of Wight, with limited opportunities for leisure on the island. A large training exercise on the mainland offered greater scope for interest. Collier's role, as a doctor, was to act as a medical referee, deciding if people were wounded and needed to be evacuated. The first two days were spent sitting with a group of people in a chalk pit in torrential rain, with little action. Collier took matters into his own hands to provide some variety and amusement:

> I decided to start a food poisoning epidemic and get a little action going. So I started going round pointing at various people and saying 'you are out of action. You have got food poisoning and drop out of the exercise.' I remember going to one chap. I couldn't see his rank really because he was wearing a groundsheet and I said 'you have got food poisoning. You are out of the exercise.' He said 'but you can't do that to me. I am the Brigade Major' and I said 'well,

> I am sorry Sir but you have just been invalided out,' and apparently it caused an enormous amount of trouble, but we thought it was all a bit of a joke.[80]

Aside from the prosaic nature of army pay, hygiene and tedious field exercises, other medics underwent training for more dramatic wartime roles. During a brief posting to the 13th/18th Hussars, a cavalry regiment, Captain John Forfar had taken part in training exercises in removing casualties from tanks. At that time, in late 1942, it was still customary to use a small phial of chloroform to render the injured man unconscious, should he not already be so.[81] That practice was subsequently abandoned. Forfar was then posted as medical officer to the 10th Battalion, Royal Marines, subsequently reformed as No. 47 (Royal Marine) Commando.

At the time of his arrival in August 1943, the unit was being prepared to operate on a new second front to be opened in north-west Europe the following summer. The training for this role was arduous. Forfar recognised the necessity of the one-month basic commando course, held at Achnacarry, Scotland, to place recruits under a great deal of physical and psychological stress, much of the latter coming from the constant fear of being 'RTU'd' (returned to unit) should the individual not make the grade. For Forfar, this would have represented the 'ultimate hurt and stigma'. Instructors were purposely arbitrarily aggressive and exercises included transferring from ships to landing craft in churning seas.

The training undertaken by RAMC recruits was designed to fit them into a range of roles within a developing system of evacuation and treatment of battlefield casualties. This system ran to eight main centres of treatment and informed the training that different units undertook:

1. The wounded solder himself should, where possible, have tried to administer First Aid, such as field dressings, on himself. This could be supplemented by his fellow troops and stretcher-bearers from his own unit. He would then either walk or crawl, or be taken by his comrades, to a Regimental Aid Post for further emergency treatment from the Regimental Medical Orderly. Stretcher-bearing

parties could consist of two, three or four men. The RAP was the most forward point at which the RAMC was expected to operate. Laying just behind the front line, although out of range of enemy rifle and machine-gun fire, rudimentary treatment could be administered here. This might include a splint or tourniquet or a morphine injection. The RAMC orderly would fix a medical card to the injured man and then evacuate him back to an Advanced Dressing Station.

2. From the RAP he would be transferred to RAMC stretcher-bearers belonging to a Field Ambulance or Light Field Ambulance and taken back to an ADS. The route between the RAP and ADS was signposted, and the latter was situated as far forward as military conditions would allow, typically just over a mile behind the front line. This could still be within the range of medium artillery. The ADS had to be accessible by ambulance and provide shelter from enemy shells and gas attacks, and were often situated in commandeered buildings. Here any immediately necessary blood transfusions could be given and the severity of the wound classified. From the ADS the casualty would be transferred in one of three ways according the nature of the wound.
3. If the soldier was suffering from severe shock and not fit for a long journey back to a Casualty Clearing Station, he would be taken to a Divisional Field Dressing Station for resuscitation and possible further blood transfusions. He would remain there until deemed fit to be moved to an Advanced Surgical Centre for an operation, or on to the Casualty Clearing Station.
4. If he was able to be moved but required an urgent operation, he would be moved to an Advanced Surgical Centre where Field Surgical Units (FSUs) would carry this out. Usually, the casualty would then remain there a few days until he was fit enough to be transferred by an Ambulance Car or Ambulance Train.

5. If he was not severely wounded, and still robust enough to travel, he would be taken by Ambulance Car to a Casualty Clearing Station for treatment and stay there until his journey back to base could resume.
6. In addition to an Ambulance Car, an Ambulance Train, Hospital Ship or even an aeroplane, could be used for evacuation.
7. Treatment was continuous by RAMC staff in Field Surgical Units. Sulphonamide drugs and later penicillin ensured that bacteria did not spread as much as in previous wars, ensuring the casualty arrived at base in a better condition.
8. Once he reached the base, the wounded man would be admitted to a General Hospital and, after a sufficient period of recovery, transferred to a Convalescent Depot and then home, if there was not immediate prospect of a return to active service for the foreseeable future.[82]

Sometimes a Walking Wounded Collecting Post (WWCP) was established behind the ADS for those who could walk despite their injuries. The ADS could accommodate about fifty casualties. Here, urgent treatment such as surgery to control a haemorrhage could be given. A wounded man would then be evacuated further down the line to a Main Dressing Station. The MDS was the headquarters of the field ambulance and was meant to be situated 2 to 5 miles behind the front line.[83] Two to four ambulances would move casualties between the ADS and the MDS.[84] These vehicles were driven by RASC men. The MDS could accommodate 400 to 500 sick and wounded, dispersed across buildings such as schools and hospitals and benefitted from proximity to a good road and water supply.

At the Main Dressing Station men were divided into those who would be evacuated back to a Casualty Clearing Station and those to be retained for a swift return to their units. It was undesirable for casualties to be retained too long at the MDS, as they would restrict the station's mobility during battle. A divisional rest station (DRS) could be established for those suffering from fatigue and strain but needed no further medical treatment.

Within this system there was great flexibility, with field ambulances and field dressing stations able to divide themselves into smaller self-contained units to meet the changing needs of the battlefield. The role of the field ambulance was to follow the infantry brigade to which it was attached and collect, treat and evacuate the brigade's and all other wounded, whether friend or foe. A field ambulance had to be constantly mobile, and was organised 'to effect the rapid evacuation of the sick and wounded'.[85] However, they were not equipped to provide anything other than the 'simplest accommodation and treatment'.[86] A light field ambulance was to consist of over 200 men: thirteen officers, 165 other ranks of RAMC men, 58 other ranks of RASC men, a dental orderly, a chaplain and a chaplain's batman. RAMC men were classed as non-combatants, protected by the Geneva Convention, and were entitled to wear Red Cross brassards and display that emblem on their vehicles and treatment centres.

Airborne and commando medics

The Second World War saw the development of airborne and commando units, with the associated need to have dedicated medical staff provided by the RAMC. Rather than the conventional method of evacuating patients to the surgeons, the idea behind airborne medical units was to parachute the surgeons right up to the casualties. Dropped alongside the surgeons were anaesthetists, nursing orderlies, operating tables, instruments, dressings, plaster, blood plasma, sterilisers and medicines. Parachute field ambulances were composed of parachute and glider regiments and a 'sea tail' of heavy transport that moved with the divisions attacking to link up with the parachute division. (Pic 8) All ranks were qualified parachutists who had volunteered for the task. They were required to know fieldcraft, map-reading, direction-finding by the stars and self-defence, and be capable of doing more than one medical job.

By 1943, David Tibbs, a medical student at Guy's Hospital, London, had grown frustrated at not being able to play a more active role in the war effort. Under wartime regulations, he qualified as a doctor six months earlier than normal and applied to become a parachutist with the newly formed 6th Airborne Division. He was assigned to No. 225 (Parachute) Field Ambulance and put in charge of a section of twenty medics.

Throughout July and August 1943, members of the field ambulance undertook a parachute jumping course. This consisted of two initial jumps from a static balloon 800 feet from the ground, followed by five jumps from a Whitley bomber, exiting through a centrally placed hole in the floor about the size of a dustbin. Having successfully completed these jumps, Tibbs became a qualified parachutist, which entitled him to wear the coveted parachute wings on the right arm and an extra two shillings per day on top of his normal army pay.[87]

First employed in the North African Campaign in late 1942, parachute field ambulances were also used in Sicily, France, Holland, Belgium, Germany, Italy, Greece and Burma. Parachute training was also essential for the medical officers and orderlies who accompanied forces supporting the partisan forces in Italy and Yugoslavia. Nursing orderlies were frequently the sole medics in their parties and had to be able to perform a broad range of duties.

Civilian recruits from all walks of life had to be drilled, dressed and moulded to support fighting forces in widely differing climates, in advance, retreat and static conditions. Many, particularly in the ranks, resented the immersion into an alien military culture and took a long time to come to terms with the demands on their minds and bodies. Nevertheless, firm foundations of physical and psychological fitness were laid, which enabled the RAMC to become an outstanding part of the British Army from 1939 to 1945.

Chapter 2

Medicine in Retreat: Norway and France

Norway

The Norwegian Campaign, fought from 9 April to 10 June 1940, marked the end of the 'Phoney War'. Advancing through Denmark, the Germans landed 2,000 troops in the port of Narvik, signifying the start of open warfare. In response, the Allies sent a naval force which overcame the German navy, then landed troops at Narvik, Namsos and Åndalsnes. Narvik was liberated by the Allies by the end of May, but the other two landings failed to achieve their objectives. Poor planning and organisation, exacerbated by a freezing climate and mountainous terrain, served to thwart efforts to oust the Germans. Eventually, Allied forces were withdrawn in order to assist with the defence of France, and the Norwegian government was forced into exile in London.

This ill-fated campaign proved to be a frustrating one for the RAMC. One principal hindrance was the severe lack of medical supplies, some of which had been loaded onto the wrong vessels, and some lost to enemy action on land and at sea. Additionally, a number of medical units were diverted at short notice from their original destinations. Landing on Åndalsnes at the mouth of the river Rauma, without any transport, RAMC units found that evacuation of casualties had to be carried out by the Norwegian medical services.

Ernest Sampson, an RASC driver attached to No. 147 Field Ambulance, recalled that the total amount of transport allocated to the unit was five 3-ton lorries, six ambulances, three motorcycles and two or three staff cars.[1] Sailing from Scotland on 14 April, Sampson landed at Harstad, 300 miles above the Arctic Circle, six days later. However, the contingent of vehicles did not arrive until 10 May as they were on another boat. When they did arrive, it was found that the ambulances could not be driven on the road. Sampson amplified the impression of disorganisation that many men felt during the campaign: 'It was chaos. Information was negligible. Nobody knew where anybody was and how things were working round. How can I explain it? You were working from day to day not knowing what was happening.'

Communication links were poor, with telephone, signal and wire methods proving inadequate. Lines were operating through local civilian exchanges, which caused long delays and heightened the risk of German spies listening in.[2] There was an initial lack of co-ordination between the naval and army medical services, and the multi-national nature of the Allied forces, containing Norwegians, Poles and members of the French Foreign Legion, caused language difficulties. However, as many Norwegians spoke good English, co-operation between British Army medical officers and their local counterparts was good, although this was not always the case between British and French medical officers. Colonel Ernest Scott, who commanded a Territorial field ambulance at Narvik, noted that the chief medical officer of a French aid post was a 'supercilious perisher' who tried to insist on Scott's ambulance carrying some of his healthy men, despite protests that he should only carry the wounded.[3]

Lieutenant J.W. Wayte, commanding officer of No. 189 Field Ambulance, bemoaned the lack of aerial cover for his hospital and the inadequate communication systems:

> Our stay in Norway resolved itself into one long endeavour to escape bombs. I took over a grand school & with beds, sheets, blankets etc. from a nearby hotel, we rigged up a hospital. We operated on local casualties & filled up some sandbags as a protection. Immediately the German planes spotted us and down came the bombs – the building cracked and shook. The patients couldn't be protected and we had to clear. We were harried from pillar to post …We could not function very well as a field hospital for we had no transport, no ambulances, no real lines of communication at all & no protection.[4]

The evacuation of casualties across the snow-capped mountains and valleys around Namsos and Åndalsnes proved problematic. Detachments from British field ambulances used a relay system, with intermittent resting posts en route. Nevertheless, the rugged terrain made stretcher-bearing a laborious and tiring endeavour, especially in the slush and ice that formed as a spring thaw set in. One medical officer described this work. He had 'taken seven casualties by one motor ambulance to Snåsa, a terrible journey as the road was in a shocking condition due to combined effects of thaw and military traffic. It was more like a farm track than a main road. The 40 kilometres took 3½ hours.'[5] Compared to future campaigns, the number of casualties was light, despite many troops succumbing to frostbite.

Once casualties had been moved down to landing posts on the fjords, most were taken by steamboats either to one of the two ships that were serving as dressing stations, or the Casualty Clearing Station at Taorstad or the General Hospital at Harstad. Some needing immediate evacuation were taken to naval destroyers. The steamboats, known as 'puffers', were a convenient method of moving patients around such a mountainous area, although they were often difficult to find as they had been requisitioned for the transportation of rations and military hardware. Moving at a speed of about 7mph, they were often sitting ducks for keen Luftwaffe pilots.

Something that was to become a depressing feature of warfare across many theatres was the lack of respect shown by some members of the German military towards a clearly displayed Red Cross emblem on medical transport and accommodation. The official War Office report into the Norway Campaign noted:

> It should be borne in mind that the water evacuation was at all times liable to interference by bombing. The Germans took no notice whatever of the Red Cross with which the larger ships were marked, and ultimately it was found necessary to substitute trained naval crews for the Norwegians, who deserted rather than face the fierce and frequent air attacks to which all the craft were subjected.[6]

Lessons were learned from the Norway debacle, the dramatic failure of which cost Prime Minister Neville Chamberlain his job. Rigorous planning and organisation were essential, and great thought had to be given to the evacuation of the wounded in relation to the geographical surroundings. Medically, the importance of early resuscitation opportunities for wounded men was highlighted, with the inadequacy of only having blood transfusion facilities available in one General Hospital and one CCS leading to men suffering from the lack of provision. Medical officers agreed that blood transfusions needed to be available closer to the front line, and more plentiful, to have maximum impact in lessening the effects of wound shock.

France and Flanders: the calm before the storm

Although the period before the German Blitzkrieg of May–June 1940 was largely a waiting game for British Expeditionary Force troops stationed in northern France and Belgium, the RAMC was in action during the winter of 1939–40. The first casualty encountered was a dead soldier brought into a Main Dressing Station being run by No. 3 Field Ambulance, along with several wounded. Thoughts had turned among senior medical officers on how to treat wound infections in the most efficacious manner. A medical society was formed in the Dieppe area, and in late 1939, this was addressed by Colonel Lionel Colebrook, Bacteriological Consultant to the British Expeditionary Force, who stressed his hopes for the new drug sulphanilamide in combating streptococcal infections. Major General Priest, Consultant Physician to the BEF, spoke of the electrocardiograph, X-rays, test meals, the gastroscope, and the chemical testing of stools.[7] Specialist Army Health units were established: No. 1 Advanced Depot of Medical Stores under Major Martin, No. 1 Mobile Laboratory under Major Francis, and No. 1 Mobile Hygiene Laboratory under Major Berry.

Field ambulance staff mainly dealt with normal medical complaints, as well as venereal disease and an outbreak of scabies, which affected 280 patients who had to be sent back to No. 8 CCS as they were too numerous to be kept by the field ambulances.[8] Elsewhere, Private Walter Hart of No. 6 General Hospital was under the direction of two nursing sisters, one of whom came with a reputation for high-handed treatment of those under her command. Hart found she fully lived up to this standing, as he was assigned to bathe a patient with scabies. The man had to be placed in a large zinc bath filled with warm water and then scrubbed with a hard brush and soft soap wherever scabs were visible. These were generally in pairs as the parasite bored its way in and out of the skin. The idea was to open the scabs so that they could be painted with Gentian Violet.[9]

Hart had arrived in Dieppe in late 1939 with the No. 6 British General Hospital, initially occupying some derelict houses on the Rue Général Chanzy. Hart's house was:

> absolutely bare and damp. We had no beds. We had to use our groundsheet and blanket for sleeping, so Jim and I shared and in that way we had two blankets. It was very cold at night and was to get progressively colder until it snowed. We were in Dieppe for a month and, while there, although there was no shortage of food in the shops, all we had was a packet of hard biscuits and half a tin of bully beef to last us the whole day.[10]

Eventually the unit moved up to the coastal village of Mesnil-Val, to establish a tented hospital in a large field in nearby Flocques. Roads were built to provide access for ambulances. This proved a challenge as the Normandy country roads were some 6 to 12 feet below the level of the farmland. The men had to strenuously dig through the steep verges to make inclines, while intermittently gazing over to a cemetery containing men who had fallen during the First World War. Hart reflected, 'This was typical of the army of that time.'[11]

Sometimes Hart and his comrades ate in a local hotel, but most of their food was cooked at base in large Soyer stoves. As they provided the only means of obtaining hot water, they also took baths in the stoves. 'It looked as if we were being boiled for cannibals to eat.'[12] Eventually, the No. 6 General Hospital opened and Hart was assigned as a general duty orderly to one of the wards.

Lieutenant Forde Cayley (Pic 9), attached to No. 11 General Hospital, looked after 100 medical beds and 3,000 Auxiliary Military Pioneer Corps (AMPC) troops, mainly unemployed elderly dockers from Liverpool. Originally housed in a warehouse, the Pioneers had to be split up. 'We had to board most of them out, especially as the Pernod started to rot their livers.'[13] Cayley bought a bicycle in order to be able to move between the different establishments, dealing with epidemics of flu, cerebrospinal meningitis and German measles. Even though hostilities were yet to begin in earnest, Cayley found himself having restricted access to resources. He had to fill in forms for every egg and glass of milk used, and he ran out of aspirin. Despite these exigencies, the 100 cases of meningitis he treated all survived.

Those field ambulances operating in France and Belgium during this pre-Blitzkrieg period were not fully mobile, being unable to transport their equipment and personnel without becoming overburdened and experiencing transport breakdowns. Overloading of vehicles was common, leading to broken springs and overheated engines as RAMC trucks and ambulance cars sought to keep to predetermined timetables. At times, stretcher-bearers were made to march, which only served to transfer the strain from machines to men.

Approximately 250,000 troops were put into the forward areas in France and Belgium in anticipation of a German attack. They were served by their own regimental medical officers and stretcher-bearers, as well as twenty-five field ambulances, fifteen General Hospitals and various convalescent depots along the lines of communication.[14] Six ambulance trains and Motor Ambulance Convoys (MACs) moved casualties across longer distances. There were also mobile laboratories, hygiene stations and CCSs. The port of Dieppe served as the main British medical base, with several specialist hospitals and depots.

Medical arrangements resembled those utilised in the same area two decades previously, although with a realisation that the further forward a casualty could be treated, the better. The chain of evacuation stretched from the Regimental Aid Post, via field ambulances and Casualty Clearing Stations to the General Hospitals back at base. It was estimated that the BEF would incur about 38,000 casualties, and only those requiring more than twenty-eight days of treatment and convalescence would be evacuated back to England.[15] Provision was made for complex maxilla-facial and orthopaedic cases to be given preliminary treatment in hospital in Dieppe.

Medical units would be more widely dispersed than in the First World War, as German air power would pose a considerable threat to tightly concentrated troops on the ground. However, this created the potential for additional communication problems, with telephone exchanges, as in Norway, proving unreliable. Senior medical officers therefore spent considerable time moving between their different units.

Lance Corporal Reg Gill of No. 18 General Hospital arrived at a bitterly cold Le Havre to be transferred onto a train with wooden seats and crushed up alongside his comrades. There was little room for themselves beside all their gear – kitbags, valises, haversacks, water bottles, respirators, tin helmets and spare boots. The train was unheated and the men were frozen stiff. After a seemingling interminable wait they were off, and despite the physical discomfort, Gill experienced 'a certain thrill that we were in the country our fathers had fought in and on much the same route'.[16] After a thirty-six-hour journey, with only one meal to sustain them and no sleep, Gill and his mates arrived at Étaples and were marched to a collection of a dozen or so Nissen huts. Men's boots froze to the floor overnight and had to be loosened by a mallet in the morning. They wore every stitch of clothing they possessed – up to three pairs of socks, balaclava helmets and knitted scarves. Gill recalled, '[We] tried to sleep, which was virtually impossible. It was pure misery.'

Once fresh water had been obtained by melting snow on a stove, the only standpipe having frozen solid, the men were told that the icy wilderness was to be the site of No. 18 General Hospital. This meant marquees had to be erected, roads built, and an electrical supply arranged. The hospital was to have a pharmacy, an X-ray department and a pathology laboratory. As a lance corporal, Gill found it difficult to balance the demands and expectations of his role:

> At that time I was a lance corporal, probably the worst position in the army because, although you got an extra 2d per day, there was a lot more responsibility. You were blamed for everything that went wrong by the corporals and Sergeants without any privileges at all. I was ticked off by the Sergeant Major for 'fraternising' as he called it. An NCO was not allowed to be friendly with the chaps that were in his squad. Ridiculous! A First World War idea I think.[17]

Gill and his party of six privates were put to work building a road from the main gate through the camp. The picks they were issued with made little impression on the frozen ground. Massive eighty-bedded marquees had to be erected by men with no experience of this task, and whose three months of training prior to embarkation to France had been wasted practising drills, 'Quite typical of the army'. Eventually these tasks were handed over to a nearby Pioneer Corps section.

Another problem that presented itself to Gill as the unit's radiographer was an unfamiliarity with the field X-ray machine, which had arrived at the hospital in February 1940. He was provided with a 4-kilowatt generator to power it and was left to his own devices to assemble the equipment. 'The radiologist, Major Lees, was a nice chap but I hardly saw anything of him. He appeared from time to time, said "How are you getting on?" and so on and disappeared again.' Gill was sent to the No. 17 General Hospital in Camiers, 8 miles away, to receive further advice. After being told how to assemble an X-ray machine, he was advised by a sergeant radiographer that when X-raying a spine, he would not find it powerful enough. Therefore, the patient would need to be strapped down to wait for the generator to deliver the necessary power, at which point it would start to cough due to overloading. Having developed some scans in the X-ray department of No. 17 General Hospital, Gill returned to Étaples to find himself promoted to the rank of sergeant.

For many of those playing a waiting game in France and Belgium, a strong Christian faith enabled them to better endure familial separation. Private Arthur Rowland was a 37-year-old printer from Croxley Green, Hertfordshire who had been a member of the Territorial Army before the war, In September 1939 he was sent to the No. 4 General Hospital at La Baule on the Atlantic coast of France. His letters to his wife demonstrated a faith that recast itself into a new situation. On 28 October he told her: 'Last night I had a thoroughly good hour with about six others on an old American organ, hymn singing. ... The Chaplain is trying to form a choir, I hope duty won't get in the way too much. Will you pray that God's blessing may rest on the word spoken and sung here.'[18]

It was common for the home churches to maintain contact with men on active service, Rowland reporting on 18 November that he had received a letter from Reverend J.L.V. Houghton, as well as one from the Army Scripture Readers. Following a Christmas away from his young family, Rowland exhorted his wife to remain strong in the faith: 'Now Darling for the New Year read Romans 15–13 & then remember all we have been through together & come out smiling, we can still do the same. May everything be for Him, & every blessing be yours.'

A regularity of religious observance remained possible in the months before the unleashing of the Blitzkrieg. On 18 February 1940, Rowland wrote:

> We had a grand time at service tonight. Three of the patients from my ward were there & they admitted to the uplift from the season of Fellowship.

> Oh that more would praise the Lord for His Goodness & for His Goodness towards the children of men. ... You & I may be separated from each other but never from Him & with Him & at His feet we can meet. ... May we be worthy followers of Him & may never be ashamed to confess the faith of Christ crucified but manfully fight under his banner.

Rowland's son Donovan was awarded a first class in a Scripture exam: 'Always remember you cannot know enough about the "Book of Books". "This Book will keep you from Sin, or Sin will keep you from this Book."'

Venereal disease

It had been remembered by the military authorities that VD had been a considerable problem amongst troops in France and Flanders during the First World War, and the dispersal of British troops in scattered formations across the countryside, often billeted close to or with civilians, exacerbated the risk of it being an even greater issue in 1939–40. It was more difficult for officers to monitor the sexual behaviour of their men as they were not quartered in camps. Men had little organised activity to occupy their leisure time, creating the opportunity for boredom, drunkenness and sexual promiscuity.

The first month in France produced an infection rate of three per thousand troops, a higher rate than during the First World War. To address this, the system of regulated brothels, *maisons de tolerance*, was reinstated. The War Office issued a *Memorandum on Venereal Diseases*, which advised abstinence based on a soldier's personal morality and his duty to family, regiment and country, but also recognised the reality of the situation in ordering the establishment of ablutions rooms, where two attendants could administer disinfectant for men to rub into their genitalia following sexual intercourse. Condoms were made available in some regiments, these being the ones with the lowest reported incidents of VD.

Lieutenant Forde Cayley, attached to No. 11 General Hospital, was one of those tasked with controlling the spread of VD. The unit was spread around Le Havre, with a surgical unit in a casino, an operating theatre elsewhere in the town and a VD clinic in a hut on the shoreline.

He recalled, 'The younger troops and those in transit through the port made for the brothels and I had to take over the VD ward. ... We had the highest rate of VD ever reported in the history of the British Army.'[19] For those stricken with various sexual ailments, the shame did not end with the illness. Every soldier was required to fill in a questionnaire describing the appearance and clothes of the woman with whom he had liaised, and where they had met. Staff from the unit then collected local French health officials and went by ambulance to the brothel to arrange treatment. It was found that one girl had infected ten men in one night.

German attack

At dawn on 10 May, the Germans began their invasion of Belgium and the Netherlands. Accordingly, convinced that they were facing a repeat of the German strategy of 1914, Allied commanders moved the bulk of their forces from the Franco-Belgian border into defensive positions within Belgium to await the continuation of the German attack. In so doing, they fell right into Hitler's trap. Rather than repeating the Schlieffen Plan of 1914, the Wehrmacht and Luftwaffe of 1940 advanced with their main thrust through the Ardennes Forest, in order to smash the vulnerable flank of the Allies. As twenty-nine German divisions advanced through the Netherlands and Belgium in the north, forty-five further divisions, including about 2,400 tanks in seven divisions, burst through the Allied right flank and drove towards the English Channel.

The German advance south from Belgium was swift and decisive and by 21 May, this thrust had reached the English Channel and encircled thirty-five Allied divisions, including the BEF. Although the French army put up valuable resistance for several more weeks, it was a rearguard action designed to support the imperative to rescue as many Allied troops as possible from German-occupied territories. During the initial phases of the German advance, from 10 to 18 May, the system of evacuation from Regimental Aid Posts via Casualty Clearing Stations back to base hospitals was followed, but once the BEF was in rapid retreat, medical units had to be innovative. CCSs had to hold casualties for far longer than planned, becoming mini General Hospitals. The planned casualty evacuation route via Dieppe or Étaples was cut off by the German advance, so Dunkirk had to be used instead.

Towards the front line, with aid posts being overrun, the men within them and the field ambulances that transported the sick were increasingly in danger. As the Wehrmacht smashed through the Allied positions there was no longer a definite front line behind which medical staff could feel protected. In the flat landscape of France and Flanders, medics were often hopelessly exposed as they hurried their patients from Regimental Aid Posts to Main Dressing Stations. Their ambulances often proved inadequate, with many being either mechanically unreliable or unable to cope with the weight of a full load of patients. Stretcher-bearers had to march towards the front line as the vehicles were unable to transport them. Furthermore, there was no room to carry a piece of equipment as basic as a bedpan on the ambulances, even if there had been one available, as was frequently not the case.

On 14 May, No. 10 Field Ambulance was ordered to move into Belgium to provide front-line support for troops facing the Germans. The unit established an MDS in a school building but had to withdraw three days later, and then found itself in constant retreat until reaching the Belgian coastal resort of Coxyde-les-Bains on 29 May. Here, a CCS was set up in the Grand Hotel Regina. The unit's commander, Colonel Arthur Cox, reported: 'All cases on arrival were taken into a large room on the ground floor, which was also used as a ward capable of holding eighty stretcher cases. In this room, they sorted those requiring immediate and urgent treatment.'[20]

Patients were taken into a large room where three medical officers worked continuously. From there, those requiring an operation were taken to the kitchens, where an impromptu operating theatre had been set up. By noon the following day, all three floors of the hotel were crammed with patients, and the corridors were jammed with men waiting to be treated. As the threat of capture drew ever closer, on 31 May the order came to evacuate all patients and staff to Rosendaël, a few miles from Dunkirk, to await evacuation. In order to get the casualties out to a paddle steamer anchored offshore, medics dragged down rowing boats from the dunes above the beach and transported them through the treacherous waters. Two members even rowed their patients all the way back to Margate.[21]

In previous conflicts, the field ambulance had travelled at the rear of the brigade it was attached to, but the nature of mobile warfare meant that brigade columns often stretched out over 20 miles along a road.

This made them vulnerable to air attack at any point over that distance, meaning that medical aid posts had to be made available at frequent points throughout the column. During the rapid retreat of May and June 1940, it was found that Advanced Dressing Stations were often sited too far behind the front line, in anticipation of making further moves. Field ambulances did not have a sufficient number of vehicles to maintain a good evacuation service, and it proved challenging under new conditions of warfare to strike the balance between siting medical posts within close enough range of the growing number of casualties and being far enough out of the range of field gunfire.

Once motor ambulances had been distributed by commanding officers, it was difficult to maintain control of them in a shifting battlefield. Even if the drivers had been given orders to rendezvous at a particular time and place, sometimes the roads had been made impassable, and at other times the headquarters had been moved at short notice, without the ambulance crew being informed. The supply of petrol was also a concern, and RAMC vehicles could often run out of fuel at inopportune moments. In addition, medics experienced poor communication with the battalions they were meant to be supporting, meaning they were not always at immediate hand for those fighting troops in the most need. It was in this dynamic, dangerous and difficult situation that officers and men of the RAMC sought to execute their duties in conditions for which they had received little training.

In the early spring, reinforcements, including a battalion of Welsh Guards, were sent forward to defend the front line. Lieutenant Forde Cayley of No. 11 General Hospital was sent with them. When the train transporting the men to the front pulled into a siding, there was some 'larking about' in the carriages, and one man's tin helmet was thrown overboard. The owner went to collect it but, on getting back in the carriage using the wheel as a step, the train started to move. His leg was nearly torn off and Cayley had to give the casualty a swig of rum, apply a tourniquet and then amputate the leg and dress the wound, sending him off by ambulance. When Cayley finished the emergency treatment, he found his bottle of rum had been stolen.[22]

Another task Cayley had to undertake was to provide a medical report on a Private O'Toole, who had made as if to strike an officer in the hold of a ship, before shinning up the mast and appearing ready to throw himself into the water. He had been admitted to hospital with delirium tremens, but Cayley's judgement was he 'was just a wild Irishman who had lost his temper'. This offended the man's Celtic officers, and Cayley was soon dispatched to another location to take command of a dressing station.

Cayley encountered a field bakery unit at Bolbec. There was a plentiful supply of local cheap champagne, and members of the unit would frequently become drunk. Many of them were placed under arrest in a military prison at Yvetot, facing a court martial for cheeking their commanding officer. Cayley reckoned they were 'old lags … let out of prison on condition they joined up'. Once in France some had gone AWOL 'and a high old time stealing, raping and even murdering in Northern France till arrested'. Cayley's role was to conduct daily examinations of those on punishment diets in the 'glasshouse', a task he found intimidating, feeling relieved when he was moved back to Le Havre.

Captain Edwin Goodridge, Quartermaster for the No. 183 Field Ambulance, fretted over the rapidity of British reversals. After his unit set up a Main Dressing Station in a conservatory on 18 May:

> It began to look as though we would have to function from midnight and if we had casualties which could not be got away some one of us would have to remain and be captured. The situation looked extremely ugly – Brussels had been evacuated the previous day and enemy patrols had crossed the canal a few miles to our south.[23]

Goodridge and his men then turned out their pockets and destroyed any papers that might have been of use to the enemy. They evacuated by night drive, 'one of the worst experiences we had … our drivers were now exhausted by their efforts of the past five days and it is a nerve-racking task to drive in convoy in absolute darkness and endeavour to keep in sight of the preceding vehicle.'

In addition, the exhaustion of constant stress and movement was taking its toll on RASC personnel: 'Three drivers fell asleep over their wheels and had to be relieved. It seemed to me it would be an advantage for RAMC ambulance car orderlies to be trained to take over vehicles in an emergency and a year later, while employed at the War Office, I had a part in drafting an Army Council Instruction authorising such training.'

With gunfire surrounding them and the roads crammed with traffic – military vehicles, refugees in cars, farm wagons, bicycles, wheelbarrows, prams and pedestrians – the men of No. 183 Field Ambulance found themselves back in France after just forty-eight hours across the Belgian frontier.

Corporal R.H. Montague of the No. 6 Field Ambulance was in charge of a four-man RAMC stretcher party at an ADS. As many Cameron Highlander casualties were being treated, a shell hit the dressing station. The wounded were hastily transferred to ambulances and the medical supplies loaded onto a truck. Montague and his men retreated to the Hotel Haute Maison in Brussels, where he found the Belgian civilians in a blissfully unaware state of the enormity of the situation unfolding around them. The unit was carrying fifty casualties in need of surgery, a fact that shocked the hotel's manager into allowing the medics to transform the ballroom into a reception area for stretchers and the dining room into an operating theatre. The hotel napkins and tablecloths were torn up for use as theatre linen, and under the light of chandeliers, two medical officers performed twenty operations.

As the Germans advanced to the outskirts of Brussels, No. 6 Field Ambulance vacated the hotel, packing their supplies into wicker panniers and their casualties into ambulances. Montague recalled, 'The rapid advance by the enemy and the fluid state of the front line rendered the old system of evacuation of the wounded impossible.'[24]

During the rapid retreat, any usable building was commandeered to serve as a temporary hospital – convent, school, brewery, chateau and farm. One night, approximately 150 casualties were brought in around 11.00 pm. One of the officers, Captain Ian Samuel, performed eighteen operations over the next ten hours, including some amputations.[25] After a short break, Samuel returned to duty exhausted, to close up a chest wound before the unit was on the move again.

As the German onslaught continued, No. 6 Field Ambulance's ADS found itself handling up to 500 new cases per day. On one occasion, Samuel was so tired that he fell asleep leaning against a barn wall, only waking up when he fell over. The judgement of the siting of temporary dressing stations during the retreat became a matter of life or death. The unit's senior officers tried to pick sites close to churches, attaching arrows and red crosses to nearby road signs. One ingenious method of alerting the wounded and those transporting them to the ADS was the use of a 4-gallon petrol drum, with a cross cut into the middle, the space covered in red paper and a hurricane lamp placed inside.

One of those who reached the temporary sanctuary of the ADS was a 19-year-old second lieutenant, whose gangrenous leg had to be removed by amputation. This was too late to save his life, and during his burial service the next morning, a German plane machine-gunned the funeral party. Another patient was an officer whose lower jaw and tongue had been shot away. Montague recalled, 'But the most horrifying part was that he was still alive and conscious, though he could not speak, only move his eyes from side to side.' Captain Samuel administered morphine and the man lapsed into unconsciousness. His suffering was over, but the psychological scars remained with the medics. Samuel recollected many decades later, 'When I think back on those terrible days, I see that half face and know how ghastly war can be.'[26]

For members of the RAMC serving as medical officers in other battalions, establishing arrangements for the movement of casualties could be problematic. Captain Richard Doll, attached to the 1st Battalion Loyal Regiment, recalled the challenge he faced in transferring a wounded man to an ADS:

> I got back to bed again about 0300 [on 16 May], but an hour later a man was brought in who had been shot by a sentry on failing to answer a challenge. He had been shot through the chest and was in a very bad way. I sent off an urgent message to the advanced dressing station at Huldenberg, which the assistant director of medical services had told me the previous day would evacuate my patients, but the station replied that they were not evacuating us and that we should go to another advanced dressing station. I sent off a message to them, but by this time the man had died.[27]

This incident created in Doll 'a steadily increasing fury' as he was unable to find any facility that would accept the responsibility of evacuating wounded men from his battalion. Expecting a heavy attack that night, and further casualties, Doll made a personal visit to the ADS. There, a friend of his agreed to take the casualties, much to Doll's relief. On the evening of the same day, a man was brought to him with a severe compound fracture of his right leg. In Doll's estimation, 'He had probably done it on purpose and had certainly succeeded in getting himself out of the war for many months.' At that point, all four casualties dealt with by Doll had been caused by British troops, and he was assigned a party of eight RAMC stretcher-bearers to assist in their evacuation.

As the withdrawal continued, chains of command and lines of communication began to unravel. On 24 May, Captain Edwin Goodridge of No. 183 Field Ambulance visited Divisional HQ and met a Major Tibbles, who had been in command of No. 32 Field Hygiene Section but had become detached from his unit and was now part of the divisional staff. Goodridge described how a dressing station received ambulance cars from units outside their Division:

> There were several cases of individual cars moving unmolested through the corridor which was supposed to be held by the enemy. These casualties were not from our Division, but we were unable to discriminate during this campaign. Ambulance drivers could not be sure where they would find dressing stations and sometimes had to drive until they found one.'[28]

The normal chain of evacuation via which the dressing station's cases should have been cleared by Motor Ambulance Convoys working forward from CCSs was not working. No. 183 Field Ambulance had extra ambulances attached to them and did their own evacuation, not in convoys but in individual ambulance cars. In such conditions, the work of ambulance drivers became perilous. 'Ambulance driving was no sinecure, with machine-gun fire and bombing to add to other hazards. Many of these drivers had been civilians a few short weeks ago, and it must be conceded that they rose to the emergency in a magnificent fashion.'[29]

Many drivers went beyond what was expected of their role, joining the medics in risking their own chances of being evacuated back to England in order to carry on their work, and drawing admiration from Goodridge:

> On one occasion a loaded ambulance was sent off to Bailleul. It returned two days later, the driver having gone

> from place to place without getting rid of his patients until he reached Dunkirk where he put them on a hospital ship. The military authorities there would not at first allow him to return but he insisted that he must report back to his unit for further duty. This incident heartened us considerably as we knew that our Lines of Communication had been cut and did not think that any ports remained open to us.

Private Stanley Cross, a native of Hull, had been a member of the Territorial Army since 1937, serving in the RASC. (Pic 10) In April 1939, he joined the regular army, undertaking his initial RAMC training at Keogh Barracks. At first, Cross's wife joined him there, before, on 18 October 1939, Cross was sent to France with the British Expeditionary Force as part of No. 150 Field Ambulance in the 50th (Northumbrian) Division. During the Battle of Arras in May 1940, Cross's comrade, 19-year-old Private George Mussared, was badly injured. Mussared was carried by Cross and other unit members for three days before being placed in an ambulance lorry during a German strafing attack. Tragically, this was not enough to save the young soldier's life as he was hit by a bullet and killed on 22 May.[30] (Pic 11)

Cross himself managed to make it to Dunkirk, from where he was able to board a converted coal carrier. The combination of the water he had swallowed during his embarkation and the sooty conditions on the vessel meant that his medical category was downgraded upon his return, and Cross saw out the remainder of the war as a nursing orderly at Edinburgh Castle, which had been converted into a PoW camp for injured enemy servicemen.

As the necessity of retreat became more urgent, No. 183 Field Ambulance was ordered to abandon its vehicles at Vyfweg, 12 miles south of Dunkirk. This presented the officers with the problem of what to do with their casualties. If a CCS could be found, they could be transferred there, otherwise a medical officer and sufficient nursing orderlies would need to remain with them. Captain Edwin Goodridge contemplated the bleak prospects for those who might have to undergo this ordeal:

> This is the unpleasant lot which befalls the RAMC in conditions such as these. Under the Geneva Convention

RAMC personnel are entitled to claim repatriation when they are no longer required to look after their own sick and wounded, but there are always difficulties about effecting this repatriation and one might face the prospect of three or four years in a prison camp. A duty such as this gives point to the Corps motto 'In Arduis Fidelis'.

German attacks on medical personnel

Although it was inevitable that RAMC personnel would be subject to general air and ground attacks in the confusion of retreat, some felt that the Germans were deliberately targeting clearly marked ambulances, dressing stations and hospitals, in contravention of the Geneva Convention. Worse still, in the eyes of many, was the carnage wrought on refugee civilians whose homes had already been destroyed. One ambulance unit received a direct hit from a German bomber, shortly after placing a large Red Cross flag on the ground.[31] The *Maid of Kent*, a clearly marked hospital ship, was sunk in Dieppe harbour by German bombers on 21 May 1940, with the loss of seventeen crew – including eleven members of the RAMC.

Corporal R.H. Montague recalled leaving an ambulance convoy to go to the aid of a stricken French soldier. He was too late to be of any assistance, but as he looked back he saw the convoy's vehicles ablaze. They had been fired on despite clearly displaying red crosses. Montague picked up the dead Frenchman's rifle along with ammunition from his bandolier. Disgusted with the attack on wounded men and those charged with their medical care, his attitude hardened: 'It appeared the Germans did not respect the red cross. I felt comfort in having something I could shoot back with.'

Other men reported seeing German doctors armed and ready for battle, again in contravention of the Geneva Convention. John Forbes Christie later wrote of seeing German ambulances being used to ferry fully armed troops into battle prior to the defeat of the 51st Highland Division at St Valery: 'From the British point of view the idea of pushing forward armed infantry in ambulances with Red Cross markings would be "just not on", even though winning the battle depended on it. In the language of the day such a move would have been classed as "just not cricket". War never was and never will be cricket.'[32]

If it were true that German forces were wont to use ambulances as weapons of war, this would partially explain the instances when they deliberately attacked British medical vehicles. One ambulance transporting wounded men from the Warwickshire Regiment was attacked. There was no mercy shown to those unable to escape. The ambulance doors were slammed shut by the Germans, trapping patients inside. It was then set on fire, killing all of those within.[33]

It was not just medical personnel who fell foul of the advancing German forces. Captain Richard Doll witnessed the tragic aftermath of a German attack that had caused many Belgian civilian casualties. On 20 May, he came across 'a refugee camp to the right of the road outside a small village [that] had received several direct hits. Though this must have been some hours before we saw it, there were still a dozen dead bodies lying out in the midst of the wrecked and burning carts, perambulators, and motor cars.'[34]

Doll looked into an ambulance that had been accompanying some Coldstream Guards. In it a Belgian boy and a girl who had been picked up by the roadside were sheltering, still suffering from shock. He administered morphine and ordered the driver to hand them over at the first town they came to.

On other occasions, the evidence suggests that German bombing of hospitals was inadvertent. Colonel C.M. Finny, Assistant Director of Medical Services (ADMS) to the 50th Northumbrian Division, recalled the case of No. 10 CCS:

> I visited a C.C.S. at Crombeke [on 28 May]. It is doing splendid work in spite of having been bombed. It has been established some days, so that its position is well known, and casualties keep on streaming in from every direction. Most of them are housed in a church, but the C.O. has to keep on taking in fresh buildings and there appears to be a hitch in getting them away. He seemed cheerful and unperturbed, and everyone, including the sisters, seemed to be working away without a thought for anything but the job in hand.
>
> The bombing of this unit appears to have been accidental. The C.O. told me that after it he hoisted a Red Cross flag, and that since then he had not been molested.[35]

In addition to the church, some houses had been commandeered, as well as the use of a few tents and a marquee as an operation room. With the Germans using an 88mm gun – a vicious weapon that could cut men to pieces – up to fifty or sixty casualties were being admitted hourly. Amputations and shrapnel wounds were commonplace.

Finny was surprised to learn that the CCS had not received any orders to move. He later learned that it was being ordered to remain in position and was to be allowed to fall into enemy hands, which it duly did. Private B.C. Miller was one of those ordered to stay behind to treat the wounded. Once the hospital had been taken, an enemy officer took charge and allowed the medics to complete their treatment of all their patients until men were able to be transferred to a prison camp or German hospital.[36]

Ernest Grainger was another orderly who served with No. 10 CCS at Crombeke, along with about eighty others. Trained as a paramedic, Grainger was allowed to stitch up wounds and administer morphine with a doctor's permission. He assisted in amputations after the surgeons had removed the shrapnel, ignoring the cosmetic aspects of surgery: 'we were just keeping them alive. It was crude, but it was effective.'[37] Clerks would work long hours keeping an accurate record of the wounded entering and exiting the clearing station, not just men injured in the fighting, but those suffering from complaints such as appendicitis.

On top of the surgical work, No. 10 CCS strove to stop the spread of infection between their patients. The most serious threat came from gas gangrene, initially caused by soil infected with animal waste entering wounds. Once a man had contracted this affliction, he immediately became an amputation case, with the stench marking out the identification of the gangrene. Alongside the British, the unit accepted large numbers of French and Belgian wounded, with treatment being as prompt and efficient as with the British casualties.

One unit that sustained significant casualties from the air was the No. 183 Field Ambulance. Having spent a miserable night sleeping in an open field, at 11.30 am on 28 May, Captain Edwin Goodridge recalled seeing about fifty Stukas approaching, followed by a:

> loud 'whooshing' noise which I can only compare with the sound made by an approaching express train. I knew instinctively that this was a shell and that it was going to land very close, but before I could throw myself down there

> was a brilliant flash and a patter of earth, and possibly shell splinters, against my tin hat. I was thrown back several yards and recovered my balance on the edge of the ditch.

Goodridge had sustained minor injuries, but others were not so fortunate, including the commanding officer of the unit, Lieutenant Colonel Alex Bremner, a native of the Shetland Isles (Pic 12):

> I saw blood running on to my right shoe and pulled up my trouser leg to find a neat little puncture on the inner side of the knee-cap. I sat down and clapped on my first field dressing and as I did so I saw the CO in the ditch a few yards away. “The B…s have hit my bloody knee,” said I. He smiled faintly and said, “They’ve broken my legs, laddie.”

Recovering from the daze of the initial shock of his injury and the instinctive action of applying a field dressing to it, Goodridge came to realise that others had been hit too. Regimental Sergeant Major Finney had had his abdominal wall ripped open and his intestines were protruding. Goodridge estimated his prospects for survival as ‘clearly hopeless’. Major Rutherford’s right leg was shattered whilst Major Hopper had sustained flesh wounds on each leg. All this carnage had been caused by a mortar bomb. Goodridge went to seek permission to accelerate the evacuation of the unit, and the casualties were allocated a motor ambulance for this purpose. However, this was too late to save RSM Finney, a veteran of the First World War, whose grave Goodridge saw being dug: ‘George Finney was a man of impressive personality and great experience. In the First World War he was badly wounded and won the Military Medal. As a Permanent Staff Instructor to the TA he had fathered several units and 183 Field Ambulance had been built round him … he was a great soldier and a splendid instructor.’

The eventual inscription on his gravestone, *Let Not Your Heart Be Troubled*, was not a sentiment that his surviving colleagues were able to share in the immediate aftermath of the attack and the loss of close comrades. Edwin Goodridge recalled that he lost his strength of will:

> Previously I had felt confident and purposeful in the knowledge that I was a necessary member of the team; now I was being taken away, no further use to anybody …

> I broke down and could hardly restrain tears; I feel rather ashamed when I look back on this period and excuse myself on the grounds of shock from the wound, coupled with the awful sight of my comrades in dire distress and fatigue of recent days.

Goodridge met an ambulance car with six of his wounded comrades. It was overcrowded, with just one ambulance orderly, a Corporal Hudson, to manage them all. The driver, who was also in pain from a previous attack, appeared confused as to the route to take, so Goodridge clambered into the cab to instruct him and administered a shot of morphine. As the road was badly cratered, the injured cramped inside the ambulance car endured a nightmare journey of bumping and jolting.

An order was received for the ambulance to head towards the CCS at Crombeke, about 16 miles from the coast, countermanding the previous order from Lieutenant Colonel Bremner to proceed directly to Dunkirk. Bridges were being destroyed to render the roads impassable for the advancing Germans. After motoring a further mile along the road, Goodridge saw a drawbridge being operated under the direction of a subaltern, who had just allowed a staff car to cross over it. Goodridge seized his chance. Wearing a raincoat that did not display badges of rank, he assumed an air of authority and ordered the subaltern to lower the bridge. When the latter began to object, 'I shouted at him not to stand there arguing – I had seriously wounded officers in need of treatment. The bridge was lowered and we were safe from Crombeke and a prison camp.'

Evacuation

For those RAMC personnel who made it to the Dunkirk beaches, a maelstrom of carnage awaited them. Corporal Montague took a wounded sergeant to a French hospital, where every corner and passageway was filled with the wounded and dying. Outside, the roads were blocked with abandoned and destroyed vehicles. Looking out to sea, Montague noted a Royal Naval destroyer with a broken back. On the sand, rows of men waited their turn for evacuation, vulnerable to wave upon wave of Stuka attacks. Montague set to work burying the dead, digging graves in the sand with his bare hands. 'We stuck each man's rifle into the sand at his head and tied his identity disc to the trigger guard.'

Sergeant Reg Gill, who had been serving as a radiographer at No. 18 General Hospital at Étaples, experienced difficulty in loading some of the French casualties who were evacuated at Dunkirk:

> We loaded the stretchers and put the French and British walking wounded aboard. Many of the French didn't want to go. When they were told we were going to 'Angleterre' they didn't want to know. Some wanted to go back down the coast and join in the fighting again but most seemed to acquiesce and go reasonably well.[38]

Just up the coast from Dunkirk, at La Panne, a large number of RAMC units had gathered and set up dressing and clearance stations in the remains of the hotels. Colonel C.M. Finny, ADMS of 50th Division, was present on 30 May and recalled:

> The sea front at La Panne is a sort of military Harley Street. Nearly everyone seems to be in the R.A.M.C. In addition to my three field ambulances, Nos -, -, and – C.C.S. and – Field Ambulance are located in hotels by the sea. No. – C.C.S. is at Rosendaël near Dunkirk and, I understand, is holding casualties prior to embarkation.[39]

Hospital ships were anchored offshore and stretcher-bearers struggled through the water to load men onto smaller transfer boats. Corporal Michael Adams of No. 11 Casualty Clearing Station was one of those at La Panne.[40] As the doctors were working round the clock performing heroic stints of endurance with their surgical skills, orderlies like Adams were left to administer post-operative care. He recollected the delirium of one soldier calling for his wife; to sooth the man's distress, Adams pretended to answer as his spouse. The pressure of the situation led him to wish the mortally wounded would die quickly, to provide relief from their mental and physical torment, and to free up space for those waiting for treatment.

Captain Richard Doll was one of the later evacuees. Having been given the order to make a final withdrawal at 2200 hrs on 1 June, he headed for the mole at Malo-les-Bains before returning to report its location to the rest of his battalion. Not being able to find them in the confusion, he returned to the beach with the small party that was accompanying him, where they dug themselves a shallow shelter in the sand. An officer then walked past asking for a doctor, as there were reports of badly wounded men the other side of the mole. Doll went to investigate but could not locate any casualties, although on his return trip he found a man with a badly broken leg. All he was able to provide was a dose of morphine, and advised the man's comrades to have him embark as soon as possible.

Realising that there was a chance that his party might not be evacuated before the Germans either overran the beach or caused much greater damage by shelling, Doll walked a short distance along the coast and found a line of men in the water, waiting their turn to board a couple of small rowing boats transporting men onto larger vessels.

> We lined up in the water and, as the empty rowing boats returned to the shore, parties of us waded out to them … the water came up to my breast before I reached the boat. …To the accompaniment of much swearing on the part of the two seamen, the boat gradually filled and was then pulled out to a paddle steamer lying a couple of hundred yards further on by a small motorboat.[41]

Upon boarding the paddle steamer, Doll's Dunkirk duties were not finished. He responded to the request of a naval medical orderly to assist with the binding and splinting of wounds of some nine or ten men: 'Some were terribly badly wounded, and I cannot understand how they got on board.' One man, who had six separate fractures on both legs, died before the boat returned to the safety of England. By this stage, Doll was utterly exhausted, but was sustained by traditional British fare: 'I must have looked terribly done up, for the orderly looked after me like a child, continually giving me steaming cups of tea, and Oxo and pieces of bread and butter.' He was then asked to treat some more wounded on deck, before being granted some much-needed rest. When he awoke he was in Ramsgate harbour. The only possessions remaining were a small haversack and a tiny kitten that had been his companion since he had found it lost and forlorn in Les Bergeus.

Captain Edwin Goodridge was in charge of an ambulance car containing six casualties, including his commanding officer, Lieutenant Colonel Alex Bremner. Having reached Malo-les-Bains, it became impossible to proceed further as all roads and bridges were blocked. Goodridge's plan was to shelter his casualties in an undamaged house, then have them stretchered across a bridge by foot after nightfall. He then spotted fifteen ambulance cars proceeding on a different road so followed them, reaching Dunkirk at 4.00 pm on 28 May.

Goodridge went to find an embarkation medical officer, from whom he learned that a hospital ship had been expected since 8.30 that morning. Two hospital ships had attempted to come in the previous day but failed; one was believed to have been sunk. A naval officer informed Goodridge that he would take any walking wounded but refused the latter's request to take stretcher cases. Goodridge assessed the bleakness of his situation, and the slight possibility of evading capture by the Germans:

> If we were not taken off I would stay until the last possible moment and then, if capture became imminent, I would dive in the quay and swim for it. I am a very strong swimmer and I thought I might be able to work my way along the coast, coming in at night for rest and to look for food until I could finally land somewhere West of the Somme on the other side of the German corridor.

One of Goodridge's casualties, Major Robert Rutherford, was in a coma brought about by a shattered leg, and died in the late afternoon, his body having to remain in the ambulance. Eventually, at 6.30pm, the hospital ship *Dinard* arrived and moored at the end of the half-mile long pier. Instructions were issued to embark the wounded. Goodridge went to the head of the queue to address those who were due to embark first, telling them he had several badly wounded officers to be carried by stretchers. Goodridge recalled their willingness to sacrifice their own prospect of evacuation: 'These men were ragged and tired but the first sixteen immediately came forward, risking the loss of their turn for evacuation.' Fortunately they all eventually got on the ship. It took half an hour to carry the stretchers on board, partly due to there being a hole in the pier, the stretcher-bearers having to pick their way gingerly over the girders.

By this time, Goodridge's knee had become very swollen from a wound received earlier in the day and he was sweating profusely. Three Stukas swooped down on the ship but did not fire, the pilots having recognised the markings of a hospital ship. He recalled the comfort he felt once in the care of the nurses on board the *Dinard*.

> At last we were on board. I remember the feeling of peace and security when I got into the war below deck. A Sister came into the ward, perfectly groomed and with starched cuffs and head veil, looking as though she were going on the morning round at Netley or Woolwich. Anything might yet happen, but the sight of the Sister, calm and unruffled, the cheery clean bed linen, and a cup of tea served on a silvery tray gave me a wonderful sense of security.[42]

Goodridge's wound was re-dressed and he was given an anti-tetanus serum. The medical orderly who had cared for the men in the ambulance, Corporal Hudson, continued to support the ship's staff, and was awarded the Military Medal for his endeavours during the evacuation. The ship eventually berthed at Newhaven on 29 May, and Goodridge was transferred to the Rainhill Emergency Hospital in Liverpool to have his damaged knee operated on. He recorded the conflicting emotions he felt in the immediate aftermath of evacuation: 'Although thankful for our deliverance I was extremely depressed at the fate of our splendid unit.'

Eric Godwin, a GP working in Ruislip, West London, had only received his commission on 10 May 1940. After ten days' training he was assigned to a field ambulance, but due to the crisis developing across the English Channel, he and two other doctors were ordered to Dover, 'and stand on a quay until a destroyer turned up, which it did and we hopped on and then we were whisked over the channel.'[43] Godwin and his companions were unaware of the scale of the emergency awaiting them, and on arriving at the Dunkirk mole, the party was dive-bombed by a German plane. The medics rushed back onto the destroyer, only to be bellowed at by the ship's captain through a megaphone to get off, as he was the target of the raid.

Reaching the shore, Godwin saw a low brick tower on which a dirty British soldier stood with a gun, mad with rage, yelling at passing planes and firing on them. Entering a door at the base of the tower, Godwin came across a group of French troops, eating, drinking and smoking as a French woman cooked them food on a huge range, a contrast, Goodwin noted, with the frantic soldier outside. Godwin began treating men in the open air at the quayside, working alone with no nurses or orderlies to assist him. During the night, as men lay wounded around him, French soldiers would come to try to rob them, Godwin shooing them off. More dead and wounded began to arrive at the quayside. 'One I can still see vividly. A Colonel in his service dress – brand new practically. And I did wish afterwards I had taken his papers to send back to his relations.'[44]

Having had very little food or water for two days, Godwin saw a hospital ship approaching, and frantically tried to evacuate as many of his patients as he could onto it.

> It was getting bombed and shelled … and the crashing of the bombs and shells in the water were getting through … we were running as fast as we could carrying these men on stretchers, one of us at each end – and it's damned heavy I can tell you. The stretcher with nothing on, it's quite heavy, and we had to run across and then up the gangplank. It's quite steep, and then into the ship.

After a couple of days of saving lives, Godwin sailed back to Dover to return to the unit with which he had only spent two days prior to his Dunkirk experience.

Operation Aerial

For those units unable to reach Dunkirk, a further escape opportunity was afforded by Operation Aerial, which ran from 15 to 25 June, with men able to leave from ports on the western coast of France. As medical units could not withdraw until their patients had either been evacuated, or provision arranged for their continuing care until capture by the enemy, the men of No. 6 General Hospital anxiously searched for transport to take them away from their tented hospital at Flocques, near the Normandy coast. The Germans had encircled the main body of the British Army and cut off any possible escape route via Dunkirk, so the unit had to retreat south-westwards. Once the evacuation order came, transport was obtained via local RASC units. However, to the dismay of Walter Hart and his comrades, this was purloined by all but two of the officers and the nursing sisters.

Eventually fresh transport was found to remove the wounded, and the remainder of the unit split in two. One party would make for Dieppe on foot, marching on the clifftops. Hart was to go with the other party making their way northwards to Le Tréport, to try to find a train to Dieppe and await the other party there. It was hoped that at least one party would get away as by this time the men had learned that the Germans were encircling the area and the only way out was by sea.

All the tents and buildings were to be destroyed by the Royal Engineers, so the group was told they were free to take anything they wanted, as it would not be regarded as looting. Hart and his friends took some tinned food and cigarettes along with a giant tin of Ovaltine and a Primus stove filled with paraffin. On arrival at Le Tréport railway station, Hart's party saw a train pulling away from the platform with the officers and nursing sisters who had previously commandeered the RASC vehicles safely ensconced in it. Undeterred by this disloyal act, the new arrivals found a goods train with open trucks and clambered aboard. It took eighteen hours for the train to edge its way along the 20-mile stretch of track to Dieppe.

Arriving at Dieppe station, Hart saw thousands of civilian refugees trying to board trains, but with the Germans blocking the line, drivers were refusing to take their trains out. To his amazement, he had only been at the station for about half an hour when the coast-walking party arrived, having lost no one on the way. The Germans had been too busy strafing the road below. Word came through that there were no more ships available to evacuate men by sea. Therefore, two options presented themselves: stay and be taken as prisoners of war, or take a chance that they could pierce the German ring by train. They chose the latter. The train managed to escape through the German lines to Le Mans and then it moved on to La Baule, where they became the temporary guests of No. 4 General Hospital, which was then operating from the town's casino. From there, Hart and his comrades moved close to the Atlantic seaport of St Nazaire, where they collected rations. They were then told by a military policeman not to bother collecting the following day's rations as there would not be any. France had capitulated, and the men were to be rescued, if possible.

Sure enough, the following morning at six, they began marching in open file along the side of the road to avoid German raiding planes, reaching St Nazaire in the early evening. At the docks they boarded MS *Sobieski*, a Polish ship designed to carry 600 passengers but currently containing ten times that number. A German raid began on the ship, but fortunately the bombs fell in the water with a terrific bang, rocking the ship and killing hundreds of fish. The overcrowding on the ship reminded East Ender Hart of Petticoat Lane market on the Sunday before Christmas. Leaving the dock to enter the outer harbour to rendezvous with the naval escort ships, the *Sobieski's* place at the dockside was taken by the ill-fated RMS *Lancastria*, which was to be sunk on 17 June with the loss of between 3,000 and 5,000 lives, the largest single-ship maritime loss in British history.

An alternative route of escape from France was undertaken by men of 'Beau Force', originally a group of 200 men comprising hospital convalescents and those returning from leave who could not get back to their units in the melee of retreat. Lieutenant Forde Cayley was assigned to this formation, the men being taken to a farm on army trucks with the idea of forming a defensive line along a 40-mile front around Rouen. Retreating to a village near Forges-les-Eaux, and digging defensive trenches, they were reinforced to 800 men, becoming Beauman's Division, named after Acting Brigadier A.B. Beauman. Cayley managed to acquire three ambulances belonging to the 51st Division, which had been left in a ditch, as the division was ordered to stay and fight to the last man and last bullet. Having seen no action for two days, the men sent back to Brigade HQ for further orders, only to find it abandoned, so they evacuated, crossing the river Seine by ferry at Caudebec. They then discovered Brigade HQ had made another retreat without giving orders, so their commanding officer ordered 'every man for himself'.

The force made for Cherbourg and were evacuated before German troops directly engaged with the Allied forces in the town. Cayley arrived back at Southampton on 18 June, eventually rejoining his unit, most of whom had been sent to Beckett Park in Leeds via Dunkirk.

Medical innovation

In the midst of the chaos and carnage, medical lessons were being learned. Major J.S. Jeffrey was working at a base hospital at La Baule, near St Nazaire, and because of its distance from the front, the hospital was able to continue functioning right up until 18 June 1940, when it was finally evacuated.

Several thousand wounded men passed through the hospital during its six operational weeks. Most of the wounds treated were to limbs and soft tissue, and were between twenty-four and forty-eight hours old. Many were dirty and had varying amounts of devitalised and gangrenous muscle. During busy periods there were three operating tables running simultaneously in a casino in the town, with surgeons and theatre staff working in relays.

Often Jeffrey and his colleagues did not have the chance to assess each case until the patient came into the theatre under anaesthetic, which was 'inevitable but undesirable'.[45] However, surgical lessons were learned during the six weeks, as Jeffrey reflected:

> To begin with, in our operative treatment, many of us younger surgeons were unduly radical. Perhaps we had heard too much of 'excision of wounds' and to some extent forgot our surgical pathology, so that we cut away devitalised tissue simply because it was devitalised, and heedless of the infection we might be spreading thereby. With experience, and guided by Colonel Max Page, Consulting Surgeon to the BEF … we soon gained better judgement, and thereafter excision of tissue was reserved for those cases of obvious gas gangrene.[46]

The great majority of wounds treated were already septic. Jeffrey developed the practice of swabbing the wound clean then packing it with sulphonamide powder, usually two heaped teaspoons. Colonel Colebrook introduced a pump to spray powder to reach all corners of the wound.

Another issue that Jeffrey and his colleagues had to deal with was the question of whether to remove bullets and fragments of shrapnel from the body. Frequently the metal could be left in situ, if not causing any other disturbance.

> Our usual practice, in the case of 24–48 hour old wounds, and with or without the aid of X-rays, was to enlarge the

> wound slightly to allow for drainage, insert a finger along the rack and seek the fragment. If the fragment could not be found, the search was discontinued and the case reviewed after five days. By that time suitable X-rays could be taken, and the wound would be either quiescent or becoming increasingly septic. In the latter case we again operated under anaesthetic and explored the wound. To open up fresh, clean and healthy tissue in any search is dangerous, though the subsequent insertion of the sulphonamide pack nullifies much of that danger.[47]

Broken bones and compound fractures were treated by closed plaster method whilst large soft tissue wounds were splinted with plaster, Cramer wire or wooden splints. Jeffrey reckoned the comfort of patients was remarkable, with none developing gas gangrene. He commented on the case of a Belgian soldier who had been shot through in mid-humeral region, causing gross shattering of the shaft and leaving an enormous exit wound. When Jeffrey's team began treatment, the injury was already ten days old and the wounded man had been continuously on the road in retreat. He had had a shell dressing and wooden splint applied, but was in constant pain, although 'brave and stoical'.[48]

Jeffrey cleaned the wound, inserted a sulphonamide pack, put the man's arm up in abduction and encased his thorax, arm and hand in plaster. He was then comfortable, but after a fortnight he began to complain of itching in the wound. Jeffrey assured him all was well, but the itching got worse. One morning, the Belgian produced two maggots in a matchbox, which had crawled out from the plaster onto his neck during the night. Jeffrey reassured him it was 'good' and 'we liked to see it'. After a few days, the plaster was removed. 'The wound was crawling with live maggots and dead flies, but otherwise looked beautifully clean.'

Jeffrey considered there was still scope for improvement in the after-treatment of wounds. 'Too often the surgeon's interest in the wound wanes during the weeks that the patient lies in hospital, whereas with proper care much can be done to speed up the process of healing.' Wounds healed best when the dressings were undisturbed for seven to ten days as persistent redressing ran the risk of spreading infection through inadequate sterilisation, or dust.

Once the Blitzkrieg began, traditional methods of providing stability for fractured limbs had to be abandoned as patients had to be ready to move at an hour's notice. For example, slinging a patient to a Balkan beam was impractical. The Thomas splint was used as a substitute, which allowed some flexion, and was easier to transport. Men of the BEF were given two tetanus injections at six-week intervals, but due to movement between units and 'rush conditions', some men did not receive their second injection. As a single injection did not confer immunity, a handful of men succumbed to the infection. Out of approximately 2,000 cases seen by Jeffrey in the hospital, four had developed a tetanus infection, two of whom died.

France and Flanders proved an effective testing ground for the new Army Blood Transfusion Service led by Colonel L.W. Proger. Blood had been taken from universal donors and flown out from England in pint bottles. In the nine days following the German invasion, 990 bottles of whole blood and 116 of plasma were sent from the Blood Supply Depot at Bristol. This could be stored for up to a fortnight, with the promptness of blood transfusion saving many lives at La Baule and elsewhere. Transfusion proved vital in the prevention of wound shock, with early treatment averting the onset of symptoms such as increased pulse rate, falling body temperature, vomiting and heart failure. Plasma in fluid in dried form was on the point of being used at La Baule when the evacuation was ordered.

Blood transfusion was provided by Field Transfusion Units with blood being carried in mobile refrigeration units. Four FTUs had opened by the time of the German attack on 10 May. The rapidity of the retreat meant that blood transfusions, although effective for those fortunate enough to receive them, were not as widespread as in other campaigns during the war. One anaesthetist, Major E.S. Rowbotham, had a supply of nitrous oxide and oxygen, but when this ran short, ethyl chloride and ether were used, administered via an intratracheal catheter. Due to the high degree of skill shown by Rowbotham, there were no fatalities in his theatre due to men receiving an anaesthetic.

Due to evacuation, Jeffrey was unable to complete a study he had begun on the value of sulphonamide powder, administering it to a group of 100, no powder to a second control group of 100, and oral sulphonamide to a third 100. In addition, many of his records were lost during the hasty evacuation, meaning he could only give his general impression and that of the senior surgeons of the value of the powder. This was that wounds that had packs administered looked cleaner after an interval of five days than those with no sulphonamide. It sterilised wounds and set them on the path to healing. Although penicillin was to become the new 'wonder drug' of the war, in early campaigns such as France and Flanders, sulphonamide was used extensively in the treatment of wounds, proving 'valuable [both] prophylactically and during the healing of war wounds'.[49] The development of the administration of the drug in powder form intrigued the surgeons of the BEF.

Major R.S. Handley, working in a CCS attached to a French hospital in Metz, was dealing with a steady trickle of casualties before the invasion of Belgium on 10 May. They were brought to him from the Maginot Line within three hours of wounding. In twenty-five cases of primary suture, he found that twenty-three remained perfectly clean with just two becoming septic.[50] Handley's work benefitted from the static nature of the CCS at that period, allowing patients' wounds to be encased in plaster of Paris and allowed to rest for ten days. Handley administered sulphonamide by mouth, on the day of the operation and on subsequent days.

Organisational lessons

Although the period spent engaged with the enemy was considerably under a month for most medical units, important lessons had been learned about organisation of medical services in the field. These were summarised by Colonel C.M. Finny, the Assistant Director of Medical Services for the 3rd Infantry Division of the BEF:[51]

1. Once a man had been carried back to his own regimental doctor, then it was nearly always possible to take him by ambulance. Enemy artillery was ineffective against the ambulance due to the speed of the withdrawal.
2. In built-up areas ambulances could come forward and save men who would otherwise have been left to die or be captured. When ambulances were not available the wounded could be evacuated in ordinary trucks, generally faring well.

3. Ambulances were distributed along columns of vehicles to deal with casualties from bombing and machine-gunning.
4. Dressing stations should only be set up when absolutely necessary. Things had to be organised so that one of the three Field Ambulances in each division was ready to move quickly in order to open up again in a safe area. When a dressing station was established, if it was moved too soon it could leave many wounded men without treatment. If, however, it moved too late, the RAMC men could find themselves captured.
5. The issue of the siting of dressing stations was addressed. It was important that they did not get in the way of the fighting troops. Sometimes the location given when planning an operation was either unsuitable or destroyed by the time the medical staff arrived there. In such cases the doctor in charge of the dressing station liaised with regimental officers or local people to find a suitable alternative.
6. Routes to dressing stations had to be well marked, so that ambulance drivers who had undertaken long journeys would not take a wrong turning. The dressing stations themselves needed to be clearly indicated by a red cross, as well as divisional signs and unit numbers.

Aftermath for those who returned

From Sunday, 26 May onwards, wounded soldiers from the BEF, evacuated via the northern French ports, began to stream into Shorncliffe, the nearest military hospital to Dover and Folkestone. The inevitable delay in operating on the wounded in England meant that even those lucky enough to escape from France had a much reduced chance of survival. The mortality rate in some civilian hospitals was as high as 25 per cent.[52] Many of the returnees were soaked to the skin, having been immersed in the Channel, whilst others carried multiple wounds, still protected by the original shell dressing. Impromptu tourniquets had been manufactured from helmet straps, puttees or string. Walking wounded and stretcher cases alike, Major James Ross noted: 'Coated with grime and filth and sand, unshaven, exhausted by lack of food and sleep, shaken by hours or days of continual bombardment, and with fearful wounds, it was amazing to us how they had survived at all.'[53]

To resuscitate, morphine, sweet tea and warmth were administered and blood transfusions, saline and glucose infusions given. Ross's opinion was that the establishment had ceased to be a hospital but was acting as a CCS in the forward zone. Surgeons triaged the wounded troops, prioritising those in need of most immediate attention, hearing grim tales of the carnage being enacted just over 20 miles away:

> 'It's murder over there, sir,' an infantry sergeant told me. 'We can't cope with it at all; our rifles and bayonets are good enough, but they're no use in the open against tanks. I saw the Guards go at the Jerries in the old style, with the bayonet; the Jerries let them come on, then mowed them down with tommy-guns.' … 'Our fellows are brave enough, none braver,' a Captain observed, 'but flesh and blood alone are no use against steel tanks of forty tons.'[54]

The medics at Shorncliffe worked around the clock using three operating tables, as stretcher-bearers brought a constant flow of wounded men. Everyone, no matter what their status or specialism, pitched in with resuscitation, transfusion, anaesthetising, admitting, clerking and assisting the surgeons. Wounds were cleansed and trimmed, and fragments removed where possible. Sometimes limbs were immobilised in plaster of Paris, but many amputations had to be performed. In all, over 500 men passed through Shorncliffe Military Hospital in the days following the evacuation. The sisters and VAD nurses frequently dealt with death – on one occasion eight men died in the main ward within half an hour following operations – along with numerous air raid warnings, heat, lack of ventilation and the stench of wounds.

The sounds of battle could be heard from across the Channel, and the hospital afforded a grand view of the numerous small ships making their way towards Dunkirk. At night the red glow of the fires could be seen. As the rush of casualties reached a climax, the hospital was told to expect about 400 cases, which would be brought over from St Nazaire on the RMS *Lancastria*, but they were among the many thousands consigned to a watery grave when the ship was sunk on 17 June 1940.

While the medical staff at Shorncliffe worked at a furious pace treating the wounded evacuees, 250 miles further north, at Beckett Park in Leeds, Private John Broom was confined to a ward suffering from impetigo. He had as companions two men whose destroyer had been sunk when leaving Dunkirk and who had had to swim for salvation. They recounted grim tales from their escape: 'Re. the B.E.F. & German cruelty. Some of the stories would make your stomach turn over. The press very mercifully, tries to dilute the sheer incomparable devilishness of the Germans. But the fellows know, & their experience is best summed up in one word "Hell".'[55]

The shock of the military reversals in France and Flanders caused a change of heart amongst many who had initially requested to serve in the RAMC for moral, religious or political reasons. Captain Edwin Goodridge noted, 'One interesting sidelight was the fact that practically all of the conscientious objectors in the unit had applied to be taken off the list of objectors – some were now definitely belligerent!'[56]

As the survivors continued to return, the Beckett Park training depot struggled to cope with their numbers. On 17 June, John Broom wrote: 'This ward is overcrowded at the moment. When I came here there were eleven beds, two of which were occupied. Now there are seventeen beds jammed in. The new patients are mainly B.E.F. & they are suffering from scabies owing to going weeks on end without a wash abroad.'

Walter Hart returned safely from St Nazaire to Falmouth, as the MS *Sobieski* continually zigzagged to avoid German submarines. There he and his comrades were reunited with the officers and nursing sisters of No. 6 General Hospital who had previously left the unit before all their patients had been evacuated. These personnel were moved on to other units soon afterwards. While at Falmouth railway station, troops were given refreshments by members of the Women's Voluntary Services, who also took messages that could be sent on to relatives. Hart's parents had received no news from him for two months, and feared that he had, at best, been taken prisoner by the Germans. They were therefore delighted to receive the WVS letter containing the words 'Safe and in England'.[57]

Whilst most medics who escaped the German onslaught were brought home via the Channel or Atlantic French ports, perhaps the most remarkable escape account from the advancing Wehrmacht was given by Lieutenant (later Major) D.I. McCallum.[58] McCallum was serving with No. 13 Casualty Clearing Station, which, on 20 May 1940, was evacuated from Domart, 15 miles north-west of Amiens, and ordered to make towards St Pol.

About forty medics and patients had to proceed on foot, due to the paucity of motorised transport, and by the time they reached Doullens, about 17 miles south of their planned destination, they found themselves cut off by the Germans. The commanding officer, Colonel Morris, decided that the only chance of escape was to divide into three parties, each one commanded by an officer. As the most junior of the officers, McCallum was allotted responsibility for twelve other men, including two sergeants.

At first, the group travelled westwards for 2 miles but were told by an agitated French civilian that German forces were in the vicinity. Despite still wearing their Red Cross brassards, they received a hail of machine-gun bullets as they dashed across a main road. A German tank prevented any chance of escape over a bridge across the river Authie, so the men had to swim. McCallum's party contained six non-swimmers who had to be assisted across by a hand bridge made with straps from their equipment. Despite one man getting into difficulties, all the party managed to reach the far bank safely and in sodden clothes proceeded to a nearby farm for a meagre meal of raw eggs.

Having rested for the remainder of the day, the men set off at 10.30 pm, surrounded by the sound of the engines of enemy vehicles. To make matters even worse, they were chased by a vicious bull. By 2.00 am, two men had to fall out through fatigue and had to be left as comfortable as possible in an evacuated farm to await capture by the Germans.

The remaining eleven men pushed on, and over the next few nights made their way through the Forest of Crecy, at one point narrowly avoiding a German patrol that passed about 20 yards from their hiding place. On the sixth night, the party had to wade thigh-deep in the mud of a marshland before finding a firm pathway. A 'kindly French official' gave the men shelter and a compass, and assured them that Mussolini had been killed, that the Turks and the Russians had entered the war and that the British would soon force their way across the Somme and take control of the area. Consequently, the party remained there for a week, well fed but surrounded by Germans.

On 3 June, the news arrived that the Germans were to occupy the billet in which they were sheltering within half an hour and a rapid escape had to be made. The following day, the men had to swim across the tidal river Somme and equipped themselves with the inner tubes of several motor tyres to support the non-swimmers. The crossing had to be made at night to pass by the German machine-gun posts on both sides of the river, and the eleven men raced across the sands, carrying their equipment and bending low, staying out of sight of the snipers. They were faced with the sound of an inrushing tide, and two men decided that they stood a better chance crossing at a different spot, so separated themselves from the group.

The remaining nine all got across safely, and by the time they reached the far bank, they had to discard all their drenched clothes but their shirts, and walked for a further six hours barefooted and almost naked. Good fortune then smiled on the men as they came across a hut recently vacated by a Highland regiment, containing jackets and greatcoats. Later that night, sufficient French civilian clothing for all nine was found in a deserted farm.

By 12 June, following a relatively uneventful few nights, the group reached Mers-les-Bains near Tréport. McCallum and Sergeant Wilson, as the two men with some knowledge of the French language, left to get some provisions, leaving the other seven resting in an evacuated house. Upon their return, they were shocked to see a German sentry guard standing at the door. One of the recently captured men managed to signal from a window to McCallum to get back down the road. McCallum and Wilson hid for eight hours in a hen house, then headed westwards towards the river Seine.

A week later, having reached the Seine, they lay at the riverbank for eighteen hours, within earshot of German sentries. Wilson managed to blow up the inner tube of a tyre with a bicycle pump, fit the tube into a sack and interlace a network of twigs into the sacking to provide a makeshift raft on which their clothes and provisions could be dragged across the river. Making the crossing at 11.30 pm on 19 June under a full moon, they were seen and fired at, but remained unharmed.

A new plan was formed to make for the island of Jersey. The pair covered from 12 to 15 miles per night, sleeping in barns during the day, sustained by food provided by French peasants. McCallum noted, 'The kindness of these peasant folks is beyond description. During the ten weeks we spent in the Occupied Zone we were refused food on one occasion only.'

At 2.00 am on 23 June, the pair were halted by a German corporal sentry with a fixed bayonet. A German officer then emerged from a staff car, spoke with the corporal and then addressed them in French: *'Qui êtes-vous?'*

'I explained that we were refugees returning to Caen. (At this time we were in civilian clothes and were complete with berets.) The officer then asked for our papers. I replied "Pas de papiers." *"Pourquoi?"* I elaborated that we had had to leave home so quickly that all our papers were left behind.'

Still suspicious, the officer had McCallum and Wilson searched, but all that was found was some food and a spare pair of shoes. He ordered them to *'Allez'*.

'To my horror, Serjeant Wilson, who had been silent up to now, politely asked in a pronounced English accent: *"Voulez-vous un fromage?"* to which the officer replied in no uncertain fashion.'

On 26 June, the pair made for the river Orne. All the bridges across the river were closely guarded, as was the Paris-Caen railway, which ran parallel to the river. Crossing the river, they eventually reached the coast of the Cotentin Peninsula, opposite Jersey. By this time McCallum was suffering from acute muscular strain, having been on the run for over a month, and was keen to cross over to the island and safety. The pair were informed that Jersey had been occupied three days previously, and that any locals in the coastal area were under penalty of death should they be caught helping the British.

Undeterred after all they had endured, after two days' rest, McCallum and Wilson headed southwards towards the Pyrenees in an attempt to reach Vichy France, unoccupied by German troops under the terms of the armistice signed by Marshal Petain. By 25 July, they were within 20 miles of Tours and were fortunately lent bicycles and accompanied through the city by a 'kindly French artisan'. By 4.00 am on 26 July, they were within 10 miles of Free France. For the final part of their journey to safety, the pair played the role of peasants working in the fields, carrying forks to make their playacting complete. At 5.00 pm, they crossed the border and turned themselves in to a French official, who explained that they would be interned 'somewhere in France'. However, he did not seem interested in carrying through with the sanction, and advised them to make for Montpellier, 300 miles away.

By hitchhiking they arrived there on 30 July and were told that if they made it to the port of Marseilles, where the Americans were in charge of British interests, they would have a greater chance of escape to Britain. Although interned in Fort St Jean, McCallum and Wilson managed to obtain false passports from a Polish ex-serviceman's organisation and escaped on a ship bound for Casablanca. From here they sailed to Lisbon and presented themselves at the British consulate, where safe passage back to Britain was arranged. One of the most remarkable escape stories of the Second World War had ended in success, despite the huge barriers the pair had had to overcome. McCullum subsequently saw action in North Africa and North West Europe, and was awarded the MC for his actions during the crossing of the Rhine in 1945.

Those left behind

Many wounded and sick men were in too serious a condition to be evacuated from France and had to be left behind as they could not be moved without endangering their health. In all, for every seven men evacuated back to England, one was either killed or taken prisoner. Some doctors, orderlies, stretcher-bearers and ambulance drivers had to remain to ensure the survival of the wounded who had been sacrificed in the retreat. Medical treatment still needed be given wherever and whenever possible. Regardless of their rank – whether senior surgeons or lowly stretcher-bearers – medical staff provided a standard of care to the utmost of their abilities long after the majority of the BEF had escaped across the Channel. Medical personnel had to be allocated to remain to care for patients until capture, and to ensure that they received appropriate treatment from the Germans. In some units, men drew lots to decide who would, literally, draw the short straws. On the early morning of 31 May, Colonel C.M. Finny visited the Main Dressing Station in La Panne, 'with written orders in my pocket to the effect that at least a proportion of the unit would have to remain behind to look after their patients when they fell into German hands; a terrible order to give to anyone.'[59]

'Ginger' Barnett was serving with No. 133 Field Ambulance supporting the 44th Division as the force fell back until a contingent reached the foot of Mont des Cats. It was here that, for Barnett and his comrades, the war would be over. The hill was held by the Germans, giving them a commanding view of the surrounding area. As Barnett's loaded ambulance drove past it came to a crossroads and took a wrong turning, delivering it straight into the path of a group of SS troops who opened fire on the vehicle.

> In the end we were surrounded. We had stopped and bullets were coming through the canvas sides of the ambulance. I said to the sergeant, 'C'mon let's get out of here!' But he told me to wait for orders. I thought 'You're joking!' He told me to pile all the blankets up the side of the lorry. But it didn't stop the bullets – they were firing tracers through the side of the ambulance. They set fire to the ambulances. So we slit the sides of the ambulances and dived out into a ditch. It was every man for himself, you just got out and ran after the bloke in front of you, hoping to get to some sort of shelter.[60]

As the ambulance crew ran for cover, their patients were trapped inside the burning vehicle. 'That was the first time I'd ever smelt burning flesh. It was bloomin' horrible!'

Reaching the temporary safety of a farm, the medics were taken prisoner with a German with a tommy gun, but Barnett later reflected that, given the fate of those in the ambulance, things could have turned out a lot worse for him and his comrades.

Ernest Grainger recalled that at the moment of capture, No. 10 CCS had been supporting the Norfolk Regiment, but the medical staff had been largely unaware of the progress of the fighting. Therefore, it came as a shock when a German medical officer entered their operating theatre with the infamous words 'For you the war is over', before proceeding to watch the CCS continue with its work.

On 1 June, the men of the No. 12 Casualty Clearing Station believed they were the last medical unit still functioning at Dunkirk. Orders came to leave three officers and thirty men to look after 230 patients who were too badly wounded to be moved. Names were drawn from a hat. There were some seventeen medical officers between whom the tense and dramatic draw took place. The three unfortunate doctors 'took their fate splendidly and cheerfully, as did the men theirs'.[61]

One of the unfortunate trio was Major Philip Newman, a surgical specialist. No. 12 CCS had been ordered to open up on a sports field in Annezin in the Bethune region of northern France. As the Germans advanced, the marquees became full of the wounded and the sports ground was strafed from the air and shelled from the ground. The unit was therefore ordered to retreat on 26 May and reopen the hospital at Dunkirk. Newman described the chaos of the retreat, he being in charge of a party of three lorries and forty men, losing their way close to the Belgian border.[62] On returning to the main road, the lorries were repeatedly strafed until the party reached Dunkirk at 1.00 am on 28 May. In the morning, Newman organised a theatre in the drawing room of the Chateau Rouge on the outskirts of Dunkirk, and within two hours had two operating teams going. Newman expressed some resentment at those who were being evacuated as he and his men continued to work round the clock in desperate conditions:

> There was an awful languid feeling about – this starting to get down to hard work again when everyone else was going home. … Bombing around us was frequent. This first day we plodded on steadily with the operating with the promise of relief in the evening by some field ambulance people. They never turned up – they had bunked off home.

Doctors and orderlies survived on tinned food, usually bully beef and biscuits, eaten standing up. A 500lb bomb fell with 50 yards of the chateau, which became packed with the wounded, the driveway becoming filled with ambulances. The commanding officer, Munro, organised the evacuation of men from the hospital to the Dunkirk mole, as those under his command gradually became worn down with exhaustion. On one day, some 700 wounded men were transferred from the chateau to the mole for evacuation. On the night of 30 May, the men of No. 12 CCS were told that they could return home, but this order was rescinded, with the instruction that only patients could be evacuated. Newman recorded, 'One of the gloomiest aspects of those days was the way anyone in authority seemed to forsake his post and jump on a boat for home.'

It was not just British soldiers whom the clearing station had to treat, but wounded civilians too. Newman recorded performing a leg amputation on a little French boy. At 2.30 am on 1 June, the ballot for those who had to remain with the wounded was drawn. Newman's name was one of the last to be drawn. As those with a chance of escape made their preparations to leave, there was a tense five hours in which there were few words spoken. One significant interaction took place between Newman and 'Cocky' O'Shea, the Roman Catholic chaplain. O'Shea gave the weeping Newman a crucifix, an item that would be passed between the two men during a lifetime of friendship through to the 1980s. Another man who was leaving gave Newman his copy of the New Testament. A short Christian service was held and then the men departed. Newman was left with sixteen other RAMC men and 300 wounded, to await the Germans.

Patients still waited in tents, corpses were strewn outside the house and there was a stink Newman likened to a cesspool. The next morning, 2 June, a German shell landed in the front room, which was being used as an operating theatre, killing or further wounding twelve patients, one of whom received a slab of concrete in his face. Outside, naked men, wounded and burnt, crawled around on the grass. Some further space on a ship was found, which enabled Newman to evacuate another few men, 'Chaps going to England in a shirt, a blanket and bare feet, some with large running wounds in their backs and legs hobbling on the shoulders of others'. Then the final British personnel who would leave Dunkirk sailed off, leaving Newman and his men standing alone, 'Forsaken by England and only the Germans to look forward to. I can never forget that moment as long as I live. It gave me the greatest feeling of desolation I have ever had.'

As the Germans neared Dunkirk, Newman and his men made an illuminated red cross to place outside the front door of the chateau to indicate that the building was being used as a hospital. A further well was found to provide water to the patients, and four of the medical staff continued to bury the dead, with Newman estimating that 150 men were laid to rest in their makeshift cemetery. Further shelling of the area created more death and destruction.

French troops began to dig in, in a park next to the hospital, where wounded men lay out in the open on stretchers, thus increasing the likelihood of the area becoming a battleground. A conversation with a French commandant averted this potentially disastrous move, and Newman posted a German pilot officer prisoner near the front door of the chateau, next to the red cross. On 4 June, the Germans arrived, and Newman rose from his sleep to find Germans sitting around the hospital, talking to the patients, showing them photographs and fetching them water. Newman felt a sense of relief, and even some warmth towards the German troops as the tension of imminent death had receded. Patients who had been trapped inside the house could now be moved into the open air, away from an increasing stench.

In the evening, German troops brought soup to the patients. Subsequently, Newman was taken to a prisoner of war camp, escaping twice and eventually returning to Britain in 1942 with the help of the French Resistance.

Elsewhere, large contingents of RAMC men were taken by the Germans. At Calais, where four battalions, mainly Green Jackets, were achieving a sacrificial delay, holding up at least two German divisions, casualties were evacuated by the navy almost to the last. The regimental MOs stayed with their own fighting troops right to the end. Three weeks later, a fresh evacuation was carried out at St Nazaire. Many of the wounded and those medics caring for them were among the many thousands lost when the RMS *Lancastria* was bombed and sunk. RAMC men searched the docks for survivors, though constantly attacked from the air. At St Valery, 8,000 troops of the 51st Division were overrun and captured, along with their medical services.

The reverses in Europe during the early phases of the Second World War had seen RAMC personnel struggle manfully to keep some semblance of order to their operations in a rapidly shifting landscape. Plans for the organisation of medical services in the field had not anticipated such a swift retreat as had happened in France and Flanders during May 1940, and medics themselves had come under repeated attack. Those who managed to return were under no illusions as to the grim struggles ahead but could reflect on their fortune of not being one of more than 200 medics who had been killed in these engagements, or amongst the 40,000 British troops taken prisoner by the Germans during these desperate operations. They lived to serve another day.

Chapter 3

Africa

The North African Campaign lasted from 10 June 1940 to 13 May 1943. It included operations fought in the Libyan and Egyptian deserts, Morocco, Algeria and Tunisia. British and French colonial interests in Africa were threatened by the Axis powers, and British and Commonwealth troops, alongside exiles from German-occupied Europe, did the brunt of the work in this theatre of war until United States forces arrived in North Africa on 11 May 1942. Following the Italian declaration of war on 10 June 1940, British forces crossed the Egyptian border into Libya and to-and-fro fighting took place between the two armies until the arrival of Rommel's Afrika Korps in February 1941. Driven back into Egypt, the crucial Allied breakout began with the Second Battle of El Alamein on 23 October 1942, where Lieutenant General Montgomery's Eighth Army inflicted a decisive defeat on the Afrika Korps, instigating the driving back of Axis forces across the desert to Tunisia. Following Operation Torch, the Anglo-American landings in North-West Africa in November 1942, the Axis powers finally surrendered in May 1943. Montgomery's exhortation to his men to 'hit the enemy for "six", right out of North Africa' had been realised. Elsewhere on the continent, medical units and RMOs served alongside the native regiments that were raised in East and West Africa.

Desert warfare innovations

In North Africa, the need for mobility in medical units became even more pronounced than in Europe, as the shape of the campaign saw armies shift repeatedly backwards and forwards across vast distances, and lines of communication became stretched. At its worst, the line of evacuation from Regimental Aid Post to General Hospital could stretch to 500 miles, much of it over very rough terrain. Therefore, major surgical treatment had to be administered as close to the front line as practicable and safe.

One medical officer described a typical evacuation for a wounded man thus:

> He probably had 50 miles back to his own R.A.P. (Going bad).
> He probably had 25 miles back to Brigade A.D.S. (Going bad).
> He probably had 30 miles back to A.M.D.S. (Going very bad).
> He probably had 30 miles back to Staging Post (Going almost impossible).
> He probably had 50 miles back to M.D.S. (Going almost impossible).
> He probably had 60 miles back to Railhead (Per motor ambulance convoy).
> He probably had 80 miles back to C.C.S. (Per hospital train).
> He probably had 150 miles back to General Hospital. (Per hospital train).[1]

Ambulance drivers were often reduced to a few miles per hour in difficult terrain, and had no easy job finding their way along lines of communication, which could stretch for 2,000 miles. Desert tracks were rudimentary and often unsignposted, with few landmarks to guide the way. One RAMC Officer noted:

> Navigating in a Ford Utility car is full of difficulties. The coil is situated so high up that when navigating from the front seat, especially on an East and West bearing, one may be anything up to 25 degrees out. In the back seat one will not be more than 10 degrees out, but exact navigation is essential. The selected bearing must be taken out of the car and the variation taken from the inside.[2]

Navigation was frequently undertaken without lights, causing some RAMC vehicles to go badly astray. Men would be given three days' rations, but not be allowed to touch them until they had been for a day without food. An Advanced Dressing Station might be anything up to 30 miles from its nearest neighbour, and often there was little for them to do except treat routine sick cases. Time would pass slowly over the course of a month. This would contrast with hectic periods such as during the Battle of Sidi Barrani, when 300 casualties passed through one ADS within seven hours.

During training there had been great attention paid to loading and unloading vehicles and erecting tents. Orders to move were often at very short notice and happened on average once per week, and sometimes two or three times in a week. During the early North African campaign, dressing stations were established consisting of tarpaulin lean-to shelters surrounding a lorry. The shelter would be dug in where possible, or comprised a low wall of sandbags round the inside wall. The lorry engine was protected by further sandbags. Slit trenches were dug to guard against air attacks. These were about 4 feet deep, 20 inches wide, at right angles with each arm about 6 feet long.

Wheels were given to formerly static units. Casualty Clearing Stations were made smaller, field ambulances were made lighter and more mobile, and a new innovation, the Field Dressing Station, was introduced. Specialised teams of Field Surgical Units, Field Transfusion Units, mobile Neurosurgical Units and other surgical teams were formed. (Pic 13) These could be flexible and attach themselves to dressing stations or clearing stations as the need arose, saving many lives in the process.

Urgent research took place during the early stages of the war to find durable substitutes for whole blood. Dried plasma and serums were developed, which were easier to handle and transport. These were flown from the United Kingdom to the Base Transfusion Unit in Cairo, and a regular supply was maintained towards the forward areas of engagement.

The journey

The transportation of the 220,000 men who were to serve in North Africa could contain moments of amusement and comradeship, but also reflected the anxiety and overcrowding that many men were experiencing.

Radiographer Charles Quant had been posted to No. 58 General Hospital, an experimental unit that possessed greater mobility than most General Hospitals but enjoyed a higher standard of equipment than a typical CCS. The unit sailed from Clyde aboard HM Troopship SS *Pasteur*, a former French passenger liner containing 5,000 people in total, including nursing sisters. The journey was not without its comical episodes: ‘Our loos were long troughs of corrugated iron where we sat in rows and a constant stream of seawater was pumped along it. Before long, some bright spark had the idea of lighting a loose bunch of toilet paper at the top end of the stream and waiting to see the heads bobbing up frantically along the line!'[3]

Walter Hart and his mate 'Monty' were separated from the rest of No. 6 General Hospital for the journey to North Africa and assigned to a sixty-bed hospital aboard the Cunard liner *Samaria*, which had been refitted as a troop carrier. Enjoying relatively luxurious quarters for someone of non-officer rank, Hart was also buoyed by the fact that one of the stewards was a fellow Jew, and able to provide him kosher food on the Sabbath. Sailing from Liverpool on 3 January 1941, Hart worked on a roster system of eight-hour shifts under a Jewish medical officer. The voyage was largely enjoyable for Hart, although interspersed with tragic episodes:

> Meanwhile our sixty-bedder rapidly filled, mostly with minor cases, but one man became a psychiatric case. He talked gibberish without pause day and night, even when sedated. After a few days, the MO told us that it was very serious. No way could we get him taken off ship and back to a land hospital. The man just lay still and talked. The MO said that the man could die. He would take no solid food and we fed him when we could with a feeding cup. We could not fit a drip feed because he had a habit of suddenly turning over. We watched him carefully, but there were not enough of us to give him constant individual attention. One day I came on duty and found his bed was empty. I was told that he had suddenly jumped out of bed, ran on deck and jumped overboard. He was never seen again.[4]

One man in Hart's care died of sunstroke before even reaching Africa:

> I was on duty one night when a bed patient called me. He had been admitted with apparent mild sunstroke after sunbathing. He complained he could not sleep and I gave him a mild sedative. All was quiet during the night, but next morning when doing the round taking temperatures, pulses and respirations, I found his temperature to be 107°F. This is extremely dangerous as it is about the temperature in an

> adult that the brain begins to agglutinate, like the albumin of an egg when heated. Children can take much higher temperatures, without that occurring. I immediately called the MO, who ordered cold showers. I learned that the patient was Jewish. His temperature came down a little, but during the day it went up again and he lapsed into unconsciousness. We worked on him day and night, but after a few days he died and was buried at sea.[5]

The first Allied victories of the war, under General Wavell in June 1940, sustained heavy casualties in the process. The unusual climate and terrain had an effect on the work required of the RAMC. Along the narrow coastal belt of North Africa the annual rainfall was a mere 4 inches, whilst inland, twenty years could pass without rain. Private F.J. 'Dick' Reynolds wrote of the intense heat and the desert winds that could wreak havoc with the tented hospitals:

> The novelty of being in Africa has now worn off, & I'm dying to get back to England now to see green fields, to feel cool breezes and refreshing rain. Rain out here is nil for months on end and then the weather breaks and it pours down for weeks on end, everywhere becomes a sea of mud. Lucky it's been hot here for the last 3 months 110 degrees to 120 degrees F in the shade. The sun just boils down all day long and there is a terrible glare with it. There is always a wind called the 'Sirocco' blowing, and although it varies in force it is always hot, just like hot air from a furnace. When it blows at gale force (every other day) we get what we call 'shit storms'. It brings so much dust with it that it looks like a smoke screen, anything in its path is either blown down or sky high. I have seen tents go flying and sheets of galvanized iron blown 100 feet into the air.[6]

It was anticipated that the ratio of sick to wounded would be eight to one, which proved to be correct. Initially there was provision for 18,000 hospital beds, but there were not enough trained medics to staff them.

New surgical procedures were implemented, supported by the remarkable innovation of the availability of fresh blood. Long before the introduction of penicillin in 1943–44, packets of sulphonamide powder were given to every soldier, with instructions on how to tip it without delay into any wound. Surgery was developed with debridement – the removal of all accessible foreign bodies and excision of dead tissue – and usually, the packing of the wound with gauze soaked in sterile grease. Interference with the dressing during transit was frowned upon, even when the patient took ten days to reach base.

For compound fractures, early traction (a steady pull towards the ankle) with secure immobilisation was essential. One innovation was the Tobruk plaster. This ingenious method consisted of a Thomas splint incorporated in a plaster of Paris shell; it provided the necessary traction to the fracture, by the pull of the adhesive plaster, and offered at the same time, cover for the wound and immobilisation at the site of fracture. (Pic 14) Due to improvements in the treatment of scalp wounds, a mortality rate of 40 per cent in 1918 was improved to a rate of primary healing of 85 per cent for patients with brain damage. The scope of skilled brain surgery was advanced by the appointment of Professor Sir Hugh Cairns as consultant in neurosurgery early in the war.

Performing medical procedures was far from straightforward in the North African desert. The all-pervasive sand aggravated every skin disease, causing desert sores, and painful and demoralising skin ulcers. These were difficult to prevent without ample soap and hot water, and harder to cure, keeping soldiers off duty for many weeks. The prevalence of tank warfare produced many cases of severe burns. The removal of badly burned or wounded patients from a 'brewed-up' tank was a hazardous exercise, and the vulnerability of such burns to the desert sand could seriously exacerbate any injuries. Raw skin and flesh had to be dressed without delay, and tannic acid was used for this early in the war. This proved ineffective, so a better alternative was quickly found in sheets of gauze impregnated with surgical jelly to which sulphanilamide had been added. Loose gloves made of waterproofed silk were sealed to the wrist, excluding infection and relieving pain during transport.

One of the earlier acts of heroism by an army medic was performed on 12 December 1940 during the Battle of Sidi Barrani. Lieutenant J.M. Muir was the medical officer attached to the 1st Battalion of the Argyll and Sutherland Highlanders. Muir was hit at about 7.00 am by a shell splinter but despite his wounds he insisted on being propped up in a sitting position beside his vehicle and refused an injection of morphine in order that his senses might remain clear. Though badly stricken himself and suffering intense pain from severe wounds in the pelvis and shoulder, he continued for about eight hours to give directions to his stretcher-bearers on how to deal with the wounds as they were brought to the RAP. He remained at his post until the last wounded man had been evacuated and only then, about eight hours after being wounded, did he consent to be placed in the ambulance himself. For this action, Muir was awarded the DSO.[7]

The treatment received by Fusilier W. Close demonstrated the various layers of medical intervention a wounded man could receive, as well as the informal support given by army chaplains and camp followers to the men of the RAMC.[8] Close had joined the army as a regular solider in 1933. He had served with the Royal Northumberland Fusiliers under General Wavell when the Italians were pushed back to Benghazi and during the subsequent British retreat to Tobruk. While manning his machine gun one evening in August 1941, a German mortar shell landed near him. Close was thrown forward but his life was saved by the corrugated iron roof and four layers of sandbags. He was temporarily blinded and blood was running into his eyes and onto his chest. Shrapnel had pierced his face.

Once the German shelling had finished, medical evacuation procedures and treatment were implemented. Firstly, he was guided, along with two other casualties, down a slit trench. They reached a gun pit filled with ammunition and spare parts. The platoon sergeant had applied a wooden splint to one of the men who had broken his arm but he was unable to help Close, who could feel the shrapnel sticking into his face. His comrades convinced him not to touch it and tried to distract him with jokes.

Next, Close was carried 600 yards by four stretcher-bearers to a South African dressing station nicknamed 'The Fig Tree'. An Australian padre was present, and he offered to cable home to Close's family to tell them he was safe. The padre also gave Close ten cigarettes and sent for the fusilier's mate, to whom he wanted to hand over his personal property.

Medical staff strapped his arms to his sides to stop him scratching his face and administered some morphine to dull the throbbing pain. He was taken on a jolting road journey by ambulance to another dressing station twenty minutes away, where he was given a cup of tea with no milk or sugar, and another shot of morphine. The staff asked if he was all right, to which Close replied, with dark humour, 'It's the rich food's my trouble.' Close was then evacuated further back to Tobruk Hospital, where he was operated on immediately. The shrapnel was removed from his face and his eyes were cleaned. When he awoke the next day his head was covered with bandages, and he was still blind. Close firmly believed that he had lost his sight for good.

The following midnight, Close was evacuated from Tobruk by barge to a destroyer, which sailed to Alexandria, where his eyes were operated on. He recuperated at that hospital for a month and was then taken to a dark room and his bandages were removed. There was a revolving wheel that staff used to try to coax Close's eyes back into use. They washed his eyes four times a day and performed different tests on them. Gradually the film of blindness was lifted from his eyes until he could eventually see again. During the rest of his recuperation, his adjutant's mother took him and two other wounded fusiliers out.

A medical report was conducted that classified Close as a 'B', which meant he would be given a job at the base depot and not be sent back out into the desert. This upset Close, as he wanted to be back with his old company, so he persuaded the medical officer to upgrade him to 'A1' He sailed back to Tobruk just in time for its relief on 27 November 1941.

Captain Eric Godwin had been transported by destroyer to Tobruk in November 1941. The coastal town had been under siege since April, and as his ship pulled into the harbour, Godwin saw the wrecks of sunken vessels, the debris of war. Godwin set up a Walking Wounded Collecting Post (WWCP) on the perimeter, 10 miles away from German guns, in an underground concrete bunker. There was a trench and a small covered area in which to place patients. Shells were aimed at a fort near the collection point, but stray ones could descend perilously close to the medical station, the nearest landing just 10 feet away. Godwin was brought both British and German troops to treat:

> The 8th Army, we got them walking in, you see, and treated them. One chap, I remember, had his arm almost severed and I just had to snip through a bit of skin and muscle. It's no good leaving that sort of thing you see. Very rough and ready First Aid. And there was this horrible German, beautifully dressed officer with his arm in a sling, and he strode up and with a horribly sort of steeling and aggressive voice, he said 'I am an officer. I demand a tetanus injection.'[9]

Godwin looked at him and made him take his turn with the others.

As well as the German guns, other dangers surrounded the WWCP. Several hundred yards behind the station, British 25-pounders aimed shells at the enemy, but some would fall short, close to the medical post. When moving up to the perimeter, a white tape had been placed to guide men along a safe passage. One night, Godwin and his line of ambulances lost contact with the tape and ended up in a minefield, becoming aware of this fact when a loud explosion was heard under one of the ambulances. Fortunately, the immediate extent of the damage was a few injured feet and startled nerves, but the next challenge was to remove the men safely from the minefield. Staying put would mean being exposed to German shells once daylight broke. Walking across a minefield in pitch darkness had its obviouse perils, but that was the course of action Godwin ordered, with no tragic consequences.

A mutual admiration developed between Private Walter Hart of No. 6 General Hospital and one badly wounded member of the Guards Armoured Division whom he treated. The man's tank had been hit and he had been burned from head to foot. The burns were covered and the patient encased in plaster of Paris. Despite his agony, the guardsman never whimpered. When Hart removed the plaster and dressings, he was amazed to find that the burns had healed, with the new skin having the pinkish red colour of a newborn baby. When he was well enough to walk, the patient insisted on helping Hart on his ward rounds, thanking him repeatedly. 'I told him that it was I who thanked him. He was fighting to keep me and others safe and free. I was only trying to repair the damage caused to those like him.'[10]

Casualty Clearing Stations were found to be too far to the rear of the front line, lacking mobility. At the beginning of 1941, casualties had to travel an average of 133 miles from an Advanced Dressing Station to the CCS, and a further 236 miles on to the nearest General Hospital, with the journeys being undertaken on poor quality desert tracks. Field Surgical Units were thus established to provide maximum mobility and flexibility. However, these needed effective transport, which did not become available until the time of the Second Battle of El Alamein in October 1942.

RAMC members serving in the desert needed to be more than medical orderlies. (Pic 15) One veteran wrote:

> If a nursing orderly can march 100 miles in 3 days on a tin of bully and a billy of tea and do a full day's work at the end of it, if he can find his way about in strange country, with or

> without a map, without losing his head or himself, can cook himself a good meal with the aid of a mess tin and a handful of wood, then he is likely to be much more of an asset to a field ambulance than the man who knows all the knots on all the bandages on a Thomas splint but who cannot fend for himself, let alone his patient.[11]

John Broom, of No. 7 Light Field Ambulance, emphasised the heavy workload undertaken by RAMC units in the desert, in conditions made atrocious by the presence of flies:

> There has been a terrific amount of work to do, and one finds but a few hours available for sleep. One of these days I will sleep the clock round! My one relaxation has been bathing in the waters of a famous sea. And what a relief to escape for a brief spell from the pestilential flies and the heat. The flies, especially, are very, very trying, and one looks forward each day to the late evening when they take their ill-earned rest.[12]

The persistent prevalence of flies was demonstrated by Private Frank Turton, who, on one occasion, decided to swat 1,000 of the insects, counting each one in turn. Upon completion of this task, he noted that his efforts had made no difference to the infestation of his surroundings.[13] Turton had embarked for the Middle East with No. 132 Field Ambulance on the SS *Orontes*, an Orient Line ship, on 28 May 1941. Due to the threat of German attack, and the fact that the vessel was on the outside of the convoy, many of the men slept on the deck as they were afraid of getting trapped in the accommodation below and potentially drowned. On arrival in Egypt, a sergeant tasked with organising the newcomers had the courage to correct an officer who wanted them to ditch their greatcoats when they went into the desert. The officer had wrongly assumed that it would be persistently hot, seemingly unaware of the exceptional night-time conditions the men would experience. The men of No. 132 Field Ambulance had good reason to be grateful to this sergeant during the long cold nights that lay ahead.

Medical staff frequently succumbed to infection and disease in the fly-infested country of Egypt. Having arrived in Alexandria, Staff

Sergeant Charles Quant swiftly contracted dysentery as a result of flies swarming all over his food. He was placed in a hospital ward with similar cases and subjected to regular doses of castor oil, 'presumably so that it should go in at one end and take everything out of the other, including the infection'.[14] After a fortnight, he was sent to a convalescent depot at Nathanya in Palestine, before being allowed to spend a few days in Jerusalem prior to returning to his unit.

The contrast between the intense heat of the day and the freezing nights took its toll. John Broom complained, 'During the past three months at different times I've been boiled, fried, roasted & toasted, & very nearly burnt. And still I'm here waiting for more! Great life this.' The hard-won physical fitness that men had attained in Britain during mile after gruelling mile of route marches, cross-country runs and the more pleasurable football and cricket matches would stand them in good stead in desert conditions. Nevertheless, it was difficult to supplement this robustness with further physical exercise:

> You will be pleased to know that I'm in the pink of condition though I wouldn't presume that even my unquestioned purity has vouchsafed me for the strength of ten. But I do feel irked sometimes when an urge to run is upon me & I gaze hopelessly upon interminable stretches of sand burning with the sun's fierce heat. Nevertheless, my figure retains its lean, supple contours, mainly on account of the unsubstantial nature of the food one eats. Not that one would feel like eating much.
>
> How I would love to see a drop of rain. I smile to remember those few days at various times that were rain free – and we proudly spoke of a drought. And now I've had a taste of what the Seven Years' Drought must have been like.[15]

By the time of the second Libyan campaign in 1941, surgeons were allowed to work right up with the field ambulances, even though there was no proper operating theatre. (Pic 16) In a 'lean-to' tent attached to a truck, a good team could still do first-class work. One hitch with this arrangement was that very little post-operative care of the patients was possible. For a casualty to lie on a stretcher soon after an operation, often with a battle going on around the tented wards, was a traumatic experience. One surgical team was captured and recaptured four times due to the ebb and flow of battle, whilst another dressing station was visited by Rommel, who found that the German patients were being well cared for and left orders that the work was not to be disrupted.[16] The need for ever greater mobility led to a trial of mobile caravans, but this did not work well and lacked the flexibility essential for forward surgery.

A clear vindication of this 'lean-to' system occurred in November 1941. A German battery had for a while advanced into a position between the tents of a surgical unit. The Germans had with them a beautifully fitted mobile theatre – 'too beautiful to risk its loss by opening it'. So when the German commander suffered a shell wound in his lung, it was in the British 'lean-to' that he had his operation. The German onlookers were astounded at the facilities, in such an austere setting, for major surgery and blood transfusion.[17]

For the Second Battle of El Alamein – an unusually static battle lasting twelve days – many of the CCSs were grouped 30 miles behind the dressing stations. Casualties amounted to about 7,000 wounded, less than had been expected. The complex arrangements proved to be entirely satisfactory. Later, for the breakout, codenamed Operation Supercharge, the mobile medical units moved forward in a strung-out line. The need to hold patients after major operations was now fully recognised, and Field Surgical Units carried ten conventional beds and ten folding canvas ones.

Once Charles Quant had recovered from a bout of dysentery, he received convoys of wounded landed by destroyers coming out of the besieged Tobruk in darkness, with very nasty stories of the appalling conditions in the town and the dock. Soon after Christmas 1942, the hospital moved westwards to Mersa Matruh and pitched their marquees, with the X-ray facilities housed in a dugout 'roofed with corrugated steel and sandbags. Very hot and airless. Electricity from generators and all water by tankers from Alex.'[18] Here, Quant and Captain Theodore Stephanides, the radiologist, used the X-ray machine to provide insights to the hospital's surgeons, which produced some surprising results:

> Casualties were from battles much nearer so we developed our techniques for depth localisation finding where bullets or shrapnel had got to after entry, often some distance away.

> At first the surgeons didn't believe us when we told them for instance that a bullet in the neck had gone as far as the abdomen, but when they began to trust our information and deductions, they got some sensationally accurate results.[19]

Walter Hart, despite his having gained the Nursing Orderly Class III qualification, was detailed to join his unit's sanitary squad. The squad's role was to tour round No. 6 General Hospital and its environs, making sure that drainage pits worked and looking for pools of stagnant water, where mosquitoes could breed. These would be treated by pouring paraffin onto the surface. Malaria could be carried by the female anopheles mosquito, which laid eggs that hatched in eight days. Therefore, stagnant water was treated every seven days to kill the eggs.

From this role, Hart was moved on to serve in the dysentery ward, of which he wryly recalled, 'I probably became the world's expert on giving enemas and I often assisted the medical officer giving sigmoidoscopies. I forget the number of bowels I have looked into.' One day, a terrific sandstorm raged around the hospital tents for several hours, bringing down electric cables, plunging the patients and medics into darkness, as the sand turned day into night. The marquee ward began to collapse, so Hart removed the patients from that part and sought help. However, it was impossible for him to know in which direction he was moving, so he took the wise decision to sit out the storm.

On another occasion, during a blazing hot afternoon, he was on duty when he heard a shout from the next ward and on looking out he could see that it was on fire at one end. A canvas marquee in the arid climate of North Africa could go up in a matter of seconds. Fortunately, the wind was blowing the fire away from the rest of the ward, but there was no way that the bed patients could have been evacuated in the few minutes before it could go up in flames. Hart ran out and grabbed the hose attached to a 30-gallon fire extinguisher, called to one of the walking patients, then climbed up and sat on the ridge pole. He instructed the patient to tip up the extinguisher, which was on wheels, and then attacked the fire from above and managed to put it out. Later, there was a board of inquiry, which Hart was summoned to attend. At the end of the inquiry, the officers in charge highly commended him for his swift and decisive action.

After one push by the Eighth Army, thousands of Libyans, who had been forced to fight for the Italians and Germans, were captured, along with about a million condoms, later redistributed to British troops. The most seriously ill and badly wounded Libyans were sent to No. 6 General Hospital, now situated at Quassassin. Walter Hart claimed that most of the QAIMNS (Queen Alexandra's Imperial Military Nursing Service) refused to nurse them and so he was left with the job of dressing and redressing all the wounds in four twenty-four-bedded wards. Due to the strain of overwork, Hart developed abscesses on the back of his neck and his forehead, eventually collapsing in a ward when on duty. He lost his sight for several days before it returned and he could continue his work.

Hart regularly saw men pass from life into death. One man died in his arms. The patient had been suffering from tuberculosis, and the medical officer had performed an artificial pneumothorax on him before asking Hart to massage the man's legs. A few days later, Hart heard another patient call him to find the TB patient trying to get out of bed. Attending to him quickly, Hart tried to return him to his bed but the man had become weak with the effort and died on the spot.

For many men relatively fortunate enough to survive to live another day, a long period of mental and physical recovery and recuperation would be needed. For this purpose, an Occupational Therapy Centre was established at No. 6 British General Hospital. Walter Hart had been sent to No. 2 BGH for a training course on occupational therapy and on his return was allocated a piece of land on which to build the new centre. Hart had it fenced off with a gateway entrance and, with support from a Colonel Roach, steps were built to provide access the separate stores, sleeping quarters and a treatment room.

The local Egyptian workmen had also laid out plots for plants to be grown, using Nile mud, and had built a small pond outside the store tent. Colonel Roach arranged for a brick chalet to be built and, when he had time to spare, would come along, take off his hat and coat and start gardening. Roach also arranged for Hart to be driven regularly to the ordnance depot at Tel El Kebir, where he could scrounge materials for the occupational therapy centre.

The military medical authorities had intended the centre to cater for psychiatric and shell-shocked patients, but Hart's vision was for patients with physical injuries to also access the facility. Before the war he had met members of the International Brigade who had returned wounded from Spain, and men who had been injured during the First World War. He had come to realise that they were crippled due to the fact that their muscles had atrophied because of lack of the right exercise during recuperation from their wounds. It took much persuasion on Hart's part, but gradually the unit's medical officers were persuaded to support this innovation, and by July 1942, the centre was thriving.

Hart was promoted to acting unpaid lance corporal by Roach, and the centre was visited by the head of the British Red Cross, who was full of praise of the treatment on offer. He reported this to senior RAMC officers, and Hart was sent to the headquarters of the British Red Cross at No. 8 Malika Farida in Cairo on Roach's behalf to meet with General Sir Henry Maitland Wilson, Commander-in-Chief of Central Mediterranean Forces, and Major General William Hartgill, Director of Medical Services, Middle East. The two eminent men had been expecting Colonel Roach, and entered a large room where about a dozen officers and Hart were gathered:

> They stood for a moment looking around and then came straight over to me. For a moment I was petrified but managed to give them a smart salute. They asked what I was doing there and, thinking it was best to tell the truth, I told them that my Colonel had said that he knew little about occupational therapy, that I was supposed to be the expert and that I should represent him. They looked at each other and burst out laughing. Then General Wilson said, 'It's a good thing that we have at least one C.O. out here that can use his common sense.'

They questioned Hart for about ten minutes, and then suggested he carry on with the good work.

Amongst the good work done by the patients in the occupational therapy centre was the manufacture, at the request of Padre Thomas, the unit's chaplain, of an altar for a Nissen hut, which was to be used as a church. Thomas had requested that the altar should serve both Roman Catholics and Protestants, but the Jewish Hart requested that the hut also be used as a synagogue, to which the padre readily agreed. Eventually, imitation leaded light windows were manufactured as well as a turntable-style altar with a Roman Catholic appearance on one side and Church of England on the other. A curtain was fixed across the hut to hide the altar during synagogue services.

Other valuable work was suggested by a surgeon, Major Semple, who approached Hart to have the patients make some surgical instruments from Perspex, as it would assist him if he could see through them during an operation. These were duly manufactured. Then an anaesthetist came and asked if a prototype anaesthetising gadget could be made. His idea was that with it, he could keep several soldiers anaesthetised at one time and so several surgeons could work to save life in the battlefield and not have to have an anaesthetist for each one. The gadget was to be a small canister that would be filled with ether. It would have an inlet and an outlet valve. The outlet would have a tube to pass into the patient's trachea. Air coming into the canister, when the patient breathed in, would pick up ether in passage and go out into the patient. This was also made, although Hart never got to know its efficacy on the battlefield.

Feeding the tens of thousands of troops in the Middle East was an enormous undertaking, and each RAMC unit had its dedicated catering team. David Jones of No. 168 Field Ambulance had volunteered to be trained as a cook in early 1940 and received a promotion to the rank of lance corporal. Having undertaken a short training course, 'All too soon I was back at Nathanya trying out my cooking skills and enjoying life in general. I had to get up at 4am and get the breakfast on the go for about a hundred men.'[20] In October 1940, the unit moved from near Jerusalem up to Nabulus, an Arab village in the mountains. This was dangerous territory, with Arab terrorists frequently blowing up railway lines. The cookhouse lorry had to go to Sarafand for rations on a daily basis and it was not allowed to move without an armed guard. The men slept in houses on the edge of the village and the cookhouse always had an armed guard around it.

The majority of the population was not averse to the presence of British troops, and some mutually congenial arrangements were entered into: 'In the course of time I learnt that every cookhouse was a magnet for Arabs, especially ones who had donkeys. They would come and plead for any scraps of food. If you let them have the contents of the waste bin then it was easy for me to get my laundry washed and back the same day.'[21]

Whilst food was strictly rationed and accounted for when not in a battle zone, once the unit was in action near Mersa Matruh, men could supply themselves with as much tinned food as they could carry, the cookhouse becoming a 'larder on wheels'.

As well as the feeding of men in the RAMC, the prosaic task of office administration consumed much of the routine of many members. John Broom worked in the office section of No. 7 Light Field Ambulance and experienced a period of torpor in the months spent acclimatising to desert conditions before the major push from 23 October 1942 onwards. He wrote:

> Nothing much happens to me these days. The flies are just about as hostile & as numerous as ever, we still rise in the mornings at unearthly hours, anticipating the sun by a good hour or so, & still feel incredibly hot during the day & quite cold at night.
>
> The day is spent in pushing the old pen along, eating fly-infested unappetising meals, bemoaning nearly everything but with such fine humour as to raise a laugh or a smile out of nearly every utterance. The day's work is not without interest & as you may well imagine there are many delightful sidelights to be seen & enjoyed of the methods used in the prosecution of the war. And at such times as these, men are to be observed as revealing their true natures naked to the appreciative eye of the student of homo sapiens. Yes there are obvious compensations in these circumstances.

Despite the grind of routine that many RAMC roles involved, they were undertaken with diligence and commitment:

> Lest you make the wrong conclusion, let me say, in all fairness to most of the fellows out here, that the manner in which they fulfil their duties & suffer unresentfully many inconveniences evokes my utmost admiration. There's no need for me to elaborate on a description of the Western Desert. You will have read time & time again of the gruelling conditions under which our men have toiled & sweated, & any man who can retain the mastery of his soul during his months in the desert, & leave it with a firm belief in the goodness of God & his honour clean is a man to whom Kipling might have said 'Yours is the earth, & everything that's in it'.[22]

In a campaign involving the movement of vehicles across thousands of miles of inhospitable terrain, the work of the ambulance drivers and mechanics was vital in keeping medical units mobile. Private Ralph Dawson, a housebuilder from Sheffield serving with No. 10 (260) Motor Ambulance Convoy, wrote to his wife:

> Yesterday I went in a long run with some Yankys to an American hospital. The heat was so bad that it stopped all the ambulances. The petrol was evaporating with the heat before it got to the engine. When we asked what the temperature had been that day it was 150 deg in the shade. So you can guess what it was like.[23]

One officer in a medical unit in Libya, interviewed in December 1941, described the nature and pattern of his duties. The work came in spasms, and he had few leisure opportunities as much time was spent replenishing supplies. In addition, the frequent moves necessitated in a mobile war caused much extra work, with one month bringing twelve different changes of location. The officer had performed 134 operations, mostly major ones. He reflected on the psychological strain of the medical role in warfare in an alien environment:

> Being mixed up in a campaign all on our own in this desolate place narrows the mental horizon. … Battlefields are sad and desolate places not because of corpses – corpses are rare, at all events by the time we arrive on the scene, and rare anyway, for one sees but few graves though these are sad enough. Just a low, long mound with rude wooden crosses and the name and number of the soldier written upon it; sometimes not that, perhaps just 'Unknown German' or 'Unknown Italian'.[24]

Another duty that came the way of the RAMC in North Africa was the medical care of captured enemy troops. Captain Eric Godwin, serving with No. 173 Field Ambulance, was sent as a medical officer to a prisoner of war camp that contained about 10,000 Libyan nationals who had been serving in the Italian Army. They had been fed on little except dried bread and nearly all of them had developed scurvy. Godwin reckoned himself one of the few men in the world who had seen so many cases of the disease at once, bringing with it swollen gums, bleeding and huge bruises. The epidemic was addressed with the simple application of 'two or three lorry loads of miserable little Egyptian oranges. Perfect cure, Vitamin C, quite dramatic actually.'[25] Men who needed further treatment would come to Godwin's medical inspection room, 'poor chaps … with terrible gumboils, sceptic teeth dripping with puss and awful pain'. The former Ruislip GP became an impromptu dentist, making the men sit on a wooden chair and hold on tight as he extracted their loose teeth with a pair of pliers.

Godwin was also tasked with filling in a voluminous ledger, listing every single pill and medicine that was issued to prisoners of war. It was expected that at the conclusion of the war, the winning side would bill the losers for the cost of the treatment.

Following the lifting of the Siege of Tobruk, Godwin contracted diphtheria. His symptoms started as desert sores, which afflicted many men as their shoes rubbed against their ankles. These 'pussy sores' never healed and it was later discovered they were diphtheritic. Godwin awoke on Christmas morning 1941 in the Beach Hospital in Tobruk, where he was working:

> looked in my mirror and I saw the dreaded grey membrane of diphtheria. Oh yes, and I was admitted and given serum, which saved my life. … I was with two other blokes, two Gunner officers, the same, and we were completely neglected. All the hospital doctors stayed in the basement and we could hear the shrapnel rattling on the roof and they never came near us. But one of the other chaps was the son of The Director General of The Medical Services for the Middle East, and he got word to his Father, who got rid of the CO of the hospital – sent him back to England.

El Alamein

When Rommel's forces counterattacked in early 1942, the desert front surged back eastwards. Charles Quant, still a radiographer with the mobile No. 58 British General Hospital, responded to the order to pack up fast as a hundred trucks arrived to move the hospital eastwards:

> We ripped down the canvases packed all the incredible kit we had for two hundred beds and the patients, but the X-ray was judged too heavy, like the generators, so we just stayed in the open pit beside the underground department, and waited, and waited. The Luftwaffe sharpened our anxiety by ground strafing everything in sight but we moved to and fro in our pit depending on the direction it came from.[26]

After a period of unease, some big trucks arrived and the X-ray equipment was loaded in double-quick time and joined the lines of vehicles of all descriptions heading east, as RAF planes engaged in dogfights with the Luftwaffe overhead.

Eventually the unit established itself in a hutted hospital at Moascar Garrison, east of El Alamein. The intense pressure of X-raying hundreds of casualties brought in during the pivotal battle caused Quant to suffer from radiation poisoning to the blood, and he was granted recovery leave, during which he took the opportunity to visit Luxor and the Valley of the Kings.

The anticipation before the major offensive of El Alamein was palpable in the heart and mind of John Broom. A week before the commencement of the fighting, the No. 7 Light Field Ambulance orderly and clerk wrote to his mother emphasising the importance of continuing communication by letters from home, which allowed him to 'soak myself in the atmosphere of a superior society in which we once lived, for one is fortified by the knowledge that what was once can be again'. He continued to articulate the significance of the twin pillars of family ties and Christian faith that sustained many men during those troubled days:

> The present situation demands the practice of 'holding fast' and 'occupying' by the 'simple faith that is more than Norman blood outworking experimentally in all places and aspects of our living, faith in one's tradition and destiny'. Here in the desert, as elsewhere, the 'family' and all that it stands for exerts a powerful influence upon one's attitude of

> mind; therefore I feel I owe a debt which can never be paid to yourself, Dad and those sisters who will always share a large part of my affections. May the good God reward you.

The night of the initial attack found Broom in further reflective mood: 'I am claiming His Protection these days. As I write this on the night of Oct 23rd events are occurring which will find a place in your newspaper. I know I have your prayers. God's Will be done.'

Meanwhile in the maelstrom of the battlefield, conscientious objector Private James Driscoll responded to an appeal for stretcher-bearers to go onto the battlefield to retrieve casualties under heavy shellfire. During one intense moment, a box barrage opened up as he and a colleague lay exposed in the field. 'I remember lying tense whilst the perspiration ran from under my steel helmet to drop off my nose on to the sand, and all the while contemplating that the next moment could be my last.'[27]

Private Frank Turton served in the reception centre of the Advanced Dressing Station of 132 Field Ambulance, attached to the 44th Division. The mobility required of field ambulances meant that tarpaulin covers measuring 40 by 40 feet were made to extend from the lorries to form a covered area for the medical work to take place. Unfortunately, the unit received far fewer casualties than they expected from the Second Battle of El Alamein, as the number of men killed in action was exceptionally high. Tragically, this did mean that the training undertaken in Kent on how to prepare a body for burial was put to good use, with Turton and his comrades sewing up the shrouds of the deceased. Greek soldiers were assigned to bury the fallen men in the desert – no straightforward task with hard rock frequently only a few inches below the surface of the sand.

Captain Charles Warner was awarded the MC for his efforts during the Battle of El Alamein and the subsequent advance across North Africa. (Pic 17) His citation read:

> For conspicuous gallantry and devotion to duty during the period of 23rd October 1942 to 17th February 1943.
>
> During the whole period of the Battle of Alamein, this officer was in command of the forward Advanced Dressing Station of the 15th Light Field Ambulance, and moved as far forward as tactical Brigade Headquarters, immediately in the area of the Regimental Aid Posts.

> All casualties come from Brigade Units and many others passed through his hands. On the 1st November 1942 he handled 123 casualties; altogether 600 before the breakthrough.
>
> During this period, his complete disdain of enemy bombing and shelling was a magnificent example to others. His skill in giving transfusions and tending wounds saved many lives. His conduct, in most difficult circumstances and his utter disregard of self, gave great courage, inspiration and cheer to all around him.[28]

The men doing the fighting had been magnificently served by their comrades in the RAMC in this most pivotal of battles.

As the Eighth Army advanced across the desert, No. 58 General Hospital followed, with the heavy equipment being transported by ship into Tobruk. This proved hazardous, as a German U-boat torpedoed the vessel, causing Charles Quant's X-ray machine to sustain irreparable damage. As the men of No. 58 General Hospital sought to unload the rest of the equipment onto the shore, they were caught in a German air raid. As the bombs fell, Quant was thrown along the dock. 'When I picked myself up I couldn't stand on my right foot and I thought "here we go again", just like the blitz in Millbank!' His foot was X-rayed by a mobile set belonging to a CCS, which revealed torn ligaments. Initially, Quant was ordered to return to Alexandria for treatment and recuperation. Having already missed action due to a previous mishap: 'I protested that I hadn't come all that way just to pull out of the war in the desert when it had got so interesting. [The doctor] grinned and put me into a walking plaster with a stirrup under the foot and that kept me going with hardly any hindrance.'

Quant's wound was healed within a fortnight.

In the breakout following the battle, No. 58 General Hospital advanced on to Benghazi, where it was allocated a site in the ground of a convent hospital untouched by the war. Fortuitously, Charles Quant was able to locate a pre-war X-ray set to replace one that had been lost at sea:

> I found that it had been operated by a nun and that the nursing nuns from an Italian benevolent organisation were still living just outside the town so I got a truck and went

> to see them. The Mother Superior was a sweet woman who after a few minutes understood what we wanted and sent for the nun in question. She spoke no English and at that stage I spoke no Italian, but we eventually established that we both could manage in Latin. It must have been the only X-ray set in the world to have instructions in Latin, as I don't suppose the Romans had X-rays.

Casualties poured in, and then out by ship, with the Royal Navy running a hospital ship between Alexandria and Benghazi. As it could not get into the harbour, which was littered with wrecks, stretchers had to be loaded onto landing craft and transported to the vessel. During the stay in Benghazi in early 1943, an American Air Force doctor gave one of the unit's surgeons, Major James Ross, a small supply of a new drug. Two men with almost identical injuries were treated, one with a sulpha drug, which failed to stop a serious infection, and one with the new drug, penicillin. The latter patient immediately recovered.

In the course of the advance across the desert, normal structures and routines of life evaporated, and few recreational opportunities were available. During a pause in action before the liberation of Tunis in May 1943, John Broom noted:

> To your question asking whether time passes as quickly with me as with you I would answer that the weeks simply fly by with me, with barely anything to mark their passing. This is possibly due to the fact that we lead such artificial lives, removed as we are out here from society (especially female) and culture. 'Society, friendship & love, how soon would I taste thee again', as Cowper wrote. Friendship, true, we have had, and this has been our sanity. The others are the 'substance of things hoped for'.

During the months between victory in North Africa and a change in location to Sicily in the autumn of 1943, Broom wrote of his sojourn in Tunisia:

> I am still chained at the Pay Desk and have not left the camp since last Sunday week. Apart from the service last Sunday

> evening which I was unable to attend because I was on duty, there has been nothing to entice me away from this sand-ridden hole. For all the benefit we have derived since the conclusion of the North African Campaign, we might as well be in the heart of the fighting. And after all, there were times near the end of that campaign when opportunities occurred of glimpsing a slice or two of civilization. To dispose of boredom I have lately started to learn Italian. Two other clerks are keeping me company, and our tutor is the R.C. Padre for the Division, an Irishman.

Corporal Paul Watts, serving with No. 6 Light Field Ambulance, attached to the 21st Tank Brigade, assisted in the supervision of Italian prisoners of war in Tunisia. (Pic 18) On 9 September 1943, he wrote to his wife of their joy at the news of the Allied invasion of mainland Italy at Salerno:

> Isn't the news wonderful about Italy? We were all so very excited last night when the news came through, even the Italian prisoners were excited, they nearly swamped me. They kept dancing round and all wanting to shake hands with me at once. My old friend, who I told you about the other day, made me feel quite bad. He came up to me and shook my hand and then held on to it without saying a word. His eyes were swimming and I felt myself beginning to feel the same way. Then he said 'Not prisoner, comrade.'
>
> It seems very strange that the Italians should be so pleased about the news, doesn't it? I think they are so war-weary that they are glad to think their people at home will be free from our bombs. Also they've found out, in this camp at least, that the Englishman isn't so bad after all.
>
> Strangely enough, yesterday was one of their feast days. The feast of the Virgin Mary I think, and we had arranged to give them a 'bit of a do'. The news came through just as they were sitting down to a meal of spaghetti and red wine. So they had a double celebration.[29]

It was unusual for Axis forces to deliberately target medical personnel during the North African campaign. Captain Norman Jevons, attached to the headquarters of the 76th Division, was riding pillion on a motorbike driven by a corporal along a straight desert road when he noticed a German plane flying very low alongside them, with a machine gun trained on their bike. Providentially, the gunner having foregone his opportunity to open fire, Jevons tapped his driver on the shoulder and pointed to the plane, at which action the driver swerved the bike into a roadside ditch, whereupon the plane flew off. Jevons reflected that the gunner had seen the Red Cross armband he was wearing, and this had saved his life. Jevons kept the brassard as a memento throughout the rest of his life.[30] (Pics 19 & 20)

Once the Mediterranean front had shifted to the Italian peninsula towards the end of 1943, medical personnel were still needed to remain in Egypt to support the troops stationed there due to the country's strategic importance. Private F.J. 'Dick' Reynolds of No. 104 General Hospital wrote in September 1943 of the numbers of wounded being brought across the Mediterranean from Sicily:

> After we get convoys of anything up to 700 patients twice or even three times per week, and this entails more work. In time, one just gets worked to a standstill, as I did. Its suicide trying to keep on when you don't feel up to it although one feels duty bound to do all they can for as long as they can for their lads that come in wounded. They certainly have done a good job of work … I haven't seen a lot of the battles in progress, but I have seen a lot of the aftermath of battles. It all makes one realise how futile war is, poor kids maimed for life, some will never see again, some will never walk other have made the supreme sacrifice, and a wooden cross marks their last resting place.[31]

As the war drew to a close, No. 132 Field Ambulance remained stationed in Egypt, and increasing time was found for leisure pursuits. One on occasion, Private Frank Turton and a friend of his wished to travel to another base to enjoy a game of table tennis. As they were below officer rank, they recruited Captain Raymond Stephenson of the Army Dental Corps to assist them in signing out an army jeep. This was far from straightforward as, during the journey, Stephenson, as an officer, could not be seen to be fraternising on a social visit with two other ranks and had to repeatedly put on then remove a sergeant's coat depending on the situation. A further complication was that the RASC driver who accompanied the party was welcomed by Italian PoW cooks at the base they were visiting and enjoyed their hospitality to such an extent that he was unfit to drive the car back to the medical unit the following day. Captain Stephenson therefore had to drive the jeep to the gates of the base before handing over to the driver, who successfully managed to navigate the couple of hundred yards back to camp without further mishap.

West and East Africa

Whilst the North African desert was the part of the continent that saw the most RAMC personnel in action, some undertook a tour of duty in West Africa for a portion of their war service, providing care for troops stationed around Sierra Leone, for members of native battalions and for some naval personnel.

Captain Geoffrey Haine was posted to the No. 34 General Hospital, landing in Freetown in late October 1941. The hospital consisted of a number of huts situated on a hill overlooking the capital's harbour and boasted a complement of nursing sisters as well as specialists in surgery, anaesthetics, medicine and pathology. Haine was appointed as a General Duty Officer to take the place of someone who had been sent home sick. His first night was eventful, as he woke the next morning to find his wallet and shoes had been stolen.

As an officer, Haine was assigned a 'boy' from the local Mendi tribe to act as his personal servant. His duties included keeping Haine's room clean, washing and ironing his clothes, warming water for his bath and checking the quality of his mosquito net. An interpreter had to be used when Haine spoke with the native troops. He found the role immensely challenging, not least because of the range of chronic illnesses amongst the African troops. Malaria was common, alongside both kinds of dysentery. Haine came across a disease called yaws, a bacterial complaint causing chronic infection that affected the skin, bone and cartilage. This had not been mentioned on Haine's tropical medicine training course. Orthopaedic surgeons originally treated it as a bone infection until it was discovered it could be dealt with medically. Another problem, the Guinea worm, used to burrow under the skin and if the natives could catch it while its tail was still showing, they would grip it with a split matchstick and give the matchstick a twist each day until the whole worm, including the head, was on the surface. Haine reflected, 'We were never stumped for a diagnosis with the Africans!'[32]

For the British troops in West Africa, malaria and dysentery were the main concerns. Men could suffer complications of cerebral malaria and blackwater fever, which carried a high mortality rate, a feature exacerbated by the inconsistency of naval personnel in using mosquito nets. 'One very severe case of cerebral malaria had so much brain irritation that he was extremely violent and had to be brought ashore in a straitjacket and to get his illness under control we had to use intravenous Quinine and heavy sedation.'

It took Haine three weeks to become acclimatised to the West African conditions:

> The electrical storms were very spectacular and noisy. I remember one quite well, when lightning struck the tennis court just behind my hut – I heard the sizzle and saw the steam rising up. Rainfall was very high, but although we were not far north of the equator, temperatures were not excessively high. The main problem was the high humidity, and heat exhaustion occurred. When we went, we were issued with pith helmets and spine pads, but later it was found that bush hats were perfectly adequate and much more comfortable.[33]

After a few months with the No. 34 General Hospital, Haine was sent upcountry to Daru, 200 miles from Freetown, to serve as a temporary duty medical officer with the 2nd (West African) Infantry Brigade. To support his work, he was assigned three native orderlies and a tin box containing various tablets. The battalion he was with then moved camp a further 80 miles inland along a long dusty track, although as the medical officer, Haine undertook most of the journey in an ambulance. Part of the force's role was to patrol from the new base camp at Twiyo up to the border with French Guinea, in order to deter the Vichy French from attacking Freetown from the rear.

In these inhospitable conditions, Haine's work had to focus on prevention as much as cure, and he oversaw the construction of a serviceable water supply by damming up the river and constructing a sand filter, and the digging of adequate latrines in order to prevent the spread of malaria. The patrols were a sight to behold: 'We had to go single file and at the rear of the column were about three hundred native carriers toting our equipment on their heads. At night a clearing would be made in the bush where we slept, and then before we moved off in the morning.'[34]

No amount of university and army medical training could prepare Haine for some of the beliefs and practices of his native charges. One day, he found one of them unconscious; then another, and another. None of them displayed any physical symptoms but it transpired they had slept on an old burial ground and their subconscious belief was that the spirits had invaded them.

Another day, back at the camp, Haine's orderlies came running to came running to relay the news that one of the native soldiers was filled with the water devil, and had 'gone for bush':

> We managed to catch up with him as he tried to throw himself into the water – but even with one man on each arm, one on each leg and one holding his head, he still struggled. We got him back to the sick bay and there I tried to sedate him with injections of morphine – the only drug I had remotely likely to help. I ended up by giving him twice the normal dose and we had to put him in the guard room as he was still violent.

The man was discharged from the army as being 'unlikely to become an efficient soldier'. 'I never knew whether the poor chap was an acutely hallucinated schizophrenic or whether it was another example of inbred tribal beliefs.' Haine returned to England on 8 September 1943 and would see further action in Northern Europe later in the war.

Across the other side, the sub-Saharan Africa, in August 1941, Captain Kenneth Hulbert alighted on the platform at Wadi Halfa in the Sudan and spied the beautiful white Khartoum Express. Hulbert climbed on board and found his berth, a spotlessly clean single cabin with a washbasin and electric fan. This train took him to Khartoum station, from where he proceeded to No. 18 General Hospital, by the banks of the Upper Nile. It was a thick, walled building with stone floors, verandas and electric fans that were whirring constantly. The defences in Khartoum were set out in Union Flag formation as it enabled a few machine guns, strategically placed, to control the town. At the centre of the 'Jack' was the famous statue of General Gordon on his camel and behind it was the palace and the cathedral.

Hulbert quickly set to work administering inoculations against yellow fever, his routine beginning at 7.00 am and taking an afternoon siesta when hot air was shut out of a room and all staff lay under a fan. After taking tea, he worked until 8.00 pm, and then took dinner. On 14 August he was dispatched to Wad Medani, the capital of the Gezira cotton growing region about 100 miles south-east of Khartoum. There was a prisoner of war camp containing several thousand Eritreans and Abyssinians who had been forced to serve in the Italian Army. The previous May, the British Army, with a large contingent of Indian troops, had defeated the Italian forces, and with it Mussolini's East African empire.

The prisoners were locked up in large barbed wire enclosures known as 'cages', containing tents, huts, latrines and cookhouses. Many of them were suffering from granuloma of the gums, which was eventually found to be scurvy. They were encouraged to eat fresh limes to combat this, which they refused to do. A medical orderly had to stand over them until they ate them. Many of the PoWs had contracted diarrhoea due to pellagra, for which the treatment was vitamin B in the form of locally grown groundnuts. However, arranging meals for a camp of prisoners containing Christians and Moslems proved tricky. The Abyssinians were Coptic Christians and wore leather armlets containing quotes from the Bible on their arms or foreheads. Some had large leather-bound Bibles, which they would read in groups. Along with these devotional practices came a refusal to eat anything that had been touched by Moslem hands, including those of Indians serving in the British Army. Thus, in order to feed them, camp guards would drive a flock of sheep into the cages for the prisoners to slaughter themselves, with the animals' heads facing Jerusalem. To the meat they would add an oatcake cooked on a hot iron plate.

After this spell at the PoW camp, Hulbert was posted to work on an ambulance train, a series of converted Sudan railway coaches, coloured fawn, with a Red Cross emblem on the side and the usual sun blinds on the outside. There were three or four converted second class coaches with a double row of bunks, upper and lower, lengthwise along the coach. The toilet was a hole in the floor, as in most trains. There was a kitchen coach with sleeping quarters for the Sudanese cook and his assistant. Other staff on the train included a sergeant, a lance corporal, two privates and a Sudanese driver. Hulbert was quartered in a first class coach with individual sleeping compartments. At the end was a surgery compartment, and right at the back was a wagon with stores and equipment. Sterilisation of instruments was achieved by boiling up water on an oil-filled stove as there was no electricity on the train.

For the next four months, the ambulance train shuttled back and forth across Sudan, passing deserts, camels, gazelles and crocodiles. It picked up patients to transport them to the nearest hospital, treating the sickest on the train. If a patient died, he had to be temporarily stored in a makeshift mortuary before being unloaded at the nearest station to a hospital, as there was no refrigeration on board: 'not the most dignified or respectful task, but necessary given the sanitation risks.'[35]

Delicate operations had to be carried out as the carriages rattled along, and the train received a consignment of forty Sudanese patients with VD. These were sent to a military prison rather than a hospital as it was classed as a self-inflicted injury and therefore an offence against military law. The treatment for gonorrhoea was 'M&B', pills produced by the May and Baker company. Small children would run alongside the train holding their hands, shouting 'M and B' because they could sell the tablets for 2/6 each in the souk.

Having served on No. 7 Ambulance Train in France from 1939–40, Captain Paul Adler embarked for service in East Africa in July 1942 and was posted to the King's African Rifles. (Pic 21) Adler recorded his impressions of treating Askari natives, and the methods both parties used to overcome the language difficulties they encountered.

> I have found that the Askaris here call me 'A Kwepeteke Keva Bas' which means literally 'It hurts much.' When they come sick I say 'Ciani?' What is it? They say 'A Kwepteke Bas,' pointing to some part of the body, usually the foot. So I say 'Eeai – A Kwepeteke Pangono Pangono.' 'It hurts by a little by a little.' So they shake their heads and grunt 'een enn' 'Kura Bas, Kura Bas' and then usually laugh thinking it a terrific joke.
>
> They are an extraordinary people but when one gets to know them, they are most likeable.[36]

Adler found that working as a regimental medical officer in the East African tropics afforded him plenty of opportunity to develop his medical knowledge and expertise.

> A most extraordinary fly has just flown in and out of the tent – I wish I knew what half these insects were …
>
> I am beginning to study mosquitoes and can tell the difference between Anophelinae (Malaria carriers) and Culicines. The lenses bought with Margaret on leave are very useful.
>
> Gradually as I get to know the language, I find there is less work and thus I have more time for refinements like testing urine, running my own sick bay and examining insects, so there is no end to the interesting things one can do out here – I only wish I had a microscope here and could examine my own slides – it is really all great fun – and is an experience well worth having if only a war wasn't at the basis of it all.[37]

Adler contemplated thc contrast between the climate he was serving in and his previous aspiration to move to live above the Arctic Circle with his beloved wife Margaret:

> I wonder if I will ever settle in the Arctic as Margaret and I planned to do – after getting used to the heat here. – I rather doubt it.
>
> Here an explorer could never be bored and the hardships he has to put up with can be tempered by excitement or an enquiring intellect, but in the Arctic one really has got to be a person who appreciates perfect silence and one has a real love for solitude. Here there is no solitude.

On 11 August 1943, Adler wrote of having a 'wonderful war'. He had visited Mwanza on Lake Victoria, 'lined with palms, the blue lake and white limestone rocks with houses perched on small hillock'. He had also been to Kigoma, a pretty town on the edge of Lake Tanganyika: 'it is like a gem. This was the town where Livingstone and Stanley met … I bathed in the lake in a small wire enclosure to keep out the crocs.'

He had had a view of Mount Kilimanjaro: 'It has a domed summit of glittering white snow with glaciers descending from it. It is usually in clouds but each morning and evening the clouds lift and one has a perfect vision.' Adler was able to buy unlimited toothpaste, chocolate and other commodities from the well-stocked shops of the Belgian Congo. For Margaret, 'I bought you a dress length and a lovely pair of crepe shoes in white green for walking but unfortunately in unloading a truck in the dark I was taking such care to see that no one else forgot anything that I forgot this parcel, it is an awful pity.'

Although many miles from home, Christmas Day for men on overseas active service offered a chance to reflect on the fundamentals of life: their faith, family and foundations. Kenneth Hulbert attended a service at Khartoum Cathedral taken by the Bishop of Egypt and Sudan, Reverend Llewellyn Gwynne. He sat on the back row with some very tall, black, southern Sudanese soldiers, all in their very best uniforms, and shared a hymn book with one of them for *Hark the Herald Angels Sing*. Following the service, lunch was taken at the British Military Hospital before listening to the king's speech on the wireless. In the evening, staff at the hospital followed the usual army custom with the officers waiting on the men for their Christmas dinner.

The staff of the No. 58 General Hospital produced a weekly journal, *Odyssey*, an eclectic and entertaining mixture of cartoons, poetry, nature, chess and bridge problems, and letters to the editor. Officers took it in turns to act as editor, whilst a long-serving managing editor was Charles Quant, a journalist in civilian life. One particularly thoughtful piece came from Private A.H. Robinson, reflecting on his experiences of Christmas Eves from 1939–44. The 1939 festival was marked by him singing carols door to door, while awaiting the 'Big Call Up', whilst 1940 had been spent in Ormskirk, watching the city of Liverpool ablaze in the distance. By 1941, Robinson was in a hutted hospital a few miles from Alexandria, which experienced an overnight downpour. 'In the morning, a scene of desolation, with collapsed tents lying in the wet, churned-up sand. Our first Christmas abroad, with the prospect of ever going home remote in the extreme.'

Christmas 1942 evoked thoughts of the nativity, and demonstrated the importance that the Christian faith played for so many British service men and women:

> That Christmas, we were no great distance from the place where the Wise Men knelt in adoration before a manger

> in a humble stable, with the rude wall of which the uncomprehending beasts in their stalls gazed down on the 'five little fingers of God' as the Christ Child stretched forth a tiny hand towards them.
>
> A simple little service in the plain room of a mission school – a tiny hand stretched forth by the Christian Church towards the uncomprehending mass of Islam. Readings from the deathless Christmas story, interspersed with the old familiar hymns and carols. Then an enormous spread of Christmas fare in the adjoining home of the mission superintendent and his ever-cheerful wife. Finally, a walk back to the camp in the white moonlight.
>
> That Christmas, one felt with an intensity hitherto unrealised the significance of the greatest event in human history, for it was but a few weeks previously that one had stood in the Grotto beneath the Church of the Nativity in Bethlehem itself and looked down on the silver star in the paving marking the traditional spot whereon God had once become Man.

On 10 November 1942, following the decisive victory at El Alamein, Winston Churchill declared in a speech at the Lord Mayor's Luncheon at the Mansion house, 'Now this is not the end. It is not even the beginning of the end, but it is, perhaps, the end of the beginning.' The pattern of advance followed by reversals across the North African desert that had occurred over the past two years or more across the north had come to an end, and victory in Africa was finally secured within a matter of months with the taking of Tunisia. Later, in the *Hinge of Fate*, Churchill wrote, 'Before Alamein we never had a victory. After Alamein we never had a defeat.' The stage was now set for the Italian Campaign to begin, with the invasion of Sicily taking place two months later. The fighting in North Africa had caused the death or injury of nearly 400,000 Allied and Axis troops. But for the dedication and skill of the RAMC men supporting the fighting troops, casualties on the Allied side would have been far higher. The outcome of the campaign might not have been the victory that formed the springboard for the successful conclusion of the war in Europe two years later, but a defeat paving the way for surrender to the Axis powers. The tide had turned.

Chapter 4

Medicine in the Mediterranean: Malta, Greece, Crete and Italy

Malta

On 11 June 1940, Italian aircraft flew over Malta for the first of what would become more than 3,000 bombing raids that the Mediterranean island would have to endure over the next two and a half years – the longest siege in British history. The territory, slightly smaller than the Isle of Wight, was one of the most important strategic pieces of land in the world, holding the key to the war in the Mediterranean and North Africa. Lying between Italy and Libya, Malta was the ideal place from which the Allies could launch attacks on Axis shipping lines supplying Italian and German forces in North Africa. Britain had to hold Malta to save Egypt, the Suez Canal and the Middle East oilfields from Nazi control.

The Axis forces were determined to annihilate the island, and Malta became the most heavily bombed place on earth. In two months, March and April 1942, more bombs fell on Malta than on London during the entire Blitz. In addition, there were big losses amongst the convoys trying to keep the island supplied with food, medicines and ammunition. Despite the starving and disease caused by the siege, the islanders held out and the whole island was awarded the George Cross in recognition of their stoicism and bravery.

During the period of the siege, torpedo bombers and submarines continued to sink critical amounts of Rommel's supplies heading to North Africa – a decisive factor in the eventual victory at El Alamein and beyond.

The only British military hospital at the time of the initial Italian attack was No. 90 BGH, situated at Imtarfa in the north of the island, perched high on a promontory. Here the medics treated a variety of diseases that troops contracted when living in roughly made shelters out in the open. By 27 June 1940, the hospital had expanded to 1,260 beds, including sixty beds in the Family Division. On 3 July, the Isolation Block, which had been used as offices, opened as an isolation hospital for families; the isolation wards in the Families Hospital were shut, and all patients transferred to the Isolation Block.

Sandfly fever, scabies and Malta Dog (a particularly unpleasant form of dysentery) were all regular features of life in the field. The first major challenge for the hospital was a batch of sixty wounded received on 10 January 1941. Naval medical staff had been transferred across to assist, with the operating theatre treating a continual stream of casualties. Many had severe burns, with their bodies pitted black, emitting the screams and groans brought on by constant agony. Nurses swabbed and sprayed the charred skin with gentian violet and acriflavine. Air raid shelters had been built for the staff, but they were reluctant to use them as it would mean leaving suffering patients unattended. Fortunately, it appeared that the Germans had no interest in attacking the clearly marked hospital. It was hit on 13 April in general bombing, with equipment being ruined but without fatalities. As well as British troops, the hospital treated Axis troops, including a group of Italians wounded by an E-boat attack on 26 July.

Two further military hospitals reached Malta in 1941. No. 45 BGH arrived in May 1941 and began admitting patients from July. It opened at Pembroke Garrison Gymnasium whilst the Sandhurst Barrack Block St Patrick's was also converted for use by the hospital. No. 39 BGH arrived in September 1941 and took over huts at St Paul's Barracks from Command Convalescent Depot. It functioned briefly from 2 February until 25 April 1942, when it was rendered non-operational by enemy action.

One of the new RAMC staff for No. 45 BGH was Reg Gill, a radiographer from Leeds.[1] Although happy to have survived the perils of a Mediterranean convoy, Gill was less than overjoyed to have been sent to bomb-devastated Malta, and experienced a sense of isolation knowing that the nearest friendly forces were about 1,000 miles away in Gibraltar or Alexandria. He was sent to a school on the north-east coast above Sliema and posted to St Andrew's barracks, from where, on a clear day, Mount Etna could been seen across the water.

Gill's fears of further heavy bombardment were quickly realised when, during his second night on the island, the Italians launched a motor boat raid, twenty of which attempted to sink the Allied convoy in the Grand

Harbour. The vessels had been detected by radar, and at 2.00 am, Gill and his comrades in the hospital were awoken by a terrific noise as every gun on the island appeared to be firing. The hospital seemed to shake and the whole of Malta was lit up by flashes of shellfire. The raid failed, leaving Gill to continue his work in setting up a functioning radiography department.

Gill was provided with a 4-kilowatt generator in addition to electric mains, which functioned intermittently between raids. X-ray films could easily be ruined by a voltage drop, so the security of a generator was essential. The machine itself lacked power, meaning that the generator struggled to provide enough power when taking a scan of a spine or an abdomen. No. 45 BGH prepared to receive naval casualties and Maltese gunners from the King's Own Malta Regiment. The hospital lacked a lift, which meant that when a patient on the second floor needed an X-ray, the machine had to be dismantled from its position on the first floor and carried upstairs. It weighed over 100 kilograms and took four men to shift it, with the efficiency of the department being adversely affected.

From July to December 1941, Gill and his comrades experienced a seemingly endless barrage of raids, mainly from the Italian Royal Air Force (Regia Aeronautica Italiana) stationed over in Sicily. Sleep was a precious commodity, with Gill learning the art of sleeping standing up where necessary. Rather than use the hospital air raid shelters hewn out of the rock, he preferred the sergeants' mess during a raid, reckoning that if a bomb dropped on it he would die instantly, but if one dropped at the entrance to the cave shelter, there would be a slow death entombed in rock.

Gill contracted sandfly fever, his temperature increasing to 40 degrees for a few days. The food situation was becoming critical, as only a few supply convoys had managed to reach the island, and by the end of 1941, Gill and his comrades were 'hungry and apprehensive', wondering how long they could hold out against the Italian fleet and air force.

The apprehension was well-founded as the Germans transferred Luftflotte II under Field Marshal Kesselring to Sicily, and early in 1942, an even bigger blitz started. Swimming became the only recreation and it was combined with the essential task of washing, which was performed using a special sea soap. This was the only way to prevent scabies, which was rampant on the island in the absence of water. A well-marked path through a minefield down to the coast was followed, and frequently when swimming, a swarm of Messerschmitts would heave into view, sending the swimmers scrambling for a hole in the rocks or otherwise risk death from gunfire.

By the spring of 1942, the islanders had resorted to killing horses to cook makeshift steaks, and the roads were blocked with debris from the bombing. Life had reached a nadir, and resistance was weakening. Sergeant Gill recalled:

> We all became fatalistic. The usual story about a bombing raid if it's got your name on it then you've had it. It's true that the hospital wasn't an intended target. We had in fact got a number of German pilot prisoners of war both in the hospital and also in a little compound just by the hospital. The Red Cross had to be informed of prisoners of war. We were sure that the Germans knew they were there and that they tried to avoid bombing the hospital which had a big red cross visible for miles in the square in front of it. The danger occurred (and this happened several times) when bombers flying over the hospital were hit by Spinola or one of the other AA batteries at Narga or Nashua on the surrounding hills. If the bomber was on fire, sheer survival required the crew to jettison the bombs to get back to Sicily.

One such bomber, a Junkers 88, circled round over the hospital then came down smoking and on fire. Two of the crew parachuted out. The plane was so low that the bombs on the bomb rack could be seen. They were released and Gill thought that was the end. Fortunately, by a split-second timing, they ended in the sea rather than on the hospital.

X-raying a patient or developing a film in the darkroom, knowing that bombers and fighters were patrolling the island, and that the whole building could collapse at any time, was challenging. Food rations were inadequate and tasted foul, consisting mainly of corned beef, dry biscuits and pilchards.

Morale, although reasonable in the circumstances, was not aided by the development of two factions within the sergeants' mess of the No. 45 BGH. On the one side were the technical staff – pharmacists, lab technicians, theatre staff, radiographers – and on the other were the regimental staff, medically less trained, who generally dealt with the convoys of wounded coming in, carrying stretchers and organising tents. Gill recalled: 'Regrettably, some of the regimental staff treated the Maltese badly and this caused a rift. The regimental staff who were mostly from London sat on one side of the mess and the medical staff, mostly from Leeds on the other and we were not a happy group.'

The tension was exacerbated by the lack of alcohol and the immense difficulty in accessing the nearest library, in Valetta, 7 miles away. Also, the receipt of mail from loved ones was sporadic or worse. Unescorted transport planes were frequently shot down, and sea mail was lost in ships sunk trying to get to Malta. Some mail got through via a submarine flotilla, with Gill receiving up to three letters at a time, providing a vital link with home.

As the siege dragged on, rations were cut yet again in August 1942. Men learned to avoid conversation about the thing that was uppermost in their minds and stomachs.

> The supply situation however got worse and worse and we were told that our rations would be cut yet again. We were really hungry. I had weighed almost 70kg and I was tall and thin but by the end of 1942 I was down to 50kg. ... I think we all were just skeletons. If you've been subjected to starvation over a long period, a key rule is never to talk about food. We all thought about it, but if anyone said 'wouldn't it be nice if we had steak and chips' they were immediately jumped on.

Gill came into contact with German pilots who were patients in the officers' ward. One was fairly friendly and spoke good English. He had suffered a fractured femur and had had a piece of shrapnel lodged in his abdomen. Gill X-rayed his femur quite often as it was very badly broken. The pilot told the radiographer he was a Czech. Gill queried why he was serving in the German air force and was told that he bitterly resented the fact that Britain and France had refused to support Czechoslovakia in their resistance in 1938 and had joined the Luftwaffe as a professional pilot. The man warned Gill that the Germans would soon capture Malta as they had Crete, and that the treatment of the British prisoners would depend on how well they had treated the Germans as captives. 'Whether he thought we would give him extra rations or not I don't know. As hard as it was for him to believe, he got exactly the same food as us!'

Despite being classed as non-combatants under the Geneva Convention, as the invasion of Malta appeared imminent, RAMC orderlies were issued with rifles.

> Most of us thought this was appalling but we were taken to the rifle range and told to practise – purely for the defence of our patients in hospital! We did of course do as we were told. We fired our rifles and so on. The powers that be probably thought that a few score Medical Corps firing into the air against paratroops would have some effect. Certainly it would have had the effect of having us all shot if the invasion succeeded as we all thought it probably would do.

Fortunately, the situation never deteriorated to the extent that medical staff had to fire in anger, as the siege was eventually ended on 20 November 1942.

As Malta underwent its torment, further east along the Mediterranean Sea, British and Commonwealth forces were experiencing heavy defeats in Greece and Crete. Having successfully repulsed an attack from the Italian Army, which had begun in late October 1940, Greece was invaded by Germany on 6 April 1941. A British Expeditionary Force was despatched to help defend the country but by 30 April, Greece had fallen into German hands, and those Allied troops who escaped capture were evacuated to Crete via the ports of Peloponnese. Here dogged resistance was put up by British and Commonwealth forces in the face of a German airborne invasion, with medical personnel performing heroics in the saving of lives and the further evacuation of casualties to the relative safety of Egypt. Sticking to their duty in the face of adversity, many RAMC personnel were themselves killed or wounded, or taken as prisoners of war by the Germans.

Having seen action in North Africa, the men of No. 168 Field Ambulance were sent over to Greece and pushed up towards the front line, not far from the Albanian border, to support the defence of the country against the German invasion. Here, a temporary hospital was set up by placing two lorries close together and draping a large tarpaulin over the top. The medics then assembled the operating table and set up all the equipment ready for the wounded when they came in. First the walking wounded arrived but it was not long before the stretcher-bearers began to bring more severely wounded men. The surgeons busied themselves with the casualties, undertaking any urgent operations before the patients were placed on an ambulance to be taken back to a base hospital some 20 miles behind the lines.

David Jones, although the unit cook, became a temporary stretcher-bearer, lining the stretchers up outside the operating tent. The doctors prioritised those needing immediate small operations and those who needed to go back to base hospital for major ones. After four days, the hospital was attacked by a Stuka dive-bomber, killing the major in the operating tent but not the man on the operating table.

On 21 April 1941, General Archibald Wavell, commander of the British Army forces in the Middle East, ordered a retreat. It was chaotic and dangerous, with men being subject to frequent strafing from Luftwaffe planes as there was little RAF presence to protect them. The withdrawal was disorderly, with units becoming split up. After moving southwards through Athens, Jones and his comrades were ordered to abandon their cookhouse lorry and walk down to the beach, where the Royal Navy would pick them up and transport them back to the relative safety of Egypt:

> Sure enough, as darkness came a large destroyer came and anchored off shore. It was not long before half a dozen small boats appeared, and we were ferried out to the destroyer. About midnight, when all the troops on the beach were aboard, we set off for what we thought to be our destination – Egypt. In the morning we found out we were in Suda [*sic*] Bay, Crete and that we were going to be off-loaded so that the destroyer could go back to Greece for more troops. We were told eventually they would come and pick us up and take us on to Egypt. We believed them.[2]

Captain Theo Stephanides was a regimental medical officer with the 66th Auxiliary Military Pioneer Corps Group in Greece. He had gone to No. 26 General Hospital in Kephisia to draw some medical supplies and was unaware that an evacuation of the country had been ordered. On returning to his headquarters at Phaleron, 'I had the very disconcerting surprise of finding the place empty and everybody gone, including my batman and all my kit. I literally had nothing except what I stood up in. Fortunately, I had my steel helmet and a first aid outfit which I always carried about with me.'[3]

Stephanides managed to evacuate on the SS *Julia*, an old Greek collier, on 23 April 1941. The 244-mile journey across to the island of Crete was beset with aerial peril over the two days during which the overcrowded vessel steered its path across the Mediterranean Sea. The ship was attacked by seven Stukas, leaving thirteen men wounded, including a sergeant with a bullet through the wrist and an Australian private whose left calf had been ploughed by a bullet that had run below the skin for about 4 inches before coming out again. Stephanides turned the ship's saloon into a sick bay where, assisted by an Australian corporal, he tended to the casualties.

A further attack shortly afterwards incurred more casualties, forcing Stephanides to use part of the forecastle and the adjoining first mate's cabin as a ward, getting his patients comfortable in a short space of time. The man whose leg had been entered and exited by a bullet had numerous fragments of trousers and sock in the wound, so Stephanides slit open the length of the tunnel made by the bullet and washed and cleaned it out thoroughly. The Australian's ordeal was made less painful by the injection of a quarter of a grain of morphine with a further quarter grain being sucked in tablet form.[4]

Crete

The evacuation from Greece placed an enormous strain on the army medical services established on the island of Crete. Medics arriving from the Greek mainland brought little more than the clothes they were wearing and occasional small pieces of equipment in their haversacks.[5] Sick and wounded men poured into the existing hospitals, causing great strain on the men staffing them, and many were placed in temporary transit camps. The chaos of the evacuation meant that many men had not had their dressings changed for over a week.

Robert Debenham had been promoted to lieutenant colonel in charge of the Surgical Division of No. 7 General Hospital in autumn 1940. Having set sail for the Mediterranean in January 1941, he disembarked with his staff and equipment on Crete on 19 April 1941. No. 7 General Hospital, largely under canvas, was laid out on a narrow strip of land on the north coast of the island. Its arrival was followed shortly afterwards by 42,000 British, Commonwealth and Greek troops who had evacuated from Greece.

The German advance through the Mediterranean continued on to the island of Crete, and during May 1941, 847 casualties were admitted to the hospital, many of them in a serious condition. Debenham and his friend and colleague Major Arnold Gourevitch split the surgical work between them, alternating take-in days.

Tragically, the hospital was hit by a German bomb, killing many staff. The official War Office report on the Battle of Crete recorded how the attack on the medics and their patients was sustained:

> A most severe attack lasing about two hours, during which time the wounded were machine-gunned in their tents by low-flying aircraft. At 11.30 hours the hospital was over-run by German troops who marched off some of the staff and those of the wounded and sick capable of walking a distance of about four miles to the region of Galtas prison where they were promptly employed in making a landing ground.[6]

Lieutenant Colonel Debenham reflected on the attack the following year: 'A deliberate attack on an Army General Hospital must be a rare occurrence and suddenly presents unexpected problems in an acute form. It is evident that the enemy do not respect hospitals if the site is of strategic importance to them.'[7]

The attack began at 7.00 am as the tents were bombed repeatedly and raked with machine-gun fire from many aeroplanes. Movement inside the hospital became impossible and anyone who had the strength threw themselves into a slit trench. After the aerial attack had lasted for two hours, 300 parachutists began to descend on a patch of land a few hundred yards from the hospital's HQ. Most of the invaders were killed before they had landed, but a number of them entered the hospital and replaced the Red Cross flag with a swastika. Staff and walking wounded were rounded up and marched down the road out of sight. Debenham claimed that most of them returned twenty-four hours later. Men daring to raise their heads from the slit trenches felt the whizz of a sniper's bullet. Eventually, New Zealand troops reoccupied the area and the rest of the day was quiet on the ground.

Debenham reckoned that this would only prove to be a temporary lull, so after dusk, all remaining patients were removed to a series of caves not far away from the tent. Fortunately, Debenham found several good hideouts along the rocky coast and initially, due to the disregard for the Red Cross that the initial wave of German attackers had shown, it was decided not to advertise the existence of the 'Cave Hospital'. The new, temporary, No. 7 General Hospital consisted of five surgical caves and one dysentery cave.

Rations had to be collected under cover of darkness, and the medical officers had to enforce blackout measures at night. The rough surface and plentiful slopes inside the caves made the arrangement of patients a challenge, an issue exacerbated by having only stretchers and mattresses on which to rest the casualties. Cooking was done on Primus stoves, with each cave responsible for its own provisions.

An operating table was set up in the largest cave, and both wounded British and German troops underwent surgery on it. Debenham remarked on the 'magnificent' attitude of all patients, despite cramped space, poor light and awkward slopes, and a lack of proper hygienic arrangements combining to make work difficult. Fresh water was carried from a well some distance away and carefully conserved, but there was an ample supply of seawater close by. The sea also acted as a natural sewage repository.

One incident that stuck in Debenham's mind was when a corpse that had to be laid outside a cave until a burial could be arranged was fired on by an eager Luftwaffe gunner. Despite this attack, Debenham eventually reversed his decision not to display a Red Cross flag after he had made contact with a New Zealand field ambulance, which had set up a Main Dressing Station in a nearby building. The New Zealanders had reported that their own flag had been completely respected. Debenham found the same respect was accorded to the Cave Hospital flag, except on one occasion when one of trucks belonging to a field ambulance bearing a Red Cross emblem was deliberately attacked by cannon from the air and destroyed.

The New Zealand field ambulance MDS allowed Debenham to evacuate casualties and thus receive new patients, with up to 500 cases being treated in the caves. This was despite a shortage of equipment and drugs, both of which had been destroyed during the raid on the hospital's dispensary. For Debenham, 'The lesson to be learned is that *two medical stores* are safer than one.'[8] For five long days Debenham and his medics worked in such conditions, until orders were received to move and a long trek across the island was to begin.

Private David Jones had arrived in Crete accompanied by the remnants of the No. 168 Field Ambulance, which had become dispersed during the evacuation of Greece. After a couple of days, the remaining members of the unit were marched off to set up a temporary hospital in an aerodrome not far from the harbour at Souda Bay, and found that more of their comrades had made their way there. There were no officers present, so a field first aid post was set up under the command of a sergeant major. After German strafing, the unit retreated towards Souda Bay, where Jones witnessed the arrival of German airborne troops: 'Then it happened; a slow freighter plane came over towing two gliders. The plane let the gliders loose out to sea just before the aerodrome. As the gliders came down our fighting troops were in good positions behind rocks. They machine-gunned the gliders as they came in to land. Not a single German got out.'[9]

Undeterred, more German gliders appeared, followed by strafing from fighter planes, and a retreat was ordered. Jones and four of his comrades walked eastwards towards Heraklion, crossing the countryside as the road was jammed with departing troops:

> Suddenly we [a group of 5] came under rifle fire and saw a company of Germans coming along the top of the hill trying to cut off half the island. The Sergeant Major told us to stop and put up our hands. In a short time they were up with us and they saw that we had Red Cross bands on and no arms. They told us to put our hands down and wait until the file of men had gone by.

A German soldier approached Jones and grabbed his haversack, which contained his small kit and a few personal items, and threw it over a wall. He did not speak to Jones but went back to the file that was passing by. 'He was a nasty looking chap and I suppose he wanted me to do something, but the sergeant major told me not to move.' After the file had gone by, Jones asked the soldier guarding them if he could go and get his rucksack, but was refused.

The remnants of No. 168 Field Ambulance were ordered to tag along behind the file of captured men. Due to the rapidity of the capture of so many British troops, there was a lack of provision for their welfare, with Jones receiving no food for four days. He was then, with three other medical comrades, picked out and taken to a hospital that had been set up by the Germans to look after their own wounded. They were issued with German identity discs and their particulars recorded. Finally, they received food, which greatly improved their morale despite their predicament, and were put to work in the German hospital wards. The patients they were charged with caring for were Austrian parachute troops, who had been so badly wounded that they could not be moved to the Greek mainland and most of whom would eventually die.

The SS *Julia*, carrying British and Commonwealth evacuees from Greece, had landed at Souda Bay on 25 April. Captain Theo Stephanides was ordered to report to Camp E, a 5-mile walk away, which transpired to be a collection of wrecked houses. He held a medical inspection of the men there, finding only a few minor ailments and unimportant cuts and bruises sustained on board ship. He found them 'still too keyed up and too thankful to be ashore to think of illnesses'.[10] The greater problem confronting the men was sanitation, there being only one pick and two shovels to dig trench-latrines for nearly 500 men but, despite the difficulties, the camp was relatively clean. There were only four cases of bad diarrhoea or mild dysentery, these caused from eating too much fruit.

On 30 April, Stephanides was ordered to a camp housed in a Greek Orthodox Monastery, where again he found deficient sanitation, just one deep-pit latrine for the whole camp. So the following day he walked to Canea to report to Lieutenant Colonel S.O. Dolan, ADMS, to see what medical supplies he could obtain. He came away with some aspirin, acriflavine, bismuth and soda tablets, and a few shell dressings. A week later, the unit was moved to a farm, where the owners put their well at the men's disposal. Stephanides faced the challenge of ensuring his troops did not dip their dirty buckets into it, contaminating the precious water supply. Despite the welcome availability of fresh water, the doctor still faced an acute shortage of medical supplies, and had to call on his knowledge of botany to make up his own medicines from various accessible plants, utilising the availability of mallow, plantain, mulberry and pine bark with 'very satisfactory results'.[11] Infusions of mallow were used to treat an epidemic of mild colds and chills, caused by the men sleeping out in the open air.

In addition to his duties as medical officer with the 66th AMPC, Stephanides took on the role of performing sick parades for the 1,005th Dock Operating Company and a company of Royal Marines, both encamped nearby but lacking a medical officer. The former contained a large proportion of shipping clerks from London, Liverpool and Manchester who had joined the company on the understanding they would be engaged exclusively on clerical work. Despite this, they had been made to unload ships. Having had their vessel bombed and sunk during the crossing from Greece, the survivors had been rescued by another ship and then told that on arrival at Souda Bay they would be doing further physical dock work. This had caused a great deal of consternation, and ninety-six out of 220 of them had reported on sick parade.

Stephanides was faced with a politically difficult situation as the men's officers wanted them classed as malingerers and punished. However, he could see that they 'were in such a state of nervous prostration from what they had been through that it would have been sheer cruelty to adopt such extreme measures'.[12] Therefore he gave the most exhausted cases a few days' light duty and persuaded the rest to comply with instructions by 'putting them on their honour'.

By this stage, the RAF had left Greece, leaving the skies over Crete open to German planes, which regularly strafed the camp. On 18 May, Stephanides received a note advising him that the No. 7 General Hospital, some 5 miles away, had obtained further medical supplies and that a 'monkey box' of a wicker basket containing instruments, drugs and other first aid necessities could be collected. Stephanides was heartened by this news, as he was running perilously low on provisions.

The hospital, situated near Maleme Aerodrome, was taking heavy bombardment. It was situated on an open piece of ground, sloping gradually down to the sea. Tents of all shapes and sizes were pitched in orderly rows, interspersed by some wooden shacks. A large red cross was displayed on the ground, to signal to German pilots that it was a medical unit, and Stephanides left with the impression of a peaceful place, a peace that was to be cruelly shattered later: 'The place looked so peaceful that it was difficult afterwards to imagine that the very next morning German parachutists descended right into the hospital area, and that a certain number of the patients and nursing staff were killed in the fighting.'

Once it was clear that Germany was mounting a serious assault on the island, Stephanides was moved southwards in retreat. On 23 May, during a short lull in bombardment, he seized the opportunity to have a medical inspection of 606th Palestinian and 1,005th Cyprus Pioneer Companies. He also accessed a tented naval first aid post under some olive trees on the left-hand side of the road from Chikalaria at the point it entered Souda village, where he was able to obtain acriflavine, bismuth, soda tablets, gauze and cotton wool. Stephanides also visited a CCS, which was under the direction of Captain E.T. Gilbert, 'an excellent surgeon as well as a capable pathologist'.[13] Assisted by only two medical orderlies, Gilbert was looking after up to a hundred casualties at a time, arranging their evacuations on board the destroyers, which were managing to slip into Souda Bay in the darkness of night. Stephanides assisted Gilbert in the extraction of a tommy gun bullet from the shoulder of a wounded Maori soldier. All the more remarkable about the work of Gilbert's CCS was that it was situated in a detached two-storey building that had had its iron roller shutters 'warped and holed by blast and splinters'.

Two days later, following heavy enemy bombing and machine-gunning, Stephanides had to attend to several civilians who had been wounded by bullets, one being a youth of 15 who was shot through both legs. It was not only physical wounds that Stephanides had to treat. He was given the case of an ack-ack gunner, aged about 20, who told him his gun had been attacked simultaneously by at least ten planes at Maleme Aerodrome, and destroyed. Virtually sleepless for a whole week, he had then been assigned to another gun near Souda Bay, again coming under heavy and persistent fire. He became excitable, shouting, 'It's sheer bloody murder!', and had to be treated with a shot of morphine, as his nerves had been strained to breaking point.

Stephanides heard of hundreds of wounded lying under olive trees at a CCS near Tobruk Avenue with practically no medical attention. The doctor himself was working in a first aid post where the floor continually heaved and rocked and the walls quivered and trembled from the force of bomb blasts. Windows were shattered and the wooden shutters had to be tied with rope to prevent them from bursting open. 'The whole landscape was eruptive earth, smoke and flame, and all our ack-ack guns had been silenced except for an occasional shot from a couple of dogged Bofors near Souda.'[14] Stephanides was able to evacuate many of his patients via lorries sent by Captain Gilbert, yet still the casualties streamed in, with the psychological damage becoming ever starker:

> There was a further deterioration of the morale of the wounded who reached our first aid post. There were more and more cases of men, and even officers, who had trifling or no apparent wounds, but who showed signs of concussion, extreme physical exhaustion, or complete nervous collapse. Some of them would fall asleep the moment I laid them down on the floor, and many had pulses very much faster or slower than the normal.[15]

A good old British cup of tea was administered to revive the spirits. Another man, Private Ironside of the Royal Scottish, was brought in by a group of slightly wounded New Zealand soldiers, having been wounded in the left breast and shoulder, the left side of his face and jaw being reduced to a mass of caked blood. The man had a high fever and had been left unattended for several days. After patching him up, Stephanides and his orderly, Corporal Tobin, gave the man some Oxo and some broken-up Dextrosan tablets found on a German parachutist, 'which seemed to do him a lot of good'.[16]

By 28 May, it was clear that the Germans had broken through the British defences and men were in full retreat, including many walking wounded. Nevertheless, Stephanides had received no orders to evacuate, therefore went to find his commanding officer. To his surprise he was told that he had left an hour or two earlier, and that Cretan civilians were removing supplies from the former HQ. Stephanides went to check on his own first aid post and found that deserted too. He returned to his first aid post, despite the anxiety he felt at the hordes travelling in the opposite direction:

> Crowds of men were pouring down the road and I felt distinctly uncomfortable to be the only person going up, especially as I was told several times not to be a bloody fool as the Germans were already in Chikalaria. I felt tempted more than once to throw away the stretcher and turn back, and I think that I would have done so had I been really certain that the enemy was in possession of the village.

> But I felt that I had to know before taking such a step or my conscience would always prick me for having left the others in the lurch. It was disturbing though to reflect that I might already be too late and that I was perhaps running into danger for nothing. My fears, fortunately, turned out to be premature.[17]

Stephanides reached his first aid post, picked up his medical box, a satchel of shell dressings and a couple of water bottles, and hastily left, he and his orderlies carrying a stretcher together. As they retreated, lorries ignored their attempts to flag them down and deposit within them the injured Private Ironside, whom they were carrying on the stretcher. As they were making slow progress, Stephanides ordered Tobin and another medical orderly to leave the party and make a more rapid retreat, as he was not certain of the treatment that, as Jews, they would have received from the Germans if captured. They initially refused, 'a very plucky decision on their part under the circumstances', but were eventually directed to depart.

In due course, two Australians volunteered to lend a hand as Stephanides continued to administer Dextrosan tablets to Ironside, still unable to eat. The stretcher broke, so the patient had to be carried in a hand chair, which was extremely tiring for the bearers. Soon, a lorry filled with wounded men passed by and although the driver seemed reluctant to respond, a padre sitting in the passenger seat ordered him to pull up, clambered down from his seat and helped to lift Private Ironside on board. It was a relief to his three carriers to see him disappear down the road.

By now the retreat had become a rout. Abandoned kit, rifles, gas masks, tinned provisions and hand grenades lay strewn across the road. Stephanides rued the loss of these, and more luxury items: 'I was greatly tempted to annex several brand new silk khaki shirts from a discarded suitcase, but compromised by tearing them to ribbons so that no Nazi should swank in them – a childish gesture which gave me considerable satisfaction at the time.' Air attacks were raining down with increasing frequency, so Stephanides abandoned the road to make for a tougher but safer hillside path. Most men insisted on sticking to the road, 'yielding apparently to a kind of herd instinct'. This presented him with a moral dilemma. Should he, as a medical officer, stick with the majority of men, or should he use the safest route in order to rejoin his unit at the earliest opportunity? Deciding on the latter course, he made for the hills and arrived at Neon Chorion village at dusk.

Here he was approached by a Greek Orthodox priest, who kept repeating, 'English sick', and took Stephanides to three British soldiers lying in front of his church. One was dead and the other two were in a bad way. He bandaged their wounds, gave them a drink and morphine injection, and wrapped them in blankets, with the intention of sending a motor ambulance to pick them up later. As night fell, Stephanides still had 25 miles to traverse to reach Imbros, so he carried on walking through the night, jettisoning everything except his medical kit, which he retained, 'as, being a medical officer, I felt that jettisoning it would lose me my self-respect like the soldier who throws away his rifle.'[18]

On reaching Imbros Gorge, he had walked nearly 40 miles in less than thirty hours, and was told to report to Major Cowen of the New Zealand Medical Corps, the senior medical officer there. Cowen informed him that their task was to receive all wounded, walking and conveyed, who came down the road, collect them in a gully under the cover of trees, administer every possible medical care and then have them transferred by lorry to Sphakia on the south coast of Crete. Throughout 30 May, the wounded continued to arrive and then be evacuated to the port. Towards midday, Major Cowen received the order to evacuate all the walking wounded, without waiting for nightfall, in lorries bearing large Red Cross flags.

This was a risky move, as the previous evening a few similarly emblemed lorries had been attacked, with a number of casualties killed or wounded again. However, it was thought that the German planes might not have been able to see the Red Cross flags in the gathering gloom, hence the decision to evacuate in clear daylight. In order to accentuate the medical nature of the convoy, men were told to discard everything that might be seen as a weapon or imply a readiness to fight, including their steel helmets.

En route they passed a wrecked clearly marked white motor ambulance. Stephanides' lorry had a large white sheet with a red cross roughly stitched to it over its bonnet, with an RAMC corporal seated in the cab with a home-made Red Cross flag fixed to a long pole, which he waved about vigorously whenever a plane appeared in the distance.

Soon the road became blocked by destroyed vehicles, so the party had to set off on foot, with the order not to scatter if aircraft appeared, but to bunch together and wave their Red Cross flag. This tactic worked: 'The oncoming planes ceased firing and circled once or twice low down over our heads; several of them even dipped their wings as they passed to signal that they had seen and understood our flag. … I will give the devil his due and that in this particular instance the Germans did respect the Red Cross.'[19]

This deliverance left Stephanides relieved but puzzled:

> I do not know how to explain this rather surprising conduct on the part of the Germans. In Greece they had bombed hospital ships and trains without any compunction, and the evening before, according to reports, they had attacked parties of walking wounded and caused a number of casualties, yet this time they merely circled us and departed without harming a hair of our heads. Did we just chance upon an unusually decent lot of Germans, or were they short of bombs and bullets at the time and did not think it worthwhile to waste them on such a miserable target? Another theory advanced was that the German purposefully refrained from attacking all the retreating troops so as to have a chance of bombing the ships which would be sent to evacuate them. I hope, however, for the good name of mankind as a whole, that the above incident was due to the fact that there were still some Germans in whom all humane feelings had not been entirely obliterated.[20]

As uninjured troops became aware of the sparing of the party of wounded men, some tried to save themselves by pretending to be part of the group. One man tied a field dressing around his forehead, leaving Stephanides with another moral dilemma – whether to dismiss them or ignore them. The situation resolved itself, with the wounded themselves objecting, and 'the unfortunate fellows slunk off.'[21]

Eventually, after joining up with another party of casualties, the enlarged group of about 130 men traversed the deep gorge of Sphakiano Pharangi, where they were met by a naval officer who guided them through the village of Sphakia and on the HMAS *Perth*. Their ordeal was not yet over, as the vessel was hit during the retreat, but not sunk, and eventually limped into Alexandria at 2.00 am on 1 June.

Other medics were not as fortunate as Stephanides in escaping capture by the Germans. Cyril McCann had landed on Crete in November 1940 with No. 189 Field Ambulance, which proceeded to set up a hospital in the Villa Ariadne at Knossos. Once the German invasion started, losses were high, and the hospital started to fill up with British and German casualties. By 1 June, of just over 600 patients, about 400 were from the invading force and just 200 were British. Both sets of men received equal treatment, with an operating theatre being established in the living room. A sense of international camaraderie prevailed. McCann recalled, 'People who had been fighting half an hour previously with every intention of killing one another were swapping fags. Daft.'[22]

Unfortunately, McCann and his comrades were unaware that the British had withdrawn and were not given the order to evacuate. When the Germans took over the hospital, the seventeen remaining men of No. 189 Field Ambulance were allowed to carry on treating the wounded for a fortnight, with the Germans arranging for the evacuation of the sick. McCann was one of five nursing orderlies left behind to complete treatment under the direction of the surgeon, Captain France. On the last night before being taken to Athens and then on to a transit camp in Salonkika before a long imprisonment in Germany, one final episode of amity occurred, as there was 'one enormous booze-up' between the German paratroopers and the remaining RAMC staff. Another member of No. 189 Field Ambulance, Private Kenneth Stalder, was captured in a cave by German paratroopers while trying to effect an escape from the island. To his surprise, he was approached by a friendly young German paratrooper who spoke English with a perfect London accent. Offering Stalder a cigarette, it transpired that he had been a shopkeeper in Tottenham before the war.[23]

Sicily and Italy

The Allied invasion of the island of Sicily, codenamed Operation Husky, was used as a stepping stone towards establishing a foothold on the European mainland. Casualties were high amongst the airborne troops sent to begin the liberation of Europe from fascism. About 30 per cent of them suffered death or injury, including some medical staff taking part in the second of the two airborne landings who died when their glider crashed into the sea. This left the MDS of the 16th Battalion, the Parachute Regiment, struggling to deal with 109 British and thirty-eight German casualties on the first day.[24] Lessons were learned from this episode: principally that airborne medical units needed to be relieved of their casualties at the earliest opportunity as they could only land with limited supplies and equipment. During the invasion of the Italian mainland this was much easier to achieve because there were excellent arrangements for evacuation by air. Within weeks of the landings, the Air Medical Transportation Service – a combined operation involving the RAF and USAAF – had managed to evacuate 40,000 British casualties from Italy.[25]

For the invasion of the island it was decided to put extra Field Surgical Units on the hospital ships accompanying the assault to provide support for the troops undertaking a seaborne invasion. The team from No. 58 General Hospital consisted of 'Dad' Hawthorne, the anaesthetist, who had been a sergeant in the Essex Regiment during the First World War, Major James Ross, the surgeon, and Messers Evans and Wagstaff as theatre orderlies. They sailed on HMHS *Amra* and were fortunate enough to avoid the fate of HMHS *Talamba*, which was bombed, despite being clearly marked with white paint and red crosses to avoid being mistaken for anything but a hospital ship.

Stan Fernando, a native of Ceylon, was serving as a junior engineer on board the *Talamba* when disaster struck on 10 July 1943:

> Imagine if you can a large floating craft full of casualties – mostly men wounded in battle and completely incapable of fending for themselves, now imagine that one of this craft is holed and filled with water – one end only. Slowly but steadily this end sinks deeper and deeper while the other end rises up until the once horizontal craft is now in a vertical position.
>
> Is it possible to imagine a worse fate that can happen to human beings already in the agony of desperation due to being incapacitated; and then imagine the whole craft sinking

> into the depths of the Mediterranean? This is just what happened when the German bombed the ill-fated 'Talamba' on that memorable night, I was one of the survivors.[26]

Amongst the staff on the ship were a number of female nurses. Sailing from Tripoli in the early morning of 10 July as part of a vast convoy of ships stretching as far as the eye could see, *Talamba* headed for Syracuse to support the troops beginning the assault and capture of Sicily. During the day a number of casualties were embarked upon the vessel and placed in wards in the ship's holds.

On the evening of 10 July, Fernando had settled down to bed with a good book when, 'We heard the screech of an aero-plane as it raced past with machine guns blasting away and there came a booming voice saying "put those lights out."' A bomb blew a hole in the ship and as men frantically tried to plug the gap, it soon became clear her fate was sealed. Lifeboats were lowered, with the ship's officers ensuring priority was given to the crew and medical personnel. However, 'About the live "cargo" of sick and wounded humans in the ship's holds (converted into hospital wards) nobody had the time or opportunity to worry.'

The men in the lifeboats desperately strove to put clear water between themselves and the sinking vessel, for fear it might drag them down as it sank: 'The sight of this once majestic ship literally standing upright with its bows pointing skywards and all three funnels unbelievably horizontal, one by one the funnels broke adrift and tumbled into the sea and the vessel herself dramatically sank below the water surface taking with her the few hundred doomed and desperate souls to their watery grave.'

Meanwhile, the *Amra* anchored off the beach at Avola, its staff dealing with badly burned casualties from the *Talamba* and other ships that had been hit, and listening to the noise of the bombs failing too close for comfort. Major Ross recalled in his diary:

> We entered the main harbour and anchored among the main vessels of the invasion fleet, the unloading of which was in full swing. Everybody looked out eagerly – the landscape was quite strange to us after the monotonous sands of the Western Desert. Here were hedgerows and trees, orchards

> and glades – how green – we were back in a world we knew – our road went up the valley of the Anapo; in the fields alongside, under the big olive trees, were tents, bivouacs, and vehicles of the numerous units which had arrived before us. The sunburnt soldiers, obviously all the old desert crown, brewing up or washing in their roadside camp, shouted greetings to our fellows speeding by.

The medical personnel who had landed in the Middle East had done so at Port Tewfik or other sites, transferring directly from ship to quay. However, for the invasion of Sicily, many would have a seaborne entry to the island. Private Frank Turton, an accomplished swimmer, had the job of teaching the non-swimmers in No. 132 Field Ambulance some basic technique. This training was undertaken in a pool of one of the more luxurious hotels in Cairo. Turton contracted pleurisy while on board the SS *Princess Kathleen* en route from North Africa to Sicily. He was given the option of returning to Africa on the ship but could not bear the thought of abandoning his comrades as they undertook the next phase of their war operations. His loyalty was rewarded as Major Mark Lindsey MC organised support for him to make his way up the landing beach, the officer even carrying the extra medical pack that Turton should have conveyed.

Once a beachhead had been secured, men of No. 58 General Hospital were quick to set up a hospital on land. Sergeant Charles Quant recalled, 'By this time we were darned good at it and within hours of setting foot on the beach we had the nucleus of a hospital established and going.'[27] The X-ray department was established in an old stone-built wine press in a lemon orchard in Floridia and casualties soon poured in. 'It was perhaps the slickest operation we ever achieved,' recalled Quant before the unit moved on to Etna.

While at the beachhead, an incident occurred involving General Montgomery, Commander of the Eighth Army, who had asked the colonel in charge of No. 58 GH to nominate three female nursing sisters to go ashore at a very early stage of the assault and work in the Field Dressing Station and Casualty Clearing Station, in rough and ready conditions.

Montgomery had also issued a General Order that any nurses in front-line areas must wear battledress, not their usual white dresses and head veils. He came ashore for a quick inspection and saw the three sisters standing in white dresses by a batch of stretchers containing wounded men. Quant recalled:

> He changed colour and sent for them. They came and stood at attention in front of him. He asked if they had not seen his General Order about dress. One of them said they had. She went on, 'But if a wounded man who may be dying on a stretcher sees a nurse bending over him in a white dress with a veil round her hair, not a crumpled battle dress, he is more likely to live than die – Sir.'
>
> Monty stood silent for a long time then said, 'You have made your point Sister. Thank you very much,' and went on with the rest of his inspection.

Moving on to Giarre, on the eastern coast of the island on the lower slopes of Etna, where a hospital was located in an old school building, Quant was introduced to anaesthetist Major Jock Harbord, who was impressed with how the X-ray department was operating.

> A fine officer absorbed in his work which was very interesting for they were delighted to use our depth localisation technique for finding bullets or shrapnel or bits of land mine embedded in the brain. They said that if they could get a casualty into the theatre within twenty minutes of being hit they could very often find the foreign body and save his life.

One particular case involved a Canadian with a penetration wound of the skull. Such wounds were usually dealt with by administering a local anaesthetic into the skin of the skull. In this case the surgeon, a Canadian, had drilled the hole and was talking to the patient, mainly to keep his confidence. Quant was standing by listening and waiting for a request for another picture with his portable set.

Suddenly it emerged during the dialogue that the surgeon and patient had been on opposite sides in the same ice hockey match in Ottawa just before they joined their army. Fortuitously, the patient lived and was sent back to base in Alexandria with the bullet duly wrapped in a bit of gauze. 'In fact, anybody who survived like that almost invariably asked for the bullet or shrapnel, and we often gave them a spare X-ray film.'

Arthur Atkin's arrival in Sicily in late 1943 was smoother than he and his comrades in No. 140 Field Ambulance had anticipated. Having embarked on the SS *City of Canterbury* equipped with landing craft, expecting to make a beach landing with assault troops, they found that the advance party had been so successful that they were able to sail straight into Syracuse harbour and disembark at the quayside. They then faced forced marches under a blazing sun to join the advance elements of the brigade. Although the condensed rations were adequate to meet the men's nutritional needs, Atkin recalled frequently suffering from thirst during the heat of the day. To avert dehydration men availed themselves of the citrus delights available from lemon and orange groves. Gorging on fruit was not without its side effects: 'John Piggott, my bivouac partner, ate so many he was violently sick. I recall discovering an enormous mulberry tree during a rest period and for a number of us khaki was subsequently well stained with purple.'[28]

As the unit began receiving casualties, Atkin was placed on resuscitation duties, using a plasma drip and keeping patients warm by means of a heater under a stretcher on trestles with a blanket draped to the floor.

Once the conquest of Sicily was secured, medical units followed the fighting troops onto the Italian mainland. Although often immune from direct enemy shelling, the force of nature could sometimes prove a challenge for medics working in General Hospitals. Charles Quant recalled being stationed in the Bay of Naples when Mount Vesuvius erupted on 17 March 1944:

> [The volcano] spouted sheets of flame, vast red hot boulders and millions of tons of black ash which spread across the sky and turned the day to near night, and gave us the task of our lives for at this time we were filling fast with casualties and the ash was pouring onto the rough old roofs, buckling them and threatening to collapse them onto the men on their stretchers and beds.
>
> We improvised a kind of squeegee – poles with bits of plank nailed across at the end and went up on our roofs

> and pushed the ash down. I don't remember for how long this went on, many days, maybe a week or more, until the black rain stopped and we could come down and start clearing paths through the feet-deep layer on all the roads. But we got it done and went on with our healing and patching up of the men who never ceased to come in on the ambulances.

Throughout the grind of the Italian campaign, Christian rituals kept men's hearts and minds close to home. No. 58 General Hospital was established in a convent school in Nocera, 12 miles south-east of Naples, during Christmas 1943. 'We had Christmas 1943 there and a very moving carol service in the old arched halls with the Sisters in their red cloaks dug out for the occasion, processing from one room to another. I saw many men weeping.'[29]

No. 226 Field Ambulance benefitted from a padre attached to the unit. Captain Leslie Collier recalled, 'He was a lovely man. He was a RC padre and he had his own bottle of gin which he labelled "the high priest's bottle". He joined in all the fun and was altogether a very fine character.' One day, as Collier and the padre were walking to the nearest village, they came across a priest and stopped to chat. As a competent linguist, Collier was delighted to hear the men converse in fluent Latin, as the British padre did not speak Italian and the native priest knew no English.

Operation Shingle, as the landings at Anzio and Nettuno were codenamed, began on 22 January 1944. This was to be a surprise amphibious attack, which experienced initial success of capturing a German garrison of 1,180 troops. However, a failure to capitalise with a drive towards Rome meant that by the end of January, 100,000 German troops encircled the 76,400 Allied troops on the Anzio bridgehead. Further attempts to advance were ruthlessly repulsed and on 3 February, the Germans launched a counter-attack aimed at driving the Allies back into the sea.

Captain Jenkin Thompson was the son of a doctor and had studied medicine at King's College Hospital, London from 1928–33. Married with two children, Thompson had already performed heroics at Dunkirk on board HMHS *Paris* and during the landings at Sicily. At Anzio, he made the ultimate sacrifice while on duty on board HMHS *St David*. He was awarded a posthumous George Cross for his work, his citation reading:

> At Anzio aboard the rapidly sinking vessel 'St. David' he organised parties to remove all the wounded to safety in nearby boats. Finally, when all were ordered to save themselves, Thompson returned alone, to almost certain death, to the one remaining patient who was still trapped below deck. Captain Thompson remained with this man and both perished together when the ship went down.[30]

William Earl of the No. 214 Field Ambulance was stationed in a Casualty Collection Point in a series of little gullies, about 70 feet deep and 150 feet wide, under constant threat from German fire. Earl recalled:

> The fighting was intense and nasty. There were few lulls during which we could collect the wounded, so it was agreed that twice a day, once in the morning after the night fighting, and once in the evening before it got dark, two orderlies would stand up in the gully and hold up a great big Red Cross. They'd stay like that until the Germans noticed and stopped shelling. That was our cue to rush out and collect the injured. When we got them all back to the C.C.P., the flag would be lowered and the shelling would start again.[31]

On one occasion, the shelling stopped and Earl was commanded, with other medical orderlies, to go through the German front lines to collect Allied wounded. This was a hazardous endeavour, as there had been reports of some stretcher-bearers having been taken prisoner, accused of spying. Earl's sergeant ordered his men not to look down to the ground when past the German line in case they saw something that would lead to arrest. Earl and his comrades stared straight ahead, not acknowledging any eye contact with the enemy, collected the wounded, and evacuated as quickly as possible.

The British medical area on the Anzio beachhead lay on sloping fields, about 300 yards off the right-hand side of the main Anzio–Rome road,

3 miles inland. Further north, a Casualty Clearing Station was situated, and on the other side of the road, a Field Dressing Station. Major James Ross arrived on 7 February 1944, two weeks into the battle, and by 8 February he was working through the night operating on casualties. The average time between the wounding and the operation was seven hours, with many men having received multiple wounds from machine-gun, shell and mortar fire. Icy gales slowed down the fighting and the evacuation of wounded had to be stopped, so Ross's CCS became full. The tented area became a sea of mud, in the midst of which stretcher cases had to be placed. Ross described the continual flow of bodies – those wounded and those working – through the CCS:

> Figures in greatcoats, tin-hats, and gas cape-waterproofs, dripping and mire-stained, stumbled in through the doorway, kicking aside the sodden blanket curtain, carrying in the wounded on their stretchers. The theatre stretcher-bearers were continually coming in from the theatre corridor, bringing patients just operated on back in to await the duty ambulance which would bear them away to the post-operation wards. The blood transfusion orderlies hurried about, carrying the transfusion stands, the bottles of blood and the plasma, the needles and rubber tubes for administering these fluids. The CCS MOs who, before the Field Transfusion Unit arrived, took turns to act as resuscitation officers, were continually bending over the patients and fixing the needles of the transfusion apparatuses in the veins and keeping the flow going once it had started.[32]

The wounded lay in two rows, caked in mud and blood and with the field dressings applied at the Regimental Aid Posts or Advanced Dressing Stations. Many were brought in at the point of near-death:

> with gross combinations of shattered limbs, protrusions of intestines and brain from great holes in their poor frames torn by 88-mm shells, mortars and anti-personnel bombs. Some lying quiet and still, with legs drawn up – the penetrating wounds of the abdomen. Some carried in sitting up on the stretchers, gasping and coughing, shot through the lungs.

1. *Above left*: Charles Quant of No. 58 General Hospital with Hypo the dog. (*Courtesy of the Quant family*)

2. *Above right*: Frank Turton of No. 132 Field Ambulance. (*Courtesy of Kay Turton*)

3. *Below left*: John Broom of No. 7 Light Field Ambulance and No. 2 Light Field Ambulance. (*Author's collection*)

4. *Below right*: Geoffrey Haine of No. 34 General Hospital and No. 49 Field Surgical Unit. (*Courtesy of Michael Haine*)

5. A tented Surgical Theatre of No. 49 FSU. (*Courtesy of Michael Haine*)

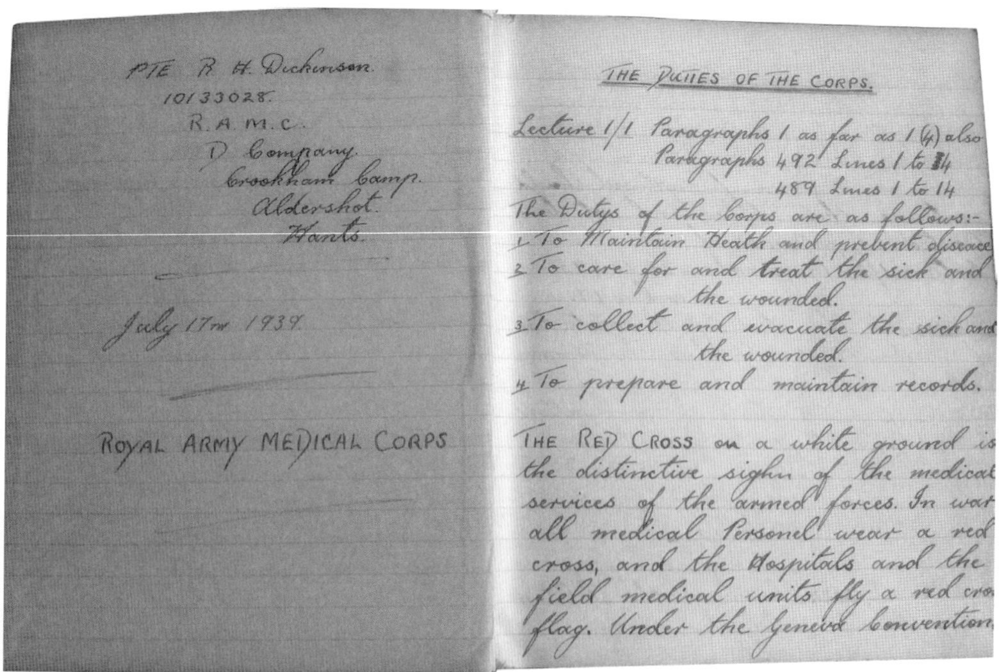

PTE R. H. Dickinson.
10133028.
R.A.M.C.
D Company.
Crookham Camp.
Aldershot.
Hants.

July 17th 1939.

ROYAL ARMY MEDICAL CORPS

THE DUTIES OF THE CORPS.

Lecture 1/1 Paragraphs 1 as far as 1(4) also
Paragraphs 492 Lines 1 to 14
489 Lines 1 to 14

The Dutys of the Corps are as follows:-
1 To Maintain Heath and prebent disease
2 To care for and treat the sick and the wounded.
3 To collect and evacuate the sick and the wounded.
4 To prepare and maintain records.

THE RED CROSS on a white ground is the distinctive sighn of the medical services of the armed forces. In war all medical Personel wear a red cross, and the Hospitals and the field medical units fly a red cross flag. Under the Geneva Convention

6. Notes taken during initial training in 1939 by Ron Dickinson. (*Courtesy of Ron Dickinson*)

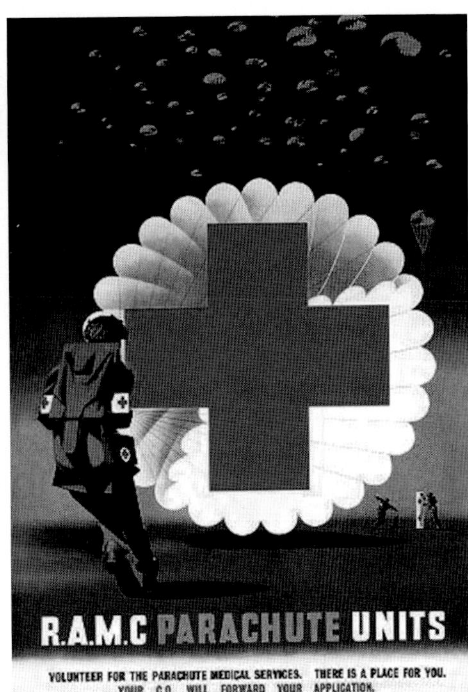

7. *Above left*: Ron Dickinson of No. 11 Field Ambulance. (*Courtesy of Ron Dickinson*)

8. *Above right*: RAMC Parachute Units volunteer poster. (*Author's collection*)

9. *Right*: Forde Cayley of No. 11 General Hospital. (*Courtesy of Michael Cayley*)

10. *Above left*: Stanley Cross of No. 150 Field Ambulance. (*Courtesy of Shelia Cox*)

11. *Above middle*: George Mussared, an early casualty of the war, forever remembered by his loving family. (*Courtesy of Laura Kitson*)

12. *Above right*: Alex Bremner of No. 183 Field Ambulance. (*Courtesy of Second World War Experience Centre*)

13. Staff of No. 49 Field Surgical Unit. (*Courtesy of Michael Haine*)

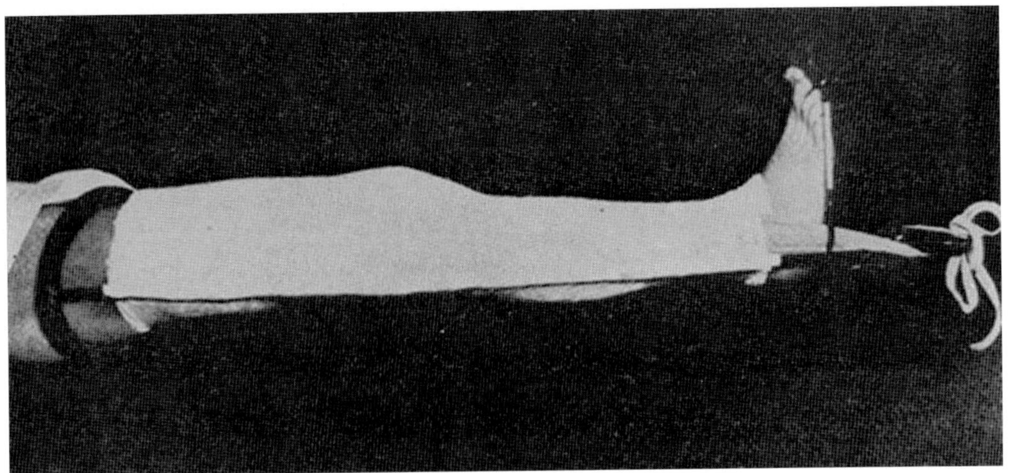

14. A Tobruk plaster, an adaptation of a Thomas splint, stabilising a leg fracture during transportation. (*Author's collection*)

15. An ambulance under attack in the desert. (*Author's collection*)

16. A Regimental Aid Post in Libya. (*Author's collection*)

17. Charles Warner (centre) operating on a wounded man in Libya. (*Courtesy of Second World War Experience Centre*)

18. *Above left*: Paul Watts of No. 6 Light Field Ambulance. (*Courtesy of Richard Watts*)

19. *Above right*: Norman Jevons. (*Courtesy of Richard Jevons*)

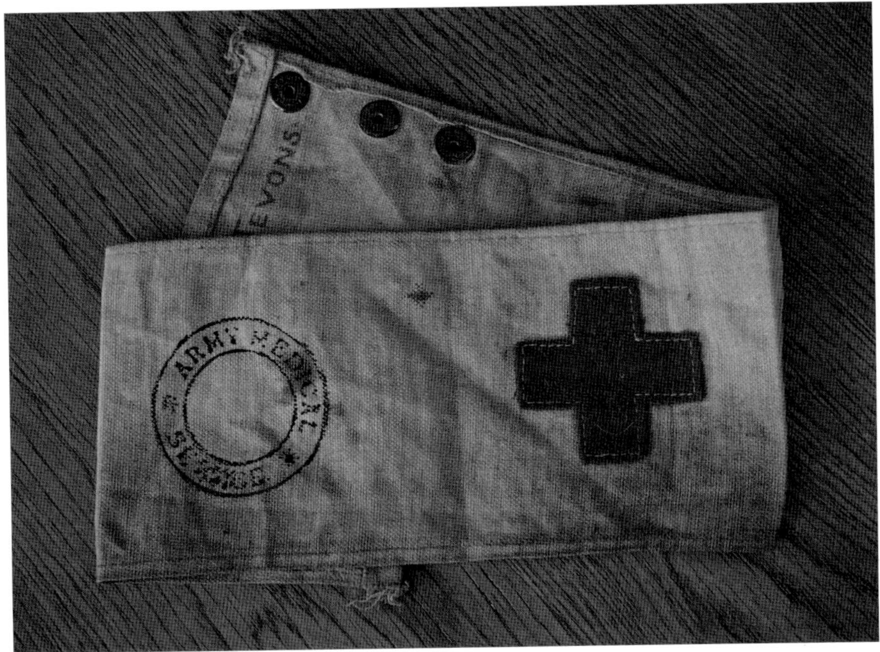

20. The Red Cross brassard, which probably saved Norman Jevons' life. (*Courtesy of Richard Jevons*)

21. Paul Adler of 13th Nyasa Battalion, Kings African Rifles and No. 6 Field Ambulance, with his wife, Margaret. (*Courtesy of Paul Adler*)

22. Bert Swingler of No. 93 General Hospital. (*Courtesy of Joan Willetts*)

23 & 24. *Above and below*: Sketches made in Italy by Arthur Atkin of No. 140 Field Ambulance. (*Author's collection*)

25. *Left*: Fred Cannell of No. 9 General Hospital. (*Courtesy of Vera Cannell*)

26. *Below*: Christmas celebrations 1945 at No. 9 General Hospital, Ranchi. (*Courtesy of Vera Cannell*)

27. *Above left*: Tom Leak, whose hopes of an early release as a PoW were dashed.

28. *Above right*: Desmond Whyte of No. 11 Field Ambulance. (*Author's collection*)

29. a & b. *Above left and above right*: David Jebbitt of No. 181 Airlanding Field Ambulance, before and after a year as a PoW. (*Courtesy of Stuart Jebbitt*)

30 & 31. *Above and below*: Ink drawings created by Gerald Hitchcock of No. 198 Field Ambulance during his time as a prisoner of the Japanese. (*Courtesy of Second World War Experience Centre*)

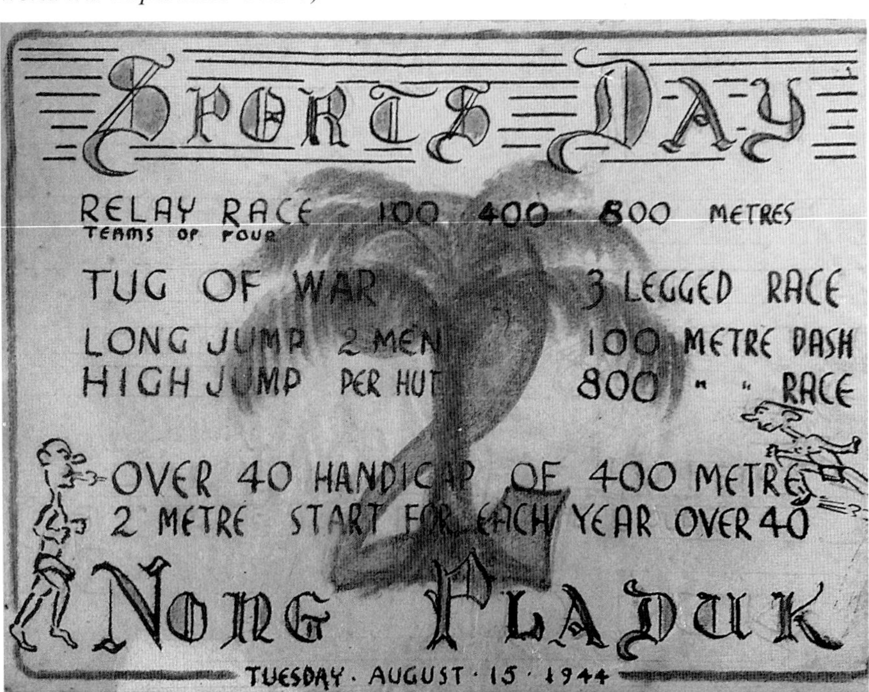

32. David Paton, Medical Officer with No. 2 Commando Unit. (*Author's collection*)

33. Engraving from *Red Devils*, an account of No. 224 (Parachute) Field Ambulance in Normandy. (*Courtesy of the Museum of Military Medicine*)

34. Casualty evacuation by jeep over Caen Canal, 1944. (*Author's collection*)

35. Jim Whitaker of No. 203 Field Ambulance. (*Courtesy of Second World War Experience Centre*)

36. Members of No. 133 (Parachute) Field Ambulance living rough to evade capture. (*Courtesy of Second World War Experience Centre*)

37. *Above left*: Eric Harden VC. (*Courtesy of Gravesend Borough Council*)

38. *Above right*: The only Second World War RAMC gravestone to bear the Victoria Cross. (*Courtesy of Julia Harden-Wells*)

39. Members of No. 11 Light Field Ambulance, including Clarence Smith (right) inspect the damage caused by a German aerial attack on Belsen concentration camp. (*Courtesy of Colin Culpitt-Smith*)

40 & 41 & 42. *Above and below*: The degradation of humanity that greeted medical personnel entering Belsen Concentration Camp. (*Courtesy of Second World War Experience Centre*)

> Others, less badly wounded perhaps, looking round with curious eyes, falling back on to their stretchers at the sights that met them there.[33]

Surgeons faced agonising choices of prioritising the wounded. An abdominal case would take at least an hour to operate on, with perhaps only a fifty-fifty chance of success, whilst a limb wound might take a quarter of that time. However, the abdomen case, if left, would face certain death and therefore no such patients went without treatment during those days on the Anzio beachhead. Most difficult of all was the decision to turn down a man for treatment when his gross wounds meant he was beyond all aid. For Ross, this felt like signing his death warrant, but not to do so would have potentially wasted precious resources for an unattainable goal. Nevertheless, most were prepared for surgery as it was better to have a death on the operating table than watch a man's life ebb away as he went untreated.

Occasionally, a second opinion would provide salvation in these cases. One morning, Ross was undertaking a pre-operation round, assigning the order of his patients when he heard a voice ask, 'What about me? I've been waiting twenty-four hours.' Ross examined the man's field card, which gave the diagnosis of a penetrating chest and abdomen wound. He had then been put on resuscitation and left, considered beyond the period when an operation stood any chance of success. Ross told the man he was not yet ready to be operated on. The patient looked round at the stretchers on either side of him, on which lay the corpses of those who had been left to die. He said 'I see', and lay back on his blankets and closed his eyes.

Ross was troubled by this conversation and gave the man an examination, concluding that the rigidity of his muscles was not due to the abdominal injury, but to the irritation of multiple fragments of shrapnel. Having had the man X-rayed, it was revealed that no operation was required beyond a minor cleaning, with no anaesthetic needed. The man was wheeled away to the evacuation ward, 'his face transformed, literally snatched from the jaws of death, in his opinion'.

As Lance Corporal Arthur Atkin approached Anzio with No. 140 Field Ambulance, 'we had the illusion of a peaceful intact town, but on landing, this proved to be little more than hollow shells and rubble.'[34] The weather had degenerated into cold wind and drizzle, and the medics experienced considerable shelling during their first night on land. The following day, much time was spent erecting the large tents, which were to form their headquarters, only to be told to take them down and move back to the sea front. 'It took much ingenuity to dig a hole as protection against enemy action and erect a bivouac over this that would stay put against the elements.' The nature of the Battle of Anzio, with its fluctuating advance and retreat, meant that Atkin's unit had to react to a fluid situation. They were ordered forward to take over a battle MDS, perilously close to the front line before dropping back to operate as a CCS. This latter hospital was situated in a flat, open expanse with no natural cover, creating 'shockingly cold' conditions for the medics and their patients.

Atkin was allocated to a resuscitation base in a marquee, which was soon packed with wounded men. As the rest of the CCS was also overwhelmed with demand, operating theatres were unable to take the cases that had been resuscitated, so the unit's commanding officer quickly assessed the situation and worked alongside Atkin in the base for the remainder of the day. Just after midnight, having finally cleared the resuscitation base, the orderlies packed up their equipment, only for the tent to leak and then collapse. In the pitch black and against a howling wind, it was a struggle to re-erect it. The following day the tent was rearranged as a holding ward for the overflow of men from the rest of the CCS. Nerves were not helped by the news recorded by Atkin: 'Hear of dive-bombing attack on an American Evacuation Hospital – some sisters and other nursing staff killed.'[35]

A few days later, on 26 February 1944, several waves of enemy planes attacked the area around the hospital, and Atkin was forced to take shelter in a bivvy hole, emerging to find a number of anti-personnel shells had been dropped within the medical area, leaving heavy casualties. Atkin was directed to treat the walking wounded, and found the department full of German casualties. After clearing these, he settled down to sleep on a stretcher, only to be woken at midnight by an intensive air attack. Unexploded bombs were found in the hospital tents, although by a miracle, no one was seriously hurt. Atkin and Piggot were moved forward to an ADS. Their ambulance orderlies were injured and their stretcher-bearer, Private Arnold Evans, was killed. Following this action, Atkin returned to unit headquarters and 140th Field Ambulance drove down to Anzio in their lorries and embarked on their Landing Ship

Tanks. The Germans gave them a farewell, 'German guns send over a few close ones as we pull out.'[36]

From 17 January to 18 May 1944, a series of assaults by the Allies were made against the Winter Line, with the intention of making a breakthrough to Rome. The western half of this line, comprising the Rapido-Gari, Liri and Garigliano valleys formed the Gustav Line. Monte Cassino, a historic hilltop abbey founded in AD 529 by Benedict of Nursia, dominated the nearby town of Cassino and the entrances to the Liri and Rapido valleys. Lying in a protected historic zone, it had been left unoccupied by the Germans, although they manned some positions set into the steep slopes below the abbey's walls.

Repeated pinpoint artillery attacks on Allied assault troops caused senior officers to conclude the abbey was being used as a German observation post. Therefore, on 15 February, American bombers dropped 1,400 tons of high explosives, creating widespread damage. The raid failed to achieve its objective, as German paratroopers occupied the rubble and established excellent defensive positions amid the ruins. From January to May, Monte Cassino was assaulted four times by Allied troops, and the German defenders were finally driven from their positions, but at a high cost. The capture of Monte Cassino resulted in 55,000 Allied casualties, with German losses being far fewer, estimated at about 20,000 killed and wounded.

No. 58 General Hospital was allocated an area of several fields near the village of San Felice, situated on one side of a hill system, with Cassino across the river on the other side. The ferocity of the fighting caused the hospital to be inundated with men from many sections of the Allied forces. Charles Quant recalled:

> Time after time the allied armies launched assaults by day and night against the steep, rocky shoulders of Monte Cassino which had a large monastery on top. Every assault brought us a fresh flood of wounded, of both sides. We now had Eighth Army, First Army … the American Army … and contingents from the Free French, including Moroccan Goums and Spahis and Foreign Legion, Canadians, Kiwis and other smaller national groups.
>
> We took the lot and patched them up before onwarding them back. Many would never have made it but for the rare

> combination of first aid and the sophisticated investigations and treatment they got in 58, as I think the finest justification for the judgement of the admin who decided to create mobile hospitals … as close as possible to the battle front.[37]

Captain Norman Jevons was a medical officer of an Anglo-French unit who had been tasked with transporting food, water and ammunition by mule to forward troops in the mountains of central Italy. They were based in a small wood facing Monte Cassino and on their right flank was an Italian unit, the country having recently moved over to the Allied side as co-belligerents. One morning, Jevons was getting ready to visit one of the company when a corporal entered his tent with the announcement 'King Umberto's here sir'. Jevons asked the corporal to let the colonel know. 'Colonel's out.' 'Well tell the adjutant.' 'He's out too. You're the only officer here.' Umberto had been looking for the Italian troops nearby and had come across Jevons' unit first. He donned his hat and emerged into a small clearing where the uniformed king, three Italian officers and a gentleman in civilian clothes were standing.

Jevons felt himself on the horns of a dilemma. Should he, as a British Army officer, salute the king of a former enemy, now a co-belligerent but not a full ally, or should the head of state of a former enemy salute an officer in the British Army? Jevons felt the eyes of a dozen of his own troops fixed upon him, eager to see who would salute first. Walking towards the group of Italians:

> I wondered if anyone in the War Office had ever thought of this situation and whether there was anything in King's Regulations about it. The moment came when a decision had to be made and I decided to salute. The King had evidently sensed the situation for at precisely the same split second he saluted too. Honour on both sides was satisfied.[38]

Jevons and King Umberto chatted pleasantly in English before the latter moved on to find his unit.

No. 132 Field Ambulance had an optometry surgical unit attached as the rocky terrain around Cassino meant that explosions caused the shattering of rock and the risk of fragmentary injuries. The medical staff had little respite over the Christmas period of 1944, with Private

Frank Turton on extended stretcher-bearing duties during that time, transporting wounded men from the Lancashire Fusiliers. A chestnut paling path, known sardonically as the 'Sunshine Trail', made walking up the muddy ground a little easier. A white tape was laid out along the hillside and stretcher-bearers were advised not to raise their head above the level of the tape for fear of snipers. Despite this, the unit sustained a handful of casualties. Eventually the men were rewarded for their efforts with an extra tot of rum and piece of fruit cake on Christmas Day. Christmas dinner had to wait until some days later but was gratefully received when finally served.

Before moving up the Italian peninsula to experience what he would describe 75 years later as the hell of Monte Cassino, Corporal Ron Dickinson and his comrades in No. 11 Field Ambulance had bedded down between rows of vineyards during their first night in the country. Unable to resist gorging on the succulent grapes after many months in the North African desert, many medical staff had to suffer the indignity of reporting sick the following day with the intestinal after-effects of their impromptu feast. This amusing interlude would soon be forgotten as the unit experienced 'hell on earth' at Cassino. Being placed in a forward area, Dickinson felt that he was in double danger, both from enemy action and RAF attempts to bomb the Axis front line. One medical casualty was a lad who went to fill a water tank and was shot: 'We thought we were protected by wearing the red cross, but that was poppycock.' During Operation Grapeshot, in the spring of 1945, Dickinson accompanied three infantry troops undertaking a recce in the hilly terrain of the Po Valley. Shells rained over them from both directions. Heavy rain had made the ground sodden, a fact Dickinson considered a 'blessing' as the four men were able to throw themselves down on it for shelter, and the mud absorbed much of the shrapnel blasts. Despite this, 'I got my fair amount of shrapnel' in addition to suffering some temporary hearing loss due to the intensity of the shelling. 'I had the bells of St Mary's ringing in my ears for two weeks.' Dickinson was flown back to No. 65 General Hospital in Naples as the war in Europe drew to an end. After a two-week recovery period, he was offered the chance to remain in Naples as the hospital was short-staffed, but he opted to return to the unit he had served with since the autumn of 1939.

Private Jack Forster had been transferred from No. 58 General Hospital to No. 1 Field Ambulance. He bemoaned the loss of the editorship of

The Odyssey, a journal produced by the hospital staff, but found solace in the comradeship of his new unit. He wrote to the publication to tell his old comrades of his progress:

> There is a grand esprit de corps in this unit. There is no Officers' Mess, Sergeants' Mess owing to the 'exigencies of the service'. The cooks are super ACC blokes, and the grub plentiful. I miss the old crowd, but most of all I miss ODYSSEY. I had never realised how much the old rag had stimulated the printing ink in my veins.

Forster had been transferred to his new unit by an American Field Service driver. He was driven through Cassino, then 5 miles further on they saw a sign advising 'This road is under shell fire'. The driver informed Forster there was another 4 miles to travel to reach No. 1 Field Ambulance HQ. 'With a queer sort of emptiness in my stomach, I asked, "That's pretty close to the line?" "Sure thing – right in the line, and if you don't watch out you get sniped or some damn thing."' Forster arrived at a small house that was acting as a forward Advanced Dressing Station for the unit and was interviewed by a Major Field:

> Casualties were coming in quite quickly in the little jeep carriers; and, whilst most of the work here is unloading the jeeps, carrying the patients into the ADS and carrying them out after dressing on to an ambulance, there are some real jobs to do inside. I was roped in on the latter staff and started working with an MO right away. There were some severe stomach wounds … and one or two traumatic amputations, but generally they were deep fleshy wounds that looked bad but that, as we know, respond to treatment.
>
> Although shells were falling uncomfortably near, I was too busy to feel much fear. The report from our own guns was deafening, and planes (identity unknown) could be heard overhead. As night crept on, the battle became more intense, and wounded come pouring in, yet they all said things were going well and so we worked all night, and by dawn Jerry had been pushed off another hill.

Forster was then transferred on to night duty in the MDS. 'Well, we were right up with the Infantry, but Jerry was moving at full speed, and upon reaching two successive locations we were told not to open. The third move brought some excitement. Our location was in the mountains, and as our convoy moved up the tortuous road, it became evident we were the first vehicles up.'

The men were forced to fill in holes in the road in order to be able to continue their advance. On reaching the summit their endeavour was rewarded as they came across twenty German soldiers who immediately surrendered.

Following the breakthrough at Monte Cassino, the 200 beds in No. 58 General Hospital were added to with anything a man could lie on, as hundreds more patients were brought in. As the unit pushed on to Trasimeno, further casualties were admitted from fighting around Arezzo. One significant admission was a man carried in on a door having been transported on the back of a jeep. Sergeant Quant noted he was a 'red-tabbed officer of high rank surrounded by staff officers who in the absence of our radiologist treated me like dirt'. Quant insisted on treating the man on the spot, and the first X-rays showed that he had extensive crush fractures of his lumbar spine. Quant began to pack sandbags beneath the small of his back to prevent it collapsing.

Astonishingly, one of the staff officers ordered Quant to stop as he was not an officer, but he continued his work. When the radiologist returned the staff officer complained that the general had been handled by 'an other rank'. The radiologist, a major, said that in his absence the entire X-ray was under the absolute control of the radiographer and that Quant's swift action had probably saved the general's life. 'Exit the general on his door and his retinue.'

Years later, Quant heard a radio appeal for the Forces Mental Welfare Society in which the speaker paid tribute to the vital help he had been given beside Lake Trasimeno. He was Field Marshal Gerald Templer, whose back had been broken when a truck had run over a mine and blown up, its rear wheel sailing through the air and crushing him against the steering wheel of his jeep. Remaining conscious, Templer turned to his ADC, Humphrey Hare, and said, 'Humphrey, get a door from that cottage, and strap me to it.'

'But Sir, it's through the minefield.'

'I know that you bloody fool. Too bad!'[39]

The orders were followed and after diagnosis of a compound fracture of the first lumbar vertebra, Templer was evacuated back to a base hospital in Naples, where his back was set and encased in plaster.

Quant also came into contact with prominent head, belly and maxillofacial army surgeons, taking X-rays to support their work. Anti-personnel landmines would usually demolish a man's legs, but would also often tear through the genitals and belly and even up to the face. There were many admissions to No. 58 General Hospital whose lower jaws had been blown away, and the maxillofacial surgeons would begin the reconstruction by slowly building up the new lower jaws with bits of bone from other parts of the body, particularly the pelvic arch. Quant considered such surgery 'miracle-working'.

Quant also found himself on the cusp of taking part in further potentially innovative work. Soon after the unit arrived in Florence, Colonel King, the Director of Radiology for the Mediterranean area, paid a visit to the hospital. He requested that Quant begin to start designing a mobile X-ray that could be placed in the nose of a glider and taken on an airborne assault. It was to be tested over the marshes close to Venice, as General Alexander was planning an airborne assault to get behind some stubborn German defences. As Quant began the design work, there was a virtual end to the fighting in Italy, so the plans for a mobile airborne hospital were put on hold.

Casualties from the Italian campaign were also treated on board hospital ships, such as the SS *Toscana*, a vessel captured from the Italians in December 1943. Pressed into service as a resource for No. 93 General Hospital, it soon began to accommodate an influx of wounded men. At the end of January 1944, Private Bert Swingler (Pic 22), whose wartime correspondence to his family exuded a generally chirpy and carefree disposition, recorded in a personal diary his grim experience of being a night duty orderly on board the *Toscana*:

> [I] am having a pretty rough time of it as things are pretty busy and there are plenty of rough cases to look after. I had my first experience of handling a dying man on the night of 8–9th of this month when a Corporal passed away from injuries. Surprised myself with the frame of mind in which

> I took that and all these other terrible wounds and injuries but think that is because there are so many. Spent a pretty sober Xmas and New Year as I couldn't take risk of getting drunk on this job.[40]

One major problem facing the Allied armies in Italy was venereal disease, especially in cities such as Rome and Naples, and the rate for both syphilis and gonorrhoea was extremely high. Captain Leslie Collier of No. 226 Field Ambulance was appointed as temporary medical officer to troops being transported by ship from Liverpool to Naples. As part of his duties he gave a lecture on health hazards in Italy, particularly focusing on venereal disease:

> I delivered what I thought was quite a good lecture covering every aspect of it and at the end of it [I asked the 200 or 300 troops] 'Are there any questions?' and there was a deadly silence. Then one hand went up. I said 'Yes?' and he said 'What is the rate of exchange of the Lira Sir?' So that was the amount of interest they showed. No wonder they all got VD later on.[41]

Having had a smooth landing at Syracuse Bay, No. 140 Field Ambulance moved up to the hilltop town of Taormina, commanding fine views of Mount Etna, remaining there for a period of some weeks. This allowed Arthur Atkin to obtain some paints and other art equipment in order to record the sights in pictorial form. (Pic 23) The stunning landscape and comforts of artistic creation were in stark contrast to the effects of warfare. Atkin was in a section manning a medical post that was open to civilians and was faced with the tragic consequences of children having strayed into minefields that had not been cleared. The treatment of Italian civilians continued once the unit had crossed the Straits of Messina and had set up a Main Dressing Station in Sessa Aurunca, a small town north of Naples.

One day a very young boy named Antonio was brought in with convulsions and a high temperature. This was soon diagnosed as being the result of tetanus infection, and Atkin and his comrade, John Piggott, alternated shifts to nurse him. (Pic 24) Antonio was placed in a darkened room that was kept as quiet as possible, with the administration of paraldehyde to control the spasms. Although the unit was dealing with other civilian cases, Antonio remained Atkin's and Piggott's main concern. Eventually, the boy's condition improved, and they were congratulated by their CO on 'a remarkable medical achievement'.[42] Antonio was taken back to his home, only for Atkin to discover that his elder sister, Lena, was very ill with a temperature of 104 degrees. A civilian doctor was called, but only visited her two days later, and three days after that, arrangements were made to send her to a civilian hospital in Naples, there being no anti-typhoid vaccine available locally. 'John and I were appalled at the apathy towards her obviously serious condition though there was little we could do about it.' After heavy action at the Battle of Anzio, No. 140 Field Ambulance was withdrawn from the line and sent to the Naples area for a short rest period. Once they had been issued with new clothing and been entertained by an ENSA concert, Atkin found the Ospedale Cotugno, where Lena had been taken. He was delighted to hear that she had been cured and had returned home.

During the advance through Italy, men from No. 132 Field Ambulance found a warm reception from Italian people. The civlilians complained that the Germans had taken everything from them, including medicines. Many had ailments that had gone untreated for a long time, which the medical staff attended to where possible. The grateful Italians attempted to pay them but the money was refused, so occasionally a bag of chestnuts was received instead as a thank you gift.

No. 226 Field Ambulance, in which Leslie Collier served, had a headquarters consisting of tents. During the Battle of the Gothic Line, which raged in northern Italy from August 1944 to March 1945, large numbers of casualties were received by the unit, whose main job was to triage them. Men would be divided into the walking wounded, those needing resuscitation and patients requiring urgent surgery. Having no facilities for blood transfusions, the most serious cases had to be treated for immediate shock before being evacuated down the line to a CCS as soon as possible. Collier found injuries caused by landmines the most gruesome. 'The Germans had these Teller mines and the box mines and they would blow people's legs off. You would get a chap with just the bones sticking out right down to his ankle. The rest of his leg was gone. They were horrible. We had a number of deaths.'

In between periods of intense action near the front line, intervals of extended leave were granted. Members of No. 140 Field Ambulance, who had seen fierce action at Anzio, were granted an extended leave period, to be spent in Egypt. During this time, they received a further TAB injection (a combined vaccine used to produce immunity against the diseases typhoid, paratyphoid A and paratyphoid B), which left some of them reeling. Arthur Atkin recalled, 'The heat, the headache accompanying the injection reaction, and the loss of sleep on night guard, had many of us staggering around in a sort of zombie trance for a while.'[43] The Cairo hotel in which Atkin and Piggott stayed was rife with insects and they had to be vigilant for pickpockets as 'A brown hand could rifle your pocket in a flash.' What made the visit worthwhile was the opportunity to see the pyramids at Giza, cruise on the river Nile and visit the Zoological Gardens at Shem-el-Nessim. Atkin availed himself of the opportunity to attend classes in drawing and Italian.

By the later stages of the war, the army was taking the education and future employment prospects of its members seriously. The amount of time allocated to training had doubled as the Army Education Corps faced the daunting task of returning a mass army to civilian occupations. Atkin remained unimpressed with how education was organised within No. 140 Field Ambulance: 'An education programme was inaugurated within the unit and John & I were on the initial committee. But the officer in charge tended to ignore all suggestions, and John & I ended up simply being delegated to run a wall newspaper.'[44]

Although nominally on a rest period, men were occasionally detailed to act as ambulance orderlies, delivering medical supplies. This task required constant vigilance: 'On these trips it was necessary to sit in the back of the vehicle with a large broom handle to fend off opportunist marauders whenever the vehicle slowed down for any reason.'[45]

Arthur Atkin returned to war-torn Italy in July 1944, reflecting, when visiting the ancient ruins of Rome's ancient Forum:

> It seemed to me like a great life-threatening convulsion sweeping up the body of Italy, and after its passage a return to near normality. But, with the scars, things can never be quite the same again. Only the ancient ruins standing silently in the moonlight seemed to acknowledge a different time scale and stood aloof to our human conflict.[46]

After visiting the opera, viewing the Colosseum and Sistine Chapel, and experiencing a visit from King George VI and attending an audience with the Pope, Atkin was assigned to convoy duties near Assisi, as his brigade prepared to attack the Gothic Line. Intensive exercises followed, including stretcher-bearing and crossing rivers with casualties using a rope hawser. This caused Atkin to fall sick and he was diagnosed with acute pharyngitis by one of his officers, Captain Weaver. He was sent to a hospital to have a blood film taken and received a further diagnosis of malaria.

Once he had recovered, Atkin advanced further across steep and exhausting country towards the front line, witnessing shellfire across the hills. A brief Sabbath pause allowed for attendance at a Christian service and the writing of letters to loved ones at home before the marching continued.

Danger lurked around every bend, and one incident left a sharp impression on Atkin:

> On a road through an open valley, travelling in a jeep, we had a sudden 'scramble' as a couple of enemy planes appeared, swooping down. We all leapt out and flung ourselves into a ditch on the roadside. The roar and splattering of gunfire crescended and passed in an instant.
>
> As I lifted my head again, my eyes were level with a culvert which ran under the road, some 15" in diameter, and faintly lit from the opposite end. At arm's length in the opening lay a plate with something piled on it and a cloth draped over it. Instinctively my arm stretched out to investigate but was stayed by remembrance of booby-trap warnings. Another thought followed: I could imagine an Italian peasant hurriedly gathering a few personal treasures and placing them here, as the battle threatened to destroy all he had worked for and hoping to return to retrieve something of value with which to start again.
>
> I left the plate untouched and returned to our vehicle which fortunately had not been damaged.

It was not just the enemy that men had to be vigilant against. Paul Watts was acutely aware of the threat of disease spreading through the war-ravaged land:

> Of course conditions in the country are worse now than in peace-time as there are so many dead cattle and horses all

> over the place. We haven't the time to dispose of them as we are far too busy looking after our own men. That's the worst of being up with the forward troops, there is no time to clean the place up and of course all these dead things are ideal breeding places for flies which means more disease.[47]

Progress became slow, with many diversions and minor attacks, until on 5 September 1944, Arthur Atkin's ambulance was attacked by a barrage. In a lull, he found Lieutenant Briggs badly injured with a penetrating chest wound, but nothing could be done for 23-year-old driver, Fred Chalk. The former was sent back in the ambulance and a burial service was held on the spot for the latter. A second barrage was encountered on the main road forward from Morciano, with Atkin treating casualties at a crossroads, before an advance on foot in moonlight to a farmhouse on the side of a hill that was the designated Regimental Aid Post. Under frequent Spandau and mortar fire, badly mutilated men were brought in on stretchers from the jeep-head throughout the day. Later, prisoners of war were used for stretcher-bearing.

Moving back to work at the CCS, Atkin found that the tent had taken a direct hit, and the station was moved back to Morciano. Intermittent shelling continued, and Atkin's recently acquired language skills were utilised to explain to an elderly couple that their rooms were now required as an extra medical space. As well as military casualties, the CCS was busy with civilian treatments. The No. 140 Field Ambulance's ADS was situated in a schoolhouse, performing blood transfusions amidst heavy shelling, before, in mid-September, an advance was made through San Savino and Mulazzano. It was then announced that, due to the heavy losses sustained during the previous weeks, 168th Brigade would cease to exist, and therefore No. 140 Field Ambulance would no long be part of 56th Division.

Atkin was put to work in a surgical dressing room in a Divisional Dressing Centre in Cesena. In order to treat an increase in skin infections among the troops, a programme of autohaemotherapy was introduced, which proved effective in increasing resistance. This procedure, carried out on the queues of men that formed outside the treatment centre, involved taking a syringe of blood from a vein in the arm, then injecting it into the gluteus maximus tissue. The whole process created great hilarity.

Captain Leslie Collier of the No. 226 Field Ambulance was a fluent German speaker, therefore used to have conversations with the walking wounded prisoners who were brought in for treatment. In a disarming manner, he would ask if they had any letters and the names of their commanding officers and was surprised to find them forthcoming. This information would then be passed on to British Army Intelligence. One particular conversation with a German prisoner was noted in a letter to Collier's sister sent on 15 September 1944:

> I had the great pleasure of being able to tell our latest prisoners that the Americans were in Germany, which, as you may imagine, shook them considerably. One young officer said – 'Well I suppose it's nearly over now. After this war, Britain, America and Germany must ally themselves and fight against World Bolshevism.' Planning the next war already! You'd have thought that they'd had enough by now.

In Collier's view, British Army doctors did not prioritise the treatment of their own casualites over those of the enemy:

> You would think there might be a tendency to look after the British soldiers first and to leave the Germans till last, and that was one thing I would never ever do. Everybody got sorted out and dealt with and treated in order of their medical priority and that was the only fact that ever counted, and if a German … needed treatment before a British person he got it.[48]

This equality of service even extended to a wounded SS officer. Collier, being Jewish, had extra reason not to like the man, especially as he started ranting about 'the international Jews and Freemasons and so on'. Collier responded, 'Well, it might surprise you to know that you are being treated by a Jewish doctor,' which produced 'the most extraordinary reaction. He just stared at me and he said "a Jew", and I said "yes", and he started crying. It was really a quite interesting reaction.'[49]

Having spent over a year slogging his way up through Italy, Paul Watts was in no mood to contemplate furthering his war service in the Far East, as the great communicator Winston Churchill misread how his speech would be interpreted by men who had endured years of overseas service:

> There is quite a lot of indignation going round the forces out here about Churchill's recent speech when he said we would help America to beat the Japs as we couldn't let America have all the fun. He just wants to come out here with our little section for just a day and see how this fun affects our men who have been wounded. They certainly don't appreciate fun of that sort. I think that Churchill will have 'had it' as far as peacetime Prime Minister is concerned. He has been a good man as far as the war is concerned but we don't want his sort of rule in peace time. It's not that we mind fighting the Japs; if we are ordered to go we will go. It's just that we object to it being called 'fun'.[50]

However, one final significant engagement awaited Watts, Operation Roast, which was conducted over 1 and 2 April 1945. The 2nd Commando Brigade succeeded in taking a narrow spit of land in the Commachio lagoon, supporting the effort to push the German army back across the river Po and out of Italy altogether:

> I see by the papers that a Commando has been awarded the V.C. and I think from the description, that he must have been killed in the action that we took part in. I couldn't tell you at the time but we have been in with the commandos. Some of the men even had to make landings with the commandos. It was when I was working in that church I told you about and we were making the attacks on Commachio from the lake and the sea and over the River Reno. We had a lot of preparations to make before the show started which accounts for the long time we spent there doing very little. The way up was under observation so the forces had to be built up very slowly so that Jerry wouldn't realise what was

> coming. When we did start it was over very quickly and that was how the final push in Italy started. From there we didn't stop moving until we were well on the way to Venice. Three of our chaps were 'mentioned in dispatches' for their work on Lake Commachio. The village where the church was is called Mandrioli, but I don't think you will find it on the map, it is very small.[51]

For those who had returned to Britain in late 1943 to prepare for the invasion of Northern Europe, the contrast between months or even years spent in the Mediterranean theatre of war and the sharpness of an English winter was striking. Having disembarked at Glasgow in January 1944, John Broom wrote of an otherness that had developed since he had left for the Middle East in the spring of 1942:

> The strangest feeling I experienced was coming down south in the train. To see English civilians was, without exaggeration, like taking a deep breath & plunging one's head in icy water. The rare wonder of it. The feeling that one did not belong, that one was part of the desert, part of lovely Italy with common experiences wholly unknown & unconceived by others, made one feel like men of a different race.[52]

For the men of the RAMC who served in Italy, the country, its landscape, its people and the intensity of the fighting left an indelible impression. For many it held fond memories of friendships made and lives saved, but for others, the recollections were of comrades whose bodies were mangled or blown to pieces, and of the heartbreak of caring for a civilian population left sick in body and soul by the treament they had received from their German allies. The war in the Mediterranean had followed a pattern of retreat, retrenchment and eventual victory. That victory, however, had cost the corps dearly.

Chapter 5

Burma, India and the Far East

The Far East campaign had the longest duration of any fought by British and Commonwealth forces during the Second World War. Beginning in December 1941, with the Japanese invasion of southern Burma, it was only ended with the dropping of the atomic bombs on Hiroshima and Nagasaki in August 1945. An initial ignominious defeat when Singapore fell in February 1942 was turned into an eventual victory via the bitterly fought Battle of Kohima of early summer 1944. The Fourteenth Army relied on the contribution of RAMC units and medical officers for its success. Preventative measures meant that rates of malaria were far lower than in the Imperial Japanese Army. The official wartime history of the RAMC claimed that 'the marked difference in the degree to which malaria was brought and held under control in the Allied and the Japanese land forces respectively during the course of the years 1943–1945 was one of the reasons, and indeed one of the most important reasons, why the Japanese were defeated.'[1] In addition to the prevention of disease, the efficient treatment of illness and injury in medical centres close to forward areas meant that many casualties could be rapidly returned to their fighting units. This in turn helped to maintain morale within the Fourteenth Army, as men knew that medical personnel were close by should they require treatment for war wounds.

As the climate and culture would prove to be very different to that experienced by those on active service in the Mediterranean and Northern Europe areas of combat, specific training was provided to those making the voyage eastwards. En route to India in October 1940, Captain Leslie Ellis faced a continuation of the brief period of physical training he had undertaken in England, as well as lectures designed to address the issues he would come up against as a medical officer on the subcontinent:

> We got chivvied around. … There was compulsory P.T. At first this was at 6.30 but later mercifully it was at 7.30. I found exercise before breakfast tended to bring

> on seasickness. I felt a bit queer each morning for the first few days after sailing.
>
> There was also two hours of lecturing each morning – an hour of Urdu then an hour of military and medical matters. We enjoyed these lectures on the whole.[2]

For other men, the consolations of Christian faith enabled them to remain strong and steadfast en route to an unknown destination and fate. Captain Kenneth Hulbert, the son of a Methodist minister, found solace in an Easter Day service in 1941 while on board the SS *Strathallan*:

> Was woken by the cabin steward with the usual cup of tea. I read the story of Easter Day. Father always used to tell us this story in his wonderful eloquent way every Easter as a sermon. The service was conducted on deck at 9.30 am. The altar consisted of a pile of ammunition boxes and we knelt on our life belts. Sang the Easter hymn accompanied by the RAOC band. At night the sea was all phosphorescent and looked very beautiful. The Milky Way is now quite brilliant and looks totally magical: I have never seen anything like it. So ends Easter Day 1941 at sea. I feel better for this day in every way and more able to face the future, which appears to be darkening. If only I could hear how they are at home, it would not be so trying. I commend them all to the Risen Lord, however, and all will be well.[3]

A stop-off in South Africa en route to India was commonplace for troops. Whilst most enjoyed the hospitality provided in Cape Town or Durban, Bill Frankland recalled an incident that left him feeling uneasy when stopping off in late 1941 when sailing from Liverpool on the *Dominion Monarch* as one of a party of thirty-five doctors destined for Singapore. Temporarily released from his duties as the ship's duty medical officer, Frankland took a tram from the docks to the centre of Cape Town. A pregnant native African woman boarded the tram and Frankland rose to give up his seat. This caused mayhem, with the woman being ignominiously ejected from the vehicle due to the racial segregation that blighted the country.[4] This was just the beginning of the inhumanity that medical staff sent to the Far Eastern theatre of war would witness and experience for the following three and a half years.

In violation of international law, as Japan had not formally declared war against the British Empire, Japanese forces began an attack on the Crown Colony of Hong Kong on 8 December 1941. By Christmas week, the colony was overrun. At this time, the Salesian Mission was the main medical store holding supplies for all the military hospitals in Hong Kong and was manned by doctors of various nationalities, medical orderlies and nine female nurses. At first, it seemed that the Red Cross flag hanging in the entrance hall would be respected by the Japanese combat troops who accepted the hospital's surrender without any resistance being offered. The women were released unharmed, but the men were forced to remove their shoes and tunics, their identification cards confirming they were medical staff were thrown aside and they were then marched a quarter of a mile up the nearby Mount Parker. On the way, the party came across a wounded man crawling towards the dressing station who was bayoneted by the Japanese.

In a clearing, medical staff were bayoneted and slashed with swords, whilst others were shot as they tried to escape. Captain Martin Banfill, the commander of the RAMC unit, was separated from the others and made to lie on the ground listening to his men being slaughtered. About eight Canadians, including a medical officer, ten members of the RAMC and three St John's Ambulance men were murdered. Apart from Banfill, there were only two survivors: Osler Thomas and Corporal Norman Leath.

Leath was struck on the back of the neck by a sword as a Japanese soldier attempted to behead him. 'It shot me into the air and spun me completely round … I fell to the ground face downwards, blood pouring into my eyes, ears and mouth.'[5] Leath suffered severe damage to his neck muscle and upper vertebrae, but miraculously not to his spinal cord. He lay beneath the corpses of his massacred comrades in a drainage ditch before later crawling away to safety. Martin Banfill was reprieved by the Japanese troops and taken as a prisoner of war.

A week later, a further atrocity took place at St Stephen's College, a 400-bed hospital housed in a former boys' school. On Christmas Day 1941, 200 Japanese troops broke in and entered the main hall and adjoining classrooms, which housed about a hundred patients. The senior medical officer attempted a formal surrender whilst trying to bar the invaders' path. He was shot in the head and then stabbed. In frenzy, the Japanese then went from bed to bed bayoneting the patients, soon killing fifty. Following this, a dozen female nurses were taken away in threes and fours and gang-raped. Some were murdered and their bodies mutilated.

The remaining men were locked into a room and then brought out in pairs to face execution. The Japanese authorities tried to excuse these brutal rapes and murders by claiming that their troops had come under fire while approaching the building, but the defilement of the nurses, and the cold-blooded killing of men who were clearly medical staff, was in clear contravention of the articles of the Geneva Convention that the Japanese government had signed up to. The protection of medical personnel had been agreed in 1907 and the humane treatment of the sick and wounded had been approved in 1929. These massacres in 1941 were to signpost the barbarism and lack of respect for human dignity that many members of the Imperial Japanese Army would display over the next four and a half years.

The *Dominion Monarch* deposited Captain Bill Frankland on Singapore on 28 November 1941, with the original plan being for him to be part of a new General Hospital at Johor Bahru on the southern tip of Malaya. These plans were changed and Frankland was posted to an Indian Field Hospital. On 2 December, a fateful event took place in the lives of doctors Frankland and Captain Lance Parkinson. They were summoned to a meeting with a senior officer and informed there were two postings that needed filling: one at the Alexandra Military Hospital administering anaesthetics and the other at Tanglin Military Hospital treating dermatology and venereal disease cases. Both Frankland and Parkinson expressed a preference for the Tanglin posting, so to break the impasse, the officer took a coin from his pocket and said, 'Frankland, you call.' Frankland correctly chose heads. Parkinson, who had hopes of developing a career as an obstetrician after the war, was one of the hundreds of medics, patients and nurses killed on 14 February 1942 in the massacre at the Alexandra Hospital.

Tanglin Military Hospital was subjected to repeated bombing raids following Japanese entry into the war on Sunday, 7 December 1941. On one occasion, Frankland was about to examine the wife of a fellow officer who had sprained her ankle when an air raid began. They threw themselves into a nearby malaria drain for shelter. Bombs fell and shrapnel flew around the area. One piece of shrapnel just missed Frankland's head and landed close to the lady. He picked it up, burning his finger and thumb: 'It was the only war injury I sustained.'[6] In between air raids, Frankland treated many men for tropical ulcers, and for gonorrhoea and syphilis, the troops having visited the ladies who plied their trade in Lavender Street.

On 11 February, as the Japanese advance continued apace, Tanglin Military Hospital was evacuated and the staff and patients moved to

Singapore City. Bill Frankland was attached to No. 1 Malay General Hospital, situated in the Victoria Theatre, where 400 beds and an operating theatre were established. Frankland assigned the sickest patients to the lower parts of the building, which contained the expensive seats, and placed the more able 'up in the Gods'. A party of drunken Australian troops was brought in and Frankland instructed one of his orderlies, Sergeant Smith, to wash out their stomachs using an enema tube. They were kept overnight then sent back sober to their units. Frankland had correctly reckoned that the Japanese would show no mercy to any troops they encountered displaying drunken belligerence.[7]

As Frankland and others struggled valiantly to treat ever-increasing numbers of casualties in the days before the fall of Singapore, on the evening of 13 February, Medical Command summoned a party of thirteen officers and five NCOs and ordered them to arrange an escape via the waterfront. Led by Brigadier C.D.K Seaver, the DDMS of III (Indian) Corps, the party included Major L.R.C. Davies, who had been second in command at the Tanglin Military Hospital. One of those ordered to attend, Captain Tom Smiley, was not present and remained on duty at the Alexandra Military Hospital. The officers remaining at the medical establishments in Singapore were only aware of this escape when their colleagues were absent from work on the morning of 14 February. This underhand behaviour caused a loss of respect amongst those left behind. When the No. 1 Malay General Hospital eventually fell to the Japanese, having taken the brunt of the surgical cases during the final days of fighting, Captain Bill Frankland sent a terse note to its commanding officer, Lieutenant Colonel D.S. Middleton. It read:

> Tanglin hospital officers doing duty at 1MGH on the 15/2/1942
>
> Sir
>
> The following officers from Tanglin remained at the capitulation
>
> Captain Hamilton-Gibbs
> Captain Frankland
> Captain Chilton
> Lieutenant (QM) Welch
> Signed A.W. Frankland
> Capt RAMC[8]

Captain Forde Cayley had been attached to the 5th Battalion, Suffolk Regiment, assigned to defend Pongol Point on the north-west coast of the Malay peninsula. Despite his medical status, 'I was issued with a service revolver and ten rounds and felt now I am really for it.'[9] Cayley had a dugout to shelter in and, when he considered it safe to do so, visited the various companies on bike. On his return, he found the dugout had been bombed, with many dead and wounded. Withdrawn to the outskirts of the city of Singapore, Cayley's battalion HQ was established at Raffles College, situated by the riverside quay, and he set up a Regimental Aid Post in the middle of one wing. The post soon became filled with wounded men:

> The mortar platoon were under a tree and the mortar hit a branch above them and blew off an officer's leg. Another was hit in the arm and I had to take it off. The Indians from the units on each side of us sent their wounded in with bullets penetrating their bowels so the night was made terrible by their cries for water. A Malay civilian came in with his sternum ripped away by a shell so that you could see his heart beating.

By this stage, the Japanese were just 100 yards away so, during a lull in the fighting, Cayley sent an ambulance with the worst wounded to a hospital further down the line. Shortly afterwards, he witnessed Japanese tanks in control of the streets, then General Percival being driven along the road to sign the terms of the British surrender. For Cayley, the war was over, but his nightmare was to last a further three and a half years.

Despite the privations they were to undergo, Frankland and Cayley were fortunate not to have been amongst the medical staff serving at the British Military Hospital, known as Alexandra Hospital, in Queenstown, Singapore. This facility, housed in an imposing white colonial-style 1930s building, had a normal capacity for 550 patients, but the fighting had swelled this number to 900. On 14 February, the hospital found itself caught between Japanese and British troops advancing towards each other. Due to the rationed supply of water and electricity, men from the 32nd Company of the RAMC were struggling to treat patients and corpses were being wrapped in blankets, remaining unburied.

At 1.00 pm, the first Japanese soldier approached the building. Captain J.E. Bartlett walked out to meet him, his hands in the air, and indicated the Red Cross brassard on his arm. The soldier ignored this and fired at him at point-blank range. Amazingly, Bartlett survived and ran back into the building. For the next hour, three groups of Japanese soldiers went from ward to ward, shooting, bayoneting and beating up medics and patients indiscriminately, killing about fifty people.

Captain Lance Parkinson, who had lost the toss of the coin with Frankland to be posted to Alexandra Military Hospital, was anaesthetising Corporal Holden of the Loyal Regiment (North Lancashire). Holden was bayoneted while on the operating table whilst Parkinson was bayoneted through the abdomen and gravely injured. He escaped to a nearby corridor but collapsed and died less than thirty minutes later. Captain Tom Smiley, who had been operating on Corporal Vetch – another victim of the Japanese bayoneted on an operating table – was lined up against a wall with several other men. He pointed to his Red Cross brassard and told the Japanese troops that the building was a hospital. In response, one soldier lunged at his chest with a bayonet, striking a cigarette case that had been given to Smiley by his fiancée. This deflected the blow onto his chest. A second soldier bayoneted him through the groin whilst a third attacked him, causing a hand injury. He collapsed onto Corporal Sutton and both men feigned death. Remarkably, both were left alone and survived.

Around 3.30 pm, 200 men were rounded up, tied into groups of eight and forced to march towards a row of outhouses some distance from the hospital. The gravely injured were not spared and were killed if they fell along the way. Upon reaching their destination the men were divided into groups of fifty to seventy and crammed into three small rooms. Here they were kept without ventilation or water, with no space to sit or lie down, and many died during the night.

The following morning, 15 February, the remaining men were told that they would receive water. By 11.00 am, the Japanese captors allowed the prisoners to leave the rooms in groups of two on the pretext of them fetching water. However, as the screams and cries of those who had left the rooms could be heard by those still inside, it became clear that the Japanese were executing the prisoners when they left the rooms. The death toll numbered approximately 100 prisoners. Suddenly,

Japanese shelling resumed and a shell struck the building where the prisoners were being held. This interrupted the executions and allowed a handful of men to escape.

Following further cold-blooded murders by the Japanese troops, a senior Japanese officer arrived at the hospital at 6.00 pm on Sunday, 15 February and ordered all movement around the hospital to stop. Pointedly, Smiley, having had his wounds dressed by Corporal Sutton, defied the order and carried on tending the wounds of the survivors, and was soon back operating. For this action, he was later awarded the Military Cross.

***

Following the fall of Singapore, British military resources continued to pour into the Indian subcontinent to defend the British Empire against further Japanese invasion and to build the strength with which it was hoped they would be able to win back the territory already lost to the enemy. By late 1944, the Fourteenth Army, comprising units and formations of the British Army and British Indian Army, had the highest number of troops of any military body in the world, reaching just over one million. These included Private Fred Cannell, who had chosen to join the RAMC as a hospital cook after his initial six weeks' training at Norton Barracks, Worcester. (Pic 25) He had then been sent to St Omer barracks at Aldershot before sailing to India on the Dutch liner *Johan van Oldenbarnevelt*, which had operated between Rotterdam and the Dutch East Indies before the war. Cannell was then posted to No. 9 Indian General Hospital at Ranchi in north-eastern India. (Pic 26) Here he learned the art of field cooking in preparation for possible work in a fighting zone.

As well as British troops in the hospital, there were Indian and Burmese patients, many of whom required special diets. Cannell also had to be prepared to help the medics if it became necessary, thus was well versed in first aid. Thoughts of home were never far away as he and his sweetheart and future wife Vera wrote to each other daily.

Claude Jennings, a medical orderly, arrived in Bombay on 28 July 1942, and the former trainee surveyor recalled his first taste of India as 'the stench, the filth and bright robes. The fine buildings and the crazy scaffolding used to build them.'[10] From here, Jennings went by train via

Deolali (whose mental hospital gave rise to the phrase 'Deolali Tap', meaning suffering from mental health problems) then on to Poona. The platform on Poona station left a further impression of the spectrum of Indian society: 'Indian soldiers in various head gears, char wallahs with trays of cups and saucers held high about their heads, respectable Indians in white ducks and topees, crippled beggars with legs like matchsticks, women beating their washing by the wells.'

Jennings was posted to an orthopaedic ward in a new barracks, treating patients injured by gunshot wounds in Burma. As he was on night duty, he took the opportunity to purchase a bicycle and pedalled around the hospital area by day. One of the places he and a colleague came across was an Indian leper colony:

> This was a walled enclosure with a house outside for the Indian doctor. An English-speaking nurse and a ward boy took us round. There was a large well-lit operating theatre. There were two huts for women who were nearly cured. The floors were swept clean and the cooking vessels were highly polished. In the more advanced cases, limbs were amputated and the faces grossly deformed. The staff consisted of the Indian doctor, an Indian missionary and a 'compounder'. The Rev Peacock visited every month …

Jennings took a course in physiotherapy and was then posted to a combined Indian and British hospital in Asansol, West Bengal. He was responsible for the day-to-day care of two patients in the British wing of the hospital. The first had a fractured tibia and fibula in plaster whilst the other had a badly crushed spine and had been encased in a complete body plaster. The more badly wounded man had suffered loss of continence, so Jennings had to attend to his nursing needs, as well as ensuring his legs and arms received regular exercise. He was catheterised and an enema had to be given daily, and his limbs had to be massaged. After six or seven weeks of such intimate treatment, it was pleasing for Jennings to see the man have his plaster removed, and eventually to walk unaided.

Indian patients were cared for in a separate ward from the British casualties, and Jennings nursed eight of them, including cases of gunshot wounds and a cracked lumbar vertebra. In order to aid the rehabilitation of his patients, he procured wood and tools and manufactured some rudimentary exercise equipment. However, the overpowering humidity often made it too difficult for patients to spend much time on them. Another aspect of local life that caused consternation for the hospital staff and patients were the snakes, which used to lie on the wet patio during monsoon time, making it treacherous to venture out after dark. To compensate for these discomforts, the wives of British steelworkers who were working in the area would make extra portions of steak and kidney pie for the hospital staff and entertain them with piano recitals.

The No. 14 British General Hospital at Bareilly in northern India contained a large gymnasium, a treatment room and an orthopaedic ward, in which two chartered physiotherapists, four medical orderlies and a medical officer worked. The ward was situated in a large barrack block, in which two large halls had been joined together by placing a cover over a veranda, and punkahs – large overhead fans – kept the patients and staff comfortable. In one hall, patients' broken femurs were kept in traction by weights supported by beams over the tops of their beds. Twenty such beds were provided, and the various beams and ropes put medical orderly Claude Jennings in mind of a forest. Men would have to stay in such traction for up to twelve weeks, and Jennings would tell jokes to put the men at ease, then got them to exercise their arms, then their good leg, before finishing off with some massage and general mobility exercises. For men further along the road to recovery, arm and leg classes were held in the gymnasium.

Eventually, the monsoons came and flooded the hospital grounds as torrents of patients were brought in on convoys from the bitterly fought Burma Campaign. In addition to the orthopaedic and surgical work at Bareilly, some RAMC staff undertook welfare work. Jennings recalled: 'I did a broadcast spell in the morning – a sort of "DJ" act. Two of us ran a Red X library and we had music programmes with some Red X records, a record player plugged into the hospital radio.'

Once the fighting had ended and the Japanese had surrendered, the final role of the No. 14 General Hospital at Bareilly was to care for those who had survived the Far East prison camps but were too ill to return home immediately. The hospital was then closed down, and Claude Jennings flew home in November 1945 after six years' service with the RAMC.

Edwyn 'Ted' Smart, from Dereham in Norfolk, enlisted as a private before ending the war as a sergeant. Smart served with No. 134 British General Hospital and noted some of his interactions with Indian civilians in a small pocket diary he kept throughout his time abroad. On 17 July 1942, Smart witnessed the death of a Sikh officer in this hospital and the angry grief of his parents:

> Both father and mother were at the bedside at the time which upset the whole applecart. Gordon and John were called about 4am in the morning. Away they go to the ward to collect the body, receiving a great shock to find it was missing. After intensive enquiries it was found the parents had moved it to the mortuary themselves. The body laid on the mortuary table with the old woman dancing around it brandishing a dam [*sic*] great knife about two foot long.
>
> Gordon walked up the steps to see to the body. The old girl sees him, gives one rush and brandishes the knife against his throat. Poor old Gordon gives one look and makes a headlong flight.[11]

Two months later, Smart had his first experience of handling the body of a dead woman, and the protocols that could offend cultural sensitivities:

> An Indian WAC (I) was killed near the hospital in a road accident. She was brought to the Hospital and taken to the mortuary. A pitiful sight with skull crushed and ribs broken. The Indian parents of the above girl were in a terrible state. The mother setting up a terrible wailing. She was of Hindu caste so was burnt. The police wanted P.M. [post-mortem]. A terrific fight [was put up] against this … the mother who spent a long while wailing.

Captain Kenneth Hulbert arrived at Kirkee, an arsenal town just to the west of Poona, with the No. 18 General Hospital in March 1941. This was pre-monsoon season, when the weather was at its hottest and driest and the landscape was parched, brown and dusty. Occasional whirlwinds sent dust spiralling into the air and slammed doors in the hospital camp, removing tiles from the roof.

Medics in India were operating in a volatile political situation. A mission by Sir Stafford Cripps to try to obtain co-operation from the Indian people for the British war effort, in return for the promise of post-war general elections and independence, had proved fruitless, with his proposals being rejected by both the Congress Party and Muslim League. A civil disobedience campaign led by Mahatma Gandhi and the words 'Quit India' painted on the roads and walls made for a tense environment in which the staff of No. 18 General Hospital had to work.

The daily routine in the hospital consisted of surgical rounds and treating malaria, dysentery and diabetes cases, but against this routine backdrop the domestic political situation was becoming ever more fractious. On 9 August, Gandhi was arrested and imprisoned in the Aga Khan's palace in Poona, prompting riots across the subcontinent. British troops in Poona were in a potentially dangerous situation as Indians started attacking government buildings, blowing up bridges and railway tracks and cutting telephone lines. Physical attacks on Europeans were reported, and Poona remained an unsettled town in which to provide military medicine. Gandhi then went on a fast and became extremely ill. Kenneth Hulbert's diary entry for 21 February 1943 tersely noted, 'There is a very tense atmosphere here in Poona.' Eventually India's political leader was released, but tensions between the Indians and the British, and between Indian Hindus and Moslems, continued.

In May 1943, Hulbert was dispatched from Poona to Chittagong, an arduous journey of 1,200 miles lasting nine days. From there he went on to Cox's Bazar by river steamer with an advance party of three other officers, an assortment of British and Indian troops, and a mascot dog. Hospital accommodation of 4,000 beds was to be built on an island in the estuary, an endeavour lasting six weeks. The buildings were made of bamboo, built by local labour and held together without nails or screws. In fact, Hulbert had been transferred from one perilous position in Poona to another, as from the first day at Cox's Bazar, Japanese warplanes began to attack.

> I thought that they were Hurricanes until they were right overhead and I saw the Japanese markings of the rising sun. We ran faster than ever in our lives and flung ourselves into a ditch. Then all hell broke loose. Everyone with a gun or rifle started firing into the air. I could not resist looking up

> to see one of the planes burst into flames and crash about a quarter of a mile away. Back in the camp the old sub-assistant surgeon, an Anglo-Indian, was holding up his hands saying, 'Oh my God, whatever shall I do. I have a wife and children at home.' Then the commanding officer started us off digging slit trenches.

Medical equipment remained unloaded on the barges, and to add to the difficulties in building the new hospital, on 25 May the monsoons began. Clouds that had been banking up from the south unleashed their torrents, stripping roofs and blowing down the bamboo huts. Roads were washed away as the medics faced the prospect of weeks of strong winds and up to 300 inches of rain. Frogs emerged in the rain, some as big as a human fist. They would appear on the floor of the hut and stare at the troops; some would even let themselves be tickled under the chin.

The monsoon meant that basic sanitation work went undone. Open pits full of faeces began to develop. Men's diets were poor, with low-quality meat and few vegetables. Work on the new hospital was sporadic, with the island it was to be built on containing a flooded paddy field, with men having to work ankle-deep in mud. Eventually, higher ground was reached and four tents were erected to shelter the troops and their equipment. Shallow latrines were dug and Hulbert arranged a water supply, testing it for contamination using a Horrocks Box, working out how much bleaching powder to add to chlorinate it.

The challenges facing the medics in establishing a hospital were as nothing compared to the agonies of the local population. On 1 June 1943, Hulbert recorded the sounds heard from outside the camp.

> After sunset a dull low moaning sound started up and seemed to go on all night. I asked one of the Indians what this was and he said that it was coming from the Indian village around us. He said it was the sound of people dying of hunger. What a dreadful place this is. The distressing thing is that there is nothing we can do to help them.

Hulbert was then sent to rejoin No. 18 General Hospital, a series of tents with the operating theatre consisting of two medium-sized tents together, with another one for X-rays, a pathology lab and dental workshops. Anaesthetics, administered in a small tent adjacent to the theatre tent, were mostly ethyl chloride and ether, with very limited amounts of nitrous oxide and oxygen. The hospital contained many Italian prisoners of war working as cooks and ward orderlies, described by Hulbert as 'very willing'. The hospital moved to Avadi, 14 miles west of Madras, to a large camp that had been built to house coolies who were going to Malaya to work in the rubber plantations. The site was so large that Hulbert had to purchase a bicycle in order to make his rounds. Hulbert took over the care of a ward full of Indian patients, many of them Gurkhas, 'who never moan about anything, however ill or in pain they are. So I am now fully extended and very busy indeed.'

By now the Burma Campaign was well under way, with a substantial section of the Allied army being made up of Indian soldiers, with other elements being drawn from the British colonies of West and East Africa. The cultural diversity of the hospital patients meant that religious sensitivities and customs had to be observed.

> Another large convoy of patients arrived today. The Africans have certainly livened things up. At first, we wondered what they would eat, as we have to be so careful never to give Hindus beef or Moslems pork. We were told that they ate anything – and they did. At breakfast they would have porridge, bacon and egg, all mixed up together.

One evening, a group of African patients was sitting in a circle outside the ward tent chattering away. The ward sister approached and asked them what they were talking about. One of them said: 'Sister, we are having an argument. If I was in a boat crossing a river with my mother and wife, and the boat went down in a storm, who would I try and save? He says his wife and I say my mother because you only have one mother and can always get another wife.'

One patient with a plaster on kept the doctors and nurses amused by saying:

> 'Dem bones him all broken, small, small.' If one patient has a clean plaster on, the others all sulk. The sister once said to one of them, 'If you do not stay in bed I shall smack you.'

> He answered, 'Sister, if you smack me I shall just sit here and cry like this.' He proceeded to cry so much that he had all the others laughing.

More amusement for the staff of No. 18 General Hospital was provided by Noel Coward, who offered a welcome change from the usual entertainment of a gramophone recital: 'It was a brilliant performance, which went on for two hours with an interval at half time. It was very hot and at the end he said that he just had to sing *Mad dogs and Englishmen go out in the midday sun*.'

It was not the heat of the midday sun that caused Captain Paul Adler difficulties. Adler, a medical officer with the 13th Nyasa Battalion of the King's African Rifles, had spent a year in the tropical heat of East Africa and found the change to the monsoon conditions of India not to his liking.

> Here it is raining hard again. Both pairs of my boots have rotted away – the soles have come off completely from one pair and the soles of my other pair are splitting right through. I am trying to wangle another pair through the Q.M. Yet at the moment I have no information. If my bed is wet I sleep between blankets and don't use the sheets. I am not looking forward to cool weather later. As the monsoon proceeds it gradually gets colder and colder![12]

As Adler and his men moved north-eastwards into Burma, the need to manage one's own health became more pressing. Having been transferred to No. 6 Field Ambulance, Adler wrote to his parents: 'Meanwhile I keep fit, I see no reason why I should get malaria as long as I take reasonable precaution. … As the months go on and I still keep fit, very fit, I begin to realise that you must have given me a very strong constitution.'

The intensity of the fighting against the Imperial Japanese Army meant that medics could not consider themselves safe from attack under the terms of the Geneva Convention. Therefore the men of No. 6 Field Ambulance were trained in the use of weapons. Adler wrote:

> I am used as the expert on weapons in the field ambulance. … I prime the grenades and look after the sten guns and when

> there is time keep training the nursing orderlies in the use of rifle and sten. Everyone is responsible for his own defence in this type of warfare and although a field ambulance is usually inside the perimeter of a defensive box comprised of fighting troops, one has to be prepared for all eventualities.
>
> You know this type of warfare here is something quite different to warfare at home – it is much more primitive and silent. Silence, complete and utter silence at night except for the birds and insects and frogs and perhaps occasional game and the howl of a leopard – an occasional laugh which is not to be encouraged. Any noise sounds very loud and gives the position of your base hidden in the jungle to a passing patrol. The crackling of twigs or bamboo sometimes wakes me up with a start.[13]

Sadly, these were amongst the final words that Adler would ever write. On 5 November 1944, while tending a wounded man on a bridge as the Japanese were being pushed back following defeat at the Battle of Kohima, he came under fire and was killed. A former colleague, 'J.R.B.', wrote in *The Lancet* of 10 February 1945:

> I knew Paul Adler well at the London, where we often worked together in the library and museum, and I spent many weekends with him on his boat, at his home, and in the country. He was a grand companion at all times, who put all his energies and interest into whatever he was doing, and this made him a fine soldier when war came. His letters, written as an RMO, showed his absorption in the details of his men's lives, and of the places he visited.

The necessity of arming and training in the use of weapons for medical staff operating in the Far East had been starkly demonstrated during the Battle of the Admin Box. The battle, which had taken place as troops of the Indian Army's 7th Division desperately defended a small administrative area in Arakan between 5 and 23 February 1944 against the surrounding Japanese, eventually resulted in the first decisive Allied victory in the Far East, setting a template to be used by Field Marshal Slim, head of the Fourteenth Army, for eventual triumph in the Far East.[14]

The box contained the Indian 7th Divisional Dressing Station, manned by men of No. 66 Indian Field Ambulance and the No. 12 Mobile Surgical Unit. The station was sited in the corner of the box in the shadow of hills and covered by jungle foliage, designed to offer protection from air attack and long-range shelling. At 9.00 pm on 7 February 1944, the Japanese opened fire on the dressing station with machine guns and rifles.

Captain Anthony Irwin, a member of the elite V Force, heard a voice from the MDS plead, 'Don't, for Christ's sake, don't.'[15] He then heard a single shot. Then silence. Although British troops knew an outrage was being perpetrated, they were unable to take action as they were under orders to remain in their slit trenches, as attacking during the night ran a high risk of shooting their own men. One patrol was sent towards the dressing station, but it was soon repulsed.

One of the medics inside the MDS was Lieutenant Salindra Mohan Basu of the Indian Medical Corps. He was seized by the Japanese, taken to one of their officers and asked how many patients and British officers were in the station, and what army units were posted in the box. His response was that his interest was in medicine, not military tactics. Three more Indian medical officers were taken prisoner and told they would be taken to Rangoon to join the Indian Independence League, an anti-British nationalist group allied to the Japanese.

As Basu was removed from the hospital, he saw a large number of dead, who had been stabbed, shot or slashed with swords. Geoffrey Evans, then a brigadier commanding the 9th Indian Brigade who was the most senior officer inside the Admin Box, recorded how others inside the dressing station had met their fate:

> When day came, they lay still so that the Japanese might not notice them. During the morning they heard a shout outside and the RAMC Captain asked: 'What do you want?' The shout – it sounded like 'You go' – was repeated. The Captain shook his head and lay down again. 'Who is it?' asked the Lieutenant.
>
> 'It's a Jap,' said the Captain. At that moment one of the Japanese soldiers appeared and shot him through the right thigh. The Captain shouted: 'I am a doctor – Red Cross – I am a medical officer.'

> The Japanese shot dead the Captain, the Gurkha Major, two British soldiers and a mess servant. The Lieutenant and the three surviving British soldiers lay still. They stayed like that all day, and when darkness came they managed to leave the hospital and find the safety of the nearest West Yorkshire post.[16]

Evans also spoke to a surviving RAMC private, who had been kicked, cuffed and cracked over the head by rifle butts, and used as a shield on top of a trench by the Japanese. Late on 8 February, they were taken along a dried-up watercourse to a clearing with a running stream. The Japanese troops then opened fire on the twenty men, killing seventeen of them.

Back in their slit trench, Irwin and his fellow officer Captain John Salmon presumed that everyone in the MDS had been slaughtered. However, at 7.00 am, Major Crawford, the principal surgeon of the MDS appeared with two other doctor colleagues. After being given a cup of tea, he reported how many of the staff and most of the patients had been killed. Among them was Captain John Robinson, a 28-year-old psychiatrist from Cambridge. Crawford had heard the Japanese inform him that they were in a hurry and could not afford to take prisoners, before summarily executing him.

Crawford and his colleagues owed their survival to the fact they had been in their tent during the attack and had remained silent for around two hours. They had then crawled out under the tent flap in darkness and hidden in nearby bushes. From that vantage point they had watched Japanese troops go round each tent, firing bursts of machine-gun fire to ensure there were no survivors. Among the patients who had managed to escape was one man still attached to the bottle of blood from which he had been receiving a transfusion when the attack began.

Lieutenant Basu had been wounded when a British mortar landed nearby. The Japanese shot one man and bayoneted another who had cried out too loudly. As they prepared to retreat, the Japanese stood in front of Basu and his companions, their rifles ready to fire. Basu complained, 'We are Red Cross people. We are doctors and hospital workers. We have nothing to do with actual warfare.' This plea made no difference to the Japanese, who shot at the group. Basu was injured in the ear, and put his hands in the blood of a dead comrade and smeared it over his own face and head so the Japanese would leave him for dead, which they did.

Lieutenant Colonel Gerald Cree, commanding the 2nd Battalion of the West Yorkshire Regiment, was also present in the Admin Box. He recalled the sense of helplessness he and his men felt when hearing the massacre unfold in the MDS:

> That night we heard sounds of firing and shouting, screams and yells coming from the direction of the MDS which was in the corner of this Admin Box. … But it wasn't really within the proper defended perimeter at all. … Nobody thought this dressing station would be attacked but it was and the Japs got into it and did the most appalling executions here among the wounded and the sick in the hospital. We could hear it going on, shouts and screams and shooting. I was asked by the … ADMS of the division to counter-attack the hospital and retake it. It was pitch black at that time. I said it was impossible to attack as we could not tell friend from foe.[17]

Eventually, as a result of heavy machine-gun fire on the part of the British troops, the Japanese were driven back from the MDS. Cree described the scene: 'Horrid. They'd shot men lying in their beds. They'd just shot them. They shot several doctors too. They just lined them up and shot them. I think it was just their policy of trying to terrorise us you see. It made everybody very furious and determined to get the better of them, which we did.'

In all, thirty-five medical staff and patients had been killed.[18] The battle continued for a further fortnight, with the burning anger felt by the British and Indian troops who had been helpless to avert the massacre driving them on to a famous victory.

One group of medics who expected no special treatment from the Japanese were those who had volunteered to serve in the Long Range Penetration Groups, the 3rd Indian Infantry Division, popularly known as the Chindits. The Chindits were the largest of the Allied Special Forces of the Second World War. Formed and led by Major General Orde Wingate DSO, the Chindits operated deep behind enemy lines in North

Burma. For many months they lived and fought the enemy in the jungles of Japanese-occupied Burma, relying exclusively on airdrops, which took place every five days, for their food, medical and other supplies.

There were two Chindit expeditions into Burma. The first, which lasted from February to June 1943, named Operation Longcloth, consisted of a force of 2,500 men who marched over 1,000 miles during the campaign. The second expedition, Operation Thursday, in March 1944, was on a much larger scale. It was the second largest airborne invasion of the war and consisted of a force of 20,000 British and Commonwealth soldiers with air support provided by the 1st Air Commando USAAF.

Wingate had a reputation for erratic genius, and one of the ways that he challenged established military practices was in his attitude to the medical support his forces would receive. He had been accused of ignoring medical advice and was disdainful of hygiene and sanitation. Wingate wrote: 'It will … be a waste of labour to dig latrines unless the bivouac is to be occupied for more than one week. Men should carry out their functions at distances not less than 100 yards from the perimeter.'[19] His brigade commanders were more aware of the importance of good hygiene. Great care was taken to ensure that water was purified by sterilisation tablets before drinking, although high rates of malaria were experienced during the first expedition due to insufficient quantities of mepacrine. Men became painfully thin due to the physically exacting nature of the campaign. Bill Aird, the medical officer with 5 Column, noted how starvation was slowly killing his men: 60 per cent of those captured by the Japanese subsequently died due to having already been starved of adequate food before being taken prisoner.[20]

Often the sick and wounded had to be left behind with a small quantity of food, water, morphine and dressings, or entrusted to the care of Burmese villagers. Each officer carried letters written in different languages explaining to the peasants how to care for the wounded. Over a third of the men taking part in Operation Longcloth were lost to the enemy or disease, and many of those who did return were emaciated and suffering from tropical disease. Colonel William Officer, who assumed the role of DDMS for the Chindits in April 1944, shortly after Wingate's death, observed:

> It soon became apparent from the information which I had received from Fourteenth Army and my ADMS that the task

> before me was by no means an easy one. It was common knowledge that the force in general and the late commander in particular were not particularly medically minded to say the least of it, and from the story given by the DADMS it was quite evident that my predecessor (Colonel Campbell) had been given no active support and had instead only received active opposition.[21]

Wingate's chief of staff, Major General Derek Tulloch, disagreed with this judgement, claiming that the arrangements for the evacuation of casualties was swift and effective.

The British, Gurkha, Indian and Burmese men who made up the force for Operation Thursday were detailed to disrupt enemy bases, vital centres and lines of communication. The brigades functioned in four columns, each of 400 men, self-contained in weapons, reconnaissance, communications, ciphering, and medical and animal care. For each brigade a Brigade Medical Unit (BMU) was formed, commanded by a major, with one other officer and twenty-one other ranks. The DDMS suggested that each column should have one medical officer each and eleven other ranks, but Wingate rejected this as he believed it would make the column too unwieldy. He argued that two MOs and two other ranks would be sufficient, and the column padre could be used to provide extra medical support.

Once again, Colonel Officer clashed with Wingate. The latter stated, 'I do not want anything medical with my columns though I suppose I must have one doctor with each for the sake of the morale effect on the families at home. … Every man with my force must be a fighting man.' He wanted 'no passengers or Geneva Convention people'.[22] To compensate for this low level of medical cover, the fighting troops were intensively trained in medical care.

Evacuation of wounded and seriously ill troops would be by the best means possible, with airlift not being a certainty. Operational necessity took precedence over all other considerations, and the doctors chosen for the missions fully anticipated outbreaks of malaria, dysentery, hepatitis, scrub typhus, helminthic infections and skin problems. Each column carried 100lb of medical supplies, with one side of a mule being allotted for the doctor's pannier, allowing for ready access to medical equipment without having to unload the animal. Three ponies with convertible saddles were assigned to carry casualties. Each soldier carried his own first field dressing in his 70lb load and four medical orderlies as well as a doctor were attached to each column. Due to the necessity to travel light, stretchers, extra blankets and groundsheets were not taken by the medics.

Flying from an air base at Imphal in early March 1944, Colonel Desmond Whyte, commanding officer of No. 11 Indian Field Ambulance, landed and quickly dispersed his column from an improvised airfield known as Chowringhee. (Pic 28) Whyte felt exhilaration at the task ahead: 'There was now hard foot slogging, but life was worthwhile, almost sweet, fit as we were, and ready to grapple with most things.'[23] They crossed the Irrawaddy River and marched north, with intermittent skirmishes with the enemy, outmanoeuvring the Japanese with superior training, fitness and close military intelligence sent by radio.

It had been planned that each column doctor would transfer casualties to brigade HQ column by the earliest available means consistent with fighting conditions. This meant that HQ column, with its single doctor, soon became overloaded with casualties, slowing progress. Nevertheless, the unburdening of casualties allowed each of the column doctors to be freed from the immediate worry of treatment, allowing for greater efficiency in his own column.

In the absence of stretchers, the Gurkhas displayed great ingenuity in using their kukris and bamboo poles to make their own, with one end resting on the saddle of a mule and the other end being dragged along the ground, four men in attendance to push the device up steep or slippery slopes. One early casualty, a skull injury, was transported for several days unconscious, being kept alive by doses of brandy and sugar plus an intravenous drip.

Finding a suitable airstrip in the thick jungle entailed lengthy and isolated journeys by the medical team and wounded to a prearranged spot notified by radio. Usually, a single-engined plane known as a 'Grasshopper' would arrive. On one occasion the pilot insisted on loading two wounded men as he could not bear to leave one behind. However, he crashed into trees at the far end of the runway and Whyte reloaded the two casualties onto mules, set the plane alight and slipped into the jungle to the sound of ranging mortar fire. Sadly, both casualties died soon afterwards, and Whyte read a short prayer from a cellulose-covered card as the men were buried.

In a conference of each column's medical officers, held in April 1944 after Wingate's death, it was agreed that malaria was now a significant danger to the Chindits' survival as a fighting force. Mosquito nets could not be used at night because of the need for immediate action at any time. As troops' resistance to disease began to wane, men throughout the brigade were put on two mepacrine tablets a day. Those who continued to display symptoms were given regular doses of quinine, getting most men back to a level of reasonable activity.

The men of the second Chindit mission lived on American K-rations during their time in Burma. The three separate packets consumed daily contained precooked items that could be reheated if circumstances allowed, and provided 4,000 calories per day, albeit in a monotonous diet. Due to the extreme physical demands of the campaign, men eventually began to lose body fat. The occasional drop of 'luxury' food items such as bread and tinned fruit was not enough to prevent this, and a shortage of water proved a constant problem, although the morning and evening 'brew-up' of tea proved a good morale reviver. Sepsis caused by leech bites increased, leading to chronically indurated ulcers, and infectious hepatitis slowly spread throughout the formation.

Surgical emergencies were stabilised as well as could be expected, with immediate debridement, using intravenous Sodium Pentothal as anaesthetic. This was important in conditions in which doctors often worked with few medical staff, with wet clothing and dressings, shortage of supplies, short rations and operating in darkness, in close contact with the enemy. The walking wounded usually managed with help, but serious leg injuries could prove disastrous because of difficulty with transport.

Orders were received to move east, to establish a block between enemy forces attempting to smash a way through to India via Kohima. Arriving on 7 May 1944, the men dug in within the defended perimeter of the new block, named 'Blackpool'. The enemy attacked in force and close bitter hand-to-hand fighting took place, littering the wire perimeter with enemy dead. The next night, the Japanese launched a more ferocious attack, which was again repulsed. By now the stench of dead bodies had become indescribable, with distending corpses and bursting limbs making an unpleasant sight.

The Main Dressing Station was filling up with casualties, and it was difficult to dispose of the dead, trapped inside the perimeter. Medical supplies began to run out, and sheets of parachute cloth were used as bandages and splint retainers. A load of hospital supplies did come in via air and three days of respite in the fighting allowed men to catch up on sleep and the backlog of patients. The lull in the attacks was short-lived and the Japanese brought up heavy artillery and began shelling 'Blackpool'. Within a sixty-minute period, 300 shells exploded inside the perimeter and knocked out the Chindits' four field guns. The enemy began to creep onto the airstrip and a detachment of gunners manning a Bofors gun fought to the death. The MDS was becoming overwhelmed with helpless wounded, and morphine was injected to stem the pain.

It was at this point that Brigadier John Masters had to take two agonising decisions: the first to withdraw his men before they were overrun and massacred, and the second to decide the fate of those who were too injured to be moved without jeopardising the safety of those still fighting and the walking wounded. He was taken to a row of nineteen stretchers, each containing a man from his 111 Brigade.

> The first man was quite naked and a shell had removed the entire contents of his stomach. Between his chest and pelvis there was a bloody hollow, behind it his spine. Another had no legs and no hips, his trunk ending just below the waist. A third had no left arm, shoulder, or breast, all torn away in one piece. A fourth had no face and whitish liquid was trickling out of his head into the mud. A fifth seemed to have been torn in pieces by a mad giant, and his lips bubbled gently. Nineteen men lay there. A few conscious. At least, their eyes moved, but without light in them.

Masters was told by Whyte that another thirty men could be saved, if these were left behind. 'These men have no chance. They're full of morphia. Most of them have bullet and splinter wounds beside what you can see. Not one chance at all, sir. I give you my word of honour. Look, this man's died already, and that one. None can last another two hours, at the outside.'

Masters faced the bleak choice of killing nineteen men instantly or sacrificing the lives of hundreds of others if he prevaricated. Whyte objected to the thought that he might have to carry out the killings. 'Do you think I want to do it? … We've been fighting to save that man for twenty-four hours and then just now, in the MDS, he was hit in the same place.' The brigadier ordered Whyte to give the men whose eyes were open any remaining morphine and summon his stretcher-bearers. Whyte then went back up to a ridge and heard a series of carbine shots ring out. He put his hands to his ears but nothing could shut out the sound.

Whyte was ordered to withdraw north with the remaining patients through the attacking force by any means available. He assembled the medical team from their posts and placed the walking wounded in sections under NCOs, with orders to meet at a certain map reference. Others were carried up a muddy hill as shells continued to tear men and animals apart. Enemy snipers had taken up positions either side of the only usable track, and a group of blinded men, tied together by a line of cloth, stumbled and slithered onwards.

A bullet ripped through Whyte's medical pack but the party pressed onwards, over a ridge. The Japanese failed to follow and finish off what remained of the party, having had enough of the spirited rearguard action, in Whyte's opinion. The breakout of the medical staff and their patients had lasted for three hours of shelling, mortaring, machine-gun fire and sniping, and the group had dragged itself up a 3,000-foot slope. The men were cold, hungry and mentally and physically exhausted. The next four days proved to be a nightmare, with those who could manage to move helping those who could not. The smell of sepsis and death was pervasive. One group of men was assembled at a staging section for removal by light plane, as malaria continued to take its toll on the others. They reached Mososakon, where the Gurkhas had improvised a shelter from the monsoon, and an RAF Sunderland flying boat was gradually able to remove the wounded men out to safety. In the meantime, three army chaplains – a Scottish Presbyterian, a Roman Catholic and an Anglican – assisted Whyte in moving the wounded, collecting body excreta and preparing meals.

During further action at the battle to capture Point 2171, men began to die of foot rot due to the incessant monsoon. The doctor from Force

HQ sent Whyte a message telling him that foot trouble was inevitable unless men kept their feet dry and wore dry socks at all times. Brigadier John Masters recalled:

> I found Desmond, naked except for a lunggyi and boots – the shirts were rotting on our backs – drafting a reasonable reply. I tore the message from him and wrote one myself, personal from Commander – ONE kindly arrange for rain to stop falling TWO please turn mud into dry land THREE please terminate war so that we can build huts and stay in them FOUR am confident cases of foot-rot will then naturally decrease.[24]

The chief doctor wanted to court-martial Whyte for this message, even though it had been written by Masters, but thought better of it.

The force was eventually assembled south of Magaung. Whyte reckoned it 'a spent force, many of us chronically sick after some four months of attrition. We were finally airlifted to India, conscious of the patience, endurance and unobtrusive heroism of the ordinary soldier and with a lasting memory of those who would never return.'

Whyte was recommended for a VC by Brigadier John Masters and was awarded an immediate DSO for outstanding gallantry and leadership in the face of the enemy. Masters considered him the one man who had kept the brigade going, having dashed out to rescue hundreds of men over a period of months.

The Chindit operations had stretched the men taking part to breaking point: 5,422 men were evacuated because of sickness, the majority because of malaria. Lieutenant Colonel J.N. Morris monitored the physical state of 401 Chindit patients sent to his hospital, who had been evacuated by aeroplane, flying boat, train and ambulance. Morris noted they displayed 'Chindit syndrome', characterised physically by long hair, long dirty fingernails, fatigue, hunger, pallor and loss of weight, skin sepsis, diarrhoea and malaria, and mentally by superior intelligence, morale and manners. Men had lost 2 stones or more in weight, and malnutrition caused widespread anaemia.

The medics who took part in the two Chindit campaigns underwent the most prolonged period of physical and mental deprivation of any members of the RAMC engaged in fighting operations. Their courage, dedication and ingenuity ensured that fatalities amongst the many casualties were considerably lower than might have otherwise been the case.

After early defeats in Hong Kong and Singapore, the recovery of Burma from the Imperial Japanese Army was a triumph for the Fourteenth Army and resulted in Japan's greatest military defeat to date. The attempted Japanese invasion of India in 1944 had been successfully repulsed, with the hugely symbolic defence at Kohima and Imphal in 1944 proving the turning point of the war in the Far East. Medical officers and orderlies had acquitted themselves with dignity, with many laying down their lives in the course of their duties. Whilst their endeavours eventually resulted in a successful campaign, tens of thousands of their comrades languished in Japanese prisoner of war camps, in which some of the very worst examples of mistreatment of military personnel by enemy forces during the war took place.

Chapter 6

Prisoners of War

Whilst nearly 25 per cent of British prisoners of war held by the Japanese died in captivity, the figure for those held by the Germans and Italians was much lower, at 3.5 per cent. Nevertheless, conditions in German camps were far from comfortable and medical officers and orderlies many of whom had volunteered or been selected to remain with the wounded, and submit to certain capture, strove manfully to preserve the health and lives of their incarcerated comrades.

Although medical officers and orderlies taken captive by the Germans and Italians were not technically prisoners of war, in reality, few were granted their freedom in prisoner exchanges between the Allied and Axis powers. Under the terms of the Geneva Convention, they were 'protected personnel' and should have been repatriated as soon as the military situation permitted, but both Britain and Germany complained that the other was holding doctors against their will. A War Office memorandum stated that 'When those who were "detained" in Germany over a period of years pointed out this breach to the German authorities they were met with the counter-accusation that the British Government was likewise detaining German "protected personnel".'[1]

Some medics were granted extra privileges due to their status, such as the ability to move within different sectors of a prison camp and to visit hospitals and other camps on official business. Nevertheless, the challenge of looking after the physical and psychological welfare of men facing long periods of incarceration on a limited diet, and with the hard physical labour often demanded in mines and factories, tested the resolve and ingenuity of the most skilled and committed medics.

RAMC personnel held as captives faced shortages of medical supplies and restrictions on their ability to practise medicine, although they often experienced professional fulfilment in the range of cases that were presented to them. All German camps contained some form of medical facility, which could be as minimal as a first aid post to the sophistication of a multi-ward hospital. For example, Stalag VIII-B at Lamsdorf had a hospital with 600 beds spread over six separate blocks, including two surgical wards, one medical ward, one psychiatric ward and two infectious diseases wards. In addition there were four blocks containing laboratories, kitchens and accommodation.

Although all medical work in the prison camps was overseen by German doctors, British and American patients were treated by their own medical staff. As Germany suffered from a shortage of medicines throughout the war, prisoners of war took a low precedence in their allocation. Often medical supplies could be supplemented by Red Cross parcels, which could provide spectacles, artificial limbs and surgical instruments as well as basic medicines. At Stalag VIII-B's hospital, blood plasma was sent from Britain to help men survive complex operations, although a restriction in the use of sulpha drugs and a complete absence of penicillin meant that wounds would take longer to heal, putting patients at increased risk of infection during this recuperation period.

In the smaller camps, or in work camps established outside the prisons, medical facilities were more primitive. Frequently, charcoal was used to treat common gastrointestinal problems, and Graham King, a medical orderly held in a camp in Poland, utilised the traditional practice of cupping to treat bronchitis and pneumonia. A glass jar was heated and then placed on a patient's back. The air inside cooled, reducing in volume, thus producing a vacuum effect to hold the cup to the skin. For another prisoner, complaining of 'severe arthritis', King administered an intra-muscular injection of 20cc of sterile water in the buttock. 'Next day he was enjoying full mobility and was quite embarrassed in his gratitude to the wielder of the syringe – me!'[2]

Augmenting the medical provision in German camp hospitals, a small number of specialist hospitals were spread throughout German-occupied Europe. These included a hospital at Bad Haina for the treatment of the blind, one in Rothenburg for skin diseases, and Königswartha and Elsterhorst for men suffering from tuberculosis. Some medical care was delivered less from a concern for the welfare of prisoners, but more from an apprehension that infectious diseases might spread to the German civilian population. The fear of typhus spreading from Russian PoWs was paramount; therefore British and American prisoners were regularly deloused and given a painful inoculation via the chest. The unfortunate

Russians themselves remained untreated, but the measures, along with careful care from the medical officers, ensured that typhus cases were infrequent amongst British or American captives.

More common were cases of tuberculosis, against which the Germans instituted a programme of mass radiography. Captain Archie Cochrane was used by the Germans as a TB specialist across many camp hospitals, although was under no illusion as to his value to his captors. 'I was told verbally by a German that their reason for doing this was not humanitarian, but their fear that tuberculosis would infect German civilian workers.'[3] Although the screening had some value in preventing TB becoming a major problem in the camps, many Allied prisoners did die from the disease due to inconsistencies from the German authorities in following up the results. Cochrane studied the graves in the cemetery at Hospital 1251, a mixed surgical and medical hospital, finding that '80 per cent of the graves were filled with victims of tuberculosis'.

Other doctors drew more inspiration from their work, believing it to be personally rewarding as well as life-enhancing. Lieutenant Bruce Jeffrey, a young Scottish doctor in the Airborne Division captured at Arnhem in September 1944, wrote to his parents of the variety of work in his prison hospital attached to Stalag IX-C at Bad Sulza: 'We do all sorts of exciting operations here. I assist at those and get a chance of seeing the operation all through. In fact I'm getting far more experience than I would have got if I had got back over the Rhine at the end of the Arnhem business.'[4] One of the more mundane but potentially life-saving duties that medical officers had to undertake was the protection of ill men from being sent to work by the Germans, who were generally indifferent to the individual prisoner's welfare. Doctors would be assigned a quota for the number of men allowed off work at any one time, typically a maximum of 5 per cent. If the number of genuine sick cases was below that, camp doctors would be prepared to give otherwise healthy PoWs a 'holiday' through signing for some spurious illness or complaint.

In order to avoid some of the harder work assignments such as mining or quarrying, desperate men would at times inflict real injuries on themselves. A rather unusual but officially sanctioned subterfuge that could earn some weeks off working parties was a voluntary circumcision, with medical officers claiming to sceptical German guards that the procedure was required for reasons of hygiene. According to trainee doctor H.C.M. Jarvis, the operations were in fact 'a very useful way of getting some of the lads off work parties for a few weeks'.[5]

Some medics were captured having witnessed the deaths of their comrades in action. It fell to them to write to the families of those killed to inform them of the circumstances of the loss. Hull-born Sergeant Tom Leak of No. 150 Field Ambulance was taken prisoner at the conclusion of the Battle of Gazala on 1 June 1942. (Pic 27) He spent the subsequent three years held in Italian and German prison camps. Leak received a letter after he had performed the heartbreaking task of confirming the death of a friend to anxious parents in England. Mr and Mrs Perrott of Middlesbrough wrote to Leak on 7 September 1943:

> Dear Sir
>
> Just a line in answer to your letter which was forwarded from the War Office which was a terrible shock to us all at home as he was a real good lad at home but we will have to bear the trouble along with many other parents although it is hard we always looked on the bright side of things but it has not shined for us. I hope you won't be long now before you are back home and we have the pleasure of seeing you. So until then we must thank you once again and allow us to remain your
>
> Effectionate [*sic*] Friends Mrs and Mr Perrott[6]

Their son, Private James Douglas Perrott, had been killed on the same day that Leak had been taken prisoner, and was eventually buried at the Knightsbridge War Cemetery in Libya.

Another of Leak's comrades killed that day was Staff Sergeant Frederick Frankish, like Leak, a native of Hull. Frankish's wife, Phyllis, wrote to Leak on 30 June 1943 informing him that 'I received official news of Fred on 10th of this month, also had a nice letter from Major Prosser.'[7] Phyllis commented on how she was keeping herself from 'brooding and getting depressed' by working as a housekeeper, a job that also 'helps funds'. She exhorted him, 'Well Tom keep your chin up, let's hope before long we are all having a drink and to your safe return.' She sent him some cigarettes, hoping that they would reach him.

By 20 October 1943, she reflected, 'I have now just got all Fred's business settled up have still the medal to go for, I only wish he was with you, what a homecoming it would have been.' Phyllis spoke of her son, Roy, who 'wishes to be remembered to you, he is getting a big boy much taller than I am!'

Sergeant Leak's wife, Bessie, was comforted by a letter written on 28 April 1943 by Captain Brian Rhodes, who had recently been repatriated to the UK due to his wounds. He described how Leak was working as a medical orderly caring for officers at Caserta Hospital in Italy: 'I really would like to congratulate you on your husband. He really has done wonderful work for us there.' Rhodes commented on how fit and well Leak was, but that he was anxious about post not getting through to him. A further letter was written by Lieutenant Peter Rhodes mentioning the 'very good work' Leak was undertaking at Caserta: 'we all thought a great deal of him. He was especially kind to me when I was ill and nothing was too much trouble for him.' Major J.L. Martin RAMC wrote to Bessie of how Leak was receiving a Red Cross parcel and fifty cigarettes weekly and in good health:

> I have just been repatriated and I left Caserta at the end of March where you husband Tom was helping me. He is well fit and hearty and just waiting to return home again. I hope it will be soon. Since he joined me in August at Caserta he has worked very hard in attending to the wounded officers and has done this work well – very well indeed and there are many officers grateful to 'Tom'. … He won't be so hard worked as he has been and is better off in hospital than in camp.[8]

For members of the RAMC held by the Germans, the work they were made to undertake was not always as rewarding. *The Times* reported how 'Prisoners, even members of the RAMC and of other non-combatant services, were used for various forms of labour, including work in the coalmines and saltmines. Work in the saltmines was dreaded most.'[9]

Captain Rhodes was fortunate in being repatriated, as the mutual exchange of prisoners of war between Britain and the Axis Powers only began once there were sufficient German and Italians who had been captured during the North African Campaign to make the process worthwhile for those countries. *The Times* reported the comments of another medical returnee:

> the devoted and courageous service of a British medical officer, Captain Webster, who untiringly served his fellow captives and fought for better medical treatment and camp conditions. He was constantly in conflict with the German officials, who eventually transferred him to a Russian camp, making him responsible for the entire medical arrangements there.[10]

Despite the repatriation of some RAMC prisoners, hopes frequently expressed by Tom Leak's family that he would be included in the process were in vain. Leak had to spend three long years knowing his two daughters were growing up without his presence. Leak's sister wrote on 27 September 1944: 'We were disappointed you weren't among last week's repatriates, but you will soon be home I expect.'

One medical officer unlucky enough to be captured, but fortunate enough to be released by the Germans, was Major E.R.C. Walker. He was captured, along with medical staff and patients, at Saint-Valery-en-Caux in Normandy on 11 June 1940. Walker was allowed to remain with his patients in hospitals throughout Rouen until February 1941, when they were moved to a PoW hospital in Germany. This facility was visited by a commission of observers to evaluate if any of the patients could be repatriated on medical grounds. The observers condemned conditions in the hospital, with patients only receiving 1,200 calories per day. Eventually, Red Cross parcels arrived and the prisoners' diet gradually improved. Nevertheless, Walker remained dissatisfied with the medical care his men received. 'With one or two exceptions, the German doctors appeared to be astonishingly ignorant medically,' he reported. Walker was repatriated to Britain in the summer of 1941.

To prepare for the eventual release of tens of thousands of prisoners of war at the end of the conflict, the government established an experimental rehabilitation scheme at the RAMC depot in Church Crookham. The scheme ran from November 1943 to February 1944 and included almost 800 RAMC personnel, as well as hundreds of regimental stretcher-bearers. These ex-prisoners were observed to have developed a 'stalag mentality', which was particularly pronounced in those who had been prisoners for more than eighteen months. Features of this included 'a very real but unfounded feeling that their physical or mental health had somehow been damaged', which was related to 'depression and guilt' suffered while in captivity, and to 'anxieties of re-adaption'.

Private David Jones of No. 168 Field Ambulance had been captured during an unsuccessful escape attempt in Crete and had been put to work treating Austrian paratroopers injured in the successful German invasion of the island. Having completed this work, Jones and his fellow RAMC members were taken to the harbour at Souda Bay and placed on a fishing boat with about forty other Allied prisoners, guarded by three German soldiers. By the end of the day they had arrived back in Greece, were fed and locked up for the night. The following morning, all the prisoners were herded back into the fishing boat, which was piloted by a Greek fisherman. This process was repeated as the party gradually made its way up the Greek coast. 'It was only when we were locked up that we were given food and were counted. Germans were great counters – if it moves, count it. This seemed to be one thing that the Germans were good at.'[11]

One night the party was placed under the guard of Italian troops, one of whom lunged at Jones with his bayonet, piercing the skin on his leg, as Jones had not moved fast enough. A German who was supervising operations struck the Italian, telling him to back off. After seven days inching up the Greek coast, the party arrived at Salonika, where they were placed in a large camp containing British and Antipodean prisoners captured on Greece and Crete. Jones stayed here for three months, on one occasion putting his catering skills to good use making a rabbit-tasting stew following the mysterious disappearance of the Commandant's cat.

After this lengthy period, the men were bundled into lorries, taken to a railway siding and placed in a train of twenty trucks, each with tiny windows and one plank nailed across the middle. The men in Jones's truck developed an ingenious way of loosening the nail, enabling them to make a midnight raid on the neighbouring rations wagon as the train sped through the darkness. One week later, the party arrived at Stalag VIII-B, a camp containing British, Australian and Canadian troops, as well as members of the RAF and some Russian soldiers, situated in the village of Lamsdorf.

Having been the unit cook during his time in No. 168 Field Ambulance, Jones made sure that all available food was shared out fairly between the sixty men sharing each hut. The main meal was served at lunchtime and consisted of soup, which had to be collected from the kitchen. The accompanying bread was cut having been measured into equal portions by the PoW metal tag. About twice a year, they received a Red Cross parcel containing corned beef, powdered milk, powdered egg, margarine, sardines, soap and hair cream.

Corporal David Jebbitt of No. 181 Airlanding Field Ambulance had been taken prisoner at Arnhem as the Germans took over the hospital he had been working in. On hearing the news, a family friend wrote him a poem:

Well, David, I am rather vexed
At the news your Dad told me,
That you, at nineteen years of age,
A prisoner of war should be.

But, David "Lad", it won't be long
Until you are once more free.
The Nazis are surrendering
All over Germany.

So, David, keep your pecker up,
Stick out your chest and sing
"Roll out the barrel",
Or else "God Save the King".

Now, David, I must tell you
This war we've nearly won.
You will soon be back in Blighty
With your dear old Dad and Mum.

Best wishes to you, young soldier,
Your manhood's just begun.
It seems to me a cruel shame
You're a prisoner of the Hun.

So "Cheerio!" young David,
Just show Jerry you're a man,
And when you get back to London
I will be pleased
To shake you by the hand.
J.McK.

Jebbitt's stint as a 'prisoner of the Hun' only lasted a few months before Stalag IV-B was liberated by advancing Russian troops. (Pics 29a & 29b) The German guards had fled, scared of reprisals for the mitreatment of Soviet PoWs. An order was issued by the Russians to the effect that the freed prisoners were to remain in the camp as 'mopping-up' operations continued in the vicinity. Jebbitt returned to his bed for 'a spot of happy contemplation now that for us the war was over'.[12] This contented state was not to last long, however. Jebbitt was asked by a warrant officer if he would be willing to move across to the former German Lazarette, where the hospital's facilities were being used by the Russians to treat their sick men, in order to provide additional support for their medical staff. 'I should get a decent bed up there and the thought of exchanging my louse-ridden straw mattress for a decent one was too good a bribe to refuse.' He was joined by a couple of other orderlies, including an American, and they were escorted to a small group of wooden buildings about a mile up the road, where a room recently vacated by the camp guards was made available.

The group had been assured that their stay would only last until the Russian army joined up with the American army and a route back to England was available. A week went by with no problems. The group ate with the Russian patients and medical staff – plain, simple fare, but solid and substantial, and an improvement on Red Cross parcels. Their Russian counterparts had been suffering from malnutrition as the Germans had not passed on any food parcels. The RAMC orderlies' duties consisted of making the beds, washing the floors and fetching food from the kitchens, whilst one Russian doctor and half a dozen Russian women carried out the medical duties.

After a fortnight at the lazarette, the British and American prisoners who had remained in the main camp were moved out and Jebbitt and his comrades prepared to join them. However, this anticipation was short-lived as they were told that permission had been obtained for them to stay behind for a couple of days until further Russian reinforcements arrived. Following this they would be taken down to the American lines and handed over for repatriation. Dismayed, the men returned to work amongst the apparently friendly Russians. Communication was difficult, usually taking place in broken German and hand gestures.

Gradually, it became apparent that the Russians were beginning to enjoy the sight of British orderlies on their hands and knees scrubbing floors. The presence of fit Russians in the hospital, sporting hammer and sickle cap badges and seemingly capable of work, reinforced the impression that something was amiss. This situation continued for a week, with no satisfactory reply to questions of being handed over to the American forces. Therefore the RAMC orderlies refused to scrub any more floors and decided to leave the lazarette of their own accord.

The following day they stocked up with bread and odd scraps salvaged from the kitchen, and each with a haversack, prepared for their journey. They had formed the distinct impression that should they be found moving off, they risked being forcibly detained by the Russians. Their rucksacks were smuggled out and hidden in the day, and after dark the group left the building and strolled casually down the grass verge of the roadside. Collecting their haversacks, they proceeded by moonlight, covering about 15 miles by dawn. A farmer then gave them shelter having heard their story and proclaiming, 'Ruskie nix good'. He provided a meal of hot stew before the party set off again towards the American lines.

On the road towards Riesa, the escaping orderlies caught up with a German woman who was pushing a small wooden trolley with all her worldly possessions piled on top. Recognising the group as English, the woman begged to be taken with them to the Americans. Reckoning that she spoke some English and would serve as a useful interpreter, they agreed. Rucksacks were heaped onto the trolley, with each man taking it in turns to push the cart. They passed through settlements reduced to ghost towns festooned with red flags to comply with Russian orders, and eventually reached the house of a doctor, who lit a fire for them in his consulting room and provided a meal of stew, bread and cheese. He told the group about the raping and looting that had taken place during the Russian advance. They commiserated, although Jebbitt found it strange to be sympathising with his recent enemies against a wartime ally.

Leaving the German woman with the doctor, the orderlies set off after a much-needed good night's sleep and found a bridge across the river Elbe. However, a Russian sentry stood outside a small wooden hut whilst one of his comrades paced to the centre of the bridge. An American soldier paced from the far bank to the centre, which marked the division between the Soviet and American zones. The British medics indicated to the Russian outside the hut that they were British and wished to cross over the bridge. He disappeared inside and emerged accompanied by an officer. Shortly afterwards, a US officer, seeing their predicament, came across and conferred with the Russians.

The American reassured the men that they would soon be on their way home, once the Russians had received proof of their identity. Offering their pay books and Stalag identity cards, they were allowed to cross to the American zone, where they were loaded onto a jeep and taken to an American barracks before being flown home to England the following day. David Jebbitt and his comrades had survived not just months of German captivity, but the dark menace of being held indefinitely by Soviet forces. As they waited for the jeep to take them to safety, the seeds of the forthcoming Cold War were demonstrated by a comment from one of the American solders stationed on the Elbe: 'One even said that he would have been quite willing to have continued the advance right through to Moscow. It distinctly remains in my memory that he commented "It'll save us the job in ten years' time."'

Of the 170,000 British prisoners of war captured during defeats in France, North Africa and the Balkans, 70,000 were initially housed in prisons in Italy. Spread across dozens of camps designated the initials 'P.G.', meaning *prigioniero di guerra* (prisoner of war), and frequently referred to as 'Campo', most were held until the Italian Armistice was declared on 8 September 1943. Most campos were taken over by the Germans, but many PoWs managed to escape, often encouraged and supported by their former Italian foes.

Captain Norman Rogers had been taken prisoner in June 1942 at the Battle of Gazala while serving as the Regimental Medical Officer to the 4th Royal Tank Regiment. He had been taking the wounded crew of an anti-tank gun to a field ambulance in his truck when it was intercepted by a German armoured car. Rogers ended up in Campo PG 49 at Fontanellato near Parma, which was inhabited by characters with a range of expertise from physics to forgery. He noted, 'the student could learn fascinating details about low-life east of Suez or the Danish system of pig farming.'[13]

At another camp, Campo PG 75 in Bari, Rogers experienced trying to treat men with only simple drugs and low supplies of other medical equipment. So ill-equipped was the camp that Rogers had to get men to wash their own dressings and bandages in order to reuse them. As a medical officer, Rogers was frequently moved between different camps and was sent to Campo PG 87 at Benevento alongside a fellow doctor, Donald Fleming. The camp was full of other ranks, with a warrant officer acting as the senior British presence. On arrival, Rogers and Fleming were met by an RAMC staff sergeant who was very concerned about an outbreak of a mysterious disease in the camp that was lowering morale among the prisoners. The symptoms were described as attacks of shivering and a fever, although having served in India, both the staff sergeant and warrant officer had ruled out malaria, as the indications were different to the strain of disease they had witnessed there.

Both Rogers and Fleming suspected that the camp had an outbreak of malaria, although the disease had not been seen in North Africa, where most of the prisoners had been captured. The following morning, at 7.00 am, 120 men reported for sick parade, the vast majority complaining of shivering attacks. Rogers ordered for blood samples to be taken and sent to Caserta for analysis to confirm their suspicions. Later in the morning, a group of Italian medical officers arrived at the camp, the most senior of whom regarded Rogers with some resentment as it had taken him many years of service in the Italian army to attain the rank of captain, whilst the 26-year-old Rogers had been given the rank as of right after just a year's service in the RAMC.

The Italians thought the sick men had contracted climatic fever caused by exposure to the heat of Africa followed swiftly by the cold of an Italian winter. The British doctors had noticed enlarged spleens in many of the patients, which had made them certain they were dealing with malaria, and the Italians reluctantly agreed. For two days the sick men were given doses of quinine, and following that, mepacrine. Within a month an enormous difference was noticed in the sick men. After that, apart from occasional cases of diarrhoea and an outbreak of jaundice, which also affected both Rogers and Fleming, the health of the men in the camps that Rogers worked in was relatively robust.

Some prisoners held by the Italians did not have to endure captivity until the summer of 1945. On 8 September 1943, Mussolini's successor as leader of Italy, Prime Minister Pietro Badoglio, announced an armistice. An agreement had been reached by the senior British and Italian officers at Campo PG 49 at Fontanello that in the event of any agreement between Italy's provisional government and the Allies, attempts would be made to hand British prisoners of war back to their own armies rather than the Germans. Therefore, on the morning of 9 September, the commandant of Campo PG 49 cut a hole in the fence wire surrounding the huts and the 500 officers held there marched out in companies before separating. Norman Rogers was one of the last to leave, being in a group of six men under the leadership of Company Commander Colonel Gibson of the Queen's Regiment. After two days the group became separated, with Rogers teaming up with Captain Arthur Jones to chart a course back to the Allied lines. Walking southwards along the least frequented paths and tracks, the pair walked over ridge after ridge across the Apennine Range, covering rough stony terrain and pine trees on the higher ground, and cultivated farmland at the foot of the valleys.

The pair skirted La Spezia, crossing the river Arno east of Florence. They had to avoid villages, travelling along sheep tracks and only daring to knock on the doors of isolated houses of shepherds and peasants. The Italians fed and clothed them and allowed them to sleep in barns as Rogers and Jones dodged German patrols. During the day, they tried to pass themselves off as self-demobilised Italian soldiers, on one occasion walking through a village containing about fifty German soldiers. Nevertheless, when they knocked on people's doors to seek shelter, they were candid about their identity. Rogers was moved by the fact that peasant families would welcome them unannounced, and provide a meal and shelter, sometimes giving up their own beds for the pair of escaping prisoners.

As they approached the Volturno River, near Venafro, they neared the front line of battle. The Germans were establishing a new defensive line and blowing up power stations, tearing up railway lines, demolishing houses to block roads and blasting craters in hillsides for gun emplacements. Entering the small village of Raviscanina, 37 miles north of Naples, they found it deserted. Barbed wire and rubble littered the streets and chickens roamed freely. After six weeks on the run they had reached no man's land. Up on the high ground there was a small castle that was being shelled by the Germans, who believed it to be an American observation post.

Rogers and Jones walked to the village centre, where there was a well. They began to walk up a narrow alleyway just off the main square. Just then an old woman brandishing a jeroboam bottle shouted to them not to proceed. A small boy had been killed making his way up the alley as the Germans had laid mines and tripwires along it. She had observed them and knew exactly where the perils lay, so she escorted each of them in turn along the 30-yard hazard. Rogers later reflected, 'That was a mercy that she was there at the time.'

Shortly afterwards, the duo came across a group of American GIs receiving their bread and mail issue. The conversation ran:

> 'Say, who are these guys?'
> 'We're British officers.'
> 'Where are you from?'
> 'We've come from a PoW camp in the north of Italy.'
> 'You must have come from the German lines. What's it like there?'
> 'We're here. Can we speak to your officer?'

They were then taken down to meet the colonel of the 36th Texas Division and given a meal consisting of American K-rations, for which they were extremely grateful after their privations. Apologetically, the colonel then explained that they had to be searched: 'Germans are very clever you know – you could be Germans.' After having had their story confirmed, they were interrogated and debriefed further, providing valuable information on the location of German mines and other defensive installations, before being transported to Caserta to be handed over to the British Army. From there they were taken to Naples, then on to Algiers before sailing back to the UK.

Rogers retained a fondness for the Italians, finding prison camp guards a 'comic opera lot', but one elderly doctor whom he had met was one of the most admirable men he had ever come across. During his six-week, 400-mile escape ordeal, he had found Italian country folk to be kind and courageous, risking imprisonment or worse if the Germans had found them sheltering escaped British PoWs. When he asked some of them why they had done so, they replied that it was an act of humanity that the Roman Catholic Church would have wished them to undertake.

Whilst prisoners of war held by the Italians experienced some measure of humane treatment, for those taken by the Japanese, tropical illnesses, limited diet and harsh living conditions produced a battery of severe problems for the RAMC doctors and orderlies to have to deal with, making their experience of captivity vastly different from their counterparts in Europe. Many treated patients who were suffering from diseases they had never experienced, with limited medicines and few instruments. By the time the war ended they were living off their wits as much as their medical training.

Following surrender to the Japanese, the No. 1 Malay General Hospital situated in the Victoria Theatre in Singapore continued to treat casualties. By 17 February, two days after the surrender, there were 1,847 patients spread across various buildings in Singapore City.[14] Responsibility for moving all the sick and wounded British and Australian prisoners from Singapore City into Changi Camp fell to a senior Australian Medical Officer, Lieutenant Colonel Glyn White. Whilst the British and Australians were to go to Changi, captured Indian casualties were sent to Nee Soon Camp. The senior Japanese medical officer, Colonel C.L. Sekiguchi, allocated just five ambulances for the task of moving all 9,000 patients – all this to be completed within seven days. White protested at the inadequacy of the transport arrangements and Sekiguchi agreed that if extra vehicles could be found then White could use them. The following morning, twenty 3-ton trucks, fifty-five ambulances and a car were lined up. Although only allowed to move 250 hospital beds, White managed to take 4,500 beds and 7,000 mattresses under the noses of the Japanese. Furthermore, instead of the week initially allotted, White managed to convince Sekiguchi's successor that the agreement had been a week for each of the British, Australian and Indian patients, giving three weeks in total. Thus a combination of resourcefulness, fortune and cunning ensured that most patients were safely transferred from military hospitals into the prison camps.

Changi Camp was situated towards the eastern end of Singapore Island and had been designed to accommodate 3,600 men engaged in coastal defence. By the end of February 1942, 50,000 men were crammed into the space, with the British medical services occupying the Roberts Barracks. One barrack block was designated as an operating theatre, another became an isolation ward, and two blocks were allocated as dysentery wards. The final transfer of British casualties was completed by 2 March. Following this, the Japanese ordered the Australians to move their patients from the Selarang Barracks, also within the Changi compound, to the Roberts Hospital.

The Roberts Barracks, having been close to a military target before surrender, had been heavily shelled and was in a poor state of repair. There was no electric lighting, no sewage disposal and a limited water supply initially. The paucity in the provision of basic utilities was in stark contrast to the medical expertise amongst RAMC officers, the hospital being served by specialist anaesthetists, radiologists, pathologists and surgeons. However, as most nurses had been evacuated from Singapore in the final days before its capitulation to the Imperial Japanese Army, regular soldiers, often untrained for the task, had to perform nursing duties.

Unlike in some German and Italian camps, men who were identified as in need of repatriation due to the nature and severity of their wounds and the need for specialised treatment were not sent home. This was despite medical members of the Imperial Japanese Army concurring with these judgements, and in line with the disregard Japan had shown for the Geneva Convention of 1929, which it had refused to sign.

Conditions in the Roberts Hospital were poor as medics strove to maintain the health of their patients. It was surrounded by slit trenches, which were being used as latrines, around which fly larvae had spread. Flies would invade the hospital, attracted by the pus of men's wounds and in such conditions that an inevitable outbreak of dysentery soon occurred. By 24 March 1942, the hospital housed 2,600 patients, and throughout March and April 1942 there were over 5,000 admissions for dysentery.[15] Captain Bill Frankland was responsible for one of the two newly opened dysentery wards, treating the sick and trying to control the spread of the epidemic. Captain Jack Ennis, a pathologist who had been attached to No. 1 Malay General Hospital, noted that 'we work and sleep to the sound of flies, defaecation, vomiting and the rattle of bedpans all the time.'[16]

Captain C.W. Wells, admitted as a patient in March 1942, described the conditions in the Roberts Hospital dysentery wing:

> 23 March
> Brought to the hospital 2 days ago, got dysentery, passing blood, awful belly-ache and feeling like death. 3 dysentery deaths last night, one within 3 feet of me, he died in delirium.
>
> 25 March
> Feeling a bit better. Hospital under-staffed. Still passing blood. It is essential here that one does all one can to help one's self, because individual attention is out of the question. Been put on a light diet – sweet rice pudding, shepherd's pie, porridge, savoury rice and tea. Legs feel wonky. First nightmare for years last night.

> 27 March
> Bored to hell in hospital, destitute of anything to read.
>
> 28 March
> Discharged from hospital today, had to walk back a mile and half in boiling sun to my billet.[17]

There were two strains of the disease. Bacillary dysentery was treated by intravenous administration of sterile saline. Antibacterial agents such as sulphonamide and sulphaguanidine were also used, although supplies of these soon ran out. More serious for the victim was amoebic dysentery, of which there were about ten cases per week admitted to Roberts Hospital. Untreated, the victim would suffer excruciating pain, intestinal problems and death within seven to ten days. Men often became deranged in the last few hours before death. Amoebic dysentery was caused by lack of fats and vitamins in the diet, and many of those who survived contracting the disease in Singapore continued to suffer intestinal disease long after the end of the war. As well as the skills of the medics in treating such debilitating diseases, Bill Frankland reckoned that a crucial factor in pulling through was the psychological will to survive.[18] The combined efforts of the hospital doctors and the resilience of the Allied soldiers meant that from February 1942 to February 1943, of the 15,379 dysentery admissions to Roberts Hospital, the death rate was a mere 1.5 per cent for bacillary dysentery and 2.2 per cent for amoebic dysentery.[19]

Another significant challenge that faced doctors working at the Roberts Hospital was diphtheria, with over 800 patients hospitalised at the height of a 1942 epidemic. A whole hospital block had to be assigned to treat these cases and one medical officer and fourteen orderlies also succumbed to the disease. Frustratingly, the doctors knew there were plentiful supplies of diphtheria antiserum on the island, which had been previously stored at Tanglin Hospital, but the Japanese refused to distribute them. One particularly enterprising doctor, Captain Hugh de Wardener, took blood from patients who had recovered and made his own antiserum from this. De Wardener self-administered the serum and his pain disappeared almost immediately.

Although de Wardener's discovery allowed for some supply of serum, Bill Frankland was faced with an ethical dilemma with a diphtheria patient. The man was also suffering from dysentery and malaria and stood little chance of survival. Without the antiserum treatment he was sure to die. Frankland requested the one remaining dose from Captain E.K. Cruickshank, the officer in charge of the hospital pharmacy, but was told that another patient had been admitted a few hours earlier, suffering from diphtheria and malaria, but was relatively well. Reluctantly, Frankland allowed the treatment to be given to the healthier patient, reflecting that the first man would have died anyway, even with the administration of the serum.

Captain Forde Cayley's captivity began with a 10-mile walk to Changi, during which he was spat at by Arab traders keen to enact vengeance on their previous British overlords. During his early days at the camp he contracted dysentery, and was admitted to hospital, where there was poor hygiene due to a lack of bedpans. On returning to the room that he had been allocated to share with army chaplain Reverend D.E. Davison, Cayley found that someone had stolen his stethoscope. His spirits low, and with the biblical knowledge inculcated in him during twice-daily services during his public schooldays, he reflected, 'As I had a bible I thought the Book of Job would be suitable reading.'[20]

Cayley was assigned to a work party that was sent to Bukit Timah to build a shrine for the Japanese war dead. The men were allocated a large rice ration, but little else, so most contracted beriberi, pellagra and scrotal dermatitis, with some developing brain and nerve troubles. In addition there was an epidemic of typhoid in the group.

Captain Leslie Ellis initially experienced some consideration from his new Japanese captors. Having been stationed near the Raffles Institution in Singapore City with No. 16 Field Ambulance dressing major wounds, he recalled 'no trouble' when they took over the dressing station, allowing Ellis to be admitted to a local hospital to be treated for jaundice.[21] During his two-week convalescence, he had the freedom to walk around town before being taken to Changi camp.

However, events were to take a grim turn for the worse on 30 August 1942, following an unsuccessful escape attempt by four men. Enraged, the newly arrived camp commander, General Shimpei Fukuye, demanded that all prisoners interned at the Selarang Barracks sign a pledge promising not to attempt escape. To have done so would have been contrary to the terms of the Geneva Convention, which accorded prisoners of war the right to attempt escape and not be punished if caught. Therefore, there was a mass refusal, and the vast majority of the British and Australian troops at Changi were herded into the parade square in Selarang, a barracks built to accommodate 800 men. This meant that nearly 17,000 men were squashed in, with the Japanese cutting off the water supplies to the toilets. With little food and water available, men soon started to succumb to dysentery.

Captain Harry Silman, a medical officer attached to the 9th Royal Northumberland Fusiliers, had loaded medical stores onto an ambulance, which also towed two full water tank trucks loaded with kit, sick men and tables into Selarang.[22] There were only two water points for the entire area, and water was limited to one gallon per day per man for all purposes and a prohibition on washing and shaving was ordered. An open sewer ran past the heads of officers sleeping on a ground floor veranda, creating an immediate stench and an ever-present threat of malaria.

Silman had one medical inspection room available for the sick, meaning only urgent and acute cases could be seen, and no routine dressings or treatments could be done. An Australian hospital tent had been set up, which undertook surgical operations and dentistry work. On the first night an appendix operation was performed, as the flies increased in number and the swill of excreta accumulated. Long rows of latrines were dug, 16 feet deep, and sappers made seats from the doors of the billets.

As the death count started to rise, and with the Japanese threatening to move more men into Selarang, which would have created a medical massacre, Lieutenant General E.B. Holmes, commander of the British and Australian troops at Changi, reluctantly issued the order to sign the undertaking not to attempt to escape.

The Thai-Burma Railway, also known as the Death Railway, stretched 258 miles from Ban Pong, Thailand to Thanbyuzayat, Burma, built by the Empire of Japan in 1943 to support its forces in the Burma Campaign. As well as native slave labour, thousands of British and other Allied prisoners of war were sent from the prison camps to work on its construction. A remarkable esprit de corps motivated Sergeant Leslie Brand and his comrades to volunteer to be sent up to work on the railway. As a member of No. 196 Field Ambulance, whose commanding officer had been detailed to accompany the working party, the remaining men of the unit had chosen to leave en bloc to stay together. In addition, 'We were told we were bound for "Valhalla" – plenty of food – leisure and all the good things to which a PoW was entitled. We were even told to take musical instruments to amuse ourselves during the long hours of inactivity!'[23] These hopes were soon dashed during a long train journey during which people had to sleep in shifts due to the lack of space.

Captain Harry Silman and his comrades were similarly delighted to have been chosen to leave Changi and travel to a new unknown camp as part of 'F' Force, a party 7,000 strong, half of whom were British and half Australian. 'There is a schoolgirlish atmosphere as the officers discuss their trip and future abode as though we were going away on holiday,' he recorded in his diary on 10 April 1943. 'The Japanese seem to be very lenient with us, and all luggage and baggage is allowed to be taken with us.'

During Leslie Brand's march up to the camp, locals were only too keen to steal what they could from the tiring troops. Even men of the cloth were not immune from this treatment. Brand recalled:

> What really did annoy us was the fact that our Padre – one of the finest I ever met – had all his vestments stolen on the second day. If ever a man was a shining example it was him. Padre Duckworth, or 'Duckie' as was known to us, was always there to help carry a sick man's pack and offer encouragement by his own personal example. He achieved more than any man I met.

On arrival at the camp, there was just a clearing made by local workers; no cookhouse and no hospital. Rudimentary latrines consisted of a trench with bamboo poles over the top on which people balanced: 'This was a free for all, us and the locals – including their women folk!'

Initially, RAMC personnel were made to work on the railway, until after about ten days, so many men were down with cholera that the Japanese were forced to allow them to open a hospital ward. Brand was 'put in charge of this horror'. There was little that medical orderlies could do to effect a cure for cholera. Saline was administered intravenously using half a stethoscope for a tube, and an ordinary bottle for the salt and sterilised water solution. The cholera outbreak could not, for the Japanese guards, slow the progress of railway construction. Brand recalled:

> We began losing more and more men with the dreadful scourge but the Nips were only concerned with getting men working on the railway. One morning they called for one hundred men when the most that could be produced was eighty. They ranted and raved, slapped and bashed our CO and insisted that a hundred men be produced. In the end our CO told us to carry our least sick men out to the parade ground and challenged the Nips to make them work. The Nips – completely snookered – then decreed that only working men would receive full rations, the sick would only get a reduced amount.

The sick were not to suffer this punishment, as every man, without exception, agreed that all food should be pooled and shared equally.

Captain Harry Silman became infuriated with the demands to provide a workforce from sick men:

> I knew that those who used to suffer from vitamin B deficiency, which used to affect their hearts, if they were made to work they wouldn't last very long. I used to try and explain that to the Japanese when they wanted to take people. They didn't take any notice. They would pull them to their feet … and carry his dead body back to you. That happened time and time again on these working parties. I used to stand over so many of these chaps who were desperately ill and the Japanese would try and get him. They would say 'want him'. They would push me away with their guns and bayonets, pick the fellow up and put him in the working party and then they would all march off at six o'clock in the morning, raining and cold and dark, and I knew this poor fellow wouldn't come back alive. They took no notice of me at all as long as they got their numbers. When you have got three or four Japanese with bayonets you can't argue with them very well.[24]

Even worse than the cycle of men dying was the fact that their corpses often lay next to their ailing comrades for hours on end. Twice daily, the guards would do a count in the hospital. Leslie Brand recalled: 'If a man died as the guards passed during their count, he had to remain there until after the next count. This often meant that we had four or five bodies packed alongside men who were themselves battling for their lives.'

Eventually, as cholera raged and the Japanese became fearful of the epidemic spreading to them, they decreed that the hospital should be moved to the other side of the valley, and there would be two camps – the 'fit' camp and the hospital camp. Captain Harry Silman was another medic who noted the Japanese aversion to proximity of men stricken with cholera. With 300 to 400 patients at any one time, there was little he could do for them apart from administer intravenous fluids, thus cholera became a 'death sentence'. The only blessing for Silman for such cases was the short duration of the illness prior to death. The smell from the cholera wards was terrible, 'the dead and the dying and the excreta', and the Japanese would make masks for themselves before entering the hospital camp. 'They didn't mind dying in battle, but they were so afraid of dying from a disease,' noted Silman. The daily spectre of death made medics inured to the awfulness to some extent:

> We used to make bonfires every evening and burn the cholera patients and those that had died during the day. We began to accept that it was our way of living now. We got sort of hardened to it. There is very little difference between life and death, so to speak. When you are amongst dead and dying, the narrow line between living and dying seems to sort of disappear. It's difficult to explain. You hope obviously that you are going to keep living from day to day but, living with the dying, you are not going to think about dying so much as trying to cope with the living.[25]

Captain Forde Cayley was another medical officer taken to Burma to undertake the construction of the Death Railway. Having been taken by train as far as Ban Pong, he was then marched to Chungkai. Here, Cayley and his comrades came under the command of Colonel Nakamura, 'who was a gentleman who tried to teach us his yoga exercises'. Two of the other Japanese officers, Captain Taramoto and Lieutenant Kanioka, were 'slave drivers'.[26] Due to the heavy and unrelenting work in tropical conditions, men were constantly falling sick. Malaria stalked the camps, and as one man succumbed, another convalescing from a tropical disease was forced to take his place on a working party.

Those who fell sick received no pay and were thus unable to buy any food from local traders to supplement their meagre rations. Therefore the officers, who were paid two or three times the wage of an ordinary rank, would all chip in to a fund to buy eggs and other rations for the sick. Those fit enough to work were given two tablets per day of prophylactic quinine, but this too was stopped if a man fell ill. Captain Forde Cayley recalled, 'We were lousy and the huts were infested with bed bugs.'[27]

Leslie Ellis drew lots with two fellow doctors to decide which one of them would leave a relatively comfortable assignment in Hanoi to be sent to Thailand. He went by steamer up the Mekong Delta to Phnom Penh, Cambodia, then by train to Bangkok before reaching the base of the railway. During his stint on the railway, Ellis was beaten on a few occasions for complaining about the treatment of the men in his care. 'I had a sick man and I said he shouldn't go out ... to do any work, and the Japanese dragged him out and I came out and complained and they ... beat me for it.'

During the early months of Ellis's time treating men who had fallen sick constructing the Death Railway, dysentery was the most common disease, but as the conditions worsened, vitamin deficiencies became more prevalent and then tropical ulcers appeared, which were often the immediate cause of death. The ulcers poisoned the bodies of the undernourished men. Ellis was frustrated that he could do little to help them, lacking basic medicines that could have saved lives, but occasionally, life-saving amputations were performed. For Captain Harry Silman, these amputations were heart-rending. His diary for 18 September 1943 noted: 'Our death toll is now on the 200 mark. Extensive, non-bleeding ulcers are now being treated by amputation. It seems such a tragedy to lose a leg following a scratch a few weeks previously. It is the only treatment as they otherwise die of toxaemia and inanition.'[28]

The heartache assumed a more personal hue with one case, leaving Silman distraught at his powerlessness to cure. On 27 October he recorded:

> I saw my former batman, Windmill, Royal Engineers, today. He is in the ulcer ward and looks a wreck of his former rigorous self. He pleaded with me with tears in his eyes for his leg to be taken off but as he is such a bad operative risk it will not be done. He says the pain is terrific, twenty-four hours a day, and at night he is afraid of losing his reason. What a terrible thing a tropical ulcer is. The post-operative mortality is very high owing to the general poor condition of the men.

The following day, Ronald Windmill was one of a large batch of men on whom Silman did perform an amputation, but on 3 November, the 22-year-old driver died from his wounds.

Doctors were by no means immune from the tropical diseases they were treating in ever-increasing numbers. Leslie Ellis suffered from amoebic dysentery for two and a half years alongside frequent relapses of malaria. However, he was fortunate in that he was given the first priority in treatment by the Japanese:

> If anybody was going to get treatment for malaria it was the doctor, so I was in some ways lucky because [it was] probably a good idea to keep me alive so I can keep some other people alive … occasionally I had some quinine, and, curiously enough, my worst attack of malaria I had some German Mepacrine. It sounds ridiculous.

Captain Harry Silman was another doctor fortunate enough to receive ten quinine tablets per day to treat his malaria, although immediate relief for his suffering was not forthcoming. 'Whether it is illness or the treatment, I feel bloody awful – no appetite, nausea, dizziness, cold sweats, deafness and tinnitus.'[29]

As a medical officer, Forde Cayley was at high risk of catching one of the myriad tropical diseases that troops were prone to contracting. One day he visited a branch camp and saw a man on a bamboo stretcher lying in his own watery stool, 'looking collapsed and with washerwoman's fingers'. A fly flew up from the stool and landed in Cayley's mouth. The man had cholera, one of thirty cases being treated in a separate camp 2 miles from the main base.

Japanese atrocities against medical personnel had not ceased after the attack on the Alexandra Military Hospital. On 18 October 1942, 600 men were sent from Changi as the '600 Gunner party' with two medical officers, Captain Bernard Aldridge of the 1 Malay Field Ambulance and Captain J.W. Lillico of the Indian Medical Service. They boarded the *Kenkon Maru* and were transported in atrocious conditions to the port of Rabaul in New Britain, to the east of Papua New Guinea. Working in appalling conditions, many became ill and just 517 were deemed fit by the end of November 1942. They were taken by another ship to Balalae Island, one of the Solomon Islands, to build an airstrip for the Japanese. Many prisoners were killed in an American air raid and the Japanese, believing that the island would be taken by the Americans, ordered that all remaining prisoners, including the medics, be shot. As well as Aldridge and Lillico, RAMC members executed by the Japanese were Privates Charles Robinson, Percy Neaves and Kenneth Sharman of No. 198 Field Ambulance, and Sergeant Leslie Knox.

Although he had been subjected to punishment beatings, Captain Bill Frankland survived until well past his hundredth birthday to tell his tale of captivity. Frankland left Changi on 5 November 1943 to be sent to the island of Blakang Mati, just off the south coast of Singapore Island. En route, the Japanese stole some of his personal belongings, including a watch and his patella hammer, but a new one was manufactured for him on the island by an Australian from a chair leg, with a rubber end made from an old car tyre. Deficiency diseases were common amongst the British and Australian prisoners on the island, with Frankland, as the only British medical officer present, responsible for the treatment of the British. The Japanese kept a strict demarcation between the two barrack blocks on the island, known as Australia House and English House.

During evening parade on Blakang Mati, the Japanese took great pleasure in the violent humiliation of British officers, ostensibly as punishment for the misdemeanours of their men. On one occasion, Frankland was hit across the face so hard that a molar tooth was knocked out. Hit to the ground, Frankland then got up, dazed and uncoordinated, and clenched his fists in front of him. A Japanese private made as if to bayonet him but was prevented from doing so by a Japanese officer who said they 'needed all the doctors they could get'.[30]

The island suffered from a disrupted water supply, and Frankland was able to locate supplies of fresh water using a divining rod made from two pieces of copper wire.

As happened elsewhere in the Far East prison camps, a doctor would be ordered to find enough men fit to go on work parties. Frankland frequently had his medical judgement overturned by a Japanese NCO as more men were required to work. However, of the nearly 300 men under his care on Blakang Mati, all survived until the end of the war.

Captain Forde Cayley had managed to keep his case of surgical instruments through the stress and movement of the marches to build the Thai-Burma Railway. However, one day, a Korean medical orderly discovered he had lost his dressing forceps and wanted to commandeer Cayley's equipment. When Cayley refused, the Korean took off his clogs and belted him over the head as hard as he could, then, as Cayley was barely conscious, he kicked him in the stomach. But Cayley got to keep his instruments.

Six days later, after miles of forced marching carrying his medical pannier, and supporting sick men, Cayley fell ill with malaria, exacerbated by the delayed shock from his beating. He rested at a camp and was taken by boat to rejoin his party further upstream at Conquita. Here, Cayley was able to buy medicines from a local Thai merchant named Boonpong Sirivejjabhandu, who was working undercover in 'V' Organisation against the Japanese. Due to this, a man with a perforated ulcer had a laparotomy performed on him by Captain Christison, with Cayley administering the chloroform. Providentially, the instruments that Cayley had saved by taking a punishment beating were used in the operation.

In order to maximise the chances of survival for the men in their care, army doctors devised ingenious methods of treatment that utilised the sparse supply of rudimentary materials at their disposal. At Bang Po, the site of a Buddhist monastery, Captain Forde Cayley saw Professor Jacob Markowitz of Toronto Medical School treating the prevailing epidemic of diphtheria by transfusing blood from a recovered case. The blood was caught in a clean milk tin and stirred with a bamboo paddle to catch the fibrin, before being injected into the patient. Markowitz, a Canadian, had offered his services to the British Army and was commissioned into to the RAMC. His work in the prison camps, particularly the development of blood transfusion techniques with only the crudest equipment and under constant strain, earned him the MBE. His citation read:

> As joint originator and supervisor of a fully successful transfusion service in prisoner-of-war camps in Siam, using the most primitive and improvised apparatus, this officer has shown skill and ability of an outstanding degree. His training of transfusion teams, his development of simple techniques for jungle surgery and his ingenious methods of improvisation saved many hundreds of lives. He has shown great disregard for personal danger and risk of brutality in order to serve his patients.

Markowitz performed 'jungle surgery' with instruments fashioned from table cutlery and undertook over 1,000 successful amputations with a hacksaw and small amounts of anaesthetic. Realising the importance of preserving the legacy of the conditions and medical treatments in the camps, Markowitz devised a scheme by which he buried medical documents in bottles besides the bodies of British soldiers. After the war the records were recovered and published, providing valuable insights into treating patients with minimal equipment and in conditions of extreme deprivation.

Forde Cayley was ordered on a week's march of 20 miles per day from Tarsao to Martona. Here, it had been ordered that the railway was to be finished as quickly as possible, regardless of the human cost. Cayley had been issued with a medical pannier with rope rings in which to fix a carrying pole, and he and his medical orderly, Corporal Jones, carried this for the entire journey. At Martona, Cayley used his resourcefulness to treat cases of beriberi, using sugar to brew a rice beer as an ointment, and a yeast cake to start off the urination process. This was successful. 'One man had become swollen all over with beriberi and went off his head and peed in the Korean guard tent. I tried a mug of my brew and spent all night passing water and turned from a balloon into a skeleton.'[31]

Tropical ulcers were dressed with banana leaves, whilst rock sulphur was brewed up with army bleaching powder to treat scabies and ringworm, and magnesium sulphate was used to treat dysentery. Six men went into a coma from cerebral malaria. When Cayley's intravenous quinine had run out, he squashed up an Atabrine (mepacrine) tablet in boiled water in a syringe, shook it and injected that. They all came round after three days, 'but with a bedsore the size of a soup plate from the hard bamboo platform they were on'.

Captain Harry Silman's ingenuity was demonstrated when he devised a method of infusing clean water into men who had contracted cholera:

> My problem was treating the cholera patients. You get water from the river, boil it up as best you can, and then you've got to have some infusion apparatus. With small bamboo shoots you can make an intravenous needle by cutting it tidily, fastening it to a stethoscope tubing, and you get a little pail or canister and you fasten a tube and suspend it from a bamboo shoot or rod. You put the needle in and then you bandaged it tightly to try and stop the bleeding but if you chose the vein correctly and you got the bamboo needle just the right size, there'd be very little oozing. It was all sort of makeshift. That was the only treatment that we could have.[32]

Forde Cayley attempted to treat the cholera cases with a drip of rock salt solution in a milk tin with a hole in the bottom to which he attached a Higginson syringe at the other end with a needle. Sadly, only one patient survived the cholera, and even he died shortly afterwards from beriberi. Due to dehydration, men's limbs had become distorted into grotesque postures, but their agony was prolonged by remaining conscious to the end.

Late into captivity, at Kanburi, officers were separated from the other ranks, and Cayley went to a hospital camp at Nakhon Pathom. It was populated with men no longer fit for work and a team of highly qualified doctors, including the legendary Australian medic Major Edward 'Weary' Dunlop. Amongst the skilled operations undertaken there were a craniotomy on an American sailor who had a cerebral tumour, and thoracoplasty, for which Cayley provided the anaesthetic using an improvised Junker's inhaler. Microscopes had been made from old mess tins with lenses of field glasses, blood transfusions were used to treat cases of chronic malaria, and the gastric juices of a healthy person were injected into the stomachs of men suffering from macrocytic anaemia. It was not only the level of medical expertise that was exceedingly good; 'The standard of bridge was so high that after the war the players won pots of money in bridge clubs all over the world. One of the players was Piddington, who started a thought-reading act afterwards.'

Leslie Ellis admired the ingenuity of his fellow doctors in treating cholera by distilling water and making saline solutions to replace the salts lost in rice water stools: 'That was terrific … they had little distillation plants and they sterilised this or made little injection plants and saved a lot of lives that way.'[33] Ellis also had what he felt was the honour of working alongside Major Dunlop, 'a great chap, an Australian doctor … and the last period but one I was with in the camp with him … he was a qualified surgeon and a great, a great personality. And I assisted him occasionally in doing minor operations there.'

It was not just in devising original methods of medical care that RAMC members showed creativity. Sergeant Leslie Brand of No. 196 Field Ambulance was one of a group of men who left Changi camp on Easter Sunday 1942, each carrying part of a wireless set to be reassembled later. On arrival at Camp Bam Pong, night marches totaling 100 miles were undertaken until the group reached a clearing in a jungle. Following an outbreak of cholera, the Japanese decided to split the camp into the 'fit' camp and the 'sick' camp, each section on either side of a valley. Food would be cooked in the 'fit' side and carried to one side of a stream that ran through the valley. Men from the hospital had to wade the stream, collect the food and bring it back to the hospital. As it was realised that the Japanese were scared stiff of cholera, it was decided that the wireless set would be safest in the hospital camp as generally, visits by the guards were only at set roll call times. The set was carefully reassembled and each night, news was picked up from Radio Delhi.

In addition to the wireless, the hospital had a mascot, a black dog named Etam, who hated the Japanese guards. One night, the news had finished and the four men who had been keeping watch by the door returned to the ward. The set had broken, and the officer in charge was trying to repair it by candlelight. Suddenly, Etam growled, and the candle was hurriedly blown out and everyone lay still. The guard called the officer and demanded to know why the candle was blown out when the dog barked. The officer explained that he was looking at a sick man and, having satisfied himself that he was all right, he had blown out the candle. The guard was not easily fooled and insisted that it was only when the dog barked that the light was snuffed.

The officer then offered to show the guard the sick man and brought him straight to Sergeant Brand. 'The wireless set was in the mosquito net next to mine. The officer nudged me, but I did not need any prompting. I was scared and the sweat ran off me as though I was having a bout of malaria. A few groans thrown in for luck and the guard became satisfied and went off.'

Visits by guards such as this were rare. Brand recalled that a few came looking for M&B 693 (sulfapyridine) to cure their venereal disease, but the pharmacist became wise to them and made up tablets of ordinary classroom chalk.

A few weeks later, a worse wireless scare occurred in the hospital. An arrangement had been made with the 'fit' section of the camp across the valley that if a search was being put on by the Japanese, the bugler would play 'officers' mess', a call never used normally. One night, however, the set had again broken down but it was decided to leave repairs until the following morning in good daylight. Repairs were well under way when 'officers' mess' sounded. The medics hurriedly tried to clear the wireless away, but before all the evidence could be hidden, the guards arrived. They found a soldering iron and some wire still visible.

Men were beaten, including the officer in charge, who was then taken away. The men experienced a sinking feeling as they feared, from past experience, that he would receive some very brutal treatment and possibly never be seen again. They were therefore delighted when, ten days later, he returned, if not unharmed, then at least in good spirits. He had been bashed around a lot, but had stuck to his story that what had been found was for an emergency operating lighting set, for use during the night. At first the Japanese did not believe this story and punished him further. However, his story eventually wore them down and they then asked him if the story of the operating set was true, how he got electricity for it. He told them that he had a 12-volt car battery and that when it ran down he would have nothing. The men laughed as the officer then told them that he had been instructed by the guards to bring the battery to them when it needed recharging, as they would ensure it was done. So the Japanese guards ended up charging a battery that the captives used to listen illicitly to news on the wireless.

Private Gerald Hitchcock of No. 198 Field Ambulance had been taken prisoner when Singapore fell, and was sent up the line to work on the Death Railway. During his captivity, his family only received one terse pre-printed postcard, with one short line for a personal message. Addressed to his mother in Bletchley, Buckinghamshire, it read:

> I am interned in THAILAND
> My health is excellent
> I am working for pay
> Please see that Dad's work and Ray is taken care.
> My love to you[34]

Hitchcock's mother's agony at the lack of news of her son was evident in a postcard that was sent on 13 September 1944:

> MY DARLING
>
> ALL OUR LOVE. I WRITE EVERY FORTNIGHT. WE PRAY FOR YOUR SAFETY AND RETURN. 'RAY'S MARRIED'. WE ARE WELL BUT SAD ABOUT YOU DEAR SON.
>
> WANT NEWS
> MOTHER.

To while away the long years of captivity, and to keep his mind and soul active thus increasing his chances of survival, Hitchcock gathered what artistic materials he could, designing a ticket for a sports day held at Nong Pladuk camp on 15 August 1944. Alongside the relay races and the jumping events was an 'Over 40 handicap of 400 metres. 2 metre start for each year over 40'. Hitchcock also created a beautiful representation of a camp hut, nestling in the Thai mountains, framed with the insignia of the 18th Infantry Division and the Red Cross brassard of the RAMC. (Pics 30 & 31) Out of the torment of captivity were created items that demonstrated the strength of human character.

From the spring of 1945 onwards, it became evident to the prisoners that the tide of the war in the East had decisively turned in the Allies' favour, offering hope of a release from the torment of Japanese captivity. Sometimes, though, the sight of Allied planes was not a time for rejoicing. Towards the end of the war, Captain Forde Cayley was sent to Nong Pladuk to work in a large hospital hut. One night, as Allied planes flew over, despite many of his comrades assuming they were safe from 'friendly fire', he wisely decided to take shelter in a monsoon trench as the aircraft rained fire down on the camp. Once the attack had finished, Cayley emerged from the trench to find his colleague, Captain Primrose, had had his leg blown off. The extent of the casualties was such that the mildly injured or uninjured men were operating for the following three days, with Cayley administering chloroform. A hundred men had been killed outright and 100 died of their wounds. A mass grave was dug and the bodies were taken out in a truck and buried.

Despite three years of inhumane treatment at the hands of Japanese guards, many British troops were able to rise above this and show humanity to their fellow man. A party of Japanese wounded came down to Nong Pladuk by train. They hadn't had food or water for three days, but none of the Japanese camp guards went to help them. It was the British medics and patients who shared their meagre rations with their wounded foes. Cayley got an attack of malabsorption and was admitted to the camp hospital to be fed on pap rice and onion stew, 'but it all went straight through'. Cayley thought he would die, and 'A strange peace came over me.' However, he recovered, just in time for the next Allied raid, during which he sheltered in a split trench. A bomb fell in the adjoining trench, killing all its inhabitants.

Tragically, many prisoners, weakened by years of overwork, malnourishment and beatings, died just weeks from release. Forde Cayley's last camp was by the Kra Isthmus, along with 400 other men. By this time, he had no quinine to administer to a number of malaria cases suffering from jaundice. Some of the stricken men went into a coma due to hepatic failure. As there was little to eat besides rice, even the cooks suffered from beriberi. Cayley did not experience much success in treating the malaria with a local ivy, and, as a medical officer, had to assist with the digging of about eight graves per day for the deceased.

The war came to an abrupt end for Cayley. One day, a Japanese officer mounted a soapbox and said, 'War finish, all men go home and fight Russians.' Cayley left the camp with the walking wounded, and was then taken to Rangoon, where he was issued with a new uniform and assigned to an eye specialist, who made him a new pair of spectacles. During the voyage back to the United Kingdom, a brother officer reported sick with primary syphilis. On his release, a local Thai bigwig had given a party with drink and dancing girls. Cayley took the decision, as the man was going back to his wife in a small town, to put a bandage round his head and offload him at Gibraltar with a diagnosis of otitis media, an inflammatory disease of the middle ear.

Leslie Ellis noted a distinct improvement in the treatment he and fellow prisoners received as the war in the Far East neared its end. One day, the normal work detail of making ammunition dumps in a nearby cave was not ordered, nor was any other work. At first the men were puzzled, then 'saw the Japanese scurrying about burning papers and so on. … And the senior sergeant was called over to the Japanese commander's hut … and he said "the war is over. You're now free men." That was it.' The following day the freed men went down to the local market with their meagre savings in order to purchase food, but it was several days before any significant movement away from the camp took place.

For RAMC men who had endured years of captivity at the hands of the enemy, they not only had to maintain their own physical and psychological health but support their comrades in doing so too. Those held in German and Italian camps had a broadly tolerable time as those nations were signatories to the Geneva Convention, and the Red Cross was allowed some access to the camps. For those held by the Japanese, the appalling conditions meant that nearly a quarter of the prisoners died or were killed directly by their captors.

Prisoners held in Europe were able to write home reasonably freely and frequently, but those in the Far East endured months and even years without any communication to and from Britain. For the Japanese, the act of surrendering was abhorrent and therefore troops who had allowed themselves to be taken prisoner were treated with disdain. Disease and malnutrition were their just reward for not fighting to the death. Medical facilities were rudimentary, with anaesthetics forbidden at Changi camp. The resourcefulness of medics in the Far East camps was remarkable as staff worked with minimal support from camp authorities or supervision from the Red Cross. They shone a light of humanity into the darkest corners of malevolence.

Chapter 7

Medicine in Western Europe, 1942–44

Although the liberation of Western Europe began with the launch of Operation Overlord on 6 June 1944, in the years leading up to that, a number of raids took place on the French coast, the most successful being Operation Chariot – the raid on St Nazaire. A British amphibious attack on the heavily defended Normandie dry dock at St Nazaire in German-occupied France was undertaken by the Royal Navy and British Commandos under the auspices of Combined Operations Headquarters on 28 March 1942. The choice of the dry dock at St Nazaire for the target of the raid was due to its strategic importance in the repair of the large German warships, such as the *Tirpitz*. If the dock could be rendered unusable, then such vessels would have to run the gauntlet of the Royal Naval Home Fleet across the English Channel, or take the much longer GIUK gap via Greenland and Icelandic waters in order to reach safe port. HMS *Campbeltown*, a former US Navy destroyer, was packed with delayed action explosives and, accompanied by eighteen smaller craft, left Falmouth on 26 March 1942, crossed the English Channel to the French Atlantic coast and in the early hours of 28 March, was rammed into the Normandie dock gates. The explosives detonated later that day, putting the dock out of action for the remainder of the war.

A force of commandos landed to destroy machinery and other structures, but their small craft were destroyed by German gunfire. Of the 611 men who took part in the raid, 228 managed to escape overland back to Britain, 169 were killed and 215 were taken prisoner. Five Victoria Crosses and eighty-four other bravery decorations were awarded to those who had been involved in what became known as 'The Greatest Raid of All'.

Captain David Paton had been transferred from a posting in the Orkneys to join No. 2 Commando in Ayr. (Pic 32) His initial impression of his new comrades was mixed:

> They hadn't been trained at all in these days. Some of them were ruffians. I mean some of them were jail birds – really.

> And they just couldn't stand the discipline of a Regiment with regular hours and regular drills and being confined to barracks and that sort of thing. They couldn't stand that, but many of them were brilliant chaps. Some of them were, one of them was a correspondent to *The Times* in Turkey.[1]

After a period of training in Scotland in February 1942, the unit embarked for Falmouth. A fortnight later, a large parcel arrived, a model of the docks at St Nazaire. 'A very good paper, papier mâché model of the docks, and we had got to study these.' In preparation for the treatment of casualties, Paton ordered a consignment of sulphanilamide powder and transferred it to fifty sweet bags donated by the proprietress of a local confectionary shop.

On the evening of 27 March 1942, having sailed may miles past the Loire estuary and back, Paton spotted a little blue light emanating from a British submarine to point them in the direction they were to go. The moon occasionally emerged from behind the clouds, illuminating the landscape. The *Campbeltown* was spotted by the Germans, but those on board the vessel knew the correct code to flash back to pass themselves off as a German ship.

The boat in front of Paton's had been detailed to seize control of the Old Mole, but was shot at before it could reach its objective. Men were in the water as Paton's craft passed by. It pulled up against the pier and Paton touched the structure with his hand. 'Bullets went right over it and I got a whole lot of cement in my face. And I thought "Oh Lord, don't let me be hit in the face."' The Germans began to roll bombs off the pier onto the deck of the boat, and the commandos kicked them off. 'I suddenly saw our chaps busy dancing about on deck kicking things, and I said, I said to one soldier "what is all this kicking these stones?" He said "them are not stones sir. Them's bombs." So I started kicking too.'

The commandos tried to erect their short metal ladders against the side of the pier but the Germans shoved them away. Meanwhile, casualties had started to accumulate below deck:

> I went off downstairs to attend to the wounded … half a dozen of them were wounded lying on the floor and the light was just abysmal. You could hardly see anything, and just

> as I was attending to my first wounded casualty of the war we hit something and scraped along it. I don't know what it was, but I was knocked sideways, and as I went I kicked this poor chap in the head. Luckily we had rubber boots on.

The vessel on which Paton was working made for the Atlantic. He refused to sew up any wounds:

> Everybody was cross with me because I didn't sew anybody up but that is the wrong thing to do, because in the wounds there are bits of khaki and bits of tailors clothing and bits of bullets. You have got all that. If you sew that up it's going to fester. You mustn't do it. You must wait until they get to the hospital and get them cleaned up.

As dawn broke, two Hunt class destroyers, HMS *Atherstone* and HMS *Tynedale*, came alongside but were unable to take any of the wounded on board before leaving, much to Paton's mystification. A request then came for Paton to transfer to another ship to attend to some casualties. He threw his haversack from one to the other, and then skilfully timed his own jump as the ocean swelled 15 to 30 feet. He was astonished to find the reason for him being needed on the second ship:

> Now the problem was, and you will find this incredible, and I didn't want to put it over the tannoy. Chaps who are wounded and in their bunks couldn't pee and they were bursting because a lot of them had a lot of beer inside them before the raid. I thought that would amuse you. I meant to, I ought not to have talked about that but they shouldn't. The Navy encouraged it with tots of rum. My chaps were drinking Newcastle Brown ale. I thought it was very wrong. I hadn't a drop.

Paton's services were then requested on a third ship. Here he found a man with severe chest wounds and a tourniquet round his ankle. One of Paton's RAMC orderlies, a private, reported that his chest only bled when the tourniquet was tightened. Paton ordered for it to be removed, but a naval officer put it back on shortly afterwards and the man bled to death.

The boats then came under attack from a German single-engined plane. One of the vessels fired its gun twice, both shots hitting the plane, which crashed into the sea with hardly a splash. Then a four-engined bomber appeared in the sky and opened its bomb doors. The men watched the load fall and it came down just behind the boat Paton was on, causing it to push, but with no damage sustained. Eventually Paton and his wounded were picked up by the navy and brought home on a destroyer. En route, Paton fell out with Commander Boyd, the commanding officer of the boat. There were no navigational instruments left on board as they had been jettisoned in order to speed away from danger as quickly as possible:

> I asked Boyd if he could get me an idea of where we were because if we were near the Scilly Islands I wanted to get some blood there, because one of the chaps was going to die. He said 'Well, what do you want?' I said 'I want blood.' He said 'You should have brought some with you.' I said 'Well, that wasn't on.' Blood was in glass bottles in these days. You don't take glass bottles on a Commando raid, and he said 'Well, have some of mine.' I said 'That is rubbish.' I said 'We don't do that. That doesn't work.' I said 'They did that to a Pope 300 or 400 years ago and it killed him the very day right away.' He said 'This is no time for joking Doc.' So we fell out over that. I said … Well, eventually, I went to him and said 'Look here, it's funny that a sailor who doesn't know where he is can tell a doctor how to look after his patients,' and he and I fell out.

The surviving patients were transferred to military hospitals in Devon. Paton eventually made his way back to Ayr and, as the only available officer, commanded a parade of just sixteen men who had returned fit enough to take part in the ceremony. Women lined the streets of the town weeping at the loss of life, 'Terrible thing to see … They had seen the Commandos that marched down. Four hundred of them had marched on to the ship, and this was about sixteen coming back.'

Two years after the raid on St Nazaire, 156,000 Allied troops were preparing to gain a foothold on French soil in Operation Overlord. The landings on the Normandy beaches, and in airborne assaults further inland, presented formidable challenges to the RAMC. A significant number of casualties would have to be evacuated from the beaches under heavy enemy fire, whilst men injured during the airborne drops would require great ingenuity to be cared for. Back home, beds were prepared in civilian hospitals for the care of the wounded who could be evacuated, and aeroplanes managed to remove over 100,000 injured men from front-line units to base hospitals within a few hours of being admitted, improving rates of recovery.

Stubborn resistance from German forces made for challenging conditions in which to practise medicine, with hardship and danger a common experience for RAMC troops, right from Normandy, through northern France, Belgium, Holland and into Germany.

In preparation for the Normandy landings, medics underwent specific training for the conditions that would be faced on the beaches. Captain Ian Campbell had been posted to the No. 2 Field Dressing Unit, within the 7th Beach Landing Group. In anticipation of the killing zone that would be the Normandy beaches, from September 1943 onwards, the group underwent a series of training exercises around the country, including at Troon, Bracklesham Bay and Studland Bay. Campbell estimated this to be 'pretty realistic training' as the medical unit was split into small groups and allocated to different ships for the crossing and landing on the beach. This enabled medics to work with people across different units, including a company of infantry engineers.

On 18 April 1944, Exercise Smash took place at Studland Bay, Dorset, with King George VI, Churchill, Montgomery and Eisenhower overseeing operations from the thick fortress of Fort Henry perched above the coastal cliff. Campbell recalled:

> Well, Studland Bay was the most difficult one because we went from Southampton, and usually in the winter it was very stormy roundabout the Needles and these places, and we got over to Studland Bay and the Infantry went in and I don't know what happened to them. They had a sort of simulated exercise. They had focal points to assault and take, I think, and they had their umpires to say whether they were successful or not. We, for our part, having landed usually you went up over your shoulders because there were runnels on the beach. I had to deal with fake casualties. There were

> a lot of fake casualties which we tried to simulate treatment and evacuate to a hospital which was supposed to be a military hospital somewhere.[2]

Two weeks before D-Day, Campbell and his comrades were sent to a sealed-off area in the New Forest. On a beautiful sunny spring day he was sunbathing with a handful of his mates when one of them looked up and said, 'Christ, there is Churchill.' The group stood and saluted the prime minister. The visit did not serve as a morale-booster as he appeared 'very depressed'. Churchill went into the NAAFI to partake of a glass of beer. A couple of days later, as the group embarked on a cross-Channel steamer to be berthed in the Solent for a week prior to sailing for France, Churchill appeared again on the gangway, accompanied by Field Marshal Smuts, General Ismay and Ernest Bevin. 'Churchill looked still depressed and so sad. He was really just about weeping and all he was doing was giving the V sign and saying "good luck boys. Good luck" and giving some a pat on the back.'[3]

Captain Geoffrey Haine had returned back to England from a posting in Sierra Leone to train as an anaesthetist, attached to No. 49 Field Surgical Unit. His D-Day training took place at Netley Hospital, overlooking the river Solent. 'The main thing I remember about Netley Hospital was the quarter-of-a-mile-long main corridor. The staff there used bicycles.'[4] Haine then moved on to Warminster to complete the unit's full establishment: nine nursing orderlies and three drivers, as well as Haine and Major Tuckett, in civilian life a surgeon at Tunbridge Wells Hospital. The Field Surgical Unit was to act as a mobile operating theatre treating battle casualties as far forward as possible. This mobility was to be provided in the form of two 3-ton lorries and onto these were loaded a tent to be used as an operating theatre, twenty beds, mattresses and blankets, a folding operating table and all the surgical anaesthetic equipment. All fourteen members of No. 49 FSU were to travel on the two lorries, and they were always attached to a parent unit that provided food, petrol and other supplies.

Preparation for a cross-Channel invasion was intense. Training took place in tent erection, packing and unpacking lorries, and physical fitness, including route marches of up to 25 miles. One volunteer corporal had a cut made in his leg, so Major Tuckett and his team could perform an operation under local anaesthetic, providing a suture for the wound. In April 1944, instructions were received to move to a location near Norwich, and in May the unit was moved to R6 concentration area near Ipswich. Here, the lorries were waterproofed and a night training exercise to Hayling Island was undertaken while under camouflage. The men of No. 49 FSU were then transferred to a ship berthed in the river Solent, remaining there for eight days before sailing for France.

Captain John Forfar had had advance notice about the exact nature of his D-Day role from his commanding officer, Colonel Phillips. As No. 47 (Royal Marine) Commando was going to be operating at the western extremity of Gold Beach, they would be contiguous to the Americans landing on Omaha. Forfar, as the commandos' medical officer, was then able to go and liaise with members of the US Army Medical Department long before 6 June.[5] Forfar and his comrades had reached a pitch of eager anticipation by early June. On 3 June, he boarded SS *Victoria*, and set off for France. The twenty-four-hour delay in the operation, occasioned by unfavourable weather conditions, created a sense of anti-climax, as well as the more prosaic problem of increased seasickness.

Corporal Peter Walker of No. 213 Field Ambulance enjoyed an idyllic 1 June bathing in the sea off Bexhill, 'our last day of freedom'. That night the unit moved to a marshalling area in the park at Glyndebourne: 'A most beautiful setting of Sussex countryside. Sited amongst the magnificent trees were brown canvas bell tents, well remembered from Scout camps of a few years before. The camp was sealed on its perimeter by a sprinkling of Military Police, and here we waited several days before embarkation.'

The unit's vehicles were loaded onto landing craft tanks (LCTs), but as the heroics were taking place a few miles across the English Channel, Walker and his comrades spent the next two weeks confined to the camp. Eventually they moved off down the Thames and lay anchored off Southend for a convoy to form up. Prior to sailing, a service was held on board ship by a Canadian chaplain and seven days' worth of compo ration was issued. Finally, on 19 June, the ships set sail, the convoy being shelled in the Straits of Dover. Reaching Sword Beach at 2200 hours on 20 June, the men were made to wait a further three days before the weather became calm enough to disembark. During this period, light air activity came from German planes overhead, and at night the ship had to move to Juno Beach for the men to unload. By 1600 hours on 24 June, all the transport and men were ashore and gathered at the concentration area at Rosières.

Walker himself had embarked at Newhaven and arrived at Arromanches in darkness to the shock of several explosions very close. As dawn broke, he was greeted with the sight of a huge concentration of ships and the Mulberry harbour, which had just taken a battering from a four-day storm. 'It was an amazing revelation to see such a feat of engineering, so unexpected, so full of port activity with dozens of small craft, especially the little DUKWs, unloading supplies, and on the coast was the wrecked, the wreckage of the fierce storm and a few bodies ebbing to and from on the waterline.'

During the tense hours and days that preceded the Normandy landings, the underlying importance of the Christian faith in the British Armed Services was once again in evidence. Medical Officer Ian Campbell recalled, 'One of the things that struck me was how seriously religious matters came into the fore. Whereas you know no one would very often think much about regularly going to a service, the chaplains when they had a service had a full house.'[6]

Campbell recalled the impact that the chaplains had on the beaches was 'pretty considerable'. The five chaplains attached to his division for the landing were hard-working individuals. 'Quite apart from their normal duty they were taking part in identifying any dead that weren't already identified and were collecting their personal effects, getting their background to write to their relatives and taking part in the temporary burials until they went to the final burial.'[7]

The men who sailed from the south coast on the night of 5 June, and those who followed them in the ensuing days, had been issued with a small folded card entitled First Aid for Fighting Men, 'to help him to go on fighting and to aid his friend in that cold interval between getting hit and getting help'.[8] Men were reminded, 'Wounds can look frightful. Be prepared for this. Remember modern surgeons can do wonders. Nature does her best to heal all wounds. But give Nature a chance. Stop wounds getting worse. That is your job. That is First Aid.' Advice was given on prioritising treatment and avoiding exacerbating the injury. 'There may be two or three wounded at once. Treat the most urgent first. Keep under cover. If mechanised, turn off petrol. Look out for falling walls. Any fool can be brave and get killed. Be brave, don't get killed and save your friend instead.' There was advice on how to stop bleeding by putting a fist into the wound, how to apply a tourniquet and how to tie down a broken limb.

Behind this initial advice on self-help came a strong presence of RAMC men, with at least one trained medical orderly in each landing craft. Seventy landing craft were reserved exclusively as water ambulances to evacuate the wounded. Dressing stations would be set up on the beaches as men fell, staffed by doctors, stretcher-bearers and blood transfusion units. This beach provision was inevitably quite basic, as there was no opportunity for the erection of large field hospitals until a beachhead had been secured. Each beach on which Allied troops landed on 6 June consisted of two Field Dressing Stations, two Field Surgical Units, one Field Hygiene Section, two Field Transfusion Units, one company of Pioneers for stretcher-bearing duties and half a Corps Field Dressing Station to serve as a casualty embarkation point. It had also been intended that a Casualty Clearing Station would be landed on each of the five beaches on D-Day itself, but unfavourable weather conditions prevented their arrival until the following day.

To partially compensate for the deficiency of medical facilities on the beaches, there were four field ambulances sited across the Channel, three along the south coast and one on the Isle of Wight. Acting as Advanced Dressing Stations, casualties would be resuscitated by men in these units. To compliment the dressing stations, hospitals at the Channel ports functioned as surgical centres for wounded troops who required an immediate operation. This arrangement was temporary, pending the establishment of General Hospitals on the French mainland. During the early days of the Operation Overlord, all casualties were evacuated to Britain, except for a handful cases for whom transportation would have jeopardised their chances of survival.

By this stage of the war, it was still unclear to the military authorities to what extent the Red Cross insignia on RAMC vehicles would be respected by the Germans. Jim Whitaker of No. 203 Field Ambulance recalled that on landing in Normandy a few days after D-Day, the red crosses on the white background on the ambulances and trucks were painted out, so as not to draw attention from the enemy. After a few days, it became apparent that there was 'more than a good chance' of the convention being respected, so the crosses were painted in again:

> However, this was spoiled, due to somebody taking a few cases of petrol forward in an ambulance and then was machine-gunned by a German plane and blew up making it

> very obvious that the vehicle was carrying petrol. After that the Germans were very suspicious and whatever respect we enjoyed there disappeared.

Flying over their seaborne colleagues, the airborne medical staff who parachuted into Normandy with their units in the early hours of 6 June had been extensively trained and prepared for the hazardous tasks of assisting in the removal of the wounded from the battlefield and treating them as quickly as possible. Previous airborne landings in North Africa during Operation Torch had been hampered by a lack of light wheeled transport and the difficulty in dropping medical equipment that was easily accessible to the medics. Therefore, in May 1943, an Airborne Force Development Centre was established at Amesbury Abbey in Wiltshire, with a separate medical section under the command of Major R. West. West was keen to address the problem of landing medical equipment with which airborne medics could operate more effectively during the crucial early stages of operations. He was instrumental in the design of equipment suitable for dropping from the air, including folding stretchers, trestle operating tables and reinforced plasma containers. These innovations were successfully used in the invasion of Sicily in July 1943, with glider transport being able to provide medical staff with specially adapted jeeps capable of carrying stretchers and heavier medical stores.

By the time of Operation Overlord, airborne medics were ready to play a crucial role in the success of the Normandy invasion. Three airborne field ambulances landed to support the Parachute Brigades on the morning of 6 June. No. 224 (Parachute) Field Ambulance was under the command of Lieutenant Colonel Dennis Thompson and was dropped with 3rd Parachute Brigade to establish a Main Dressing Station at Le Mesnil. (Pic 33) No. 225 (Parachute) Field Ambulance under Lieutenant Colonel Bruce Harvey was attached to 5th Parachute Brigade and set up its dressing station at Le Bas de Ranville. The two qualified surgeons on No. 225 FA were Captain Arthur McPherson and Captain Peter Essex-Lopresti, with their teams consisting of an anaesthetist and three operating room assistants. Finally, No. 195 (Airlanding) Field Ambulance, under the command of Lieutenant Colonel W.M.E. Anderson, flew to Normandy in ten Horsa gliders containing eleven officers, 109 other ranks, nine jeeps and five trailers, and rapidly opened a MDS in a large building in Le Mariquet.[9]

Alongside the trained medics and regular RAMC orderlies, there was a significant group of unusual volunteers. While forming the 6th Airborne Division, its ADMS, Colonel Malcolm MacEwan, a veteran of the North African Campaign, was disappointed with the few volunteers forthcoming from within the ranks of the RAMC. By this stage of the war, bonds of comradeship had formed within units, which made men reluctant to leave those with whom they had served for years. However, MacEwan realised that a large number of conscientious objectors had been undertaking dangerous bomb disposal work during the war and were far from being the cowards that some sections of the popular press had portrayed them. MacEwan made approaches to them and many agreed to serve with the division, on the proviso that they would never be required to carry a weapon, and would have a free hand to treat any German wounded the same as they would a British casualty. MacEwan readily agreed, as this was RAMC policy anyway. Eventually, about 190 conscientious objectors joined the 6th Airborne Division, comprising about a third of the strength of Nos. 224 and 225 (Para) Field Ambulances.

Captain David Tibbs, whose section of twenty men contained six conscientious objectors, recalled: 'These men were not allowed to have any rank other than private, but they could not have been any more exemplary. You just asked them to do what was required and they did it without the need to bark orders and indeed Christian names were often used.'[10]

No. 225 FA's dressing station came under constant sniping and mortar fire throughout 6 June, but by 9.00 pm, Major McDonald, of 3rd British Division, had established contact and the evacuation of casualties back to the beach area and on to Britain had begun. During the first twenty-four hours of operations, sixty wounded men were evacuated and within two days, a staggering 380 casualties had passed through the hands of No. 225 FA. Meanwhile, No. 195 FA had converted a cellar into an operating theatre and had performed twenty-three surgical operations by the morning of 7 June.

Working in primitive conditions with the fire of battle all around them, as they waited to establish contact with the beach landing parties, orderlies sterilised instruments by holding them over a Primus stove, and wounded limbs were placed in plaster and immobilised as far as possible, to reduce the pain, minimise shock and assist in the control of infection.

Amputations were rare, and surgeons were reluctant to perform them unless deemed absolutely necessary by the risk of infection caused by the blast effect of high explosives and basic conditions of field surgery.

J.C. Watts of No. 195 Field Ambulance recalled that his colleagues who were working in combat conditions for the first time were very quick to learn how to thrive in this situation:

> These men were learning war surgery the hard way, under terrific pressure, whereas I had been gradually initiated, with five years' experience before the Mareth Line battles, at which I had first met more cases than I could deal with. I was now astounded to see the rapidity with which a green team could settle down and almost become veterans in an afternoon. I do not recall that I have ever had to show them a procedure twice.[11]

The keenness and ability of the young surgeons under Watts's command could be ascribed in no small measure to the rigorous training they had received, in many cases for up to a year before the invasion.

The men of No. 224 FA were dropped wide of their destination, leading to a frantic search for each other and wounded men from their brigade. Confusion reigned as indiscriminate shooting was heard in the Normandy countryside. An MDS was soon established and operated amongst the constant explosion of mortar shells. All but a handful of patients were operated on within twenty-four hours of being wounded, this dropping to ten hours when a further medical officer made his way to the MDS.

Despite the dedication of the medics, some casualties died during the first few days because of the necessity of using plasma, which lacked the oxygen-carrying capacity of whole blood. It was impracticable for airborne medics to carry round supplies of fresh blood, which could only be kept for an hour without refrigeration. When fresh blood was used, it was RAMC orderlies, many of them conscientious objectors, who provided it.[12] Infection of wounds was largely prevented by the local application of penicillin and sulpha drugs, and where gangrene was present, an anti-gas gangrene serum was provided. The efficacy of these procedures is shown by the fact that out of a total of 822 casualties treated by No. 224 FA from 6 to 19 June, only twenty-two died.[13]

The force that stormed the Normandy beaches on 6 June 1944 had widespread access to penicillin. It had been trialled on wounded soldiers in North Africa in 1943 and Howard Florey, Professor of Pathology at the University of Oxford and adviser to the British Army, had established the superiority of the drug over sulphonamides; Allied soldiers in Italy had already benefitted from it. Further towards the line of fighting, the Regimental Aid Post of the 9th (Essex) Parachute Battalion was situated in an area known as 'Bomb Alley', with the medical officers finding themselves working in the thick of the fighting. The RAP was located in a stone villa on a slope facing the river Orne, with casualties brought into a small backyard to be dressed in a tool shed. The history of No. 224 FA described the yard as looking like 'the threshold of a slaughter house … blood-stained clothing and boots lay about in grim disorder'.[14]

Captain David Tibbs was among the first paratroopers to be dropped into occupied France on D-Day, and was later awarded the Military Cross for his work clearing the parachute drop zone while under heavy fire. Tibbs and his stick had an eventful crossing into Normandy in a Douglas C-47 Dakota transporter. Having taken off from England in the early hours of 6 June, in command of a section of twenty men to be parachuted into Normandy, Tibbs, as number one jumper, was by the open door surveilling the advancing coastline. At first the view was just darkness, and then a thin white line of breaking surf was visible where the English Channel met the beaches.

Tibbs and his men readied themselves to jump when suddenly their Dakota banked steeply, taking evasive action to avoid an RAF Stirling bomber that was veering into its flight path. Everyone was sent sprawling across the floor. By the time they had gathered themselves, the green jump light was on, and although they all jumped safely from the aircraft, most landed outside the designated drop zone, with only five of them reaching the rendezvous point at Ranville, north-east of Caen.

Tibbs, accompanied by his batman Frank Clark, went to reconnoitre the church at Ranville, intending to use it as a gathering point for casualties, before passing them down to the MDS of No. 225 (Para) Field Ambulance. Finding the doors of the church firmly bolted, it was decided not to use the building as Tibbs had not yet received any casualties and a dressing station would soon be opened. As the day dawned,

Tibbs's section began the search for wounded paratroopers. Fields containing wheat 3 feet high made the task of finding injured parachutists and glider-borne troops more difficult. Some wounded men tied a cloth or handkerchief to the end of a stick and waved it in the air to indicate their whereabouts. Tibbs was in charge of a handful of stretcher-bearers who systematically swept the divisional landing zone.

During the first eight hours of daylight, about a dozen men were located, mostly with fractured femurs, and they were carried to a waiting jeep and on to the dressing station at Le Bas de Ranville. Later in the day, Tibbs moved towards the far extremity of the drop zone where a group of paratroopers had taken up defensive positions by a roadside. By them, a wounded German soldier lay, with a severe thigh wound and pale from blood loss. He was being ignored by the British troops as he was disarmed and posed no threat to them. Tibbs approached him, indicating the Red Cross brassard on his arm as he did so. The German smiled at him, realising that salvation was at hand. Tibbs ordered the soldiers not to move him as he was now under medical supervision and returned with a jeep to transport him to the dressing station.

The medics worked in dangerous conditions, with a lack of cover and being subjected to light machine-gun fire and heavy sniping. At around midday, they returned to No. 225 (Para) FA's dressing station at Chateau de Guernon-Ranville to find it packed with casualties, more than the medics could cope with. To add to the challenge, heavy mortars were being fired by both sides, making it dangerous to venture out into the open. Despite the danger, Tibbs and the unit's dental officer, Captain George Holland, went out onto the road outside the chateau to bring in a wounded man. Later, Tibbs went out to assist two men carrying in a wounded officer, the remnants of whose leg was trailing behind him.

Tibbs was put in charge of a large barn adjacent to the chateau, containing eighty casualties lying on dry straw. To his disquiet, a 6-pounder anti-tank gun had been placed above the building, despite the Red Cross flag having been placed above it. As the German attack progressed, a panic-stricken RASC driver burst into the barn, shouting that the enemy was only 50 yards away at the bottom of the lane. Some of the wounded men reached for their weapons. This left Tibbs in a quandary. As an officer he carried a 9mm automatic pistol but was reluctant to use it in anger against the enemy.

Another non-combatant in the barn was the badly wounded Catholic padre Father Bill Briscoe. He beckoned to Tibbs and asked him to remove his ceremonial pistol as he reckoned he would be killed if the Germans came in and saw him carrying one. Mercifully, two of the German tanks were knocked out and the attacking Panzergrenadiers retreated. In the ensuing quiet, Tibbs reflected that it was ethically wrong for the wounded to be armed while under the protection of a Red Cross flag. Therefore, he instructed his orderlies to remove and hide all weapons:

> This was done amid grunts of annoyance, but I am sure I was right. The wounded stood a better chance if I depended on the Red Cross to protect them. Oddly, we had been given virtually no instruction about the Red Cross and the rules of the Geneva Convention. As I was to find, the Germans were pretty good in observing the Red Cross and letting us get on with our task under its protection. We looked after their wounded well, just as they often looked after our wounded.[15]

In the barn, Tibbs assessed the state of each patient and for those with severe wounds, arranged for plasma or, more rarely, a blood transfusion. One priority was to prevent haemorrhaging, with the source being dealt with and blood circulation restored to prevent the loss of a limb. In these cases, an operation had to be performed under anaesthetic. Sadly, amputations were sometimes deemed necessary for the patient to survive. Other men were brought in with severe abdominal wounds, which the surgeon would seek to repair, placing the patient in a stable state. Injuries to the chest and head also required emergency surgery so that a casualty could be safely transferred to a General Hospital. Eventually, at 9.00 pm, it became possible to begin evacuating the most serious casualties, including Padre Briscoe, to the coast and across the English Channel. However, two of them were killed and four were wounded. During the subsequent intense battle to defend the airborne perimeter, with bullets whistling by and grenades detonating, Tibbs showed complete disregard for his own safety. The citation of his MC paid tribute to 'his courage and leadership'.

One of the medical orderlies parachuted into Normandy with No. 224 Field Ambulance was Private Lacey Tingle, a conscientious objector. On the afternoon of 7 June, in the village of Douville-en-Auge,

16 miles east of Caen, a group of British and Canadian paratroopers, including Tingle, was surrounded by the enemy, nine of their number losing their lives in the ensuing battle. Company Sergeant Major Lord was wounded and taken prisoner with seven others, though he later escaped. The history of No. 224 FA recorded that 'With this party was Tingle who was presumed to have been killed, for CSM Lord did not see him again after the battle began and six months later he was still posted as missing.'[16] The dead men were buried in the village by locals before being moved to Ranville War Cemetery after the war. Tingle was buried as an unknown soldier. In 2018, after much assiduous research, it was confirmed that the unknown grave contained Tingle's body and was rededicated at a ceremony, with a new headstone being unveiled. Fittingly for the devout Methodist whose conscience had led him to refuse to bear arms against a fellow human being, the inscription from John 15:13 reads, 'GREATER LOVE HATH NO MAN THAN HE WHO LAYS DOWN HIS LIFE FOR HIS FRIENDS.'

Sometimes, captured German prisoners were placed on the staff of the airborne dressing stations. They created a very favourable impression amongst British medics and proved very useful in dealing with German patients. According to the history of No. 224 FA, 'Their punctilious behaviour towards our officers disprove[d] the Intelligence maxim that to treat a prisoner like a human being is to make him disrespectful.'[17]

The airborne medical services had their reputation significantly enhanced during the landings. Medical and combatant personnel had worked in harmony and efficient evacuation of casualties had taken place. Further lessons had been learned for future operations, notably the desirability of a trained anaesthetist attached to each surgeon, and that surgical work should be done in separate Field Surgical Units, closer to the fighting.[18]

The contribution of airborne medics during the Normandy invasion was summarised in the history of No. 224 FA:

> Those who had been conscious that the RAMC did not cut a very glamorous figure beside the fighting parachutists felt that they had come into their own; the changed attitude towards them was a matter of satisfaction, apart from the profounder satisfaction of working to save life when everyone else had the duty of destroying it.[19]

Other conscientious objectors worked with the seaborne forces on D-Day. Private David Briggs had managed to gain a transfer from the Pay Corps to the RAMC, in order that he might share the dangers that his contemporaries were facing. Interviewed on the wireless on the seventieth anniversary of D-Day, he recalled the stillness before the storm as he waited to set sail across the Channel:

> The thing that has always stuck in my mind was the sound of nightingales, the most beautiful sound, which drifted across the water into our boat. Every night we'd hear these wonderful songs from the nightingales and it was very, very peaceful. And it was the contrast between that and D-Day that has stuck in my mind.

Briggs had vivid memories of his first approach to the beaches, arriving around midday on 6 June:

> There was of course an awful lot of air activity, planes all over the place and we never knew if we were going to be torpedoed or not. Although it was only a few hours after the invasion started, there was a kind of eerie quiet on the beach. … The first thing I saw was a dead Canadian lying in the water. … The landing craft was relieved of the tanks. The tanks rolled out onto the beach and then all the space that was left … we had brackets coming out of the walls to hold stretchers. Our job as medics was to go onto the beach to rescue the wounded of all nationalities, German as well as English, and ferry them back to the UK. And then that job was finished and then we were discharged from the boat. We were told later that the boat was torpedoed and sunk.

The men from No. 223 Field Ambulance who were to land on Sword beach on D-Day were divided between two landing craft; if one was attacked there would still be enough men to operate as a field ambulance. Conscientious objector Private Jim Wisewell and his fellow stretcher-bearer decided to shelter under one of the tanks the craft was carrying. Like many, he sought strength in his religious faith: 'I remember I wasn't particularly anxious. I read my Bible before turning in that night and prayed for all of us and got off to sleep fairly quickly.'[20]

Wisewell landed at Lion-sur-Mer just after 10.00 am on D-Day. The precious tanks were unloaded from the landing craft first, then an officer said 'Come on chaps' and Wisewell went down the ramp and made for the nearest shell hole, under intensive shelling and mortar fire. As well as the joint responsibility for a stretcher, he carried a large haversack of medical equipment, including hot water bottles to help counteract the shock that the wounded would experience.

Although Wisewell could see a wounded man in the next shell hole to his, he was under strict orders to leave the casualties on the sand to a Beach Dressing Station, and to move inland to form a Field Dressing Station near a rendezvous point at Hermanville. It was on the road between Lion-sur-Mer and Hermanville that Wisewell saw his first D-Day fatalities. A mortar had landed, killing three of the division:

> One of them had practically dissolved from the waist downwards. The other one was in a kneeling position on one knee and he seemed to be unmarked. And the other one was just a shapeless mess. And I looked down at my foot and there was something which looked like a pound of steak, and this was obviously part of one of them.[21]

As the casualties started to pour in at the dressing station, the doctor had to 'play God' in deciding which men could be treated and which left to die. Wisewell, having qualified as a Nursing Orderly First Class, was splinting fractures, dressing wounds and injecting morphine and anti-gangrene serum.

Captain Geoffrey Haine of No. 49 Field Surgical Unit left Felixstowe at dawn on 6 June, eventually landing on King Beach at 2.00 am the following morning. The waterproofed ambulance lorries started up and went down the ramp and through 3 feet of water without any issues. On the beach the drivers expected to find markers to indicate where steel mesh tracks had been laid down, but they were not visible and the heavily laden lorries soon become bogged down, axle deep in the sand. Having tried to dig the lorries out, an irate beach marshall approached the unit and informed them that, as the tide was coming in, they should carry off as much equipment as possible and abandon the lorries:

> That did not sound like a very successful ending to our training and so seeing a Royal Engineer working with a Bulldozer, I persuaded him – or maybe used my rank for I was then a Captain and ordered him to pull us out. Thanks to him he soon got us back on the track and we got into the little holiday resort of Ver sur Mer as dawn was breaking.[22]

Haine then saw his first battle casualty, a young man who had been shot and instantly killed. Rigor mortis had set in quickly and he was still in sniper firing position. Although he was to see many gruesome sights during the advance through Europe, that young soldier remained in his mind.

Having proceeded to Jerusalem on the road between Bayeux and Tilly, Haine was involved in a macabre episode. One of the first casualties was a man with abdominal injuries, suffering from severe shock. As he became more shocked during the operation, Major Tuckett placed an abdominal clamp over a bad injury in the bowel and returned him to the ward with the hope that after further resuscitation he would be fit for more surgery. After completing further operations on other casualties, it was discovered that the patient had died, and had been buried with the clamp still in situ. As the clamp was essential for medical operations, after consultation with the padre, it was agreed that the grave could be opened up and the clamp retrieved. At night by torchlight and hurricane lamps, the job was quickly accomplished. On one occasion, at Aunay, Tuckett, Haine and the medical orderlies completed a continuous operation session of thirty-six hours. These laborious episodes were occasionally brightened by visits from ENSA, one party including 'Forces' Sweetheart' Vera Lynn.

Captain Ian Campbell, attached to the 7th Beach Landing Group, landed on Juno Mike Red beach at 10.00 am on 6 June. He witnessed wrecked boats and casualties strewn across the sand and lapping waves. Campbell contacted the Beach Dressing Station, which had been operational since 8.15 am. Men from the Pioneer Corps were dodging the bullets on the beach and stretchering casualties to the station. Campbell had been directed to proceed to Graye-sur-Mer, 600 yards behind the beach to set up a dressing station, with a view to establishing a Casualty Evacuation Point. However, he was not initially allowed to leave the beach due to continuing small arms fire from German marksmen blocking the small exits that the Royal Engineers had created. Eventually, at noon, Campbell was allowed to proceed up a narrow path accompanied by a sergeant. At the end he was met by a Catholic priest who asked, 'Are you medical?' Recognising the Red Cross band on his arm, the priest then explained how the villagers had been through the village hall recently vacated by the Germans, clearing it of booby traps and scrubbing it clean ready for its use as a dressing station.

Campbell set up a treatment room in the hall and casualties came flooding in. Later, a surgical unit arrived and set up an operating room in which a surgeon, an anaesthetist and ten medical orderlies began to perform a string of life-saving operations. Another Field Surgical Unit started performing operations on a wrecked landing craft on the beach. Their lives saved from immediate danger of death, the casualties were evacuated back to the UK by the Royal Navy on specially adapted Landing Ship Tanks, which contained a special nursing and medical component.

Over the next three weeks, Campbell built up the Field Dressing Station to accommodate 600 patients, moving the hospital to a chateau a mile along the road. Here the unit was joined by members of Queen Alexandra's Imperial Military Nusing Service (QAIMNS), two additional FDSs, two Blood Transfusion Units and four Field Surgery Units, which shared the imposing premises. Campbell noted that the highest number of patients treated in one twenty-four-hour period was 2,240.

This treatment included the use of penicillin – the first time Campbell had come across the new wonder drug:

> We had a ward where we had to keep patients who were critically ill and couldn't travel, but one of the main duties was just … to see that the patient was comfortable, to see that they were fit to travel and to ensure that those got the new magic drug because … Churchill decreed that the new drug penicillin would not be used in the UK until the first people had it, which were the casualties in Normandy. So they had the benefit of having penicillin first of all, and that was one of the regular things we had to do.

Further west, as dawn broke, John Forfar, medical officer of No. 47 (Royal Marine) Commando, waited 8 miles off the western extremity of Gold Beach, eager to fulfil the order to get inland as quickly as possible across sands that were to already have been captured by the Hampshire Regiment. However, the Hampshires had been unable to get ashore and had turned eastwards, away from the link with Omaha Beach and the Americans, with whom Forfar had expected to liaise. The commandos had to follow them, which lost valuable time, during which the tide rose, hiding obstacles that should have been visible from the landing craft. Five out of fourteen vessels were blown up, including Forfar's, and he was thrown into the water complete with his heavy medical rucksack. One of his medical orderlies was killed instantly. As his rucksack gradually sank beneath the water, Forfar desperately tried to push it to shore with one hand, while frantically swimming with the other. The rucksack eventually disappeared as Forfar struggled to make the hundred yards to shore.

His progress was impeded by landing craft coming from behind. Forfar could hear the rattle of machine-gun bullets scraping their sides as his head bobbed in the water. Once ashore, at 9.30 am, Forfar and his comrades waited below the sea wall at Asnelles until they were relatively safe. The 420-man commando unit had been reduced to less than 350 by losses incurred during the landing.

The commando unit then had the task of getting behind German lines, marching 12 miles, and taking Port-en-Bessin. For the rest of 6 June they traversed the countryside, engaging in a series of skirmishes with the Germans. One occurred on a sunken cart road just past Les Roquettes. As the men looked up from beneath the big banks on either side of the road they spotted three Germans on the brow of a hill, one with a sub-machine gun and two with rifles. There was a rattle of shots from the commando unit and the German with the machine gun dropped down while the other two came running down the hill with their hands in the air.

The wounded German had been hit in the stomach and liver, and Forfar was certain he was dying, as was the man himself.

> He kept on saying 'Kaput, kaput' – finished. And I said 'No, no, nein kaput', and tried to encourage him in a sense, but then he whipped out of his pocket his pay book and

> opened it up and took photographs of his wife and children as much as to say 'Look, what's going to happen?' And there was nothing you could do except commiserate with him and move on and leave him lying by the roadside.[23]

Further on in the struggle towards Port-en-Bessin, a horse-mounted German officer was suddenly seen ahead. Had he spotted the commando or not? The risk could not be taken. One shot and he fell off the horse. At La Rosière, thirteen commandoes were injured and one killed by sniper fire. As the casualties mounted, Forfar found himself conflicted in his role. His instinct was to stay and tend to the wounded, but the role of a medical officer in a commando was to press on with the unit.

A more light-hearted encounter took place with a German regimental sergeant major who was cycling peacefully along a side road unarmed:

> I wondered what he was up to … he didn't know that the Second Front had started, and all he was doing was going by bicycle to Ouistreham, which was about twelve miles away … because he had a girlfriend there and he wanted to see her before he surrendered. He had decided the war was given up. So we were very ungentlemanly. We didn't allow him to go and see his girlfriend in Ouistreham. We satisfied his second need that he wanted to get out of the war so we did that by taking him prisoner.

Due to the nature of his posting with a commando unit, Forfar carried a handgun, which he used on one occasion to ward off a German he thought might be approaching to capture him.

On the night of 6 June, Forfar and his comrades stopped at Mont Cavalier, a mile and a half from their objective. Forfar commandeered a huge bunker that was being used as a German medical post. It contained two German medical officers and many wounded, who were astonished to see their aid post being overrun by British troops, 10 miles behind the front line. The unit moved in to take Port-en-Bessin, sustaining further heavy losses in the process. Forfar continued to press on with the fighting troops, leaving his Regimental Aid Post further behind, outside the port itself. He had to bandage up the wounded as best he could and place them in the houses of the town's civilians, one of whom responded with bemusement at the demand from a wounded man to remove the shrapnel from his abdomen. Once the port had been reached, Forfar returned to the wounded he had left in a ditch outside the town. As he only had one stretcher left after the losses of equipment in the chaos of the initial landing, men were carried piggy-back into the port to an impromptu RAP inside a dirty barn. Other casualties were collected from the civilian houses and by the morning of 8 June, there were forty-eight wounded troops and civilians in the barn.

Eventually the Germans surrendered; a group of them came walking down a hill towards Forfar headed by Corporal Amos, who had been captured the previous night. The commandos had previously seen a sign on a wall stating 'All Commandos must be interrogated and shot', but Amos owed his salvation to the fact that he had stayed behind the rest to tend to a badly wounded sergeant, the Germans taking him to be a medical orderly. Forfar was finally able to link up with his American counterparts, who took many of his wounded into their care and arranged a parachute drop of sorely needed medical supplies.

Private Ronald Ritson of No. 26 Field Hygiene Section landed on Sword Beach two days after D-Day and his initial impression was, 'everything seemed lovely. The sun was shining, and it just looked as if it was a lovely seaside resort, apart from traffic moving up and down the beach.'[24] As the barges dropped their landing gear so the trucks could run off the craft, there was a wire laid out all along the beach so they would not sink into areas of soft sand. The Germans began shelling and managed to hit an ammunition dump, causing an enormous explosion and an inferno of flames. The driver of Ritson's truck panicked and turned off the wire that was running up the beach. The lorry sank into the sand, so Ritson and his comrades jumped out and crawled under a tank carrier. A young soldier who was with Ritson was petrified: 'I felt sorry for him really, because he kept saying to me, he didn't know what was going to happen to him. He said to me, "I don't want any medals for this." So I said to him, "If you don't keep your head down you won't get anything!"'

Soon afterwards a tank was brought up and the lorry extricated from the sand.

26 Field Hygiene Section then moved inland along a track that had been carefully laid, with frequent reminders to troops to stay off the minefields on either side. Arriving at the tiny village of Plumetot,

a few miles inland, the unit set to work ensuring that the men of the 3rd British Infantry Division had a supply of clean water. Some of the thirty men in the unit had been sanitary inspectors in civilian life, and took readily to the training that had been undertaken in Aldershot on water purification in the field. Water would be procured from a river, then placed in large mobile water tanks into which purification tablets would be added.

A more poignant duty was to make sure that the remains of dead troops were correctly treated and buried in a proper manner. Bodies would be wrapped in a blanket and placed in underground storage, for removal later to a Commonwealth war cemetery. Ritson recalled:

> How they used to identify these soldiers was that every soldier used to wear two discs around his neck. If he was killed, one disc was cut off to send back to the Army Headquarters. The other disc was buried with him. That way they would know that they had got the right person. Some of the work wasn't very pleasant as you can imagine.

Captain Eric Godwin advanced through Northern Europe attached to a Field Surgical Unit, a service that used plentiful amounts of blood. He recalled:

> Pre-war, the Blood Transfusion Service in England was a very small voluntary society, but the war, as always, brought on medical advances, and it was a wonderful blood service. We got all the blood we needed. And then, some months after the invasion, we got penicillin, and that was extremely expensive. About a hundred pounds a day it cost ... and it was given in a drip.[25]

The unit possessed a large tent in which men who would need operations were given time to become fit enough to undergo them. The FSU boasted a recovery rate of 60 per cent, working around the clock in twelve-hour shifts, treating twelve to sixteen patients in a twenty-four-hour period.

Corporal Peter Walker had landed at Arromanches in late June, and he and his comrades had marched to Brécy, 7 miles inland, to be reunited with No. 213 Field Ambulance's transport and drivers. Initially the men bivouacked, sleeping on verges until one of their number was hit by shrapnel and died from his wounds. Following that incident, men slept under their vehicles. The comradeship that had developed amongst the 43rd (Wessex) Division during months of training throughout 1943 and 1944 was now to stand them in good stead: 'There was a lot of noise, but strangely it did not dominate and now I can hardly recall it. We had a tremendous will to work, I remember that very well. These battalions were our own people. We had an enormous regard for them and they relied on us.'

The first action was seen during Operation Epsom, from 26 to 30 June, the aim of which was to seize the city of Caen. Walker found himself stationed at Cheux, 10 miles west of Caen:

> We opened up again and spent a very noisy night. I remember the early casualties. The first man had, rather incongruously, appendicitis. The next was our own second-in-command, Major Menzies, who came in with gunshot wounds to both legs from mortar fire, and the third chap was a case of blast injury. He died almost immediately. By the morning we had thirty casualties.

The next major engagement for Walker was Operation Jupiter on 10 July, the objective being for the division to recapture the villages of Baron-sur-Odon, Fontaine-Étoupefour and Chateau de Fontaine, and Hill 112. Situated near a quarry outside Caen, No. 213 Field Ambulance dealt with 350 cases in thirty-six hours. (Pic 34) Walker recalled, 'We lived on tea and cigarettes until we dropped. Then a MO would give you a dose of Benzedrive … and you would be able to carry on for another four hours.'

Walker and his comrades had the job of performing casualty sweeps, following up behind the fighting men of the battalion to locate casualties. There was an urgent need to observe and mark or remember where men had fallen. RAMC orderlies physically marked the position, then gave emergency treatment if the casualty was still alive. The position would then be marked with the man's rifle stuck in the ground, and if that couldn't be found then a strip of bandage would be tied to a bush as a marker. Casualties were to be left for those coming up from behind, who had to remove them from the field, but this was far from straightforward. A man's position could not be betrayed to the enemy and if possible he needed to be moved to 'dead ground'. The wounded man himself had to guard against loss of blood, while possibly frightened and not in a fit state to remember his self-treatment training. He may have felt desolation and abandonment as his mates passed over him. In the close bocage landscape of Normandy it was easy for following stretcher-bearers to miss a man. When scouting for casualties, Walker and his comrades would allow 100 yards between each of them and move closer at night. Many hundreds of wounded men were saved from possible death by exposure due to this assiduous work.

More problematic was the extraction of wounded men from a tank. To locate casualties, a regimental medical officer would scour the battlefield in a scout car and get help from other medics in the field if he could. Tanks carried phials of chloroform, which would be placed on a gauze to give the wounded man what Walker termed 'sixpenny worth of oblivion' while being taken out. Tannic acid would be used in the treatment of burns, as it relieved pain while forming a protective coating to the burnt area to avoid loss of fluid. It also prevented poisons from damaged tissue entering the blood stream, which was the usual cause of death from burns.

Regaining control of the city of Caen from the Germans proved a tough nut to crack, and Private Jim Wisewell of No. 223 Field Ambulance found himself in the thick of treating hundreds of casualties streaming in from the 185th Brigade of the 3rd Division. The RAF began a heavy bombardment of Caen on 7 July, and eight hours later, a land assault was launched. 'The bombing of Caen was something that I had never experienced before or since. The dust from the bombing rolled back. We were about four miles away, and it rolled back into our camp, and it was like a thick London pea-souper, you could hardly see your hand in front of your face.'

As the RAF had been instructed not to bomb short because of the risk of killing Allied troops, they had bombed 3 miles forward and missed most of the Germans too. At 4.00 am on 8 June, Wisewell and his comrades were wakened and given a cup of tea, and from 5.00 am they started receiving casualties in their Advanced Dressing Station.

> Now they were from the Norfolks, the Warwicks and the KSLIs and they were very cheerful. They said that they had taken their first objective and everything was going fine.

> But it was a hot day and as the day wore on so the tide of casualties rose and there was always a queue waiting for us to attend to them. And there were all sorts of casualties. There were legs without feet, there were knees without kneecaps, there were shoulders without arms. I remember one sergeant major brought in with half of his head blown away and yet he was still conscious, and the MO said to me 'give him two grains of morphia; it'll finish him quickly.' But it didn't. And chest wounds, shocking chest wounds. It was horrible. On that one day we treated 466 British casualties and 40 Germans in our ADS alone.

For Wisewell, that was the worst day of his entire war.

Sergeant Jim Whitaker (Pic 35) of No. 203 Field Ambulance, supporting the 59th Infantry Division, attended a briefing given by Lieutenant Colonel J.G. Bullock, commanding officer of the 7th South Staffordshire Regiment. Bullock's advice prior to the assault on Caen was 'The more prisoners you take lessens the chances of your own survival.' A large number of prisoners to supervise would also have interfered with the work of the RAMC units. Whitaker recalled:

> We expected to be advancing all the time and not to be in a retreating position and under these circumstances prisoners were an embarrassment. If prisoners were taken they had to be looked after until they could be passed back to the rear formations. This meant someone who should be attacking would be looking after gerries [*sic*] and this would also interfere with the evacuation of our own wounded.[26]

When the attack on Caen was launched it was the job of Whitaker's 176th Brigade, on a strict schedule, to take all the well-defended villages on the approach to Caen. Working too slowly would interfere with the overall strategy, too fast would mean walking into their own creeping barrage of shells, which was put down by heavy guns to the rear and also from ships lying off shore. Whitaker's job was to advance with the infantry and treat casualties as they arose, then sticking the injured man's rifle in the ground for the stretcher-bearers and jeeps following behind to spot and take him back to a dressing station.

Whitaker found that most of the German troops his brigade encountered were young, and a favourite trick of theirs was to lie on a revolver when injured, then roll over and pick it up after receiving treatment and shoot the man who had helped him. Due to this, Whitaker became wary and made sure his own wounded were treated first. This brought him into conflict with his medical officer, Captain Gibb. Whitaker ignored the instruction to treat all wounded equally, expressing to Gibb the wish that he did not want to learn his lesson 'the hard way'.

A common injury was a 'sucking wound' where a bullet or piece of shrapnel had made an entry or exit in the chest, causing the patient to breathe through the chest wall. This was fairly easily sealed with Vaseline gauze so his transport to the rear would be comfortable. Another was where a man had stepped on a shell and had his foot blown off. Whitaker reckoned, 'The courage of the wounded men was something of the highest order.' Disdain, however, was the order of the day for psychiatric cases, in Whitaker's view:

> In contrast was the behaviour of the men suffering from 'battle exhaustion' or 'shell shock'. We considered this to be a very poor show as this was simply that the man had lost control. Some people called it cowardice. Their behaviour was pitiable or contemptible as you prefer. I have seen them trying to hide behind a steel helmet.
>
> On one occasion one of my men just dropped a stretcher and ran. I was in such a fury that if I could have got hold of him, I would have injured him.

As Montgomery's 21st Army Group continued its advance across Northern Europe, Private James Driscoll, serving with No. 131 Field Ambulance, reflected on the ebbs and flows of the esteem in which the army was held, and juxtaposed this to the 'forgotten army' in Burma. Writing to his wife Kathleen in July 1944, he mused:

> you feel that the home folk were only interested in you when you were belting like hounds after Jerry. When you came to a stop you could almost picture them saying, 'What's up with the eighth army? I bet they get pushed all the way back again?'

> So now I'm one of those fortunate who get lavished with fame and lauded to the skies (or do the RAMC get that?) I naturally think of the poor unsung hard working lads in India and Burma … those poor blighters in the Burmese jungles, sweating their insides out, living on much less palatable rations than compo I'll bet, getting soaked in torrential rain, eaten alive by flies and mosquitoes with their omnipresent threat of malaria from the latter and dysentery from the former.
>
> And in the news? They are always last …[27]

Some medical orderlies found themselves close to or even across the front line as the forward push continued. On one occasion after the taking of Caen and before the crossing of the river Orne, when the line was temporarily static, a night patrol of 176th Brigade returned without their officer and one of the men who were so badly injured that they had to be left. Jim Whitaker set out on his motorbike, followed by a jeep, in the direction of the location he had been given where the men had been left. One of the retiring patrol volunteered to guide Whitaker, but the directions were not very accurate. Dawn had just broken and the brigade parties were in dispersed formation:

> I managed by bad luck to go straight through our own parties, without seeing them, and was almost in the enemy lines before I realised. I saw a German with his mess tin, having had his breakfast and fortunately his rifle was laid on the ground a few yards away and I was able to get away before he collected his wits. When we eventually found the two wounded they were both dead.

John Broom had found the frequent movement backwards and forwards across northern France, Belgium and Holland had led to a sense of timelessness similar to that he had experienced during the advance across North Africa in 1942–43.

> Again Sunday has come round & I haven't been to a service yet. Apart from the first Sunday ashore, near the beach head, I haven't known of any service. Another thing,

> but for two Sundays we have been 'on the move'. You have no idea of the work involved in 'moving' a big unit, & time 'wasted' as far as office work goes. Sometimes we move our location twice a day, & the extent of some of our moves would stagger you. In these days of highly mobile warfare, operational troops get very little rest at all. 'No time' for this, or that. The extent to which we are occupied would stagger most people.
>
> Most days go by without a thought as to what part of the week they belong. Dates we remember, but not days, apart from weekly 'returns' (office). I've known chaps to be five days out in their reckoning.[28]

Notwithstanding the lack of rest, RAMC men were among the Allied troops receiving a rapturous welcome in Belgian towns and villages. John Broom wrote:

> When we were forced to make slight halts for blown bridges and traffic blocks we were being mobbed by delirious crowds. Sometimes we even had to fight to eat our food. Somebody took a snap of Sgt. Griffiths 'brewing up' in the historic Square of a large Belgian town, absolutely surrounded by thousands of people. And I was busy being kissed and autographing books and all the rest of it. What a time![29]

However, danger was ever present despite the German Army being in retreat:

> Later that day Jerry returned to the place and started tossing a few toys about. He was soon dealt with. There were actually too many Jerries around, for besides those whom we were chasing before us were those whom the Canadians and Poles were pushing from the coastal areas, and these were constantly astride our communications. We had a thrilling time in pockets of our own! And one must admit it was a very good show.

The warm welcome accorded to British troops in Belgium was replicated in Holland. Frequently the feeling was mutual, with admiration being shown for the brave work of those patriots who had done their utmost to resist the German occupation.

> You'll be pleased to know that we have had more 'embarrassing' welcomes from recently liberated Dutch territory inhabitants. Just the job. I'm writing this in a café-garage in which we have temporarily installed our office. It's the HQ of the local Underground Movement & last night I saw a chap being 'sworn in'. The lady here was in Antwerp for 18 years & speaks voluble French. She is 47 yrs old & looks 35, has a daughter of 13 who is about twenty miles away in a town that was liberated some 5 weeks ago. … Until the latest push started I was able to sleep in the houses of friends I had made in the town where the parsonage is situated. Nevertheless, though continually on the trot, I have managed to get a good civilian bed since then, for each night.

Quite apart from the high esteem in which members of the Dutch resistance were held, Broom quickly developed an admiration for the general population, which contrasted starkly with his summation of the actions of the Germans during the long occupation of the country:

> I wish now to record that the attitude of the Dutch we have met in our latest breakthrough is beyond criticism. They are dears, very patriotic with an intense hatred of the Germans whom they call Moffen. Nothing is too much trouble for our comfort & the people I have promised to visit in Holland is mounting rapidly in numbers. I love to watch the Dutch with their wonderful orange decorations. Sometimes whole frocks are made of orange silk, or hats, bows, sashes, lapel facings; windows are gay with the national flag with its companion strip of orange, & orange bunting. Freedom has gone down very well with these folk. The Germans were such thieves. Hadn't the manners of swine.

Arnhem

The high mutual regard between Dutch civilians and British soldiers was to be hugely enhanced by the events around the town of Arnhem in September 1944. By this time the tide of the war had decisively turned in the Allies' favour. Given the view that the German war effort was almost on the point of collapse, it was agreed that a single army should be given priority of resources to execute a plan that would deal the final blow and win the war before the end of 1944. Progress by land had been slowed by an exceptionally wet summer. John Broom wrote:

> The chappie you heard on the radio about a fortnight ago didn't spread his icing too thickly when he spoke of the frightful weather we were having at the time. You would have wept to see the shocking state some fellows were in, caked with mud & very well soaken. Roads were unusable, vehicles, including our ambulances, couldn't move an inch, & altogether it was like a very merry party. To cap the effort we were continuously shelled for days on end & bombed at night for nights running. After the worst weather had disappeared, & some unexploded bombs near some of our vehicles made it necessary to shift the vehicles, one of them ran over a mine, which sent another chap away 'down the line'.[30]

Field Marshal Montgomery proposed a highly ambitious plan to fly three divisions of glider and parachute troops (35,000 men) and land them in various parts of Holland to capture five key bridges. British tanks would simultaneously break through the front line and link up with the airborne divisions one by one to properly secure these bridges. The plan – the largest airborne assault in the history of warfare – was codenamed Operation Market Garden.

The capture of the final bridge at Arnhem, the 'Bridge Too Far', the ultimate goal of Market Garden, was entrusted to General Roy Urquhart and his 1st British Airborne Division. Opposition was believed to be light, but unbeknown to them, two elite German SS panzer divisions had recently been billeted in and around the town. These units were well trained, fresh from battle, and were equipped with tanks.

The 1st Airborne Division was medically supported by No. 16 (Parachute) Field Ambulance, No. 133 (Parachute) Field Ambulance and No. 181 Airlanding Field Ambulance. (Pic 36) In addition there were regimental medical officers supported by about a dozen RAMC orderlies in each fighting unit. The division was also supported by the Polish Parachute Brigade and its own field ambulance.

On the first day, No. 16 (Para) FA and No. 181 Airlanding FA were dropped, supporting No. 1 Parachute Brigade. The task was to capture the main road bridge over the Rhine and then to secure the drop zones for the following day's landings. On the second day, No. 4 Parachute Brigade and the remainder of the divisional troops were to land with No. 133 (Para) FA and move forward to the town to consolidate a bridgehead with the covering party that had been protecting the drop zones. On the third day, the Polish contingent were to drop south of the Rhine to take over an area east of Arnhem.

At the age of 19, Corporal David Jebbitt RAMC, a medical orderly, was at the epicentre of one of the most courageous and bloody battles of the war. Jebbitt was attached to No. 181 Airlanding Field Ambulance and was part of the first lift of the operation, which took place on 17 September 1944. He flew in a Horsa glider towed by a Dakota from Down Ampney Airfield in Gloucestershire and landed at the drop zone near Wolfheze outside of Oosterbeek. On landing, Jebbitt was based at the MDS in the Schnoord Hotel in Oosterbeek, where a heavy load of casualties soon accumulated, and medics struggled to treat them with a dearth of medical supplies. He was assigned the role of anaesthetist, supporting the surgeons. Amputations were carried out using saws issued for PoW escape purposes and these were little more than hacksaw blades. The fighting was house-to-house and at close quarters, and sometimes the Germans would be right across the street, so stepping outside, even for a moment, to collect casualties was always dangerous. On one occasion Jebbitt was outside as a German tank came down the road and drove straight past him without incident. His belief was that his Red Cross armband had saved him.[31]

After a week working in the Main Dressing Station, the number of patients had increased to over 1,200, with medical teams working under horrendous conditions as the hotel was targeted several times with mortars. Being at the centre of the fighting, dressing stations were frequently drawn into the line of fire, so a temporary truce was arranged for the wounded to be evacuated to a German hospital. Remaining behind with the patients, Jebbitt was one of the RAMC staff taken prisoner and initially taken to Dutch army barracks at Apeldoorn before being transferred to Stalag IV-B in eastern Germany.

The encumbrance of jumping with a kitbag of medical equipment strapped to the leg was skilfully dealt with by Private John Battley. Battley had volunteered as an airborne medic when his division was being disbanded at the end of the North African Campaign to make up the numbers in other units for the fighting in Sicily and Italy. After training, he was assigned to No. 16 Parachute Field Ambulance. His descent from the Dutch skies was perilous:

> When we did jump, the slipstream caught my right shoulder and spun me round so that the lift-webs were twisted right down to my helmet, and the canopy very restricted. I had a kitbag of medical equipment strapped to my leg, which I let down on a line to give me some freedom to get rid of the twists, but this simply created a counter-twist down below, and I landed in this awkward position. Fortunately, it was a warm sunny day, with plenty of up draught, and the landing was no heavier than usual. The first thing I saw was someone running towards me — not a German soldier, but a Dutch woman after the valuable prize of my parachute as a source of dress material.[32]

On landing, the medics were to clear the drop zones and landing zones of casualties, with No. 181 Airlanding FA establishing a temporary dressing station. No. 16 (Para) FA was to go to Arnhem with No. 1 Parachute Brigade to set up a medical facility at St Elisabeth's Hospital. Regimental officers and their orderlies were to remain with their battalions throughout the battle and organise the evacuation of casualties for the nearest dressing station. These plans did not come to fruition. The first lift landed safely with very few casualties, with the 1st Brigade forming up quickly and moving towards Arnhem with No. 16 (Para) FA in attendance. Part of the brigade managed to reach the bridge and stayed at the north end of it for four days in the face of overwhelming odds. Eventually they were all killed, wounded, captured or dispersed.

The No. 16 (Para) FA reached St Elisabeth's Hospital at 10.00 pm on the first day to find casualties already awaiting them on the steps. Within ten hours of landing, surgeons were performing operations in the hospital. No. 181 Airlanding FA established a dressing station in the area of the drop zones and had admitted over 150 wounded within twenty-four hours. The second lift was six hours late and the Germans put up fierce resistance. This increased the number of casualties admitted to the dressing station to 250. By the evening of the second day, the rest of the brigade moved towards Arnhem and by nightfall were concentrated at Oosterbeek, where they were prevented from advancing by a large enemy force.

By the third day, the battle was in two clear parts. The 1st Parachute Brigade were at the bridge fighting stubbornly but its medical support, the No. 16 (Para) FA, had been captured and moved out of the hospital, although the two surgical teams were allowed to stay to treat the 100 most severely wounded. The fighting at Arnhem was to cost the unit five lives, with the remainder spending the rest of the war as prisoners. One member was awarded an MBE, another a Military Cross, and there were two Distinguished Conduct Medals, three Mentioned in Despatches, one Dutch Bronze Lion and two Dutch Bronze Crosses.

No. 4 Parachute Brigade were on the divisional perimeter at Oosterbeek supported by the No. 181 Airlanding Field Ambulance, with five officers and thirty other ranks of No. 133 (Para) FA in support. This area measured half a mile across by 1 mile in length, with the medical area occupied by these units and four Regimental Aid Posts. The original dressing station was sited in a large hotel with a surgical annexe in a nearby emergency hospital of thirty beds, but this spread to over ten buildings as the wounded poured in. Conditions were treacherous, with consistent shell and mortar fire hitting the buildings, one being burnt to the ground and two rendered uninhabitable. When the Germans captured any building being used as a dressing station, they allowed the staff to remain due to the acute injuries they were treating. Colonel Graeme Warrack, the ADMS of the 1st Airborne Division, was full of praise for the stoicism of the patients under such appalling conditions:

> I cannot speak too highly of the extreme bravery and self-control shown by the wounded under these most appalling conditions; even when mortaring was at its height, when

> glass and plaster were falling in profusion and when bombshell fragments were whistling through the windows, there was never a murmur or sign of hysteria from the wounded. It is one of the most shattering experiences to see men who have been wounded in battle being killed and rewounded in bed where they should be safe. It is felt, however, that the damage caused to the hospital buildings was not wilful as the whole area was extremely small and the medical buildings were on the edge of the perimeter.[33]

Casualties were brought into the dressing stations from the RAPs by jeep and hand-carried stretcher. Although drivers had been trained to drive jeeps slowly to avoid undue shock to the wounded, in the circumstances it proved safer to arrive with a shocked patient from driving too fast than not to arrive at all.

One of the buildings used was the Schoonoord Hotel, into which Colonel Warrack moved his office on 22 September, working with the other medics to treat an increasing number of casualties in deteriorating circumstances. These medical facilities were often in the firing line and remarkably, in certain cases were in front of British positions so casualties had to be evacuated forwards rather than back down the line.

By the fifth day, no proper surgery could be carried out as the buildings had been wrecked, and by day seven it became perilous to admit more patients to the overcrowded dressing stations, so the wounded were kept in the more dispersed Regimental Aid Posts. On Sunday, 24 September, a week after landing, Colonel Warrack was sent to a dressing station occupied by the Germans to request that the seriously wounded be moved to their safe hospitals. Accompanied by a Dutch interpreter, he was taken to the German Divisional Headquarters, where General Blaskowitz agreed to evacuate all the British wounded and stop firing towards the dressing stations and RAPs. The German HQ staff then gave Warrack a bottle of brandy and allowed him to return to the perimeter. Two days later, the hotel and other buildings were overrun by the Germans.

One of the wounded who had been evacuated by the Germans on Warrack's request was Brigadier John Hackett, commander of 4th Parachute Brigade. He had been hit in the belly by a mortar bomb fragment and admitted to St Elisabeth's Hospital. There, the surgeons opened him up and found he had fourteen holes in his small intestine.

These were sewn up, the wound was closed and a drain left in situ. He was given blood transfusions and put back to bed with careful instructions given to the medical orderlies who were to tend him. By this stage the Germans had completely taken over the hospital and one of their doctors wanted to administer a lethal injection to Hackett because he thought that the case was hopeless. However, he was operated on by Captain Alexander Lipmann-Kessel, who, with superb surgery, managed to save the brigadier's life.[34]

Ten days later, a member of the Dutch resistance visited the hospital and asked the British surgeon if he had any cases fit to travel and be cared for by them. Hackett was selected as being the most senior soldier there. Still weak from his wounds, he was not very keen to get up at first but made a big effort. He was dressed in civilian clothes and a bloody bandage was wound round his head. He then walked out of the hospital on the arm of the Dutchman, who drove him away under the eyes of the Germans to a safe place. Four months later, Hackett returned to the British lines after a long and perilous journey. Colonel Warrack summarised: 'This I think is a great tribute to his personal courage, to the efforts of the surgeon who operated, to the staff who nursed him and to members of the Underground Movement who sheltered him.'

The following day, Warrack was informed that Montgomery had issued orders for a night withdrawal by the division. It was further pointed out that it would be impossible for the medical units to evacuate their 2,000 wounded, so the medics should stay behind to look after them. Warrack tried his best to delay the captured men being removed immediately to the heart of the Reich. Initially the wounded and their medics were moved back to a barracks at Apeldoorn, where 1,400 were admitted to the huts and the surrounding hospitals. They were surrounded by barbed wire and guarded by elderly members of the Wehrmacht known as 'Bismarck Youth'.

Warrack established the First Airborne Divisional Military Hospital in Occupied Europe, staffed by twenty-four medical officers and about 200 orderlies. This was provisioned by food and medical stores from the local Dutch population, and occasional contributions from the Germans. Relations with the German medical officers were so cordial that their chief doctor suggested that the British be allowed to fly in medical supplies to treat their wounded, although this was rejected by Field Marshal Model, the Commander of German Forces on the Western Front.

Warrack had hoped that their captivity would be relatively temporary, and that an Allied advance would bring swift liberation. When it became clear that this would not materialise, some wounded were loaded into cattle trucks with straw, little food and no sanitary arrangements and moved to Germany. After strong protests were made to the commandant, the remaining patients were transported on a fully equipped hospital train. Eventually, after most patients and medics had been moved into German prison camps, with a few medical officers managing to escape, the hospital was closed.

One of those who effected an escape was Warrack himself. He discovered a hiding place in his office that could be reached through a panel in one of the cupboards. He disappeared into this on 17 October with the intention of coming out later and reaching the Allied lines. After making contact with the Dutch resistance he eventually rejoined the Allied forces in February 1945. He was later awarded a DSO for his work at Arnhem.

Derrick Randall, who had received an RAMC commission on 6 November 1943 and was serving as the Regimental Medical Officer of the Royal Artillery in the 1st Airborne Division, landed at 1.30 pm on 17 September and established a temporary aid post with his two medical panniers by some bushes on the edge of the landing zone. One of his first casualties was a sergeant who had sustained a crush fracture of a lumbar vertebra. Whilst the usual treatment for this was total immobilisation in a full-length body plaster, this was impossible in the circumstances and Randall advised the man to carry on moving, but with minimal activity. Fortunately, Randall was later to learn that the man had survived and that this impromptu 'mobilisation treatment' had become standard practice in such cases.

The next day, divisional headquarters was moved away from the landing zone and set up in the Hartenstein Hotel. Randall set up an RAP in a room in the basement, with some light provided by a Tilley lamp. Casualties soon began to pour in as the perimeter tightened and other medical aid became overstretched. As an RMO, Randall did not have a medical orderly of his own, but Colonel Warrack assigned him one of his own corporals. The casualties had sustained wounds from all types of small arms, mortar and shellfire. Treatment was primary care with the administration of morphine as necessary, control of bleeding and treatment of wounds by cleaning and application of field or shell dressings with splinting as required. There was little opportunity for comfort and rest for the patients, although tea was given regularly, and food was donated by various units.

Initially, casualties requiring operations were transferred to the dressing station at the Hotel Schoonoord, either by walking where possible, or by jeep, with patients either sitting or lashed onto stretchers fixed to the top of a stripped jeep. Despite the intensity of the fighting, Randall experienced no psychiatric casualties. Later in the battle, a few cases of 'battle exhaustion' were admitted, where twelve hours' rest was allowed, with the men being able to sleep soundly despite the noise of nearby fighting.

At times, the close proximity of the two armies left the medics in direct contact with the Germans. One day, Randall's corporal set out with some casualties when he was unexpectedly stopped by a very smart SS lieutenant and asked in excellent English where he was going. The corporal replied he was taking casualties to the dressing station and hoped that he would be allowed to proceed. The SS officer replied, 'If I do I suppose you will give away my position.' The corporal replied, 'Yes, Sir.' After a pause the officer told him to 'carry on'.[35]

Once the Germans occupied the dressing station, Randall stayed with his patients in the basement at Hartenstein, to where General Urquhart and his staff had also had to relocate. Therefore the casualties had to be moved to nearby houses, where local Dutch inhabitants assisted the medical orderlies in their care. To compensate for the loss of his orderlies, Randall received the support of various army chaplains in tending to the wounded. Eventually these houses too became overcrowded, and in many cases untenable, as indeed by this time were most of the remaining medical stations. Randall's supplies of shell dressings and morphine had become exhausted, and they had to rely on troops donating their own personal allocation of two shell dressings and two ampoules of morphine.

The water supply soon dried up and once again, men from surrounding units donated their supplies, which they poured into trailers carried by jeeps. Tragically, this precious resource, obtained at great risk, was holed by shell or mortar fragments and drained away before it got to the aid post. Occasional top-ups to medical equipment came via an airdrop, including some penicillin. This was the first time that Randall had come across the new drug, which he administered to two men with severe abdominal wounds who were then evacuated through the lines. They made a complete recovery.

As the days wore on and sleep became rare, men's sense of time became blurred. Randall became more confident that the XXX Corps would eventually relieve the airborne troops. These hopes were dashed when, early in the evening of 25 September, he was informed of the intention to evacuate, but he was to remain with the wounded on the order of General Urquhart. As most of the troops withdrew, Randall fell into a deep sleep despite the thunder of battle. Waking at dawn the following day, he was struck by an unreal quietness as German stretcher-bearers made their way around his RAP. Randall spent the day collecting local casualties, before being loaded onto a truck, trundling through the 'sad tattered streets of Arnhem' and on to Apeldoorn. Here locals would gather at the gates to try to pass in food and medical supplies, which even included some bottles of much-needed blood.

Through negotiation with the Germans, cooking facilities were allowed through and a limited dressing station was established. Randall was taken to Stalag XI-B in Germany on the hospital train provided for the transportation of prisoners, after protest at the initial use of the cattle wagon.

No. 213 Field Ambulance, attached to 214 Brigade, part of the 43rd (Wessex) Division, were concentrated near a bridge over the Lower Rhine at Nijmegen and had moved in small groups to a convent school in which they were treating local civilian sick. They received an urgent demand for medical supplies for the 1st Airborne Division at Arnhem. A 3-tonner was loaded with all available reserve dressings, bandages, cotton wool, sutures, gauze, Thomas splints, surgical wire, tetanus and anti-gas gangrene serum, sulphanilamide powder and morphine. Blood and plasma was also sent, and medical comforts such as milk and sugar, cocoa, malted milk, blankets and fifty stretchers. This load was transferred to a DUKW at brigade headquarters and sent forward. Although thirty ambulance cars in total were sent from the various RAMC units in the 43rd Division to the desperate 1st Airborne Division, only a small number reached them.

Early on the morning of 18 September, No. 3 Light Battery drove down from the landing zone to Oosterbeek church in order to deploy their guns to provide closer support to the 2nd Battalion force at Arnhem bridge. Later in the morning, Captain Randall Martin, RMO of the Light Regiment, followed. He asked a local lady, Kate ter Horst, if he could set up an RAP in her house. He told her, 'We don't need much … only the lightly wounded will be treated here … hope we won't have many casualties.'[36] This remained the case until Tuesday, 19th, when the casualties started to pour in. For the next six days, as the battle drew closer to Oosterbeek church, Martin's RAP, in which he only had a handful of medical orderlies and no fellow officers, coped with hundreds of casualties. Lacking much surgical equipment, the best he could offer most of the wounded was first aid. Martin managed to dispatch a few of the more seriously wounded to the MDS at the Tafelberg Hotel, but this later became impossible as enemy fire had destroyed most of the available jeeps.

The whole house soon became crammed with casualties, and the furniture was placed in the garden to create more space. Alongside the furniture, the dead lay, awaiting burial. Kate ter Horst had five young children in the house, as well as a refugee family sleeping in the cellar, but she went round the wounded men, giving what food and drink she had. As well as sustenance for the body, she gave comfort for the soul, ending each day with the reading of a psalm from the Bible of the Light Regiment's padre, Reverend Thorne. One evening she read the beautiful words of Psalm 91: 'Thou shalt not be afraid for the terror by night nor for the arrow that flieth by day.'

Kate ter Horst noted in her memoir:

> All around they are dying and must they breathe their last breath in such a hurricane? Oh God! Give us a moment's silence: give us quiet – if only for a short moment, so at least they can die in peace. Grant them a moment of holy silence while the pass on to eternity.
>
> It's a great prayer which breathes from us all – give us silence in this place of death. And again comes the night: and again follows the day: we scarcely look up at the dawn. And now, what the orderlies have feared for some time has happened – the doctor is wounded. They have taken him upstairs and he is lying in the corner of the nursery.[37]

The long corridor of the old rectory was filled with wounded, lying side by side on linen stretchers, leaving barely enough room to walk between them. In the kitchen, medical orderlies gave the wounded morphine injections and wrote on the patient's forehead the time and the dosage.

Fresh water was brought in from a pump in a neighbour's house 60 yards away. The wounded filled the kitchen, dining room, study and garden room and were even placed in the lavatory. Kate observed Reverend Thorne, 'a kind little man with curly hair and spectacles', cleaning out the filthy lavatory.

The house was hit repeatedly by mortar fire, tank shells and machine-gun fire. Some of the wounded in the house were killed or re-wounded. Soon there was no food, water or medical supplies and the house was pockmarked with bullet and shrapnel holes. All the windows were smashed and there were gaping holes in the walls.

On 25 September, a German tank fired a shot through the house. Bombardier Ernest Bolden, a medical orderly, and Padre Thorne ran out brandishing a piece of white cloth and the tank withdrew. For his tireless work, Captain Randall Martin was mentioned in despatches. Fifty-eight of the approximate 300 soldiers who were cared for in the house, cellar and garden died of their wounds.

After the perimeter had been breached, the Germans forced the local inhabitants to evacuate and Kate ter Horst was sent off with her children, eventually to be reunited with her husband, Jan, who was working with the Dutch resistance.

RAMC units and regimental medical officers had played an indispensable role in the Normandy landings and the subsequent advances through France, Belgium and Holland during the summer of 1944. Outstanding acts of bravery had co-existed alongside the daily grind of routine medical work. Each member of the RAMC had played his part in ensuring that the tide of the war in Western Europe had swung decisively in the Allies' favour. However, there was still a great struggle ahead – a struggle that would be tinged with much heartache as the full extent of the horrors of Nazi rule became apparent.

Chapter 8

Medicine in Western Europe, 1944–45

Following the setbacks at Arnhem, the Allied armies settled in for the winter of 1944/45, before launching a final thrust into Germany in early spring. Although victory seemed likely to occur in 1945, it was by no means a foregone conclusion, and the Wehrmacht continued to put up stiff resistance against the Allied armies. John Broom's New Year started with a bang:

> The recent Jerry offensive hasn't really affected us much round here. The chief thing is that he knew where not to strike. He tries to tickle us up now & then with bombs & shells. Two shells landed in the garden of the house where I was staying, at 3 mins past midnight, before the New Year could get its breath. It didn't disturb me greatly as only a window was broken. Actually I didn't go to bed until five & twenty minutes to five in the morning! Certainly saw the New Year in.[1]

For Corporal Peter Walker, that winter was bitter. The tank from which he and his comrades in No. 213 Field Ambulance drew water froze up, leaving twelve men to share one bucket of water to wash in, and Walker to shave himself in a mug of hot tea on the bonnet of a 15-hundredweight truck. White flags hung from the houses of German citizens and the roads were crammed with escaping slave labourers as the country was gradually liberated from Nazi control. Germans plundered their own factories for food and supplies. One particular sight stayed with Walker for many decades:

> Another persistent memory is of a ploughman plodding his weary way across the stubble with two horses, but with a

> white flag mounted on the beam. Here was a man trying to sustain life with bread while at the same time we were killing each other. Do we ever notice these absurd contradictions?[2]

As the advance into Germany gathered pace, many forward medical units found themselves almost on the front line. When an attack was about to begin, the forward medics would be sited about 300 yards behind the front-line troops. As the fighting men advanced, so would the medics. Walker recalled:

> One medical unit would leapfrog over another, and so the reason for that was that you don't want too much space to develop between where the casualties are occurring and the first casualty post otherwise you've got problems of carrying people long distances, so we tried to keep up as much as we could.

During this long and bitter campaign, one problem that afflicted some men was what had been known in the First World War as shell shock and was now termed battle fatigue or psychiatric cases. In February 1944, a small network of psychiatrists had been established, allowing one per corps, spread across six General Hospitals. They provided some training in psychiatry to medical officers in RAMC units so the latter could be aware of the prophylactic need, pulling men out of action before their symptoms got to the acute stage and endangering them and their comrades.

At field ambulance level, an Advanced Dressing Station would pass such cases to a Field Dressing Station, which was sometimes attached. Walker described the presentation and treatment of these cases:

> They would come in weeping and jittery, unwashed and unshaven, disheveled and dusty, and some were apathetic, some were noisy. They started like hares at the least noise. Some sat and shook almost too scared to move. Some wanted to dart off to a more substantial shelter than mere canvas would offer. Mild sedatives, warm drinks, a clean bed and sleep were prescribed. A period of sedation and the complete rest that it entailed brought wonderful changes to many.

For those whose symptoms were not cured by this period of rest, no official shame was attached. It was recognised that a man could be a very good soldier for months and then suddenly crack. There was a finite limit to most men's courage, different in each individual. As treatment developed, it was concluded that the period of sedation and rest was best carried out within the sound of gunfire. Men recovered and were RTU'd much sooner when this practice was adopted than if they had been sent further back to a tented hospital.

Early in 1945, the only Victoria Cross won by a member of the RAMC was earned. Three divisions of Lieutenant General Neil Ritchie's XII Corps were tasked with carrying out Operation Blackcock, an attempt to clear German troops from the Roer Triangle on the Dutch-German border. The operation had begun on 14 January and was in its final stages when Lance Corporal Henry Eric Harden, attached to No. 45 (Royal Marine) Commando, performed an extended act of bravery that won him his unique accolade. (Pic 37) At the time of this action Harden was 32 years old, married with two children. He had been born in Northfleet in 1912, the seventh of eight children. He was a keen sportsman who excelled at swimming, tennis and football and also played the violin. He had taken over his brother-in-law's butcher's business and had become a sergeant in the Northfleet St John Ambulance Brigade before being conscripted into the army in 1942. Although initially assigned to the Royal Artillery, his medical aptitude was soon recognised and he was transferred into the RAMC.

Harden soon grew restless with the inactivity of home service and volunteered for the Commandos, being posted to the Achnacarry Commando training depot in the Lochaber region of Scotland. Having successfully completed his training there, he was posted as a medical orderly to 45 RM Commando in January 1944. After taking part in the D-Day landings, Harden returned to the UK, expecting to be sent to the Far East, but on 7 January 1945, orders were received to return to Europe for Operation Blackcock. Attached to the 7th Armoured Brigade, the task for 45 RM Commando was to cross the Juliana Canal and drive on through Maasbracht and Brachterbeek to capture the town of Linne.

On the freezing night of 23 January, 45 RM Commando had pushed forward to occupy the small village of St Joostburg, setting up their headquarters in a house situated behind the church, which offered protection from enemy fire. The Able Troop was ordered forward to occupy the railway station at Maasbracht, but became trapped by an enemy ambush at a crossroads. Some men lay seriously injured in the snow-covered fields whilst others took cover in houses and outbuildings. Among this group was Captain John Tulloch, who arranged for jeeps displaying the Red Cross emblem to be sent out to retrieve as many of the wounded as possible. On their return, despite being clearly marked as medical vehicles, they were fired on by the Germans. One jeep was destroyed and all its occupants killed.

Therefore by the morning of 23 January, four men lay seriously wounded out in the open in freezing conditions, and a previous attempt at rescue had been met with deadly fire. With no regard for his own safety, Lance Corporal Harden ventured out into the open under intense mortar and machine-gun fire. Advancing across 120 yards to reach the wounded men, Harden bound up the wounds of three of them and dragged one marine to safety, sustaining a wound in his side on his way back to the aid post, which had been set up in one of the houses along the Stationsweg in Brachterbeek.

Two more attempts were made to rescue the other wounded men, one using tanks and the other with the aid of a smokescreen, but both failed. Against orders, Harden arranged for a stretcher party to go out into the open, carrying a white flag with a red cross. Again, despite the clear signal that this was a medical aid party, it was fired at by the Germans and the man being carried was killed. Despite this, Harden went out a third time and was bringing in Lieutenant Corey when he was hit in the head and mortally wounded. His body lay out in the open until the next day. His eventual burial stone was inscribed with the words from the Gospel of John 15:13: 'Greater Love Hath No Man Than This, That A Man Lay Down His Life For His Friends.' (Pic 38)

Medics could find themselves wrapped up in the high tensions that existed between the German army and Dutch civilians. Early in 1945, some staff of No. 223 Field Ambulance were allocated to a military hospital in a former school building at Nordhorn, on the Dutch/German frontier. A number of German medical personnel had remained to tend their own patients, and the RAMC men found themselves treating Allied and German casualties together. One dead German had been laid out on a stretcher with a label attached to his chest, which said 'Obergerfreiter Schmidt', with the date of his death. Private Jim Wisewell and his colleagues were told to arrange his burial, so they took the body to a civilian cemetery and dug a grave. The Roman Catholic padre performed a perfunctory burial service. Then:

> A woman with two children from across the road who we had seen watching the funeral came across with a big bunch of flowers and she held them out and she said to us 'for your English comrade'. So we said 'well he's not actually an English comrade. He was German' and she snatched the flowers back and she said 'I'm Dutch. I live the other side and I was caught here during the war and couldn't get back. No flowers for a German.'

After crossing the Dutch/German border, one of the most harrowing tasks facing RAMC members was the medical management of German concentration camps, in which people had been systematically starved, left to succumb to disease and killed. No. 11 Light Field Ambulance crossed the Rhine in early 1945 and the four previously separated sections came together at Neustadt on 13 April 1945. Rumours began to circulate within the unit that Brigadier Glyn Hughes, the Chief Medical Officer of the Second Army, was to assign a special task, according to Major D.T. Prescott, 'something about a concentration camp infected with typhus'.

At 12.15 am on 17 April, orders were received to be ready to move within twelve hours and anxiety began to manifest itself in the men. They had come through the entire North-West Europe Campaign virtually without a scratch and were wary of entering a typhus infected area so near to the end of the war. The unit entered a 5-mile square neutral area agreed between the British and German High Commands as the Germans did not want to see a chaotic evacuation of the camp, with typhus and other diseases spreading throughout the north-east German native population.

Belsen camp was very closely camouflaged with wooded areas, and members of No. 11 LFA caught glimpses of huts and barbed wire fencing as they passed by the perimeter of the camp en route to the entrance. A detachment of Hungarian troops had been assigned by the Germans to act as camp guards, wearing a white armband.

No. 11 LFA joined No. 32 Casualty Clearing Station under the command of Lieutenant Colonel J.A.D. Johnston MC, the senior medical officer at the camp. Later they would be joined by No. 163 Field Ambulance, No. 9 British General Hospital, No. 35 Casualty Clearing Station and the No. 29 British General Hospital. Assistance was also received from 567 Company American Field Service Unit. Major D.T. Prescott of No. 11 LFA was shocked by the sight that confronted him:

> The scene which met us as we entered the camp was one of utter chaos with dead and dying everywhere and an estimated 6–10 thousand people dead on site. The fitter ones seemed to be wandering about – a lot of them aimlessly – in the blue and white prison pyjamas which offered very little protection from the elements.[3]

Captain Eric Godwin took a series of photographs of conditions at the camp and many of the harrowing scenes that the liberators witnessed. (Pics 40, 41 & 42) He recorded on the back of one: 'Belsen. We drove along the road & wondered what the people were. The local Germans must have known what went on.'[4]

Some prisoners could hardly shuffle, and Major Prescott saw some inmates collapse and die as they lay on the ground. Inside some of the huts, hundreds of people were crammed together without bunks. In the dormitories there were two to three people to a bunk, without a mattress. Often one of them was dead, with the survivors lacking the strength to remove the body. The vast majority were suffering from diarrhoea, and typhus and tuberculosis were rife. People resembled human skeletons. Death and human excreta were everywhere.

Belsen's inmates had not been sent there to be directly exterminated, but to be interned and to endure harsh forced labour. As well as Jews, there were many political internees. The camp possessed just one single-chamber crematorium, presenting a challenge in the disposal of the infected corpses. An attempt was made by British troops to raise the morale of the inmates by encouraging them to make small fires in the open, on which to cook the small amounts of food provided for them. Many inmates could not bear the smell of the Bengal Famine mixture (a rice and sugar mixture successfully used to address the 1943 famine) provided and rejected this fare.

It was decided that everyone would have to be evacuated and the camp completely destroyed. Bulldozers were brought in to dig enormous pits that could hold about 5,000 bodies. The machines then shoved the bodies into the pits, which were marked by minefield tape. Members of the SS who had been running the camp prior to liberation were made to do a token burial of the dead by loading the deceased into lorries, taking them to the pits and throwing them in.

Jewish rabbis who were internees spent their days conducting funeral services for those who had been recognised by friends or family. A hospital was established at a large cavalry barracks a couple of miles from Belsen. At its entrance a large stable was turned into a 'human laundry', in which the men of No. 11 LFA were dressed in anti-typhus suits, dusted with DDT powder under the direction of Captain Douglas Peterkin and Captain Paddy O' Donnell and sent into the camp in ambulances to evacuate the inmates who were most seriously ill. Their clothing was removed and they were wrapped in army blankets and taken to the 'human laundry'. Here, German female nursing orderlies bathed and deloused the patients, who were then wrapped in clean blankets and transported to makeshift hospital wards in the barrack area. Every day, 650 to 750 survivors were dealt with under this system.

RAMC personnel located German medical supplies, and these were brought together in a dispensary under Prescott's leadership. He had working under him a German army pharmacist and a camp inmate who spoke five or six languages. The hospital staff included Major Max Griffin of No. 32 CCS, in charge of the 'human laundry', and Major Winterbottom, an anaesthetist. Any local or continental doctors and nurses who were available were commandeered to staff it.

Despite displaying a large Red Cross emblem on the ground at the point where No. 11 LFA was camped, between the concentration camp and hospital barracks, a German Focke-Wulf aircraft strafed the tents and ambulance vehicles with machine-gun fire, fatally wounding one man and injuring two others. (Pic 39) On another occasion, Prescott sent his orderly off with a message and was curious as to why it had taken him so long to return. The man replied that he had seen Marlene Dietrich, who had been at the camp searching for her sister who had run a canteen in the troop cinema that SS officers used to frequent.

Two RAMC privates were given the job of decontaminating any visitors to the camp by spraying them with a gun filled with anti-louse powder on the head, arms and down the front of the trousers. Famous visitors to be treated this way included Field Marshal Montgomery, Marshal of the Royal Air Force Lord Tedder, and Richard Dimbleby, the BBC correspondent who reported on the horrors of the camp to the British wireless audience.

After three or four weeks, the tasks of decontaminating and treating were near completion. On 21 May 1945, Prescott witnessed the Royal Engineers using flame-throwing tanks to perform a ceremonial burning of the evacuated huts.

A Special Order of the Day, issued by the commanding officer of No. 11 LFA, Lieutenant Colonel M.W. Gonin, referred to the work undertaken at Belsen:

> You then undertook what, for this unit, was the thankless and unspectacular task of clearing Belsen Concentration Camp. Our American friends and yourselves … have moved well over 11,000 sick from Belsen. To do this, 63 of you have worked for a month amid the most unhygienic conditions inside huts where the majority of internees were suffering from the most virulent disease known to man. You have had to deal with the mass hysteria and political complications requiring the tact of diplomats and the firmness of senior officers. During the first 10 days of the Concentration Camp and before any organised attempt had been made to feed the sick in those huts you distributed 4,000 meals twice daily from what RSM Marno could scrounge by initiative and subtlety.
>
> By collecting medical equipment from all over Germany you produced a dispensary which has supplied drugs for 13,000 patients a day and has met the demands of excitable medical officers of all races requiring the most exotic drugs in half a dozen different languages. You may have, without hesitation, acted as undertakers, collecting over 2,000 corpses from the wards of the hospital area and removing them to the mortuary – a task which the RAMC can never before have been asked to fulfil.
>
> The cost has not been light; 20 of you contracted typhus – a disease causing great personal suffering. Thank God all the patients are doing well.

> One of us will never leave Belsen – the dawn attack by the German Air Force on our lines was the price he paid to come here.
>
> Life can never be quite the same again for those who have worked in the Concentration Camp but you will go with the knowledge that the 11(Br) Lt Fd Amb has once again done a good job.[5]

Lieutenant Colonel Ian Campbell was placed in charge of a 600-bed hospital in Delmenhorst, near Bremen in north-western Germany, which, as well as treating wounded German soldiers who had been graded according to the nature rather than severity of their injury, received patients coming in from Belsen. These included American troops who had been taken in the crossing of the Rhine and sent to the concentration camp. The camp victims 'were really absolutely skin and bone and in a very bad way and we had to try and get fluid, limited fluid, into them so that they could survive, but we were glad to get them off to an American unit for proper treatment if I might say.'[6]

Further evidence of the German tendency to inflict mistreatment on prisoners based on nationality or ethnicity was found at Stalag X-B camp near Sandbostel in Lower Saxony. During the war, several hundred thousands of prisoners of war from fifty-five nations passed through the camp, with estimates of those who died ranging from 8,000 to 50,000. There was a clear hierarchy among prisoners. At the top were British and American PoWs, generally treated correctly in accordance with the Geneva Convention and receiving numerous aid packages from the International Red Cross. As a consequence, they were well fed until the very end of the war, when transportation and supply links broke down. Prisoners from Western Europe were also accorded prisoner of war status but received less outside help and were not as well nourished. However, they were allowed contact with international help organisations. Eastern European nationals from countries such as Serbia and Poland were denied access to outside observers. Italians, who arrived after their nation's surrender in September 1943, were deemed traitors by both the German guards and the other prisoners, and were towards the bottom of the hierarchy. Consequently, they were ill-fed and from the autumn of 1944, were forced to work with the Wehrmacht or be treated as civilian forced labour.

One step from the lowest position in the German hierarchy, just above the Jews, were prisoners from the Soviet Union. They were denied PoW status and consequently received no outside food, and were denied access to international observers. German guards operated a shoot-to-kill policy and there was a lack of adequate shelter. Thousands had already died from disease, starvation and brutal treatment from German guards before the camp was liberated on 29 April 1945 by troops from the British XXX Corps. What was discovered was so horrific that when the commander of the corps, Lieutenant General Brian Horrocks, paid a visit, even that most hardened of soldiers was physically revulsed by what he saw:

> The floor of the first large hut was strewn with emaciated figures clad in most horrible striped pyjamas. Many of them were too weak to walk but they managed to heave themselves up and gave us a pathetic cheer. Most of them had some form of chronic dysentery and the stench was so frightful that I disgraced myself by being sick in a corner. It was difficult to believe that most of the hardly human creatures had once been educated, civilised people.[7]

Horrocks was so angry that he ordered the burgomasters of all the surrounding towns and villages to supply a quota of German women to clean up the camp and look after the prisoners. He expected an indication of horror or remorse from those Germans sent to the camp. 'Not a bit of it. I never saw one tear or heard one expression of pity from any of them.'

Major Hugh McLaren was a surgical specialist serving with the No. 10 Casualty Clearing Station, which arrived in the camp on 6 May. McLaren submitted a typewritten report later that month to Sister Freda Laycock, chief of C Block in Sandbostel's hospital.[8]

Initially, the medical aid that a fighting force could spare to address the horrendous conditions in the camp was small. No. 168 Light Field Ambulance, No. 31 Field Hygiene Section and McLaren's CCS were assigned to the task of dealing with the 'pig-sty' that had been found. The camp hospital consisted of one hut containing a dark central corridor from which twenty small rooms led off. The accommodation huts were similarly designed, with each room containing a dozen shelves where the prisoners would lie in close-packed rows, forty to sixty to each shelf. The Scottish doctor noted, 'The most chaotic slum dwelling on Clydeside was luxurious in comparison.'

Although the hut McLaren was working in was designed to accommodate eighty patients, on average, 320 were housed there. Conditions were foul:

> On arriving at C block to begin work, my first sensation was one of nausea. The latrines had been blocked for days without discouraging the patients from using them. The wards were equally offensive. Standing on the floor or hanging onto the bunks for support were the merest skeletons of men. They were naked, unshaven and dirty. They defecated onto the floor where they stood. They had sunk so low that no trace of embarrassment was occasioned by the presence of British or German sisters.

Each nurse had sixty patients to care for with only one bedpan, and people were dying unnoticed where they lay.

One section of Sandbostel was termed the 'Horror Camp' and contained about 8,000 political prisoners of the Nazis. Lieutenant Colonel Prym, commanding officer of No. 168 Field Ambulance, was assigned the grim task of retrieving the remnants of life left by the SS guards. The mass of dead, dying and befouled humanity had received an occasional cartload of turnips or potatoes, with those with the strength left to do so winning the mad scramble for the scraps. The men of the field ambulance unit removed the likely survivors from this human pigsty and passed them on to the 'human laundry'.

The laundry was a large marquee in which were placed rows of trestles supporting stretchers. The survivors of the Horror Camp were washed on these stretchers and covered in DDT (anti-louse) powder. Wrapped in a clean blanket they were transferred to an unsoiled stretcher and delivered to Major McLaren and his staff in No. 10 Casualty Clearing Station by ambulance. This work was done by the conscripted German women under the supervision of RAMC personnel. This initial screening and sanitising ensured that very few lice found their way into the hospital. Of the 8,000 prisoners found in the horror camp, No. 10 CCS treated 4,000, with 1,500 having to be buried and 2,500 evacuated.

The survivors sent to McLaren were severely emaciated and curiously apathetic, with inmates' brains having been affected by starvation. The Major found that there was evidence of considerable derangement, with 50 per cent being in such a depressed state of mind that the news of liberation brought about little or no emotional reaction. Their focus was on their basic needs, with shouts of *'Wasser, wasser!'* and *'Kein essen!'* reverberating down the corridor. Their pasts and futures had become blank. This manifested itself in the sangfroid with which the prisoners regarded death occurring in a neighbour. McLaren noted this was often merely a signal to request the crusts or cigarettes from under the dead man's pillow. There were patients who would interrupt a medical examination with a remark like *'Zwei tage, Herr Doktor … und kaput'*. 'How often they proved correct,' recorded McLaren.

Occasionally a macabre humour manifested itself in the face of death. One skeletal survivor beckoned McLaren to his bedside and, pointing up to the bed above, he asked, *'Ist er tod?'* He examined the man above and found that he was dead. Relaying this information to the man in the lower bunk, McLaren was met with the merest trace of a smile, *'Gott sei dank'* (Thank God!), then the patient proceeded to detach the groundsheet that he had used to protect himself from the droppings of the dead man above.

Not all victims of the Nazis remained as phlegmatic. They were frequently encountered in the corridors searching for food and twice McLaren was summoned to quieten a melee in the ward. On both occasions a crazed Russian had plunged his head and shoulders in a food pail, and had to be forcibly removed by the medics, his face streaming with soup.

For the first four days, No. 10 CCS personnel lived through a nightmare of the immediate effects of Nazi callousness and the constant demands for care from its survivors. Each man required at least five large cupfuls of water per day as a minimum, and with sixty patients in each hut that meant that the one medical orderly and two assistants could not keep up with the demand, even with a system of 'pani-wallahs' assigned to deliver the water. McLaren therefore devised a mechanism whereby drinking bottles of saline transfusion sets could quench the thirst of the feeblest patients, who could not drink unaided. Slowly, however, the situation began to ease; the shouting and wailing of the patients abated and an air of hope came over the hospital.

Over time, the food provided became more nourishing. Initially, in order to feed over 2,000 mouths thrice daily, Sergeant Williams RAMC had to provide soup, but as extra supplies reached the camp, the soup became a stew, and occasionally eggs, milk and butter were added to the diet. The black bread that accompanied the soup aggravated the diarrhoea that most patients suffered from due to the famine. Sulphaguanidine cured the condition in twelve to twenty-four hours and it also improved quickly with careful dieting and kaolin/opium mixture.

There was one group of patients who were a long way from hope. McLaren listened to a Jew who had seen SS guards push their elderly kinsmen from the second-floor window of Lublin General Hospital in Poland, then cart off the stunned or dead for burial. Another had seen the SS mow down his wife, father, mother and two sisters. The Jews in the hospital looked more helpless and pathetic than the rest, and McLaren soon learned not to enquire after their families, restricting his conversation to practical medical matters.

One group of people in the camp with whom McLaren did speak about the treatment of the Jews in Nazi-controlled Europe was the German females who were among the 300 assorted European nationals supporting the RAMC units in caring for the sick. In contrast to Brian Horrocks's impression of a lack of remorse, McLaren found them hardworking, although ascribed this to the example set by the British nursing sisters of the QAIMNS. Several times he found the Germans weeping and not getting on with their work, saying they were terrified of contracting typhus. McLaren would lead them to where Sister Laycock was working in the middle of typhus cases, 'calmly doing whatever she had to do'.

When questioned about their response to what they had seen in the camp, most expressed the view that they could have done little to stop the horror that had occurred in the concentration camps. However, one lady, Fraulein Bittner, the 35-year-old 'Over-woman' of the German girls, give a blunt assessment in a conversation recorded by McLaren:

McLaren: Fraulien, you have been a great help to us in the camp. But do you feel ashamed of its being here?

Bittner: No. The Fuhrer must have had good reason to create it.

McLaren: Do you condone the starving of those men, then?

Bittner: The Fuhrer said, first I must feed my soldiers, then my workers, then my mothers and children. If there is anything left, others may have something.

McLaren: Do you condone Hitler's killing of three million Polish Jews?

Bittner: The National Socialist Party decided this policy was the best for our country, so I agree with it. The Jews can go and live in their own country, which The Bible says was set aside for them.

McLaren: Do you really agree with gassing Jewish children?

Bittner: (hesitantly) Well, if they are allowed to grow up they will be a problem later, so perhaps it is better for them to die now.

Just hours after this conversation, Field Security drove up to the camp with Fraulein Bittner's name on their wanted list.

McLaren was full of pride in his unit:

> That 10 CCS did not crack with fatigue during the intensive work from May 18th was, I think, due to the fact that everyone was given full scope to use their own initiative. Even accepting that everyone knew his or her job, it was quite remarkable how few orders had to be given. The Germans were astonished at this.

This pride was tempered with the horrifying thought of the scenes at Sandbostel being repeated in Britain, had the war against Germany not been won:

> Our V-Day celebration was replaced by Sandbostel. Although most of us did not doubt that Germany had to be beaten, we did not appreciate the savagery of the enemy until we reached here. I am sure we all shuddered as we pictured the possibility that might have been, this wilderness

of barbed wire and huts on the Stockiemuir in Scotland, or on Hampstead Heath. … And the skeletons would then have been … who?

As RAMC personnel came into regular contact with German civilians during the advance through the country and the subsequent occupation, they expressed hugely varying views on the native population, depending on the context of the war. Having previously denounced the German 'swine' for their actions during the occupation of Holland, John Broom's view shifted as the war came to an end and he became part of the occupying forces in that ravaged nation. On 14 April 1945, he wrote:

> One doesn't see the best side of the German race in conditions that obtain at present, but I must say that I haven't been at all impressed with the bearing of the Masterfolk. Most of them look pretty criminal – possibly from a sense of guilt in some cases though I should say that on the whole they are incapable of feeling any responsibility for their crimes. Their moral standards never existed.[9]

A week later, Broom's unit, No. 2 Light Field Ambulance, took over a large farmhouse whose civilian residents were confined to the cellar. Here the men found a book entitled *Two Wars, Two Victories*, with large photographs of the German war leaders and maps of the German advances day by day in Norway, France, Denmark, Belgium, Holland and Poland. Broom noted that 'All houses seem to possess books glorifying German conquests. How they must mock the people as they handle them! Vain boastings of a crooked people.'[10]

By June 1945, his tone had softened:

> Naturally one's instinctive attitude to all Germans is one of distrust. However, I have met some who are genuinely anti-Nazi, some who spent years in Concentration Camps, etc. Personally, I believe in intelligent, selective fraternisation with approved non-Nazi people, but at the moment conditions aren't conducive to a proper understanding of the issues involved.

A visit to Hamburg in the middle of June, during which Broom could enjoy a visit to the theatre, brought home to him the devastation that had been wreaked on German civilians:

> Yesterday afternoon I paid my first visit to Hamburg since about May 6th (this unit entered, I think, on 4th, & a couple of days later were well north of the main city) the object being to see ENSA's representation of *Richard III* in which Sybil Thorndike & Laurence Olivier were appearing. He's one of the best-known film stars, it seems.

Although the theatre was largely undamaged, it was one of the few buildings in the city to escape destruction:

> I think that nowhere will you find such widespread devastation for five hundred thousand people lost their lives there in the raids, two hundred thousand in one raid. It's colossal. Many streets have disappeared utterly, & rubble is piled higher than the height of ordinary 6-roomed houses. Quite often, too, one catches whiffs of dead bodies, for most of the 500,000 slain lie buried beneath the huge masonry

As the deprivations of the civilian population became more acute with the onset of the first war-free winter since 1938–39, Broom severely chastised his mother for her 'unchristian' attitude to those Germans whose travails he was daily witness to:

> I find it frightfully difficult to understand your views on the Germans. Apart from your unchristian attitude (Love your enemies: I find it quite impossible to worry overmuch about the dear Germans) you seem to be singularly dense in appreciating the food situation out here. This I assess by virtue of your use of the words 'the very meagre amount that we are able to procure'. If your amount is meagre, for high heaven's sake how would you describe the amount the Germans have to live on when for a tin of bully-beef a gold watch will change hands, for 50 marks (25/-) a small, plain bar of army chocolate, for 400 marks a pound of coffee

(£10)? Of course these are Black Market prices, but how else can the people live? I have at various times striven to acquaint you with the German ration scale, which is so much lower than the British as to make the British appear as callous hogs, but believe me that the official weekly ration scale is never obtained. The ration cards are there all right, but the goods just aren't available in the shops. I'm heartily sick of labouring the subject to people who seem unable to grasp the situation intelligently, but at the risk of repeating myself I would say that the sight of unused ration cards in respect of past & current months is eloquent evidence of the discrepancy between entitlement and distribution. *Compris?*

Try, if you will, to think of the Germans as individuals or as members of family 'cells', not as a nation whose economic frustrations in the closed markets of the world led them to find the outlet for their inferiority complex by a policy of self-justification leading to all the horrors of the Nazi prison camps & brutal war.

Take the average German woman. Her man is either dead or a prisoner of war. If the latter, she isn't aware of it, unless he were captured before the end of 1944. Few women have their men with them. If they have, they are either men who were discharged from the German forces during the war on account of grave disability (chiefly loss of a leg, a very common practice in German field surgery) or in extreme cases, men of good health who were farmers or other vital civilian workers. So you see that the average woman has lost her husband. She has at least two or three children. Her main problems are care of the children, the procurement of food & fuel. To obtain any hope of getting any food she must queue all day long & then often has to go away home unsupplied. But how can she queue properly with young children to look after, & no help available? Getting trees chopped up is utterly beyond her powers, so the fuel situation settles itself by her having to go without. All very nice for Christians to contemplate whilst getting dug in on a fair-sized meal in a fairly warm room.

The RAMC had done a grand job in adapting itself to serve a highly mobile fighting force during the North West European campaign. John Broom reflected on the huge distances covered by the office lorry of No. 2 Light Field Ambulance from July 1944 to May 1945:

> This heavy office lorry is nearing its eighth thousand mile since it landed with this Unit's Rear Party in July 44 and as it has never been used for any job other than purely operational moves of the whole unit, you can understand that some of our lighter vehicles have done thirty or forty thousand miles. I suppose that I have done at least twelve thousand miles. That, I think, is a considerable under-estimate.[11]

The comradeship that had been formed during those long, dangerous miles meant that many RAMC men found it heartbreaking when, due to the changing demands of peacetime, divisions, brigades and units were broken up. John Broom witnessed the final days of No. 2 Light Field Ambulance, a unit he had served with from Tunisia through Sicily, Italy, the UK, France, Belgium, Holland and Germany:

> Already we have had about 120 new men come & about a corresponding number depart. It's all so unhappy. Strong men with rows of medal ribbons, with tears falling down their cheeks to be leaving their friends & their 'home' of the past 6 years or so. The GHQs are not very sentimental; all they work on are cold facts & nominal rolls. They can never understand the spirit of a unit which has borne the burden of England in many lands. Soon there will be very few left – even I must go (under this scheme all under Group 32 are affected) whither I know not as yet. Wherever it is, you may guess that I shall be taking a dim view. It does seem a shame that chaps won't be allowed to finish their army service in the Unit which so unforgettably is moulded by the individual character of its members. Some chaps have signed on for one or two years' extra service rather than lose the Unit. Rather selfishly, perhaps, they say 'Maaleash [too bad] the wife & kids. It's 2LFA for me!'

Broom also witnessed the disbanding of the famous 7th Armoured Divison, the 'Desert Rats':

> We have met dozens of Desert Rats making their way to new units as far afield as Paris, Brussels, Rotterdam. They are practically the last of their units' old men, & all speak with horror of the red tape being woven into the fabric of the 'new div'. There have been some rare scenes, and even the War Office itself is protecting the interests of certain personnel who, on leaving the div, refused to conform to the current stupidities in the new unit like putting brown boot polish on Bakelite cap badges!

Broom himself, and his staunch comrade and fellow-Christian George 'Geordie' Dunn, found themselves transferred from No. 2 Light Field Ambulance to No. 121 British General Hospital. On 23 December 1945, he wrote:

> The day after Geordie & I arrived at the 121 we were told to take down our Rats & put up the 21 Army Group sign. We've taken down the Rats, but not put up the 21 A G efforts. However, we remain true Rats at heart whatever our sleeves bear, & the new chaps in the Div who wear the Rat may know that they haven't got the soul of a Rat whose outstanding qualification is the few pounds of sand lying in the stomach.

Despite this upheaval, Broom, who had been outspoken recently of military discipline and routine throughout 1940–41, toyed with the idea of staying in the RAMC following the cessation of hostilities. Writing to his mother on 14 November 1945, he advised of the difficulty he anticipated in returning to civilian life:

> I'm still strongly considering signing on for a couple of years. I'm sure that this won't meet with your approval, but then, if we spent all our lives trying to please people we shouldn't get very far. … I love freedom of action & independent thought, & I really find a lot of irksomeness in

> listening to the opinions so often illogically & prejudicially presented by people with civilian experience only. In writing this I'm not directing my thoughts to the members of my own estimable family all of whom are protected by ties of blood & love from adverse criticism. However, I haven't yet decided what to do. I suppose you think I'm crazy, dear. Maybe I am! I won't dispute the point. We all make mistakes, & those I make I prefer to make on my own initiative.

The 'freedom of action & independent thought' that the army had nurtured in its medical personnel had underpinned the victory in Europe. Men of the RAMC had played an indispensable role in the overthrow of a tyrannous and evil regime, which had threatened to blight the freedoms and independence of millions for many decades to come. Theirs was the victory, but at a heavy cost.

Chapter 9

Homecoming, Demobilisation and Reflection

'The Second World War was, on the whole, a triumph of military medicine. Only one British soldier died of disease for every four that were killed by the enemy.' This was the government's summation of the efforts of the RAMC and other medical services during the conflict.[1] This triumph was not uniform, with Burma proving the great exception to that story of iatric progress, 'the one theatre of war that modern pharmacology never mastered'. For all of the achievements Slim's army made in the battle against malaria, Burma remained a deadly place for human beings to traverse in large numbers.

Not all RAMC members shared this sense of collective achievement. By October 1944, Private Ralph Dawson was expressing cynicism about his role in the army, and a resentment of the hierarchical nature of the organisation he had been brought into.

> Also, have you noticed they can give us more money now and let us wear ties to look a bit more respectable now they know the war is nearly over. Marvellous isn't it? I can only say one thing – the sooner they kick me out of it the happier I shall be. I've had enough of being kicked from pillar to post and domineered by men who perhaps in civvy street were 2½ d shop assistants.[2]

Dawson, an ambulance driver, reflected in 1945 that the years of sacrifice needed to be repaid by the government in the form of a fairer society with a greater equality of opportunity:

> 3 years ago today I joined up in his majesty's army. 3 years of the best, wasted. Let's hope it's for a better cause than the last one. The lads will want something worth coming

> back to after this lot won't they And make up for the years they've lost sweating and toiling through the African desert and wet cold and slosh of Italy. They won't forget it in a hurry.[3]

For Lieutenant Colonel Ian Campbell, who had entered the RAMC as a 23-year-old newly qualified doctor, the experience of war educated him in the backgrounds and perspectives of men of different classes: 'Well, the personal aspect was that you got to know people. You got to know life by other persons rather than your own life. You got to know the troops very well and you got to know about their families, their activities, and this was a great education.[4]

One of the routine tasks he undertook as an officer gave him a further insight into the inner lives of his men. This enabled him to have 'a good gain in confidence because we had to censor letters, and you had to glimpse through the various letters written by the troops and you saw really, you learnt a lot about life, and that was one of the things.'[5]

On 22 September 1944, Ernest Bevin, Minister for Labour and National Service, announced the details of the national demobilisation programme. Based mainly on men's ages and the length of time they had been in uniform, the proposals drew a mixed reaction from the ranks of the RAMC. Nearly a month after the proposals were set out, Ralph Dawson wrote to his brother-in-law complaining about its perceived unfairness:

> What do you think about the demobilisation scheme? I don't altogether agree with it. For one thing they haven't taken into consideration overseas service. Secondly they haven't given any priority to a man's compassionate means. Such as large families, and conditions at home. For instance, is it right that a single young man who has done the same time as me in England all the time gets discharged as soon as me?[6]

For Dawson, despite the opportunities his war service had given him to experience the cultural delights of Italy, his release could not come soon enough. Four days after VE Day he wrote: 'I wonder what the programme is now. And how long we are going to stick in the army before we get out. Of course we all can't get out, somebody's got to go and settle up with the little yellow man, but I hope I'm not one of them. I've had enough.'[7]

Private Jim Wisewell's reminiscence of VE Day was one laced with sorrow rather than anger:

> We were at Delmenhorst … when the war actually ended. And I've always tried to analyse my feelings. Siegfried Sassoon says that when November the eleventh came in 1918 instead of going wild and drinking and celebrating, he said he spent the day sobbing and cursing and thinking of the dead … apart from the cursing I did the same.

Private Kenneth Stalder, who had been captured in Crete in May 1941 along with most of his comrades in No. 189 Field Ambulance, harboured lingering resentments of the enemy. Discharged from the RAMC upon his release as unfit for further active service, he continued to hold an antipathy towards Italians: 'One day I saw an Eyetie with an English girl and I went for his throat. It took my brother and two others to pull me off.'[8]

Gradually, men who had spent years in close mutual companionship began to be separated as units were broken up. Those who had served on hospital ships, such as Private Bert Swingler, would feel the departure of valued comrades particularly closely. Writing from H.S. *Toscana* following the successful conclusion of the war in Europe, he described the send-off given to some of those he had served alongside in No. 93 British General Hospital:

> We have had eight of our company go back home this week and they have done there [*sic*] full whack out here 4½ years and the Commanding Officer went as well as he's due for de mobbing and we were sorry to see him go as he was a really good sort and never bothered us about anything and was the best C.O. we have had since I came in the army for he would always look after us, you know what I mean Dad. We had a good night before they went for we had a bit of a 'do' with a good issue of beer and sandwiches and a sing song and they went on most of the night and I think they were all half

> carried when they went off the ship the next morning but we all gave them a lift with their gear onto the lorry that was waiting for them so that they had a good start off.[9]

For others, the end of military service could not come soon enough. Private Hubert Manning, who had enlisted in October 1940 and had served in the Middle East with No. 76 General Hospital before being transferred to northern Europe in July 1945, was released from the army in May 1946 with the testimonial 'A very good Nursing Orderly and a willing and conscientious worker, who has experience of operating room work, of good appearance and forthright manner'.[10] The final comment served as a polite reference to two incidents during his post-war service. In early August 1945, Manning went absent without leave for a week, for which offence he was confined to barracks for the same duration, and in February 1946, he received a two-day confinement for the following incident:

> Conduct to the prejudice of good order & military discipline in that he had an untidy kit lay-out on the Ord / Officers Billet inspection, viz. Dirty mess tins, appearance of food on eating utensils.

Clearly, Manning considered he had played his part in the successful conduct of the war, and he had little time for the continuation of the irksome restrictions and expectations military life imposed upon his behaviour.

For older men, such as Sergeant Samuel Thorley, it was a relief to go home. Thorley had been called up in July 1944 when aged 38, and returned to his wife and young son after a relatively short period of service in the Far East. Before enlistment, Thorley had served in Civil Defence and with the Home Guard. Once his overseas service commenced, he had been twice promoted within two months, his conduct being graded 'exemplary' and who 'when called on to perform the duty of a much senior person, he did so at very short notice and performed the duty in a very efficient manner with confidence'.[11]

Once men were demobilised, many began to reflect positively on the lessons their war experience had taught them. John Forfar thought that, as an officer with a commando unit, men would tell him things that they would not confide to other people: 'I learnt a tremendous lot about human nature, a tremendous lot of how men reacted to stress and to what extent there was a degree of resilience in them, particularly, of course, in my chaps who were all volunteers, against stress.'[12] His medical repertoire was greatly enhanced, on one occasion having to remove a man's leg with a pair of scissors without any anaesthetic after a booby trap had exploded under him. Ultimately, Forfar reflected, 'from a medical, from a human point of view, from a kind of almost emotional, social point of view, yes, you learn an awful lot. You learn a tremendous lot about human nature.'

Captain Forde Cayley recalled his homecoming after three and a half years as a prisoner of the Japanese. It was a dull autumn day as his ship pulled into Liverpool docks. Cayley handed in his uniform, drew a demob suit, twenty clothing coupons and a book of ration tickets. He bade farewell to his comrades and went home to Ealing to find his wife, father and sister, his mother having died during his incarceration. Cayley contemplated his situation in life; 'I was thirty, weighed about seven stone, wanted children, and had to find a job, get rid of my diseases, get my psyche settled down, and bring my medical knowledge up to date.'[13]

To that end, Cayley was examined at Middlesex Hospital and diagnosed as having hookworm and threadworm, the latter of which would take a decade to clear. He was offered a post as supernumerary registrar, working at St Stephen's Hospital in Chelsea, starting work almost immediately on his return to Civvy Street. However, it would take time for some of Cayley's army ways to fade. During a month's stint working at the Chelsea Workhouse with unwanted babies, 'The doctors' maid ticked me off for swearing like a trooper. Having been with the men all those years, I didn't notice I was doing it.' Over time, his attacks of malaria grew less frequent but, sadly, 'My terrible dreams and the fear took a long time to go.'

Although initially holding a grudge against those who had fought for the axis powers, this perspective was altered when encountering medical colleagues from Germany and Japan: 'My hatred for the Germans and the Japanese vanished when I went to the World Medical Assembly in Paris and met people from those countries who had been on the other side in the battles in which I had taken part. … They too had suffered, and we had compassion for each other.'

Geoffrey Haine, having served in West Africa, Northern Europe and the Far East, was demobbed in December 1945. Having undertaken a long series of plane journeys through the Middle East, he thought that once he arrived in England, the demobilisation process would be over in a matter of minutes. He could then board the train home to Gloucestershire and his waiting family. However, army procedure meant he had to first go to Millbank and then to the RAMC depot at Aldershot. Then, he had to travel all the way back to Taunton to collect his demob suit before finally being allowed to travel home.

Leslie Ellis endured an extended wait for his demobilisation after his release from Japanese captivity. Stricken with sinusitis and amoebic dysentery, he spent a few months recuperating at No. 107 British General Hospital in Bangalore. However, this stay was not without its high points, as he wrote to his mother in November 1945:

> Saw Leslie Henson & Co on Friday last with dinner after with 3 charming 'Wrens' – a dance at the club on Saturday, pictures on Monday – a very good dance at the Club in Bangalore with Mary Braithwaite and a friend of hers plus dinner beforehand in a friend's bungalow, a gramophone recital on Wednesday and a dinner at the Red Cross H.Q. tonight. There was also a cocktail party last week to meet Mrs Supremo – Lady Mountbatten. It was given by the local Red Cross Chief and a party of patients and Red Cross girls went from the hospital. Someone was able to introduce about 6 of us and then ran out of names. I was the first of the unknowns to shake hands with Lady Louis – so she said we should introduce ourselves American style and announce our own names – 'My name is Mountbatten.'

Ellis also availed himself of this extended period of slack time to relay to his mother the missing three and a half years of his life since she had last heard from him. He sent eleven 'Liberty Letters', which told her of his movements and the work he had undertaken. In his second missive, written on 2 September 1945, he reflected on the gains the previous few years had brought: 'About the best thing of our life has been the friendships we have formed. … I plan a tour around England and stop every 50 miles at a friend's house and many may turn up in Harrogate.'

Despite seeking to draw some positives from his recent experiences, Ellis could not immediately forgive or forget the way he and others had been treated by his captors:

> I have seen men sick and dying through sheer ignorance, mismanagement, malice or calculated brutality. The Korean guards are just as bad as the Japanese. I never thought people could get as bitter as we prisoners are. If I let myself go I could keep up our stories for ages. However, it is all over now; we are wondering what the future holds. England seems a queer place now.

Lance Corporal Arthur Atkin, having spent most of his war in Italy with No. 140 Field Ambulance, realised that by 1945 the country had to begin 'the monumental task of re-adjustment and rebuilding'.[14] On a personal level, men's thoughts turned to demobilisation and, for many, a need to find new skills or refresh the ones that had previously provided civilian employment. Centres of training were set up to fulfil this need, but also to modify the rate of release into civilian life. Atkin, as a commercial artist, could hardly have found himself in more propitious surroundings.

> I counted myself particularly fortunate to apply and be accepted for a month's rehabilitation art course in Florence. All the bridges across the Arno had been destroyed except the Ponte Vecchio and even here the approach on each side of the river had been badly destroyed so that the rubble had hindered its use during the fighting. However most of the Uffizi Gallery largely escaped damage and the central area still held its evocation of the spirit of its artistic vitality.

There were lectures on Italian painting, tours of Florentine churches, and a visit to the basement of the Uffizi, where much of the priceless collection had been in wartime storage for protection. Drawing classes were also provided, 'Yet in spite of this course, I still felt ill-equipped to fit into the world of commercial design and illustration. I resented the big gap in career development, and even contemplated a return to academic and school training.'

However, Atkin had the offer of work, which in turn meant he would be in a position to marry his sweetheart, Mary, so he returned relatively smoothly to his pre-war occupation.

Kenneth Hulbert had risen to the rank of major during his service in East Africa and India. In later years he reflected positively on how the war had shaped him:

> It was a great adventure and I was entirely thrown back on my own resources. I was able to see the world in a way that I would never have done in any other way. Then there was the comradeship, having to meet and mix with people from different backgrounds and, at the same time, maintain my Methodist roots. … The long separation from home was painful, but my home was all the more precious as a result. The long journeys, so often spent on my own, and the opportunity to see people of other lands have enriched my life ever since.

Lieutenant Colonel Geoffrey Wooler was in no doubt that the war, although a terrible endeavour, was immensely worthwhile as it rid the world of monstrous regimes. 'I think any person hates war, hates to see these young people dying, but it was either that or living under a dictatorship regime which would have been far worse.'[15] Nevertheless, Wooler's initial keenness for his work waned as the toll of disease, damage and death mounted:

> At the beginning of the war I got involved with great enthusiasm, but towards the end of the war I got a bit tired of it. I used to call them 'blood and plaster parties'. It really got me down a bit. In fact, when I came home after I was demobilised I remember telling my parents I didn't want to do any more surgery. I had had enough. I got tired of seeing so many young people mutilated.

At the end of the war, Wooler's zest for life took months to return as he enjoyed walks in the countryside. Gradually, he forgot the unpleasantness he had experienced and fixed his mind on the positives that the war had brought him:

> War certainly does bring out the best in people; the comradeship that you had, the feeling that everybody was trying to help everybody else. It didn't matter how much trouble it took to do things, they wanted to try and help other people and you had such loyalty. You were all working together and there was no need to discipline people because they would discipline themselves. I made a lot of friends during the war, really true friends, and you don't often find that in civilian life – a very deep and strong friendship – and they still are my friends.

Captain Bill Frankland arrived back in England on 13 October 1945 after four years abroad, three and a half of them as a prisoner of the Japanese. Disembarking at Liverpool, he was asked if he would like to see a psychiatrist. His reply was emphatic: 'No I want to see my wife.' Having been sent to a camp at Huyton, Frankland and a colleague walked 5 miles to a nearby village where the vicar was allowing returning prisoners to use his telephone, and spoke to his wife after many painful years of separation.

Frankland resumed his medical career at St Mary's Hospital, London, and went on to achieve eminence in the field of allergies. For many decades he chose not to speak about his wartime experiences, either in public or to most of his family. Frankland reckoned that dwelling on the past, rather than looking positively at the life that lay ahead, could lead to depression. Despite the brutal treatment he had received at the hands of his captors, Frankland's Christian faith meant that he bore no ill will to those who had tormented him and tens of thousands of other prisoners: 'You must not go on hating people; it does you harm but it does not do them any harm. I am a Christian who was taught to love, not hate. That's how I live my life. You feared the Japanese. I feared them. I would not use the word hate.'

Sergeant Charles Quant was working at No. 58 General Hospital, which had established itself in an old Fiat factory in Torino, when the war in Italy ended. In one regard, Quant regretted that his war was over, 'having spent several exciting, hardworking years doing a job that in retrospect had saved the lives of thousands of men of all nationalities, including Germans and Italians'.[16]

This disappointment was short-lived, as the joy and admiration with which their efforts have been regarded by the local population became clear. Quant and some of his comrades took a trip up to the Alpine village of Balme, which comprised a collection of small stone shacks:

> It was hot, and not surprisingly there were few people about, but when we pulled up in the square, they poured out of every house, thirty or forty of them. They rushed at us, flung greetings at us and the lucky ones among us got great luscious kisses. I explained that we were British troops. They said that we were the first they had seen in that remote spot. They said most of their men had gone off to join the *partigiani*, the partisans. We said we had a partisan in our unit and handed them loaves of army bread and tins of army jam and bully beef.

Then something very strange and beautiful happened. An old woman stepped out of the crowd, gazed at the medics for a while then dashed to a house and picked up a bucket by the door. She turned again and ran out into the surrounding patches of grass and grabbed the head rope of a tethered cow.

> Towing the cow behind her she ran back to us, squatted on her heels and began milking the cow. With a pint or so in the bottom of the bucket, she went to the nearest soldier and offered him the bucket. He took it with a warm *Grazie* and drank, handed it on to another of us who emptied it. She took the bucket again and milked some more into it. In turn we all got a drink. It tasted just like ordinary milk, but it was different in almost a spiritual way. We did our best to tell her that we knew what she meant. I hope we got our message over.

For Quant, the incident of the peasant woman and her cow forever symbolised 'the achievement, the simple fact of victory, the liberation. It was not high technology. It was the encounter between a handful of the soldiers who had travelled thousands of miles, and an old woman of a liberated country.'

Corporal Peter Walker of No. 213 Field Ambulance ended his war in Germany. However, 'I decided that I would apply for a commission. I thought I hadn't been ambitious enough myself, and I thought I should.' He trained in the Officers' Cadet Training Unit in Wrotham, Kent before being posted to Bangalore. After a year he came out of the army. 'We went home and I forgot about the war for fifty years. I was quite pleased to forget about it and I tried to forget about it in a way.' Walker recognised that the army had developed in him a more rounded view of life due to his war experience: 'Oh yes, I think you grew up fast in the war. And I think I was quite slow to mature really. I think, I think the period in the ranks was really quite good for me.'

Unlike many men who found that their Christian faith was strengthened during the travails of wartime service, Walker suffered a loss of faith:

> I mean it's very difficult to maintain your faith when you see the things that we saw in the war, and that had a profound effect on me. I remember very clearly trying to stand on parade at the end of the war in Germany, I think with my foot in a rabbit hole trying to stand to attention, and we were outside a German church, and we were brought up on parade and we waited for a very long time and the doors were shut and then suddenly the doors opened and to our surprise a German civilian congregation filed out. And … I realised then, of course, that this was quite absurd, you know, that was God really on one side or the other, and, of course, you have to start to think about things. … I searched and searched for a very long time until I found something that was a bit more intelligent to believe as a philosophy, yes.

Acting Sergeant Frank Turton emerged from the war with his understanding of anatomy and physiology greatly enhanced, having never had the opportunity to study medicine before 1940.

This fascination stayed with him through the rest of his life, although he decided against pursuing a career in medicine, returning to work his way into the management structure of the Brightside and Carbrook Co-operative Society in Sheffield. Turton recalled, 'You just wanted to go back to your old life and what was familiar after the war,' as the importance of picking up on the familiar ties of family, workplace and community had been reinforced during his six years away from home.

Corporal Ron Dickinson found transition back to civilian life was not easy, but the process was aided by the interest his family and colleagues in Barnsley showed in his wartime experiences. This had first been in evidence when he had returned from Dunkirk: 'People came out of their terraced houses and wanted to talk to you. You got used to the attention.' After demobilisation in 1945, Dickinson returned immediately to his pre-war employment. 'The biggest problem. You weren't overpaid for doing the dirty work, and had no money behind you, so you had to knuckle down to working and earning.' Family connections at a local glass works meant that he had the promise of future promotion, a prospect he saw as giving him an objective in life, 'salvation'. However, Dickinson also had to work three nights per week in a local fish and chip restaurant to supplement his income. Compared to the twenty-one men of No. 11 Field Ambulance who were never to return from war, he considered himself 'lucky to survive. You daren't look back on all that that didn't survive.'

Private F.J. 'Dick' Reynolds, who served in a series of General Hospitals in England and North Africa, was less effusive about his medical work and knowledge:

> You say we shall get an African Star. Yes! We will get our African Star, but as far as I'm concerned they can keep 'em. I'll never wear mine or any other form of decorations given. In years to come I shall need nothing to remind me of the years spent in the army. Give the star to them that fought in the battles – I just helped to nurse some of the wounded.[17]

In contrast to Reynolds, Private Stanley Cross was keen to use the skills he had learned in the army to benefit his community. Cross received an early medical discharge on 5 May 1945, upon 'ceasing to fulfil army medical requirements' after health problems caused during his evacuation from Dunkirk. His testimonial read: 'An industrious honest and sober man whose work and general conduct has been completely satisfactory throughout his service.' Cross returned to his native Hull to work as a dock labourer. This heavy manual work was too taxing for him to sustain all year round, and for three months out of twelve he would be taken to Chapel Allerton Hospital in Leeds, which specialised in the care of ex-military personnel. The skills Cross had learned in the RAMC never left him. In the crowded terraces around the docks of East Hull, if a child had a fall they would be brought to the Cross residence as 'Mr Cross will sort it'. He would even be asked to assess children's loose teeth, and if necessary, 'Mr Cross will pull it for you'.[18]

Although Cross was able to continue with a relatively normal life, the young comrade who had been killed beside him in May 1940, Private George Mussared, left an enormous hole in the life of his devoutly Methodist family and friends. (Pic 11) A former pupil of Kingston School on Hull's Boulevard, Mussared had a school prize named in his honour, and his family continued to insert private notices in the pages of the *Hull Daily Mail* each 1 January, Mussared's birthday, as the years turned to decades. The family also sought to understand their loss through their Christian faith. For Mussared's gravestone, situated near Outtersteene on the Franco-Belgian border, they chose the epitaph 'SAFE IN THE ARMS OF JESUS. LOVED AND LONGED FOR ALWAYS BY MAM, DAD AND OLIVE'. An RAMC comrade named 'Cyril' inserted a tribute in the *Hull Daily Mail* reinforcing Mussared's faith: 'He died as Christ would have him die.' 'Charlie' of the RASC wrote, 'So we part sadly to meet in sweet Jerusalem', and Mussared's sweetheart, 'Emmie', recorded that she felt he was 'Safe in God's haven of peace'.[19] A decade later, his cousin Tom would recall 'The wonderful memory of his smiling face and loving disposition' which 'will ever be an inspiration to those who loved him'.[20] Mussared's parents, who like so many hundreds of thousands, had to carry the memory of their son's life cut cruelly short, beseeched God to 'Hold him, O Father, in Thine arms and let him for ever be a messenger of love between our aching hearts and Thee'.

The men who served in the Royal Army Medical Corps during the Second World War came from all walks of life. Some would go on to eminent careers in medicine and surgery, whilst others would return to their pre-war civilian occupations. Although a few autobiographies were produced in the decades immediately following the cessation of hostilities, it was not until the fortieth, fiftieth, sixtieth and seventieth anniversaries of the major events of the war arrived that many were drawn to record their reflections. Their records tell of a job well done, of evil conquered, of lives saved, and lifelong friendships made. In the midst of the most terrible conflict the world has ever seen, the work done by the RAMC brought out the best in humanity. Selfless devotion and courage was the hallmark of the corps, whose members remained 'Faithful in Adversity', saving lives throughout the world.

Notes

Glossary for notes

IWM	Imperial War Museums
MMMA	Museum of Military Medicine Archive
SWWEC	Second World War Experience Centre
TNA	The National Archives

Chapter 1

1. Francis Crew, *Medical History of the Second World War: Army Medical Services. Administration, Vol.1* (HMSO, London), p.15.
2. Crew, p.32.
3. Ibid, p.198.
4. Ibid, p.16.
5. Ibid, p.189.
6. Ibid, p.157.
7. Ibid, p.157.
8. Ibid, p.51.
9. www.britain-at-war.org.uk/ww2/alberts_war/html/to_leeds.htm.
10. Ibid.
11. Museum of Military Medicine Archive, Alexander Adamson.
12. Crew, p.116.
13. G.D. Jones, *Memories* (Cwmsychpant Press, Llanybydder, 2000), p.11.
14. BBC People's War, Ronald Ritson.
15. Family papers, Paul Watts.
16. SWWEC, Jim Whitaker.
17. Walter Hart, *In Arduis Fideles* (privately published, 1999), pp.3–4.

18. Charles Quant, *Old Forgotten Far-Off Things and Battles Long Ago* (privately published, 2002), p.8.
19. Sean Longden, *Dunkirk: The Men They Left Behind* (Constable, London, 2009), p.212.
20. Family papers, Frank Turton.
21. Longden, p.214.
22. Family papers, John Broom, March 1940.
23. William Earl & Liz Coward, *Blood and Bandages: Fighting for Life in the RAMC Field Ambulance, 1940–1946* (Sabrestorm Publishing, Sevenoaks, 2016), p.27.
24. Geoffrey Haine, *This is what Dad (or Grandad) did in the War!: My Story* (privately published, 1994), p.3.
25. Haine, p.15.
26. SWWEC, David Parton.
27. BBC People's War, Reg Gill.
28. James Driscoll, *Memories of an Old Man* (privately published, 2006), p.32.
29. *Birmingham Daily Gazette*, 30 August 1940, p.6.
30. SWWEC, Jim Wisewell.
31. Family papers, John Broom, March 1940.
32. SWWEC, Leslie Ellis.
33. Family papers, John Broom, 29 Sept 1940.
34. Ibid, March 1940.
35. Family papers, Paul Watts, 18 April 1940.
36. Interview with the author, 9 June 2018.
37. Ibid, 25 July 2018.
38. Hart, p.6.
39. Family papers, John Broom, March 1940.
40. SWWEC, Ian Campbell.
41. Ibid, John Forfar.
42. Jones, p.14.
43. Family papers, John Broom, 8 July 1941.
44. Family papers, Paul Watts, 13 July 1940.
45. Author's collection.
46. Family papers, John Broom, 31 March 1940.
47. Family papers, Pall Watts.
48. Family papers, John Broom, 26 April 1940.
49. Ibid, 15 September 1940.

50. Ibid, 11 November 1941.
51. Ibid, 12 October 1940.
52. Ibid, 3 November 1940.
53. Arthur Atkin, *An RAMC Sketchbook* (privately published, n.d.), pp.1–6.
54. BBC People's War, Reg Gill.
55. IWM, Department of Documents, Captain F.E. de W. Cayley, 7888.
56. Earl & Coward, p.29.
57. Ibid.
58. Family papers, John Broom, 13 February 1941.
59. Earl & Coward, p.34.
60. Ibid, p.34.
61. Family papers, John Broom, 4 February 1941.
62. SWWEC, Peter Walker.
63. Ibid, Ian Campbell.
64. Ibid, Ian Campbell.
65. Ibid, Eric Godwin.
66. Family papers, John Broom, March 1940.
67. Second World War Experience Centre, Claude Jennings.
68. BBC People's War, Kenneth Hulbert.
69. Hart, p.4.
70. Hart, p.4.
71. MMMA, Robert Debenham.
72. James Ross (J.A.R.), *Memoirs of an Army Surgeon* (Blackwood & Sons, Edinburgh & London, 1948), p.3.
73. BBC People's War, Ronald Ritson.
74. Ibid, Kenneth Hulbert.
75. Ibid, Kenneth Hulbert.
76. Watkins, p.98.
77. SWWEC, Alexander Keay.
78. Author's collection.
79. SWWEC, Leslie Collier.
80. Ibid, Leslie Collier.
81. Ibid, John Forfar.
82. Anthony Cotterell, *RAMC* (Hutchinson, London, 1945), p.17.
83. T.B. Nicholls, *Organisation, Strategy, Tactics of the Army Medical Services in War* (Balliere, Tindall & Cox, London, 1937), p.89.

84. Ibid, p.106.
85. RAMC Training Manual (HMSO, 1935), p.101.
86. Ibid, p.82.
87. Neil Barber (ed.), *Parachute Doctor: The Memoirs of Captain David Tibbs MC RAMC* (Sabrestorm Publishing, Sevenoaks, 2012), pp.25–6.

Chapter 2

1. SWWEC, Ernest Sampson.
2. TNA, WO 222/1480, 'Campaign in Norway, April–June 1940', p.19.
3. MMMA, Colonel Ernest Scott, Diary, 14 May 1940, 478/1.
4. Ibid, Lt Col J.W. Wayte, 1952/2.
5. TNA, WO 222/1480, p.9.
6. Ibid, p.8.
7. J.S.G. Blair, Centenary *History of The Royal Army Medical Corps, 1898–1998* (Lynx Publishing, 2001), p.284.
8. Blair, p.284.
9. Hart, p.15.
10. Ibid, p.11.
11. Ibid, p.12.
12. Ibid, p.13.
13. IWM, F.E. de W. Cayley.
14. Harrison, *Medicine and Victory*, p.41.
15. TNA, WO 177/1, 'Report of Committee on Evacuation of Casualties'.
16. BBC People's War, Reg Gill.
17. Ibid.
18. Joan Lightning (ed.), *With All My Love: Letters of Arthur Rowland, 1939–41* (privately published, 2016).
19. SWWEC, Forde Cayley.
20. MMMA, Col Arthur Cox, 801/13/3.
21. Ibid.
22. IWM, F.E. de W. Cayley.
23. SWWEC, Edwin Goodridge.

24. MMMA, Captain R.H. Montague.
25. Ian Samuel, *Doctor at Dunkirk: With the 6th Field Ambulance at War* (Autolycus Pubs, London, 1985), p.48.
26. Samuel, p.50.
27. Richard Doll, 'Dunkirk Diary: "Experience of a Battalion Medical Officer at Dunkirk"', *British Medical Journal*, Vol. 300, 1990, p.1186.
28. SWWEC, Edwin Goodridge.
29. Ibid.
30. Family papers, Stanley Cross.
31. John Nichol & Tony Rennell, *Medic: Saving Lives from Dunkirk and Afghanistan* (Penguin, London, 2010), p.41.
32. Sean Longden, *Dunkirk: The Men They Left Behind* (Constable, London, 2009), p.220.
33. Longden, p.221.
34. Doll, p.1259.
35. C.M. Finny, 'An ADMS's Experiences with the B.E.F – May 1940', *Journal of the Royal Army Medical Corps*, Vol. 76, No. 2, February 1941, p.72.
36. MMMA, B.C. Miller.
37. Longden, p.215.
38. BBC People's War, Reg Gill.
39. Finny, p.80.
40. IWM, Department of Documents, Corp F.C.M. Adams.
41. Doll, p.1452.
42. SWWEC, Edwin Goodridge.
43. Ibid, Eric Godwin.
44. Second World War Experience Centre, Eric Godwin.
45. Maj J.S. Jeffrey, 'Treatment of War Wounds in France, May–June 1940', *Edinburgh Medical Journal*, November 1940: 47 (11), p.730.
46. Ibid, p.732.
47. Ibid, p.733.
48. Ibid, p.734.
49. Ibid, p.727.
50. Ibid, p.730.
51. Anthony Cotterell, *RAMC* (Hutchinson, London, 1945), p.65.
52. McLaughlin, p.64.

53. Ross, p.6.
54. Ibid, pp.6-7.
55. Family papers, John Broom, 5 June 1940.
56. SWWEC, Edwin Goodridge.
57. Hart, p.17.
58. D.I McCallum, 'Personal Experiences in France', *Journal of the Royal Army Medical Corps,* 1 July 1941, pp.32–6.
59. Finny, p.81.
60. Longden, p.213.
61. McLaughlin, p.63.
62. BBC People's War, Richard Newman.

Chapter 3

1. Cotterell, p.67.
2. Cotterell, p.68.
3. Quant, p.9.
4. Hart, p.24.
5. Hart, p.25.
6. Mitchell family papers.
7. Cotterell, p.73.
8. Ibid, pp.69-72.
9. SWWEC, Eric Godwin.
10. Hart, pp.33–4.
11. McLaughin, p.69.
12. Family papers, John Broom, 13 August 1942.
13. Family papers, Frank Turton.
14. Quant, p.9.
15. Family papers, Broom, 31 August 1942.
16. McLaughlin, p.73–4.
17. Ibid, p.74.
18. Quant, p.13.
19. Ibid.
20. Jones, p.15.
21. Ibid, p.16.
22. Family papers, John Broom, 9 October 1942.

23. Family papers, Ralph Dawson, 7 July 1943.
24. Cotterell, p.73.
25. SWWEC, Eric Godwin.
26. Quant, p.13.
27. Driscoll, p.67.
28. SWWEC, Charles Warner.
29. Family papers, Paul Watts, 9 September 1943.
30. Family papers, Norman Jevons.
31. Family papers, Mitchell family.
32. Haine, p.7.
33. Ibid, p.8.
34. Ibid, p.10.
35. BBC People's War, Kenneth Hulbert.
36. Family papers, Paul Adler, 9 November 1942.
37. Ibid, 16 November 1942.

Chapter 4

1. BBC People's War, Reg Gill.
2. Jones, p.21.
3. Theodore Stephanides, *Climax In Crete* (London: Faber & Faber, 1946), p.15.
4. Stephanides, p.25.
5. TNA, WO 222/1481 'Report on Medical Services in the Battle of Crete, May 1941', p.5.
6. Ibid, p.7.
7. Lt Col R.K. Debenham, 'A RAMC Hospital in Crete', *Journal of the Royal Army Medical Corps*, 1 April 1942, p.183.
8. Debenham, 'A RAMC Hospital in Crete', p.184.
9. Jones, p.23.
10. Stephanides, p.33.
11. Ibid, p.41.
12. Ibid, p.52.
13. Ibid, p.71.
14. Ibid, p.100.
15. Ibid, p.102.

16. Ibid, p.105.
17. Ibid, pp.108–109.
18. Ibid, p.132.
19. Ibid, p.148.
20. Ibid, p.149.
21. Ibid, p.151.
22. IWM Sound Archive, Cyril McCann, 4689.
23. Ibid, Kenneth Stalder, 10933.
24. Lt Col Howard N. Cole, *On Wings of Healing: The Story of Airborne Medical Services, 1940–1960* (William Blackwood, Edinburgh & London 1963), pp.34–50.
25. Harrison, *Medicine and War,* p.161.
26. Sunday Times Sri Lanka, 24 February 1980.
27. Quant, p.18.
28. Atkin, *Sketchbook*, p.23.
29. Quant, p.22.
30. *London Gazette*, 2 February 1945.
31. Earl & Coward, p.102.
32. Ross, p.208.
33. Ross, p.209.
34. Atkin, *Sketchbook*, p.36.
35. Ibid.
36. Ibid, p.41.
37. Ibid.
38. Family papers, Norman Jevons
39. John Cloake, *Templer: Tiger of Malaya* (Harrap, London, 1985), pp.139–40.
40. Family papers, Bert Swinger, diary entry 31.1.1944.
41. SWWEC, Leslie Collier.
42. Atkin, *Sketchbook*, p.30.
43. Arthur Atkin, *Drawing to the End* (privately published, n.d.), p.2.
44. Ibid.
45. Ibid.
46. Ibid, p.4.
47. Family papers, Paul Watts, 20 September 1944.
48. SWWEC, Leslie Collier.
49. Ibid.

50. Family papers, Paul Watts, 20 September 1944.
51. Ibid, 13 June 1945.
52. Family papers, John Broom, 11 January 1944.

Chapter 5

1. F.A.E. Crew, *The Army Medical Services: Campaigns: Volume V,* Burma (HMSO, London, 1966), p.647.
2. SWWEC, Leslie Ellis.
3. BBC People's War, Kenneth Hulbert.
4. Watkins, p.106.
5. Rennell & Nichol, p.64.
6. Watkins, p.117.
7. Interview with the author, 9 May 2015.
8. Watkins, p.166.
9. IWM, F.E. de W. Cayley.
10. SWWEC, Claude Jennings.
11. Family papers, Ted Smart diary.
12. Family papers, Paul Adler, 4 June 1944.
13. Ibid, 23 October 1944.
14. James Holland, *Burma '44: The Battle That Turned Britain's War in the East* (Bantam Press, London, 2016), pp.363–4.
15. Anthony Irwin, *Burmese Outpost* (Collins, London, 1945), p.95.
16. Geoffrey Evans, *The Desert and the Jungle* (Kimber, London, 1962).
17. IWM Sound Archive, Gerald Cree, 8245.
18. Louis Allen, *Burma: The Longest War* (J.M. Dent, London, 1984), p.183.
19. MMMA, 'Special Force: Report on Medical Operations for the Period 1943–4', 816.
20. P.G. Stibbe, *Via Rangoon: A Young Chindit Survives the Jungle and Japanese Captivity* (Leo Cooper, London, 1994), p.101.
21. MMMA Archive 'Special Force'.
22. Ibid.
23. Desmond Whyte, 'A Trying Chindit', *British Medical Journal*, Vol. 285, Dec 1982, pp.1176–80.
24. John Masters, *The Road Past Mandalay* (Harper & Bros, London, 1961), p.277.

Chapter 6

1. TNA, WO 222/245 'Memorandum on Position of British MOs in Captivity'.
2. Adrian Gilbert. *POW: Allied Prisoners of War in Europe, 1939–1945* (John Murray, London, 2006), p.222.
3. A.L. Cochrane, 'Tuberculosis among Prisoners of War in Germany', *British Medical Journal*, 10 November 1945.
4. Quoted in www.pegasusarchive.org/arnhem/Bruce_Jeffrey.htm.
5. George Moreton, *Doctor in Chains* (Corgi Books, London, 1970), p.138.
6. Family papers, Thomas Leak.
7. Ibid.
8. Ibid.
9. *The Times*, 20 October 1943.
10. *Ibid.*
11. Jones, p.23.
12. Private family papers, David Jebbitt.
13. IWM Sound Archive, 4755, Norman Rogers.
14. Watkins, p.169.
15. TNA, WO 222/1383 'P.O.W. Camp Changi, 1942–3'.
16. Watkins, p.181.
17. IWM Dept of Documents, C.W. Wells.
18. Interview with the author, 9 May 2015.
19. TNA WO 222/1838.
20. IWM, F.E. de W. Cayley.
21. SWWEC, Leslie Ellis.
22. Ibid, Harry Silman.
23. Ibid, Leslie Brand.
24. Ibid, Harry Silman.
25. Ibid, Harry Silman.
26. IWM, F.E. de W. Cayley.
27. Ibid.
28. SWWEC, Harry Silman.
29. Ibid.
30. Interview with the author, 9 May 2015.
31. IWM, F.E. de W. Cayley.
32. SWWEC, Harry Silman.

33. Ibid, Leslie Ellis.
34. Ibid, Gerald Hitchcock.

Chapter 7

1. SWWEC, David Paton.
2. Ibid, Ian Campbell.
3. Ibid.
4. Haine, p.15.
5. SWWEC, John Forfar.
6. Ibid, Ian Campbell.
7. Ibid.
8. Author's collection.
9. Cole, p.86.
10. Barber, p.29.
11. J.C. Watts, *Surgeon at War* (George Allen & Unwin, London, 1955), pp.88–9.
12. MMMA, 'Red Devils: a parachute field ambulance in Normandy' (6 June–6 Sept 1944), typescript account by members of 224 Parachute Field Ambulance, p.26, RAMC/695.
13. Ibid, p.53.
14. Ibid, p.45.
15. Barber, p.51.
16. MMMA, 'Red Devils: a parachute field ambulance in Normandy' (6 June–6 Sept 1944), p.116, RAMC/695.
17. RAMC/695, p.27.
18. Cole, *Wings of Healing,* p.107.
19. Ibid, p.45.
20. SWWEC, Jim Wisewell.
21. Ibid.
22. Haine, p.17.
23. SWWEC, John Forfar.
24. BBC People's War, Ronald Ritson.
25. SWWEC, Eric Godwin.
26. Ibid, Jim Whitaker.
27. Family papers, James Driscoll.
28. Family papers, John Broom, 4 August 1944.

29. Ibid, 18 September 1944.
30. Ibid, 4 August 1944.
31. Family papers, David Jebbitt.
32. BBC People's War, John Battley.
33. Graeme Warrack, *Travel By Dark: After Arnhem* (Harvill Press, London, 1963), p.112.
34. John Hackett, *I was a Stranger* (Houghton Mifflin Company, Boston, 1978), pp.27–44.
35. BBC People's War, Derrick Randall.
36. Kate ter Horst, *Cloud Over Arnhem: September 17th–26th 1944* (Allen Wingate, London, 1959), p.14.
37. Kate ter Horst, *Cloud Over Arnhem: Setember 17th–26th 1944* (Allen Wingate, London, 1959), p.50.

Chapter 8

1. Family papers, John Broom, 2 January 1945.
2. SWWEC, Peter Walker.
3. Maj D.T. Prescott, 'Reflections of Forty Years Ago – Belsen 1945', *Journal of the Royal Army Medical Corps*, 1986, Vol. 132, p.48.
4. SWWEC, Eric Godwin.
5. IWM, Dept of Documents, Mervyn Gonin, 9589.
6. SWWEC, Ian Campbell.
7. Lt Gen Brian Horrocks, *A Full Life* (Collins, London, 1960), pp.264–5.
8. SWWEC, Hugh McLaren.
9. Family papers, John Broom, 16 April 1945.
10. Ibid, 22 April 1945.
11. Ibid, 20 May 1945.

Chapter 9

1. TNA, WO 162/299.
2. Family papers, Ralph Dawson.
3. Ibid.
4. SWWEC, Ian Campbell.

5. Ibid.
6. Family papers, Ralph Dawson.
7. Ibid.
8. IWM, Kenneth Stalder.
9. Family papers, Bert Swingler, 22 July 1945.
10. Family papers, Hubert Manning.
11. Family papers, Samuel Thorley.
12. SWWEC, John Forfar.
13. IWM, F.E. de W. Cayley.
14. Atkin, *Drawing to the End*, p.27.
15. SWWEC, Geoffrey Wooler.
16. Quant, p.27.
17. Mitchell family papers.
18. Family papers, Stanley Cross.
19. *Hull Daily Mail*, 11 June 1940.
20. Ibid, 1 January 1950.

Sources & Bibliography

Museum of Military Medicine Archive

Personal memoirs

Alexander Adamson
Robert Debenham
B.C. Miller
R.H. Montague
Ernest Scott
J.W. Wayte

Other documents

'Red Devils: a parachute field ambulance in Normandy' (6 June–6 Sept 1944), typescript account by members of 224 Parachute Field Ambulance, RAMC/695

'Special Force: Report on Medical Operations for the Period 1943–44', RAMC/816

Imperial War Museum Archive

Department of Documents

M.J. Pleydell, 337
D.I. McCallum 18970

Sound Archive

Cyril McCann 4689
Norman Rogers 4755
Kenneth Stalder 10933
Desmond Whyte 12570

BBC People's War Website

John Battley
Reg Gill
Kenneth Hulbert
Philip Newman
Derrick Randall
Ronald Ritson

Family papers

John Broom
Stanley Cross
Ralph Dawson
Geoffrey Haine
Norman Jevons
David Jebbitt
Thomas Leak
Hubert Manning
Charles Quant
Ted Smart
Bert Swingler
Samuel Thorley
Frank Turton

Interviews

Ron Dickinson
Ruggles Fisher
Bill Frankland

The National Archives

WO 32/10757
WO 162/299
WO 177/1
WO 222/245
WO 222/1383
WO 222/1480
WO 222/1481

Second World War Experience Centre

Arthur Atkin
Leslie Brand
Alex Bremner
Ian Campbell
Forde Cayley
Leslie Collier
John Forfar
Edwin Goodridge
Claude Jennings
Alexander Keay
Jim Whitaker
Jim Wisewell

Pegasus Archive

Bruce Jeffrey

Primary Published Sources

Atkin, Arthur, *An RAMC Sketchbook* (privately published, n.d.).
Atkin, Arthur, *Drawing to an End* (privately published, n.d.).
Barber, Neil (ed.), *Parachute Doctor: The Memoirs of Captain David Tibbs MC RAMC* (Sabrestorm Publishing, Sevenoaks, 2012).
Cochrane, A.L., 'Tuberculosis among Prisoners of War in Germany', *British Medical Journal*, 10 November 1945.
Cotterell, Anthony *RAMC* (Hutchinson, London, 1945).
Debenham, Lt Col R.K., 'A RAMC Hospital in Crete', *Journal of the Royal Army Medical Corps*, 1 April 1942, pp.183–6.
Doll, Richard, 'Dunkirk Diary: Experience of a Battalion Medical Officer at Dunkirk', *British Medical Journal*, Vol. 300, 1990, pp.1183–6.
Evans, Geoffrey, *The Desert and the Jungle* (Kimber, London, 1962).
Finny, C.M., 'An ADMS's Experiences with the BEF – May 1940', *Journal of the Royal Army Medical Corps*, Vol. 76, No. 2, February 1941, pp.67–83.
Hackett, John, *I was a Stranger* (Houghton Mifflin Company, Boston, 1978).
Hart, Walter, *In Arduis Fideles* (privately published, 1999).
Horrocks, Lt Gen Brian, *A Full Life* (Collins, London, 1960).

Irwin, Anthony, *Burmese Outpost* (Collins, London, 1945).
Jeffrey, Major J.S., 'Treatment of War Wounds in France, May–June 1940', *Edinburgh Medical Journal*, November 1940: 47 (11), pp.727–42.
Jones, G/D., *Memories* (Cwmsychpant Press, Llanybydder, 2000).
Lightning, Joan (ed.), *With All My Love: Letters of Arthur Rowland, 1939–41* (privately published, 2016).
Masters, John, *The Road Past Mandalay* (Harper & Bros, London, 1961).
McCallum, D.I., 'Personal Experiences in France', *Journal of the Royal Army Medical Corps*, 1 July 1941, pp.32–6.
Moreton, George, *Doctor in Chains* (Corgi Books, London, 1970).
Nicholls, T.B., *Organisation, Strategy, Tactics of the Army Medical Services in War* (Balliere, Tindall & Cox, London, 1937).
Prescott, Major D.T., 'Reflections of Forty Years Ago – Belsen 1945', *Journal of the Royal Army Medical Corps*, 1986, Vol. 132, pp.48–51.
Quant, Charles, *Old Forgotten Far-Off Things and Battles Long Ago* (privately published, 2002).
RAMC Training Manual (HMSO, 1935).
Ross, James (J.A.R.), *Memoirs of an Army Surgeon* (Blackwood & Sons, Edinburgh & London, 1948).
Samuel, Ian, *Doctor at Dunkirk: With the 6th Field Ambulance at War* (Autolycus, London, 1985).
Stephanides, Theodore, *Climax in Crete* (Faber & Faber, London, 1946).
Stibbe, P.G., *Via Rangoon: A Young Chindit Survives the Jungle and Japanese Captivity* (Leo Cooper, London, 1994).
ter Horst, Kate, *Cloud Over Arnhem: September 17th–26th 1944* (Allen Wingate, London, 1959).
Warrack, Graeme, *Travel By Dark: After Arnhem* (Harvill Press, London, 1963).
Watts, J.C., *Surgeon at War* (George Allen & Unwin, London, 1955).
Whyte, Desmond, 'A trying Chindit', *British Medical Journal*, Vol. 285, Dec 1982, pp.1176–80.

Secondary Sources

Allen, Louis, Burma: *The Longest War* (J.M. Dent, London, 1984).
Allport, Alan, *Browned Off and Bloody-Minded: The British Soldier Goes to War, 1939–45* (Yale University Press, 2015).

Blair, J.S.G., *Centenary History of the Royal Army Medical Corps* (Lynx Publishing, 2001).

Cloake, John, *Templer: Tiger of Malaya* (Harrap, London, 1985).

Cole, Lt Col Howard N., *On Wings of Healing: The Story of Airborne Medical Services, 1940–1960* (William Blackwood, Edinburgh & London, 1963).

Gilbert, Adrian, *POW: Allied Prisoners of War in Europe, 1939–1945* (John Murray, London, 2006).

Harrison, Mark, *Medicine and Victory: British Military Medicine in the Second World War* (Oxford University Press, 2008).

Holland, James, *Fortress Malta: An Island Under Siege, 1940–1943* (Orion Books, London, 2003).

Holland, James, *Burma '44: The Battle That Turned Britain's War in the East* (Bantam Press, London, 2016)

Longden, Sean, *Dunkirk: The Men They Left Behind* (Constable, London, 2009).

Lovegrove, Peter, *Not Least in the Crusade* (Gale & Polden, Aldershot, 1951).

Nichol, John & Rennell, Tony, *Medic: Saving Lives – From Dunkirk to Afghanistan* (Penguin, London, 2009).

Sebag-Montefiore, Hugh, *Dunkirk: Fight to the Last Man* (Penguin, London, 2006).

Watkins, Paul, *From Hell Island to Hay Fever: The Life of Dr Bill Frankland* (Brown Dog Books, Bath, 2018).

Index